Egon Ronay's
PUB GUIDE
1987

Bar snacks

Bed & Breakfast

Pub restaurants

D1080838

Establishment research conducted by a team of full-time professional inspectors, who are trained to achieve common standards of judgement with as much objectivity as this field allows. Their professional identities are not disclosed until they seek information from the management after paying their bills. The Guide is independent in its editorial selection and does not accept advertising, payment or hospitality from establishments covered.

Egon Ronay's Guides
Second Floor, Greencoat House
Francis Street, London SW1P 1DH

Editor Moyra Fraser
Copy editor Julanne Arnold
Chief copywriter Peter Long
Research editors Michèle Roche
                 Coreen Williams
Publisher William Halden

Cover and design of introductory pages Michael Leaman
Illustrations Margaret Leaman

Cartography by Intermap PS Ltd. All road maps are based on the Ordnance Survey Maps, with the permission of the Controller of HM Stationery Office. Crown copyright reserved.

The contents of this book are believed correct at the time of printing. Nevertheless, the publisher can accept no responsibility for errors or omissions or changes in the details given.

Distributed in the United Kingdom by the Publishing Division of The Automobile Association, Fanum House, Basingstoke, Hampshire RG21 2EA and overseas by the British Tourist Authority, Thames Tower, Black's Road, London W6 9EL.

ISBN 0 86145 405 7

AA Ref 54726

Typeset in Great Britain by William Clowes Ltd, Beccles and London
Printed by Cox & Wyman Ltd, Reading

CONTENTS

How to use this Guide   6
Explanation of symbols

Publisher's summing up   8
N.U.T.S. to the brewers

Pub of the Year   12
The three finalists

Outstanding bar food   14
Star-quality snacks

Outstanding cheeseboards   18
A cut above the rest

Outstanding French wine lists   22
The pick of the bunch

Children welcome   23
Pubs for families

Waterside pubs   29
Sipping by river, sea or lake

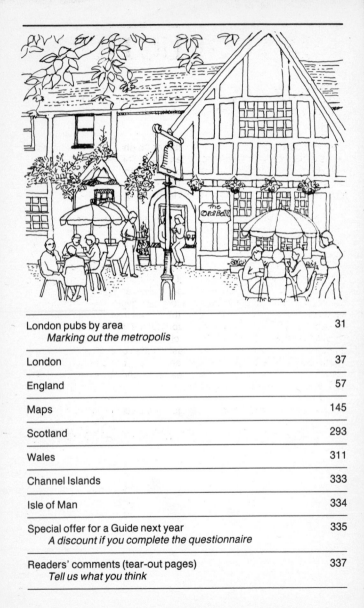

London pubs by area *Marking out the metropolis*	31
London	37
England	57
Maps	145
Scotland	293
Wales	311
Channel Islands	333
Isle of Man	334
Special offer for a Guide next year *A discount if you complete the questionnaire*	335
Readers' comments (tear-out pages) *Tell us what you think*	337

INTRODUCTION

Changing of the guard is successful if it is executed smoothly, with organised precision, and if it is imperceptible to the outside world. This is exactly how the change in the publishers of this Guide has taken place.

I am particularly pleased that the publisher's philosophy continues to place quality above all other considerations. The traditional, stringent criteria of judgement have been applied by the inspectors and the thoroughness of their inspections has been maintained. A guide is always as good and as reliable as its inspectors.

A further guarantee of continuity is that most of the previous key staff – inspectors, editors, writers and researchers – have been taken over with the Guide and are directed by a publisher as dedicated as I have been.

All this is a remarkable achievement if one considers the nature of a guide publishing operation, far more complex and demanding than is generally supposed. Starting from scratch every year, drawing up terms of reference for the research, the almost military organisation of inspectors, the gruelling task of vetting the inspectors' long and detailed reports, attending to them clerically and – most important – evaluating them to arrive at a just classification of establishments, not to mention the task of marketing and sales, are vital parts of the machinery necessary to enable a reader to choose a reliable dining venue or a good room for the night.

As you will see, the changing of the guard is a success.

Egon Ronay

HOW TO USE
THIS GUIDE

GOOD BAR FOOD

We include establishments where our team of professional inspectors found excellent-quality bar food. Such pubs are indicated by *Food* following the locality. Reference may also be made to the pub's restaurant, but our chief concern has been with bar food.

Two typical dishes are listed, with prices valid at the time of our visit. Prices may, however, have risen a little since then.

We indicate when bar food is not available and give the time of last food orders in the evening.

Those establishments serving outstanding food are shown with a star alongside the description.

GOOD ACCOMMODATION AT PUBS

We also inspected the accommodation, and those pubs recommendable for an overnight stay are indicated by *B&B* following the locality. We list the number of bedrooms, and a symbol shows the minimum price (including VAT) for bed and a cooked English breakfast for two in a double room:

£A   over £45
£B   £35–45
£C   £25–35
£D   under £25

If residents can check in at any time, we print *all day*; if check-in is confined to certain hours or if it's advisable to arrange a time when booking, we print *restricted*.

ATMOSPHERIC PUBS

Some pubs are recommended as pleasant or interesting places for a drink rather than for their bar food or accommodation.

CHILDREN WELCOME

Those pubs we suggest as suitable for families are ones that have a room or indoor area where children are allowed whether eating or not. Many pubs welcome children if they are eating bar food and some pubs make a feature of outdoor play areas, but readers should note that these are not the qualifications on which we base our category. Restrictions on children staying overnight are mentioned in the entries.

DRAUGHT BEERS AND CIDER
We print whether an establishment is a free house or brewery-owned. After the 🍺 symbol are listed the names of a number of beers, lagers and cider available on draught. We print *No real ale* where applicable.

OPENING TIMES
Opening hours vary throughout the country. Some pubs have a six-day licence. Any regular weekday closure is given in the entry. As most pubs close at some time during Christmas and New Year, it is advisable to check during that period.

ORDER OF LISTING
London entries appear first and are in alphabetical order by establishment name. Listings outside London are in alphabetical order by location within the regional divisions of England, Scotland, Wales, Channel Islands and Isle of Man.

MAP REFERENCES
Entries contain references to the map section in the middle of the Guide.

SYMBOLS

Food	Recommended for bar food
B&B	Recommended for accommodation
★	Outstanding bar food
Children welcome	Suitable for families
Credit	Credit cards accepted
£A–D	Cost of B&B
🍺	On draught
🧀	Good cheeseboard (see pages 16–17)
♀	French wine pubs (see pages 20–21)

N.U.T.S.* TO THE BREWERS

What makes a good pub? The traditional answer is a friendly welcome, an inviting atmosphere and a well-kept pint of beer. But times are changing. Opening hours, at least in England, look likely to be extended, the enforcement of drink-and-drive laws is bound to become stricter and the EEC is looking for changes in the way our pubs are run. All these influences must mean that pubs will have to pay much more attention to the role they play and the food and accommodation they offer. The time cannot be far away when to justify its licence a pub must offer good food and its landlord have at least basic training in food handling.

One in a hundred

There are 70,830 pubs in Britain at the last count. In this 1987 edition of the Pub Guide we feature some 875 – just over one in a hundred.

Obviously, we have not visited all 70,000 – at least not this year. Far too many just do not serve food at all. But last summer and early autumn we visited not just existing entries but hundreds and hundreds of pubs recommended to us either by readers' letters or by researchers burrowing through newspaper cuttings and trade magazines or, best of all, by word of mouth from locals in a particular area.

These new recommendations are vital to replace the 10% of entries which are dropped from every new edition of the Guide because of changes of ownership, declines in standards and so on. This year these 'drop-outs' reached even higher proportions and it became even more difficult to find new entries. All this at a time when the demand from the public for good pub food continued to increase and beer consumption in pubs stayed in decline.

Is it us? Do we expect too much? Well, the briefing this year to the inspectors was the same as it has been since we launched our first Pub Guide in 1979: 'Food that is wholesome, well prepared, well cooked and tasty'. It does not matter whether the pub serves just filled rolls and not much else or whether it offers a full restaurant-style menu – each will find a place in this Guide.

*Not up to standard, an abbreviation used by Egon Ronay's Guide inspectors in their official reports.

Following the publication of last year's Guide several breweries asked if we could undertake inspections for them and so lift the quality of food they served in their pubs. The idea was good but that is not our role: we operate as consumers and our job is to recommend worthwhile establishments without fear or favour.

However, one of those brewers did supply us with the names of the 20 of its 200 pubs which they thought deserved to be included in the Guide. Significantly, our inspectors approved only two.

N.U.T.S.

Perhaps it would be useful if those brewers who constantly express interest in making their pubs more attractive and welcoming read the following samples of inspectors' reports which are tucked away in our files marked appropriately 'N.U.T.S. – not up to standard'.

The frustrations of our inspectors could best be summed up with this report on an inn in the Highlands of Scotland, in this case a new recommendation from a reader:

At first sight this inn looks fine for the Guide. But one needs to stay here to find the problems. It took an hour to find a key to my room, the door of which sticks so badly it's a struggle to open, and the shade then fell off the bathroom light. As I sit here and write this at 11pm I can hear pop music from the room next door, the noise of a lively public bar below me and the tramp of feet on the ceiling above. We cannot send people here.

Good food does not mean lengthy, elaborate menus – far from it. In Wales this was one inspector's experience:

The recommendation said that this pub has the largest menu in the area. It was a book of Bible size with heavy cardboard pages and voluminous descriptions of ingredients. None of the fresh fish and poultry dishes were available and no alternatives were offered. Settling for a 'Crispy Sweet and Sour Pork with rice' I was served a bowl of stodgy, unwashed rice (straight from the microwave) on which rested charred chunks of deep-fried, unseasoned pork, covered in lukewarm sweet and sour sauce from a tin.

Far too many pubs, although they advertise accommodation, treat visitors almost as intruders, and housekeeping is often non-existent. This Welsh inn is far too typical:

The pub was dirty and deserted when two of us, both total strangers, arrived. We wandered around the bar, dining room and kitchen looking for someone to greet us. This was 5.30pm and the bar reopened at 6pm without being cleaned from lunchtime. We were served breakfast next morning in the same public bar next to an uncleaned, unlit grate; the carpet had not been vacuumed from the previous morning; the 'easy' chairs were covered in dog hairs, and dirty ashtrays abounded on the adjacent tables.

And a similar experience of another inspector, this time in Sussex:

I had to boil a kettle in order to get hot water to shave. I was told the reason was because two other guests had had a bath. Given that they offer seven rooms, all with private bath, the situation was intolerable. Also they were so mean with the central heating that I awoke shivering at 6am. The bedding for the time of year was totally inadequate.

The quality of staff in pubs has to be an overriding problem, and it is surprising how many owners or tenants do not seem to exercise any management standards. This, a rustic and historic inn in the High Street of a famous tourist area town, is typical:

An unfortunately bloody-minded and surly 'manager' did little to create a good first impression. The upstairs bedrooms, with pleasant traditional furnishings, tea/coffee making facilities and colour televisions, were spoilt by lack of cleanliness. Bar food not recommended: celery soup – a turgid watery broth; steak pie – fatty lumps of gristle, frozen peas and commercial croquette potatoes; hazelnut meringue – an appalling stale slice of solid commercial rubbish. Suggest re-visit next year as 'problem' staff have since, apparently, been removed.

There was a similar story in the next town. Even more sadly, this inn had had several years of good reports:

This establishment has no right to be in business. My stated time to book in was mid-afternoon. The premises were deserted until 7pm and the barman had to break in to open up. No food available whatsoever. No bath towels, no soap. No hot water – evening or morning. No indication with regard to breakfast times but at just before 8.30am I was rudely advised: 'My breakfast was spoiling'. Aggressive, unprofessional and unpleasant staff. Not recommended.

The way standards can fall dramatically from one year to another is demonstrated by this report:

Last year's story is now pure fantasy. This is now a run-down pub with paper peeling off the bedroom walls. Certainly not a place where I would willingly spend the night. The bar is equally tired with the poor food display offering unappetising ham and dried-out turkey and the only pud a wilting bought-in gâteau. Ugh!

Or this pub in the Isle of Wight:

This attractive little village pub was once undoubtedly very good. Now it is neglected and has a very sorry appearance. Bar food was of the instantly forgettable variety – burgers, chips and basket meals. I ordered the seafood pie but my worst fears were realised – hardly any fish, about three peas and loads of inedible potato. I did not bother to order anything else as it would have been a waste of time and money.

And so it goes on. It would be good to think that there was a theme to these reports – a common fault that, once corrected, would mean perfection for customers and double the amount of entries in this Guide overnight.

Certainly, we have strengthened the emphasis on food in this year's edition and we will go on doing so, but the real change can only come from the brewers and the publicans themselves.

Just before writing this summing up, I received a phone call from a publican who complained bitterly that he had been writing to us for two years because he felt his pub not only deserved an entry in the Guide but served such good food that he would undoubtedly win our 'Pub of the Year' award.

Hoping to put a more optimistic ending on this article, I made an anonymous visit myself. It was just before Christmas: 'No food', I was told, 'we're too busy today'.

And that just about sums up everything.

William Halden, Publisher

PUB OF THE YEAR

The Pub of the Year Award is a hand painted and gilded octagonal decanter by Mason's Ironstone, engraved with the winner's name and retained for a year. As previously, the main criteria for the award are a very high standard of bar food and a congenial ambience. The three pubs described below are the finalists for the 1987 award, and the winner will be announced on the day of publication. The runners-up will receive barrel-shaped decanters.

Monksilver, Somerset
NOTLEY ARMS

Alistair and Sarah Cade are dedicated and most agreeable landlords, but it's chef Sally Wardell who carries off the major honours here. Nothing commercial goes into her kitchen, just high-quality fresh produce. And what comes out is a series of super dishes, including pasta with various sauces, steaming bowls of delicious soup, splendid curries and mouthwatering sweets. Further pluses are a good wine list, a family room and a beautiful stream-bordered garden.

Llowes, Powys
RADNOR ARMS

Very much a restaurant with pub rather than a pub with food. It's in the excellent hands of Brian and Tina Gorringe, and in any one week you'll probably find 100 items on the menu – all home-prepared from freshest ingredients. Some typical delights: carrot and orange soup served with hot wholegrain bread, kidney omelette, succulent beef and mussel pie, treacle and walnut tart. There's also a fine cheeseboard.

Little Walden, Essex
CROWN INN

A really appealing little pub, with a single cosy bar where customers can enjoy some terrific snacks with a glass of well-kept ale. Fresh and smoked fish, home-cooked beef and ham, super soups – it's all of the very best, and besides the interesting regular menu there are tempting seasonal specials like venison casserole and game pie. The friendly people who run this delightful place are Chris and Gillian Oliver.

OUTSTANDING BAR FOOD

ENGLAND
Brightling, E Sussex: Fullers Arms
Burham, Kent: Golden Eagle
Burton, Wilts: Plume of Feathers
Dartmouth, Devon: Cherub Inn
Fossebridge, Glos: Fossebridge Inn
Fulking, W Sussex: Shepherd & Dog
Great Waltham, Essex: Windmill
Grimsthorpe, Lincs: Black Horse Inn
Kirkby Stephen, Cumb: King's Arms Hotel
Little Walden, Essex: Crown Inn
Longparish, Hants: Plough Inn
Maidensgrove, Oxon: Five Horseshoes
Monksilver, Som: Notley Arms
Moulton, N Yorks: Black Bull Inn
Oakwoodhill, Surrey: Punchbowl Inn
Old Dalby, Leics: Crown Inn
Pitton, Wilts: Silver Plough
Shenington, Oxon: Bell
Shipston-on-Stour, Warwicks: White Bear
Staddle Bridge, N Yorks: McCoy's at the Tontine
Stanford Dingley, Berks: Old Boot Inn
Stanton Harcourt, Oxon: Harcourt Arms
Stapleton, Co Durham: Bridge Inn
Stuckton, Hants: Three Lions Inn
Yattendon, Berks: Royal Oak

SCOTLAND
Dulnain Bridge, H'land: Muckrach Lodge Hotel
Tarbert, S'clyde: West Loch Hotel

WALES
Llanfihangel Crucorney, Gwent: Skirrid Inn
Llowes, Powys: Radnor Arms

- Dulnain Bridge
- Tarbert
- Kirkby Stephen
- Stapleton
- Moulton
- Staddle Bridge
- Old Dalby
- Grimsthorpe
- Shipston-on-Stour
- Shenington
- Little Walden
- Llowes
- Llanfihangel Crucorney
- Fossebridge
- Stanton Harcourt
- Great Waltham
- Maidensgrove
- Burton
- Yattendon
- Stanford Dingley
- Burham
- Longparish
- Pitton
- Oakwoodhill
- Monksilver
- Stuckton
- Brightling
- Fulking
- Dartmouth

The Dairy Crest Symbol

DAIRY CREST FOODS, the leading manufacturer of cheese in Britain, has joined with Egon Ronay's Guide to identify 'Pub Guide' establishments where the quality and presentation of cheese is excellent.

The inspectors for Egon Ronay's Guides have awarded the Dairy Crest Symbol of Excellence for standards which project the many characteristics and qualities of cheese. And these will be evident however cheese is served, whether as part of a tasty lunch-time snack or on an appetising cheese board.

The inspectors are also awarding the Dairy Crest Symbol of Excellence to establishments in the two other major guides, the Hotels & Restaurants Guide and the Just a Bite Guide. For all these awards the inspectors are particularly interested in those who, like Dairy Crest Foods, are applying the highest quality standards.

Wherever you see the Dairy Crest Symbol of Excellence, you will be sure that particular attention has been given to:

# of Excellence...

QUALITY OF TASTE – through careful selection, expert handling and correct storage

QUALITY OF CHOICE – by offering traditional cheeses as well as new and local varieties

QUALITY OF VISUAL APPEAL – by using colour, texture and shape to create a mouth-watering and attractive presentation

QUALITY OF INFORMATION – by enthusiastically passing on knowledge and understanding

Dairy Crest Foods' own excellent cheeses include soft cheeses such as Lymeswold, White Lymeswold, Melbury and Medley; the reduced-fat Tendale range as well as prize-winning Cheddars, Stilton and the full range of English and Welsh traditional regional cheeses.

DAIRY CREST

OUTSTANDING CHEESEBOARDS

LONDON
Admiral Codrington, SW3
Lamb & Flag, WC2

ENGLAND
Bedford, Beds: Park
Biddenden, Kent: Three Chimneys
Bridport, Dorset: George Hotel
Chenies, Herts: Bedford Arms Thistle Hotel
Corton, Wilts: Dove at Corton
Empingham, Leics: White Horse
Fossebridge, Glos: Fossebridge Inn
Great Waltham, Essex: Windmill
Grimsthorpe, Lincs: Black Horse Inn
Hatherleigh, Devon: George Hotel
Hildenborough, Kent: Gate Inn
Horley, Surrey: Ye Olde Six Bells
Knightwick, H & W: Talbot Hotel
Ledbury, H & W: Feathers Hotel
Levington, Suffolk: Ship
Little Langdale, Cumbria: Three Shires Inn
Longparish, Hants: Plough Inn
Melmerby, Cumbria: Shepherds Inn
Moulton, N Yorks: Black Bull Inn
Oldbury-on-Severn, Avon: Anchor Inn
Philleigh, Corn: Roseland Inn
Pitton, Wilts: Silver Plough
Plymouth, Devon: Unity
Saffron Walden, Essex: Eight Bells
Shalfleet, I of W: New Inn
Slaithwaite, W Yorks: White House
Sonning-on-Thames, Berks: Bull Inn
Stamford, Lincs: George of Stamford
Staple Fitzpaine, Som: Greyhound Inn
Stretton, Leics: Ram Jam Inn
Stuckton, Hants: Three Lions Inn
Tarrant Monkton, Dorset: Langton Arms
Timperley, Ches: Hare & Hounds
Washbrook, Suffolk: Brook Inn
Weobley, H & W: Red Lion Hotel
Yattendon, Berks: Royal Oak

SCOTLAND
Glasgow, S'clyde: Babbity Bowster

WALES
Felingwm Uchaf, Dyfed: Plough Inn
Hay-on-Wye, Powys: Old Black Lion
Llandissilio, Dyfed: Bush Inn
Llowes, Powys: Radnor Arms
Llyswen, Powys: Griffin Inn

ENJOY A TASTE
OF FRANCE

Buying a glass of wine in a pub 20 years ago was virtually impossible and the chance of it being a French wine was also remote.

Today, however, French wines are a common sight across the bar of many public houses and they are drunk either on their own or to complement the ever-increasing 'cuisine' of many pub menus.

As well as the reliable Vins de Table wines, the choice sometimes includes a selection of Appellation Contrôlée wines, with their individual tastes and bouquets.

This change in English drinking habits during recent years, and the general interest in French wines has been greatly aided by the introduction in 1963 of an organisation called Food and Wine from France Ltd.

As the UK branch of SOPEXA (Société pour l'Expansion des Ventes des Produits Agricoles et Alimentaires), this team of over 20 people based in London aims to create a better understanding and awareness of French products through a number of generic promotional campaigns – from advertising to in-store demonstrations, tastings and the provision of general information to the wine trade, retailers and members of the public.

Unlike most marketing boards, Food and Wine from France does not own, sell, distribute or control any of the products it promotes. It serves merely to offer objective advice and assistance in the marketing of French food and drink products, including fresh fruit and vegetables, cheese, charcuterie, wines and spirits. With approximately 44% of all wines sold in the UK today coming from France, it should not be difficult to discover a local pub that offers a good selection of French wines.

To make life easier, Egon Ronay's Pub Guide has this year introduced an easy method of identifying such establishments by the use of a small wine glass symbol. This will be included in the entry of those pubs offering the choice of at least four different French wines, whether they be red, rosé, white or sparkling.

Sampling French wine is always a pleasure, and it is hoped that this simple system will enable you to experience a taste of France in your local pub.

FRENCH WINE CLASSIFICATIONS

France was the first country to establish regulations for the production of wine, for the purpose of protecting the professional wine producers and the consumer by controlling the quality, quantity and price of French wines. Other countries have since followed suit with their own regulations.

APPELLATION CONTRÔLÉE (AC):
the best wines, with prices varying according to vineyard, year and region. The classification was established in 1935 to provide guarantees of origin and authenticity.

VINS DÉLIMITÉS DE QUALITÉ SUPÉRIEURE (VDQS):
regulation established in 1949, for very good wines, aiming for AC status, and carefully nurtured. VDQS wines are often unusual and are modestly-priced.

VINS DE PAYS:
this category was created in 1973, for wines from specific named areas – mostly from the South of France and the Loire Valley – and by law cannot be blended with wine from other regions. Characteristics vary enormously but all are good value for money.

VINS DE TABLE:
usually blended from several different areas within a large region, not named after an area or château but may be given a brand name. Ideal for everyday drinking.

OUTSTANDING FRENCH WINE LISTS

LONDON
White Horse on Parsons Green, SW6

ENGLAND
Alsager, Ches: Manor House
Appleby-in-Westmorland, Cumb: Royal Oak Inn
Beaulieu, Hants: Montagu Arms Hotel
Beauworth, Hants: Milbury's
Biddenden, Kent: Three Chimneys
Bishop's Lydeard, Som: Rose Cottage
Brightling, E Sussex: Fullers Arms
Chilgrove, W Sussex: White Horse Inn
Chipping Campden, Glos: King's Arms Hotel
Clare, Suffolk: Bell Hotel
Doddiscombsleigh, Devon: Nobody Inn
Dorchester-on-Thames, Oxon: George Hotel
Fotheringhay, Northants: Falcon Inn
Fowlmere, Cambs: Chequers Inn
Kintbury, Berks: Dundas Arms
Lancing, W Sussex: Sussex Pad
Moulton, N Yorks: Black Bull Inn
Oakwoodhill, Surrey: Punchbowl Inn
Port Gaverne, Corn: Port Gaverne Hotel
Saffron Walden, Essex: Eight Bells
Saffron Walden, Essex: Saffron Hotel
Scole, Norfolk: Crossways Inn
Shelley, W Yorks: Three Acres Inn
Shipston-on-Stour, Warwicks: White Bear
Shipton-under-Wychwood, Oxon: Lamb Inn
Southwold, Suffolk: Crown Hotel
Staple Fitzpaine, Som: Greyhound Inn
Stuckton, Hants: Three Lions Inn
Whitewell, Lancs: Inn at Whitewell
Yattendon, Berks: Royal Oak

SCOTLAND
Dulnain Bridge, H'land: Muckrach Lodge Hotel
Eddleston, Brds: Horseshoe Inn
Invermoriston, H'land: Glenmoriston Arms
Strathblane, Central: Kirkhouse Inn
Troon, S'clyde: Sun Court Hotel
Wester Howgate, Loth: Old Howgate Inn

WALES
Crickhowell, Powys: Nantyffin Cider Mill Inn
Whitebrook, Gwent: Crown at Whitebrook

PUBS FOR FAMILIES

LONDON
Anchor, SE1
Bull's Head, W4
City Barge, W4
Cock Tavern, EC1
Fox & Anchor, EC1
George Inn, SE1
Glasshouse Stores, W1
Grenadier, SW1
Mayflower, SE16
Old Ship, W6
Prospect of Whitby, E1
Samuel Pepys, EC4
Slug & Lettuce, W2 & N1
Spaniards Inn, NW3
Swan Tavern, W2
White Horse on Parsons Green, SW6
Yacht, SE10
Ye Olde Windmill Inn, SW4

ENGLAND
Abberley, Bell at Pensax
Alford Crossways, Napoleon Arms
Alrewas, George & Dragon
Alsager, Manor House
Alswear, Butchers Arms
Ansty, Fox Inn
Appleby, Royal Oak Inn
Appletreewick, Craven Arms
Armathwaite, Duke's Head Hotel
Ascot, Stag
Ashburton, Exeter Inn
Ashbury, Rose & Crown
Ashcott, Ashcott Inn
Ashwell, Bushel & Strike Inn
Ashwell, Three Tuns Hotel
Askham, Punch Bowl
Askham, Queen's Head Inn
Askrigg, King's Arms Hotel
Aston Cantlow, King's Head
Axbridge, Oak House
Axminster, New Commercial Inn
Bainbridge, Rose & Crown Hotel
Bamford, Rising Sun Hotel
Bantham, Sloop Inn

Barbon, Barbon Inn
Barnard Castle, Red Well
Bassenthwaite Lake, Pheasant Inn
Bathampton, George Inn
Beauworth, Milbury's
Beer, Anchor Inn
Beetham, Wheatsheaf Hotel
Belford, Blue Bell Hotel
Belsay, Highlander Inn
Berkeley Road, Prince of Wales Hotel
Bewdley, Black Boy Hotel
Bibury, Catherine Wheel
Biddenden, Three Chimneys
Bidford-on-Avon, White Lion Hotel
Blakesley, Bartholomew Arms
Bledington, King's Head
Blickling, Bucks Arms
Bollington, Church House Inn
Boot, Woolpack Inn
Bowland Bridge, Hare & Hounds
Box, Chequers Inn
Bratton, The Duke
Bray, Crown Inn
Breage, Queen's Arms
Bredwardine, Red Lion
Brendon, Stag Hunters
Brendon Hills, Ralegh's Cross Inn
Bridgnorth, Falcon Hotel
Bridgwater, Admirals Landing
Bridport, Bull Hotel
Bridport, George Hotel
Brightling, Fullers Arms
Brighton, Black Lion Hotel
Bristol, Jolly Cobblers
Brockton, Feathers Inn
Brome, Oaksmere
Bromham, Greyhound Inn
Broom, Broom Tavern
Buckler's Hard, Master Builders
    House Hotel
Burford, Bull Hotel
Burford, Inn for All Seasons
Burnham-on-Crouch, Ye Olde White
    Harte Hotel
Burton, Plume of Feathers

Burtonwood, Fiddle i'th Bag Inn
Burwash, Bell Inn
Calderbridge, Stanley Arms
Cambridge, George Inn
Carey, Cottage of Content
Carthorpe, Fox & Hounds
Cartmel Fell, Mason's Arms
Casterton, Pheasant Inn
Castleton, Castle Hotel
Castleton, Moorlands Hotel
Cerne Abbas, New Inn
Chaddleworth, Ibex
Chagford, Globe Inn
Chale, Clarendon Hotel
Charlbury, Bell at Charlbury
Chedworth, Seven Tuns
Chelsworth, Peacock Inn
Chenies, Bedford Arms Thistle Hotel
Chester, Ye Olde King's Head
Chiddingfold, Crown Inn
Chiddingfold, Swan
Chilham, Woolpack
Chipping, Dog & Partridge
Chipping Norton, Crown & Cushion
Chipping Norton, Fox Hotel
Chiseldon, Patriots Arms
Chorleywood, Sportsman Hotel
Christow, Artichoke Inn
Church Enstone, Crown Inn
Churchstow, Church House Inn
Cirencester, Crown
Clare, Bell Hotel
Clearwell, Wyndham Arms
Clifton Hampden, Barley Mow
Cobham, Plough
Cockwood, Ship Inn
Coleford, Speech House Hotel
Colesbourne, Colesbourne Inn
Coleshill, Coleshill Hotel
Coleshill, Swan Hotel
Collyweston, Cavalier Inn
Congleton, Lion & Swan Hotel
Constable Burton, Wyvill Arms
Corsham, Methuen Arms Hotel
Cousley Wood, Old Vine
Coxwold, Fauconberg Arms
Cranborne, Fleur-de-Lys
Croscombe, Bull Terrier
Damerham, Compasses Inn
Darrington, Darrington Hotel
Dedham, Marlborough Head
Devizes, Bear Hotel

Dorney, Palmer Arms
Dragons Green, George & Dragon
Driffield, Bell Hotel
Dummer, The Queen
Dunsfold, Sun
Eartham, George Inn
East Dereham, King's Head Hotel
Edge, Edgemoor Inn
Elkstone, Highwayman Inn
Elslack, Tempest Arms
Elsworth, George & Dragon
Elterwater, Britannia Inn
Empingham, White Horse
Eskdale, Bower House Inn
Ettington, Houndshill
Evercreech Junction, Natterjack
Ewhurst Green, White Dog Inn
Exford, Crown Hotel
Eyam, Miners Arms
Eyam, Rose & Crown
Fairford, Bull Hotel
Faringdon, Bell Hotel
Faugh, String of Horses
Fawley, Walnut Tree
Felixstowe, Ordnance Hotel
Fen Drayton, Three Tuns
Fenny Bentley, Bentley Brook Inn
Fiddleford, Fiddleford Inn
Fingest, Chequers Inn
Fiskerton, Bromley Arms
Fittleworth, Swan
Fletching, Griffin Inn
Fonthill Bishop, King's Arms
Ford, White Hart at Ford
Fossebridge, Fossebridge Inn
Fotheringhay, Falcon Inn
Fovant, Cross Keys Hotel
Fovant, Pembroke Arms
Fownhope, Green Man Inn
Framfield, Barley Mow
Frampton Mansell, Crown Inn
Frilford Heath, Dog House
Friskney, Barley Mow
Fyfield, White Hart
Glastonbury, George & Pilgrims Hotel
Goldsborough, Bay Horse Inn
Gomshall, Black Horse
Goostrey, Olde Red Lion Inn
Gosberton, Five Bells
Great Chishill, Pheasant Inn
Great Ryburgh, Boar Inn
Greenhalgh, Blues

Greta Bridge, Morritt Arms Hotel
Grimsthorpe, Black Horse Inn
Guisborough, Fox Inn
Guisborough, Moorcock Hotel
Halford, Halford Bridge Inn
Hallaton, Bewicke Arms
Hambleden, Stag & Huntsman Inn
Harrietsham, Ringlestone Inn
Harrogate, West Park Hotel
Haslemere, Crowns
Hatherleigh, George Hotel
Hawk Green, Crown Inn
Hawkhurst, Tudor Arms Hotel
Haytor Vale, Rock Inn
Helmsley, Feathers Hotel
Helston, Angel Hotel
Henley-on-Thames, Little Angel
Hexworthy, Forest Inn
Highclere, Yew Tree Inn
Holt, Old Ham Tree
Holton, Old Inn
Holywell, Ye Olde Ferry Boat Inn
Holywell Green, Rock Hotel
Honley, Coach & Horses
Hope, Poachers Arms
Horringer, Beehive
Horton, Horton Inn
Horton in Ribblesdale, Crown Hotel
Hubberholme, George Inn
Huntingdon, Old Bridge Hotel
Ilmington, Howard Arms
Keswick, Pheasant Inn
Kettlewell, Racehorses Hotel
Keyston, The Pheasant
Kineton, Halfway House
Kingscote, Hunters Hall Inn
Kingston, Scott Arms
Kingston, Juggs
Kintbury, Dundas Arms
Kinver, Whittington Inn
Kirk Langley, Meynell Arms Hotel
Knapp, Rising Sun
Knightwick, Talbot Hotel
Knowl Hill, Bird in Hand
Lacock, Red Lion at Lacock
Lamberhurst, Chequers Inn
Lamberhurst, George & Dragon Inn
Lancaster, Farmers Arms Hotel
Lanchester, Kings Head
Lancing, Sussex Pad
Langdale, Pillar Hotel, Hobson's Pub
Langham, Noel Arms

Langthwaite, C. B. Hotel
Leafield, Old George Inn
Ledbury, Feathers Hotel
Ledbury, Verzons Country House
 Hotel
Ledbury, Ye Olde Talbot Hotel
Ledston, White Horse
Leek, Three Horseshoes Inn
Leigh on Mendip, Bell Inn
Leominster, Royal Oak Hotel
Lickfold, Lickfold Inn
Lifton, Arundell Arms
Limpley Stoke, Hop Pole Inn
Lincoln, Wig & Mitre
Linton, Windmill Inn
Little Langdale, Three Shires Inn
Little Washbourne, Hobnails Inn
Liverpool, Philharmonic Dining
 Rooms
Long Compton, Red Lion
Long Melford, Black Lion Hotel
Long Melford, Crown Inn Hotel
Long Melford, Hare Inn
Lowdham, Springfield Inn
Lower Woodford, Wheatsheaf
Loweswater, Kirkstile Inn
Lowick Green, Farmer's Arms
Ludlow, Angel Hotel
Lurgashall, Noah's Ark
Lyddington, Marquess of Exeter
Lydford, Castle Inn
Lyonshall, Royal George Inn
Madingley, Three Horseshoes
Malham, Buck Inn
Malton, Green Man Hotel
Manaccan, New Inn
Marhamchurch, Bullers Arms
Market Drayton, Corbet Arms Hotel
Market Weighton, Londesborough
 Arms
Marlborough, Sun Inn
Marshside, Gate Inn
Mayfield, Rose & Crown
Mellor, Millstone Hotel
Mere, Old Ship Hotel
Metal Bridge, Metal Bridge Inn
Metherell, Carpenters Arms
Middleham, Black Swan
Middleton Stoney, Jersey Arms
Midhurst, Angel Hotel
Mildenhall, Bell Hotel
Milton Abbas, Hambro Arms

Pubs for families

Minster Lovell, Old Swan Hotel
Molesworth, Cross Keys
Monksilver, Notley Arms
Moreton-in-Marsh, Redesdale Arms Hotel
Moretonhampstead, White Hart Hotel
Morval, Snooty Fox Hotel
Moulton, Black Bull Inn
Murcott, Nut Tree Inn
Nantwich, Lamb Hotel
Nassington, Black Horse Inn
Needham Market, Limes Hotel
Needingworth, Pike & Eel
Nettlecombe, Marquis of Lorne
Newark, Robin Hood Hotel
Newton, Queen's Head
Newton, Red Lion Inn
Newton, Saracen's Head
Newton-in-Bowland, Parkers Arms Hotel
North Bovey, Ring of Bells
North Cerney, Bathurst Arms
North Petherton, Walnut Tree Inn
North Wootton, Crossways Inn
Northiam, Six Bells
Nunney, George Inn
Oakwoodhill, Punchbowl Inn
Ockley, King's Arms
Odiham, George Hotel
Old Dalby, Crown Inn
Ollerton, Dun Cow
Ombersley, Kings Arms
Onecote, Jervis Arms
Orleton, Boot Inn
Oswaldkirk, Malt Shovel Inn
Ovington, Bush Inn
Oxford, Perch
Oxford, Turf Tavern
Parkgate, Ship Hotel
Pelynt, Jubilee Inn
Pembridge, New Inn
Peppard Common, Red Lion
Perranarworthal, Norway Inn
Petworth, Angel
Pewsham, Lysley Arms
Philleigh, Roseland Inn
Pickhill, Nag's Head
Pin Mill, Butt & Oyster
Pitton, Silver Plough
Plumley, Smoker Inn
Pocklington, Feathers Hotel
Poole, Inn in the Park

Porlock Weir, Anchor Hotel & Ship Inn
Powerstock, Three Horseshoes
Priors Hardwick, Butchers Arms
Pulborough, Waters Edge
Pulverbatch, White Horse
Pyrton, Plough Inn
Ramsbury, Bell at Ramsbury
Ringmore, Journey's End Inn
Ringwood, Original White Hart
Ripon, Unicorn Hotel
Ripponden, Old Bridge Inn
Risplith, Black-a-Moor Inn
Rockcliffe, Crown & Thistle
Rotherwick, Coach & Horses
Running Waters, Three Horse Shoes
St Dominick, Who'd Have Thought It Inn
St Margaret's at Cliffe, Cliffe Tavern
St Mawgan, Falcon Inn
St Neots, Chequers Inn
Saffron Walden, Eight Bells
Saffron Walden, Saffron Hotel
Salisbury, Haunch of Venison
Salisbury, King's Arms
Sandon Bank, Seven Stars Inn
Sandside, Ship Inn
Sandwich, Fleur-de-Lis
Scole, Crossways Inn
Scole, Scole Inn
Sedgefield, Dun Cow Inn
Sedgefield, Nag's Head Inn
Semley, Benett Arms
Sennen Cove, Old Success Inn
Shalfleet, New Inn
Shave Cross, Shave Cross Inn
Shelley, Three Acres Inn
Shenington, Bell
Shepperton, Anchor Hotel
Shepperton, Thames Court
Shepperton, Warren Lodge
Shepton Mallet, Kings Arms
Shipston-on-Stour, Bell Inn
Shipston-on-Stour, White Bear
Shiplake, Baskerville Arms
Silk Willoughby, Horseshoes
Skidby, Half Moon Inn
Slaidburn, Hark to Bounty Inn
Slaithwaite, White House
Sleights, Salmon Leap
Smarden, Bell
Snainton, Coachman Inn
Snettisham, Rose & Crown Inn

South Dalton, Pipe & Glass
South Leigh, The Mason Arms
South Zeal, Oxenham Arms
Southwold, Crown Hotel
Staddle Bridge, McCoy's at the
 Tontine
Stafford, Swan Hotel
Stamford, Bull & Swan Inn
Stamford, Crown Hotel
Stamford, George of Stamford
Standerwick, Bell Inn
Standish, Foresters Arms
Stanton Harcourt, Harcourt Arms
Staple Fitzpaine, Greyhound Inn
Stapleton, Bridge Inn
Starbotton, Fox & Hounds
Staveley, Royal Oak
Staverton, Sea Trout Inn
Stewkley, Swan
Stoke Lacy, Plough Inn
Stoke St Gregory, Rose & Crown
Stony Stratford, Bull Hotel
Stow Bardolph, Hare Arms
Stow-on-the-Wold, Royalist Hotel
Stretton, Ram Jam Inn
Sutton, Sutton Hall
Sutton Howgrave, White Dog Inn
Sutton-upon-Derwent, St Vincent
 Arms
Symonds Yat West, Old Court Hotel
Talkin Village, Hare & Hounds Inn
Tarporley, Swan Hotel
Tarrant Monkton, Langton Arms
Teddington, Clarence Hotel
Temple Grafton, Blue Boar
Terrington, Bay Horse Inn
Testcombe, Mayfly
Thetford, Historical Thomas Paine
 Hotel
Timberscombe, Lion Inn
Timperley, Hare & Hounds
Toot Hill, Green Man
Tormarton, Compass Inn
Trebarwith, Mill House Inn
Troutbeck, Mortal Man
Turville, Bull & Butcher
Tutbury, Ye Olde Dog & Partridge
Twickenham, White Swan
Upper Oddington, Horse & Groom Inn
Upton Grey, Hoddington Arms
Uttoxeter, White Hart Hotel
Walkern, White Lion

Wansford, Haycock Hotel
Wanstrow, King William IV
Warfield, Cricketers
Wark, Battlesteads Hotel
Warmington, Wobbly Wheel Inn
Warminster, Old Bell Hotel
Warwick-on-Eden, Queen's Arms Inn
 & Motel
Wasdale Head, Wasdale Head Inn
Wath-in-Nidderdale, Sportsman's
 Arms
Welford-on-Avon, Shakespeare Inn
Wentworth, George & Dragon
Weobley, Red Lion Hotel
West Ilsley, Harrow
West Lavington, Wheatsheaf
West Witton, Wensleydale Heifer
Weston, White Lion
Wetherby, Alpine Inn
Whatcote, Royal Oak
Whitewell, Inn at Whitewell
Whitney-on-Wye, Rhydspence Inn
Wickham, Five Bells
Wilmcote, Swan House Hotel
Wincham, Black Greyhound Hotel
Winchcombe, George Inn
Winchelsea, Winchelsea Lodge Hotel
Winchester, Wykeham Arms
Winfrith Newburgh, Red Lion
Winkfield, Olde Hatchet
Winkton, Fisherman's Haunt Hotel
Winsford, Royal Oak Inn
Winslow, Bell Hotel
Winterton-on-Sea, Fisherman's
 Return
Wisbech, Rose & Crown Hotel
Withington, Mill Inn
Witney, Red Lion Hotel
Wixford, Three Horseshoes
Woburn, Black Horse Inn
Wolvey, Axe & Compass
Woodbridge, Bull Hotel
Woodhall Spa, Abbey Lodge Inn
Wooler, Tankerville Arms
Woolverton, Red Lion
Worcester, Slug & Lettuce
Wye, New Flying Horse Inn
Wykeham, Downe Arms
Yarde Down, Poltimore Arms
Yarmouth, Bugle Hotel
Yattendon, Royal Oak

Pubs for families

SCOTLAND
Airdrie, Staging Post
Anstruther, Craw's Nest Hotel
Ardentinny, Ardentinny Hotel
Busby, Busby Hotel
Castle Douglas, King's Arms Hotel
Catterline, Creel Inn
Comrie, Royal Hotel
Dulnain Bridge, Muckrach Lodge
  Hotel
Dysart, Old Rectory Inn
Eddleston, Horse Shoe Inn
Elrick, Broadstraik Inn
Fochabers, Gordon Arms Hotel
Glamis, Strathmore Arms
Glencoe, King's House Hotel
Glendevon, Tormaukin Hotel
Glenfinnan, Stage House Inn
Inverbeg, Inverbeg Inn
Invergarry, Inn on the Garry
Invermoriston, Glenmoriston Arms
Killin, Clachaig Hotel
Kippen, Cross Keys Inn
Linlithgow, Champany Inn
Loch Eck, Coylet Inn
Lochgair, Lochgair Hotel
Lybster, Bayview Hotel
Melrose, Burts Hotel
Melrose, George & Abbotsford Hotel
Moffat, Balmoral Hotel
Moffat, Black Bull
Muir of Ord, Ord Arms Hotel
New Abbey, Criffel Inn
Onich, Onich Hotel
Portree, Rosedale Hotel
Spean Bridge, Letterfinlay Lodge
  Hotel
Strathblane, Kirkhouse Inn
Tarbert, West Loch Hotel
Tayvallich, Tayvallich Inn
Troon, Sun Court Hotel
Uig, Ferry Inn
Ullapool, Argyll Hotel
Weem, Ailean Chraggan Hotel

WALES
Aberaeron, Harbourmaster Hotel
Abergavenny, Llanwenarth Arms
Betwys-yn-Rhos, Ffarm Hotel
Cardigan, Black Lion Hotel
Cenarth, White Hart
Chepstow, Castle View Inn
Cowbridge, The Bear
Crickhowell, Bear Hotel
Crickhowell, Nantyffin Cider Mill Inn
East Aberthaw, Blue Anchor
Felindre Farchog, Old Salutation Inn
Ffairfach, Torbay Inn
Henllan, Henllan Falls Hotel
Llanarmon Dyffryn Ceiriog, West
  Arms Hotel
Llandissilio, Bush Inn
Llandovery, King's Head Inn
Llanfihangel Crucorney, Skirrid Inn
Llanfrynach, White Swan
Llangorse, Red Lion
Llangollen, Britannia Inn
Llangurig, Blue Bell
Llanrug, Glyntwrog Inn
Llantilio Crossenny, Hostry Inn
Llantrissent, Royal Oak Inn
Menai Bridge, Gazelle Hotel
Nottage, Rose & Crown
Pembroke, Old King's Arms Hotel
Penmaenpool, George III Hotel
Pentwynmawr, Three Horseshoes Inn
Raglan, Beaufort Arms Hotel
Three Cocks, Three Cocks Hotel
Trecastle, Castle Hotel
Whitebrook, Crown at Whitebrook
Wolf's Castle, Wolfe Inn

CHANNEL ISLANDS
Pleinmont, Imperial Hotel
St Aubin's Harbour, Old Court House
  Inn

ISLE OF MAN
Peel, Creek Inn

WATERSIDE PUBS

LONDON

Anchor, SE1
Angel, SE16
Bull's Head, W4
City Barge, W4
Dickens Inn, E1
Dove, W6
Grapes, E14
Mayflower, SE16
Old Ship, W6
Prospect of Whitby, E1
Trafalgar Tavern, SE10
Yacht, SE10

ENGLAND

Armathwaite, Cumbria: Duke's Head Hotel
Bathampton, Avon: George Inn
Bedford, Bedfordshire: Embankment Hotel
Beer, Devon: Anchor Inn
Bidford-on-Avon, Warks: White Lion Hotel
Bledington, Oxon: King's Head
Brendon, Devon: Stag Hunters
Bridestowe, Devon: White Hart
Bridgwater, Som: Admirals Landing
Brockton, Shrops: Feathers Inn
Buckler's Hard, Hants: Master Builders House Hotel
Burnham-on-Crouch, Essex: Ye Olde White Harte Hotel
Burton upon Trent, Staffs: Riverside Inn
Calderbridge, Cumbria: Stanley Arms
Cambridge, Glos: George Inn
Cockwood, Devon: Anchor Inn
Cockwood, Devon: Ship Inn
Elslack, N Yorks: Tempest Arms
Eskdale, Cumbria: Bower House Inn
Exford, Som: Crown Hotel
Fen Drayton, Cambs: Three Tuns
Fiskerton, Notts: Bromley Arms
Ford, Wilts: White Hart at Ford
Fossebridge, Glos: Fossebridge Inn
Helford, Corn: Shipwright's Arms
Holywell, Cambs: Ye Olde Ferry Boat Inn

Horley, Surrey: Ye Olde Six Bells
Hubberholme, N Yorks: George Inn
Huntingdon, Cambs: Old Bridge Hotel
Kettlewell, N Yorks: Racehorses Hotel
Kintbury, Berks: Dundas Arms
Knightwick, H & W: Talbot Hotel
Lamberhurst, Kent: George & Dragon Inn
Langdale, Cumbria: Pillar Hotel, Hobson's Pub
Llanfair Waterdine, Shrops: Red Lion
Loweswater, Cumbria: Kirkstile Inn
Marshside, Kent: Gate Inn
Metal Bridge, Cumbria: Metal Bridge Inn
Monksilver, Som: Notley Arms
Needingworth, Cambs: Pike & Eel
Newenden, Kent: White Hart
Newton-in-Bowland, Lancs: Parkers Arms Hotel
North Cerney, Glos: Bathurst Arms
North Dalton, Humb: Star Inn
Onecote, Staffs: Jervis Arms
Ovington, Hants: Bush Inn
Parkgate, Ches: Ship Hotel
Pin Mill, Suffolk: Butt & Oyster

Porlock Weir, Som: Anchor Hotel & Ship Inn
Port Gaverne, Corn: Port Gaverne Hotel
Pulborough, W Sussex: Waters Edge
Ripponden, W Yorks: Old Bridge Inn
Sandside, Cumbria: Ship Inn
Sennen Cove, Corn: Old Success Inn
Shepperton, Middlesex: Thames Court
Shepperton, Middlesex: Warren Lodge
Stockbridge, Hants: Vine
Testcombe, Hants: Mayfly
Thames Ditton, Surrey: Albany
Trebarwith, Corn: Mill House Inn
Twickenham, Middlesex: White Swan
Wansford, Cambs: Haycock Hotel
Wasdale Head, Cumbria: Wasdale Head Inn
Wath-in-Nidderdale, N Yorks: Sportsman's Arms
Whitewell, Lancs: Inn at Whitewell
Winkton, Dorset: Fisherman's Haunt Hotel
Withington, Glos: Mill Inn
Withybrook, Warks: Pheasant
Wixford, Warks: Three Horseshoes
Woodstock, Oxon: Black Prince

SCOTLAND
Anstruther, Fife: Smugglers Inn
Ardentinny, Argyll: Ardentinny Hotel
Canonbie, D & G: Riverside Inn
Catterline, Gram'n: Creel Inn
Edinburgh, Loth: Cramond Inn

Glencoe, H'land: King's House Hotel
Inverbeg, S'clyde: Inverbeg Inn
Killin, Central: Clachaig Hotel
Loch Eck, S'clyde: Coylet Inn
Lochgair, S'clyde: Lochgair Hotel
Onich, H'land: Onich Hotel
Portree, H'land: Rosedale Hotel
Spean Bridge, H'land: Letterfinlay Lodge Hotel
Tarbert, S'clyde: West Loch Hotel
Tayvallich, S'clyde: Tayvallich Inn

WALES
Aberaeron, Dyfed: Harbourmaster Hotel
Cenarth, Dyfed: White Hart
Dolgellau, Gwynedd: Gwernan Lake Hotel
Felindre Farchog, Dyfed: Old Salutation Inn
Llanarmon Dyffryn Ceiriog, Clwyd: West Arms Hotel
Llangwm, Gwent: Bridge Inn
Llantrissent, Gwent: Royal Oak Inn
Menai Bridge, Gwynedd: Gazelle Hotel
Penmaenpool, Gwynedd: George III Hotel
Penybont, Powys: Severn Arms

CHANNEL ISLANDS
Pleinmont, Guernsey: Imperial Hotel
St Aubin's Harbour, Jersey: Old Court House Inn

ISLE OF MAN
Peel, Isle of Man: Creek Inn

LONDON PUBS BY AREAS

BAYSWATER & NOTTING HILL
Slug & Lettuce, W2
Swan Tavern, W2
Victoria, W2
Windsor Castle, W8

BLOOMSBURY & HOLBORN
Lamb, WC1
Museum Tavern, WC1
Princess Louise, WC1
Ye Olde Mitre Tavern, EC1

CHELSEA
Admiral Codrington, SW3

CITY
Black Friar, EC4
Cock Tavern, EC1
Dirty Dick's, EC2
Fox & Anchor, EC1
Hand & Shears, EC1
Railway Tavern, EC2
Samuel Pepys, EC4
Ye Olde Dr Butler's Head, WC2
Ye Olde Watling, EC4

COVENT GARDEN
Lamb & Flag, WC2
Nag's Head, WC2
Nell of Old Drury, WC2
Salisbury, WC2

EAST LONDON
Dickens Inn, E1
Grapes, E14
Prospect of Whitby, E1

FLEET STREET
Old Bell Tavern, EC4

Printer's Devil, EC4
Seven Stars, WC2
Ye Olde Cheshire Cheese, EC4
Ye Olde Cock Tavern, EC4

KNIGHTSBRIDGE
Grenadier, SW1
Paxton's Head, SW1

MAYFAIR & MARYLEBONE
The Audley, W1
Prince Regent, W1
Red Lion, W1
Shepherd's Tavern, W1
Ye Grapes, W1

NORTH & NORTH-WEST LONDON
Albion, N1
Eagle, N1
Flask, N6
Jack Straw's Castle, NW3
Old Bull & Bush, NW3
Slug & Lettuce, N1
Spaniards Inn, NW3

ST JAMES'S
Red Lion, SW1
Two Chairmen, SW1

SOHO & TRAFALGAR SQUARE
Glass House Stores, W1
Sherlock Holmes, WC2
Tom Cribb, SW1

SOUTH-EAST LONDON
Anchor, SE1
Angel, SE16
George, SE1
Mayflower, SE16
Trafalgar Tavern, SE10

Yacht, SE10

SOUTH-WEST LONDON
Ship, SW14
Sun Inn, SW13
White Horse on Parsons Green, SW6
Ye Olde Windmill Inn, SW4

VICTORIA & WESTMINSTER
Albert, SW1
Cardinal, SW1
Cask & Glass, SW1
Orange Brewery, SW1
Slug & Lettuce, SW1
Two Chairmen, SW1

WEST LONDON
Bull's Head, W4
City Barge, W4
Dove, W6
Goat, W8
Greyhound, W8
Old Ship, W6

With a brew like this, it's just as well the Bavarians can hold their lager.

A Bavarian barmaid never has her hands full remembering an order.

In a keller, everyone drinks lager. And you can't blame them.

Their beloved Löwenbräu gains strength and character from brewing skills that date back over 500 years.

The locals call it the 'Pride of Bavaria.'

Which probably explains why the sight of a barmaid with her fists full of Löwenbräu is such an uplifting experience.

And why the local Hans don't have any trouble keeping their hands to themselves.

LÖWENBRÄU
STRONG ON TRADITION

*HOW MANY TEAS DO YOU NEED TO MAKE
A FINE QUALITY BLEND?*

Brooke Bond

PG tips

As many as twenty eight different teas are used to create PG Tips, because no single tea can produce that unique taste. Crops vary in quality from day to day and country to country and a great deal of skill is required of Brooke Bond blenders to balance the qualities of one leaf against another. Their skill and experience is evident in each day's blend of PG's ✺ famous flavour. ✺

A week in the life of one of our Cards

Monday 14 AMERICAN EXPRESS	Book train, car for Birmingham — Amex Travel. Book theatre tickets — for 19th.
Tuesday 15 AMERICAN EXPRESS	gift, fill — Fenwicks Bond St. Lunch Julian — Cork & Bottle.
Wednesday 16 Full Moon AMERICAN EXPRESS	Birmingham, lunch David — Bobby Browns.
Thursday 17 AMERICAN EXPRESS	new shirt and suit — Hornes. Summer hols, book Supertravel.
Friday 18 AMERICAN EXPRESS	Lunch Sarah — Tara, Poachers new tie — Tie Rack. Restaurant.
Saturday 19 AMERICAN EXPRESS	Order hamper Fortnum & Mason Nat. Theatre — Cerri & Pat, dinner & show.
Sunday 20 AMERICAN EXPRESS	Golf — fees due. Lunch — The Old Bakery.

M T W T F S S | M T W T F S S | M T W T F S S | M T W T F S S | M T W T F S S | M T W T F S S | M
1 2 | 3 4 5 6 7 8 9 | 10 11 12 13 14 15 16 | 17 18 19 20 21 22 23 | 24 25 26 27 28 29 30 |

AMERICAN EXPRESS®
3742 00001 728
VALID DATES ∀
09/84 THRU 08/86 AX
CHARLES FROST

Don't leave home without it.

American Express Europe Ltd., incorporated with limited liability in the State of Delaware, U.S.A.

LONDON

Admiral Codrington (Food)

17 Mossop Street, SW3 · Map 13 B1
01–589 4603

Brewery Bass
Landlords Melvyn & Irene Barnett

Credit Access, Amex, Diners, Visa
🍺 Bass; Charrington's IPA; Stones Bitter;
Guinness; Carling Black Label; Tennent's Extra;
cider.

Well-prepared snacks can be enjoyed in the bar or plant-filled patio of this convivial Victorian pub. Lunchtime dishes span soup, potted shrimps, savoury mince, and a variety of grills, with fish and chips popular on Saturday. Traditional Sunday lunch. Similar, more formal evening choice. Sandwiches, cheeses and salads always available on request. *Typical prices:* Steak & mushroom pie £3.95 Fresh asparagus £2.50 (Last bar food 10.30pm. No bar food Sat & Sun eves) ☕

Albert

In a street dominated by modern office blocks, this handsome Victorian pub is all the more striking for its survival. It opened for business in 1867 and retains many fine period features, including engraved glass windows, carved woodwork and a set of Victorian prints depicting – incongruously, perhaps, in this setting – the evils of alcohol.

52 Victoria Street, SW1 · Map 13 C1
01–222 5577 *Owner* London Hosts *Landlords* Mr & Mrs E. Jones
🍺 Watneys Combes Bitter; Stag Bitter; Webster's Yorkshire Bitter;
Guinness; Foster's; Budweiser.

Albion (Food)

10 Thornhill Road, N1 · Map 11 C1
01–607 7450

Brewery Hamden Hosts
Landlords Michael & Shirley Parish

Credit Access, Visa
🍺 Ruddle's County; Webster's Yorkshire Bitter;
Combes Traditional; Watneys Special; Holsten;
Foster's; cider. ♀

A charming Victorian pub notable for its lovely flower displays. The regular bar menu of fish and chips, quiche, sandwiches, etc, is backed up by daily specials such as oxtail soup, salt beef (Monday & Friday), sausage toad and chicken, bacon and mushroom casserole. Good sweets, too, like rhubarb crumble or bread and butter pudding. *Typical prices:* Salt beef £2.95 Steak & kidney pudding £2.95 (No bar food eves or Sun).

Anchor

Superb views across the Thames to St Paul's can be enjoyed from the terrace of this famous Southwark inn. The Globe Theatre and Clink Prison once stood nearby, and Dr Johnson was a regular and appreciative customer. The present Georgian building features some fine pine panelling and a minstrel's gallery.

1 Bankside, Southwark, SE1 · Map 12 C2
01–407 1577 *Free House* *Landlord* T. Henry
Children welcome *Credit* Access, Amex, Diners, Visa
🍺 Courage Directors Bitter, Best Bitter; John Smith's Bitter; Guinness;
Kronenbourg; Hofmeister; cider.

Angel

There's been a tavern on this site since the 15th-century, when the monks of Bermondsey Priory spotted the potential of the superb view of the Thames. Notable customers have included Samuel Pepys, Captain Cook and the notorious Judge Jeffreys, while Laurel and Hardy are said to have been regular patrons. Today's pub has a modernised interior, and they've modernised the view, too.

101 Bermondsey Wall East, SE16 · Map 11 D2
01-237 3608 *Owner* THF *Landlord* N. Parker
Credit Access, Amex, Diners, Visa
🍺 Courage Best Bitter; Directors Bitter; John Smith's Bitter; Guinness; Kronenbourg; cider.

The Audley (Food) **New Entry**

41 Mount Street, W1 · Map 12 A2
01-499 1843

Free House
Landlords Mr & Mrs C. H. Plumpton

Credit Access, Amex, Diners, Visa
🍺 Webster's Yorkshire Bitter; Ruddle's County; William Younger's Scottish Bitter; Carlsberg; Budweiser.

Salads and sandwiches are the things to order at this busy pub, where ornate ceilings and much dark wood give a Victorian feel to the bar. Smoked salmon, mixed seafood, roast beef, roast turkey, ham carved off the bone in generous portions – all this can be enjoyed at the counter or at a comfortable table. Affable Australian staff. *Typical prices:* Seafood salad £6.95 Double-decker roast turkey sandwich £3.95 (Last bar food 10.30pm) ☕

Black Friar

Admirers of Art Nouveau will enjoy the turn of the century decor – carved woodwork, marble and mother of pearl inlay, stained glass windows and bas reliefs of friars – which gives a unique charm to this unusual wedge-shaped pub dating back 300 years and modernised by the Victorians. Closed weekends except Saturday lunchtime Mar–Oct.

174 Queen Victoria Street, EC4 · Map 12 C1
01-236 5650 *Owners* Nicholsons *Landlords* Mr & Mrs McKinstry
🍺 Adnams Bitter; Bass; Tetley's Bitter; Boddington's Bitter; Guinness; Tennent's; Castlemaine; Löwenbräu; cider.

Bull's Head

On the towpath beside the Thames at Chiswick, this popular pub dates from the 17th century. Its chief historical interest is that it was on more than one occasion used by Oliver Cromwell as his headquarters during the Civil War. Relax in the panelled bar or sip outside on the terrace.

Strand-on-the-Green, W4 · Map 10 A2
01-994 1204 *Owners* London Host *Landlords* Mr & Mrs R. D. Smart
Children welcome (lunchtime) *Credit* Access
🍺 Watneys Stag, Combes Bitter; Webster's Yorkshire Bitter; Guinness; Carlsberg; Holsten. ⚲

Cardinal *(Food)*

23 Francis Street, SW1 · Map 13 C1
01-834 7260

Brewery Charrington/H.H. Finch
Landlords Barry & Stella Rutson

Credit Access, Amex, Diners, Visa
🍺 Bass, IPA; Stones Best Bitter; Worthington Best Bitter; Guinness; Carling Black Label; Tennent's Extra. ♀

This smart, half-panelled pub offers cosy refuge from the bustle of nearby Victoria Street. Hot and cold tastes are catered for, with a blackboard menu of traditional favourites and an appetising display of home-cooked ham, game pie and quiche, with nice fresh salads. *Typical prices:* Steak & kidney pie £2.25   Sirloin & salad £5.95 (Last bar food 9pm. No bar food Sat & Sun) 🍽

Cask & Glass *(Food)* **New Entry**

39 Palace Street, SW1 · Map 13 C1
01-834 7630

Owners Chef & Brewer
Landlords R. & M. Beatty

🍺 Watneys Special Bitter, Yorkshire Bitter; Carlsberg.

A sandwich and a half of bitter (no pints sold) is the usual order at this pretty little corner pub presided over by kindly Mr and Mrs Beatty. Generously filled brown-bread sandwiches are made in advance for the lunchtime trade, to order in the evening. Outside snacking in the summer. *Typical prices:* Cream cheese & chive sandwich 95p Corned beef sandwich 95p (Last bar food 10.30pm. No bar food Sun). Closed Sunday evening. 🍽

City Barge

Although largely rebuilt after wartime bomb damage, this agreeable riverside pub still retains plenty of period charm. It takes its name from the Lord Mayor's staff barge, which used to be moored nearby. There are two bars and a terrace.

Strand-on-the-Green, W4 · Map 10 A2
01-994 2148 *Brewery* Courage *Landlords* Mr & Mrs Hitchings
Children welcome *Credit* Access, Visa
🍺 Courage Directors Bitter, Best Bitter, JC; Guinness; Hofmeister; Kronenbourg; cider.

Cock Tavern *(Food)*

Poultry Avenue, Central Markets, EC1
Map 12 C1
01-248 2918

Free House
Landlord Mr A. Burrows

Children welcome
Credit Access, Amex, Diners, Visa
🍺 Young's Special; Charles Wells Bombardier; Courage Best; Red Stripe Lager; cider. ♀

A cellar pub right in the heart of Smithfield Market, notable for its excellent food and long opening hours. Breakfast, served from 5.30am, offers anything from kippers to kidneys, from toast to a T-bone steak. Grills, roasts, game birds and salt beef sandwiches are lunchtime favourites, and in the evening there's a cold table. *Typical prices:* Hot salt beef sandwich £1.50   T-bone steak £9 (Last bar food 8pm). Closed Sat, Sun & Bank Holidays 🍽

40

Dickens Inn

In the heart of St Katharine's Dock redevelopment area, this popular pub is an 18th-century warehouse that's been reconstructed in the style of a balconied inn. The timber shell and many other features are original, and the decor, including antique marine bric-à-brac, is very much in keeping. It's on three floors, with a terrace.

St Katharine's Way, E1 · Map 11 C2
01–488 9936   *Free House*   *Landlord* Adrian Hyde
Credit Access, Amex, Diners, Visa
🍺 Dickens Special; Courage Best, Directors; Oliver's Bitter; Guinness; Kronenbourg; cider.

Dirty Dick's

The name is the sobriquet bestowed on an 18th-century landlord, one Nicholas Bentley. This worthy gentleman gave up cleaning his person and his premises after the death of his bride-to-be. The stone-floored cellar bar is startlingly true to his period of tenure, whereas the main bar is Victorian in style. Closed Sat & Sun eves.

202 Bishopsgate, EC2 · Map 11 C2
01–283 5888   *Owner* Mr Hardy   *Landlord* Mr Hardy
Credit Access, Amex, Diners, Visa
🍺 Charrington's IPA, Bass; Greene King IPA, Abbot Ale; Courage Directors; Guinness; Carling Black Label; Foster's; cider. ♀

Dove

This pleasant pub stands beside the Thames in a group of handsome Georgian houses. It has long been a popular watering hole, and there are fine river views from the terrace. Famous names associated with the Dove include the painter Turner and James Thomson, who wrote the words of 'Rule Britannia'.

19 Upper Mall, W6 · Map 10 A2
01–748 5405   *Brewery* Fuller, Smith & Turner   *Landlord* Mr Lorrey
🍺 Fuller's ESB, London Pride; Tennent's Lager; Heineken.

Eagle

'Up and down the City Road, In and out of the Eagle': this is the Eagle in question, immortalised in those words from 'Pop Goes the Weasel'. Marie Lloyd made her bow here when it was one of London's best-loved variety theatres.

2 Shepherdess Walk, N1 · Map 11 C1
01–253 4715   *Brewery* Charrington   *Landlord* Mr L. Deadfield
🍺 Charrington's IPA, Bass, Toby Bitter; Guinness; Carling Black Label; Tennent's Extra; cider. ♀

Flask

A pub of considerable character, with beams and panelling in the cosy bars and a pleasant hedged forecourt for summer sipping. It takes its name from the flasks filled with Hampstead's spa water which could once be obtained here.

77 Highgate West Hill, N6 · Map 10 B1
01–340 3969   *Brewery* Taylor Walker   *Landlord* Mrs G. Light
Credit Access, Visa
🍺 Taylor Walker Bitter; John Bull's Bitter; Ind Coope Burton Ale; Guinness; Löwenbräu; Oranjeboom; Castlemaine; cider.

Fox & Anchor   *(Food)*

116 Charterhouse Street, EC1 · Map 12 C1
01–253 4838

Brewery Taylor Walker
Landlord Mr O'Connell

Children welcome
Credit Visa
🍺 Taylor Walker Bitter; John Bull Bitter; Burton Ale; Guinness; Skol; cider. ♀

Hearty breakfasts served from 6am keep the workers from nearby Smithfield market happy at this friendly, late-Victorian pub. Not surprisingly, the meat here is first class – superb sausages, chops, prime beef and lamb – but you can also have something lighter such as soup, sandwiches and salads. Patio. *Typical prices:* Steak & kidney pie £5.50   Rump steak £6.85 (No bar food eves). Closed weekends & ten days Christmas. ⊖

George Inn

Built around a courtyard where Shakespeare's plays were once performed, London's sole surviving galleried inn stands no more than 500 yards from the site of the Globe Theatre. Oak panelling, beams, and leaded windows create a richly atmospheric ambience.

77 Borough High Street, Southwark, SE1 · Map 12 C2
01–407 2056   *Brewery* Whitbread   *Landlord* Mr John Hall
Children welcome   *Credit* Access, Amex, Diners, Visa
🍺 Flowers Original; Wethered's Bitter; Greene King Abbot Ale; Guinness; Fremlins; Stella Artois; cider.

Glasshouse Stores   *(Food)*   **New Entry**

Brewer Street, W1 · Map 12 A2
01–734 4771

Brewery Taylor Walker
Landlords Robert & Christine Cook

Children welcome
Credit Access, Amex, Visa
🍺 Taylor Walker Best Bitter; Burton Ale; Guinness; Skol; Löwenbräu; cider.

Frequently busy but rarely too crowded, so you can snack in relative comfort at this Edwardian-style Soho pub, whose most notable feature is its ornate bar ceiling. Snacks cover a standard spread and preparation is careful, from sandwiches and salads to hot lunchtime dishes such as lasagne, chilli or steak and kidney pie. Vegetable dishes, but no puds. *Typical prices:* Lasagne £1.15   Vegetable provençale £1.15 (Last bar food 10.30pm. No bar food Sun) ⊖

Goat (Food) *New Entry*

3a Kensington High Street, W8 · Map 13 A1
01–937 1213

Free House
Landlords Jane & Stuart Davies

Credit Access, Amex, Diners, Visa
Webster's Yorkshire Bitter; Younger's Bitter, IPA; Guinness; Carlsberg; cider.

There's been a pub here for over 300 years, and the present building dates from 1771. In the long, narrow bar they serve typical pub fare – ploughman's, sausages, steak and kidney pie, beef and pasta bake, a decent quiche served with a simple salad selection. Limited choice Sunday lunchtime. *Typical prices:* Cornish pasty with vegetables £1.50 Beef & pasta bake with vegetables £2.50 (Last bar food 9pm. No bar food Sun eve) ⊖

Grapes

Down by the Thames in the heart of dockland, this pleasant little 16th-century pub is a peaceful spot for a drink. Ties with the dockland life and the literary world are strong, and the Grapes was reputedly the model for the 'Six Jolly Fellowship Porters' in Charles Dickens' *Our Mutual Friend*.

76 Narrow Street, E14 · Map 11 D2
01–987 4396 *Brewery* Taylor Walker *Landlord* Mr Frank Johnson
Credit Access
Taylor Walker Bitter; Ind Coope Burton Ale; Friary Meux Bitter; Guinness; Löwenbräu; cider.

Grenadier

Once the mess for the Duke of Wellington's officers, this famous pub stands in a quiet cobbled mews, its position signalled by a smart sentry box outside. The military theme continues within, and in the cosy little bar you can enjoy a pint of well-kept ale or one of the long-serving barman's justly popular Bloody Marys.

18 Wilton Row, SW1 · Map 13 C1
01–235 3074 *Owner* London Hosts *Landlord* Mr A. R. Taylor
Children welcome *Credit* Access, Amex, Diners, Visa
Ruddle's County; Webster's Yorkshire Bitter; Watneys Stag, Combes Bitter; Guinness; Holsten; Carlsberg; cider. ⚲

Greyhound (Food) *New Entry*

1 Kensington Square, W8 · Map 13 A1
01–937 7140

Free House
Landlord Mr J. Dougall

Charles Wells Bombardier; Greene King Abbot Ale; Yorkshire Bitter; Guinness; Foster's; cider.

Built in 1899, this friendly pub faces a pretty square just moments from the clamour of High Street Kensington. The bar food is very reasonable and covers quite a good range, from sandwiches, cold pies, Scotch eggs and simple salads to hot specials like Somerset sausage casserole or spicy stuffed peppers. Tables outside in fine weather. No sweets. *Typical prices:* Steak & kidney pie £2.75 Somerset sausage casserole £2.70 (Last bar food 10pm) ⊖

Hand & Shears

Named after the emblem of the Guild of Merchant Taylors, this little corner pub was a favourite haunt in Tudor times of tailors from nearby Cloth Fair. Later on, a less happy association developed with prisoners from Newgate, who were allowed to take their last drink here. Closed Saturday & Sunday.

1 Middle Street, EC1 · Map 12 C1
01–600 0257   *Brewery* Courage   *Landlord* Mr Latimer
🍺 Courage Directors Bitter, Best Bitter; Guinness; Hofmeister; Kronenbourg; cider.

Jack Straw's Castle

A leader of the Peasants' Revolt of 1381 is commemorated in the name of this striking weatherboarded pub on the top of Hampstead Heath, near the Round Pond. The haunt of highwaymen and Victorian artists and writers – including, of course, Mr Dickens – the old Castle was damaged in the 1940 blitz and completely rebuilt in the 1960s.

North End Way, NW3 · Map 10 B1
01–435 8374   *Brewery* Charrington   *Landlords* Brian & Alva Hillyard
Credit Access, Amex, Diners, Visa
🍺 Charrington's IPA, Bass; Stones Bitter; Guinness; Tennent's Extra; cider. ♀

Lamb

Victorian cut-glass snob screens are a noteworthy feature of this warmly inviting pub, which Charles Dickens was wont to pop into, as his house was just round the corner. The walls are covered with sepia photographs of Victorian and Edwardian stars of theatre and music hall. Small area for outdoor drinking.

94 Lamb's Conduit Street, WC1 · Map 12 B1
01–405 0713   *Brewery* Young   *Landlord* Mr R. White
🍺 Young's Bitter, Special Bitter, Winter Warmer; Guinness; John Young's London Lager, Premium Lager; cider.

Lamb & Flag   (Food)

33 Rose Street, WC2 · Map 12 B2
01–836 4108

Brewery Courage
Landlord Terry Archer

🍺 Courage Best Bitter, Directors Bitter; John Smith's Yorkshire Bitter; Guinness; Kronenbourg 1664; Miller Lite; cider.

Cheese is king at this famous old pub, where customers frequently spill out from the tiny bars on to the street. Somerset Brie and blue Cheshire have recently joined stalwarts like Stilton, Cheddar, Caerphilly and sage Derby, and they can all be enjoyed with baguettes or slices of delicious hot bread. There's also the odd hot lunchtime dish. *Typical prices:* Ploughman's £1.60   Two-cheese ploughman's £2.60 (Last bar food 10pm) ©

Mayflower

In 1611 the captain of the *Mayflower* was enjoying a pint at this characterful dockland pub when he received his commission to transport the Pilgrim Fathers to America. The century is faithfully recalled in the beamed bars with their fascinating collection of nautical memorabilia, and the jetty commands splendid views of the Thames.

117 Rotherhithe Street, SE16 · Map 11 D2
01–237 4088 *Owner* Vintage Inns *Landlord* Mr Emslie
Children welcome *Credit* Access, Amex, Diners, Visa
🍺 Charrington's IPA, Bass; Guinness; Carling Black Label; Tennent's Lager; cider.

Museum Tavern

Karl Marx is said to have taken refreshment breaks from his studies at this handsome corner pub opposite the British Museum, and it is a popular haunt today with both students and tourists. The large, bustling bar is a veritable extravaganza of Victorian-style gilded columns, carved wood and stained and frosted glass.

49 Great Russell Street, WC1 · Map 12 B1
01–242 8987 *Free House* *Landlord* Mr Clark
Credit Access, Amex, Diners, Visa
🍺 Greene King IPA; Brakspear's Special; Ruddle's County; Charles Wells Bombardier; Guinness; Carlsberg; Foster's; cider.

Nag's Head

Close to the Royal Opera House, this 18th-century pub attracts a fashionable pre-theatre crowd to its plush, Edwardian-style bar that's decorated with etched mirrors and playbills. Its first customers were, in contrast, market porters taking a break from their early-morning duties in Covent Garden market.

10 James Street, WC2 · Map 12 B1
01–836 4678 *Brewery* McMullen *Landlords* Mr & Mrs Grant
🍺 McMullen's Country Bitter; Guinness; Steingold; Hartsman; cider.

Nell of Old Drury

The lady in question is Nell Gwynn, one-time orange seller – her pitch the steps of the Theatre Royal across the street from this pub – and later on the mistress of Charles II. Playbills decorate the walls of the pub's simply appointed bar, where dramatist Richard Sheridan is said to have drunk. Closed Sunday.

29 St Catherine Street, WC2 · Map 12 B1
01–836 5328 *Brewery* Courage *Landlord* Mr Dunphy
Credit Access, Diners
🍺 Courage Directors Bitter, Best Bitter; John Smith's Bitter; Guinness; Kronenbourg; Hofmeister; cider.

Old Bell Tavern

Journalists and printers pack the simple bar of this busy Fleet Street tavern, where once Sir Christopher Wren's workmen quenched their thirst during the building of St Bride's next door. The excellent and exceptionally well kept real ales are a great attraction. Closed Saturday evening and all Sunday.

95 Fleet Street, EC4 · Map 12 C1
01–583 0070   *Free House   Landlord* Mrs N. Healy
🍺 Old Bell Bitter; Wadworth's 6X; Tetley's Bitter; Boddington's Bitter; Guinness; Castlemaine; Löwenbräu; cider.

Old Bull & Bush

Once the home of the painter William Hogarth, this former farmhouse was immortalised in the music halls by Florrie Ford's song 'Down at the Old Bull and Bush'. Pictures of her and of many other artists provide the main decorative theme. The pub stands on the edge of Hampstead Heath and has a pleasant beer garden.

North End Way, NW3 · Map 10 B1
01–455 3685   *Brewery* Taylor Walker   *Landlord* Graham Dove
🍺 Taylor Walker Bitter; Burton Bitter; Guinness; Löwenbräu; Skol; cider.

Old Ship   New Entry

The Old Ship dates back in parts to the 16th century, which makes it the oldest pub on this stretch of the river. The two traditional-plush bars are adorned with various nautical trappings, including rowing sculls and blades. The cosy fires are an attraction in winter, the Thames-side patio a summer draw.

25 Upper Mall, W6 · Map 10 A2
01–748 3970   *Brewery* Watneys   *Landlord* Mrs M. McCormack
Children welcome (lunchtime)
🍺 Watneys Stag, Combe; Webster's Yorkshire Bitter; Guinness; Budweiser; Foster's; cider.

Orange Brewery   *(Food)*

37 Pimlico Road, SW1 · Map 13 C2
01–730 5378

Owner Clifton Inns
Landlords John & Avryl Fletcher

Credit Access, Amex, Diners
🍺 Orange SW1, SW2, Pimlico Light (summer), Pimlico Porter (winter); Guinness; Foster's; Holsten; cider.

Home-brewed bitters are a popular feature of the simple cheerful Pimlico pub. Snacks are available in both bars and range from freshly made sandwiches and ploughman's to hot dishes such as lasagne and chilli con carne. A special favourite is the hot roast beef sandwich, generously filled and tingling with horseradish. Tasty soup for starters and cheesecake for afters. *Typical prices:* Hot roast beef sandwich £1.85   Beef bourguignon £3 (Last bar food 10.30pm) ✍

46

Paxton's Head

Named after the multi-talented Sir John Paxton, who designed the original Crystal Palace for the Great Exhibition of 1851 in nearby Hyde Park, this is a popular and lively pub with great atmosphere. The mock-Victorian main bar has comfortable plush velvet seats and polished mahogany walls decorated with lovely etched mirrors.

153 Knightsbridge, SW1 · Map 13 B1
01–589 6627   *Owner* H. H. Finch & Co.   *Landlord* George Redgewell
Credit Access, Amex, Diners, Visa
🍺 Ind Coope Burton Ale, Special Bitter; John Bull; Double Diamond; Guinness; Skol; Löwenbräu; cider. ♀

Prince Regent

Portraits and caricatures of the Prince Regent abound in this smart and ever-popular corner pub, whose decor also features warrants, medals and many other princely memorabilia. Of interest, too, is the collection of little brass plaques engraved by a former landlord with the names of his faithful regulars. Patio.

71 Marylebone High Street, W1 · Map 12 A1
01–935 2018   *Brewery* Charrington   *Landlord* Mr Thomas MacCormick
Credit Access, Amex, Diners, Visa
🍺 Charrington's IPA; Bass; Worthington Best Bitter; Guinness; Tennent's Lager; Carling Black Label; cider.

Princess Louise   *New Entry*

A pub of great character, and a real gem of late Victoriana. Ornate moulded ceilings, etched mirrors and painted tiles take the eye in the bar (along with the pretty barmaids), and the loos sport some original marble and brass. The food here comes a distant second to the beer. London Standard Pub of the Year 1986.

208 High Holborn, WC1 · Map 12 B1
01–405 8816   *Brewery* Vaux   *Landlord* Ian Phillips
🍺 Vaux Samson Ale; Ward's Sheffield Bitter; Greene King Abbot Ale; Brakspear's Bitter; Guinness; Tuborg Pilsner; cider.

Printer's Devil

Named after the traditional nickname for a printer's apprentice or errand boy, this busy old pub is not surprisingly much frequented by workers from nearby Fleet Street. The main bar features a fine display of woodcuts, old books and models of printing presses. Rare in the City, there's also a public bar. Closed Saturday and Sunday lunchtimes.

98 Fetter lane, EC4 · Map 12 C1
01–242 2239   *Brewery* Whitbread   *Landlords* Mr & Mrs Gibbs
Credit Amex, Diners, Visa
🍺 Whitbread Best Bitter, Trophy Bitter; Wethered's Bitter; Flowers Original; Greene King Abbot Ale; Guinness.

Prospect of Whitby

One of London's best known and best loved riverside pubs, once a den of
thieves and smugglers, now a must for thousands of tourists every year.
Turner and Whistler came to paint river scenes, Dickens to drink, Judge
Jeffreys to dine while watching pirates hang.

57 Wapping Wall, E1 · Map 11 D2
01–481 1095   *Owners* London Hosts   *Landlord* Mr Trevor Chapman
Children welcome   *Credit* Access, Amex, Diners, Visa
🍺 Watney's Stag, Combes Bitter; Webster's Yorkshire Bitter; Ruddle's
County; Guinness; cider.

Railway Tavern

Railway buffs should get up a head of steam and make for this busy pub
near Liverpool Street Station. It's full of pre-electric memories, with
photographs and models of old locomotives and crests of 19th-century
railway companies. Closed Sat, Sun, Bank Holidays and eves after 9pm.

15 Liverpool Street, EC2 · Map 11 C2
01–283 3598   *Brewery* Whitbread   *Landlord* Mr Hanley
Credit Access, Amex, Diners, Visa
🍺 Flowers Original; Wethered's Marlow Bitter; Whitbread Trophy;
Boddington's Bitter; Guinness; Stella Artois.

Red Lion   (Food)

23 Crown Passage, Pall Mall, SW1 · Map 12 A2
01–930 8067

Brewery Watney Combe Reid
Landlord Michael McAree

🍺 Ruddle's County; Webster's Yorkshire Bitter;
Guinness; Budweiser; Foster's. 🍷

A welcoming and very popular pub in a
passage off Pall Mall. The trade in bar food
is brisk, with most people opting for the
excellent home-made pies (chunky chicken,
steak and kidney, beef and ale). There's a
good choice of salads and sandwiches, but
no starters or sweets. *Typical prices:* Chunky
chicken pie £3.10 Beef & ale pie £3.95 (Last
bar food 11pm). Closed Bank Holiday Mondays ⊝

Red Lion

Built in 1723 to accommodate the builders constructing Chesterfield
House, the home of Lord Berkeley, this cosy pub was the headquarters of
the US Airborne Division during World War II. Today, its darkly panelled
interior, leaded windows and old pub prints make it a favourite haunt of
many, and the little front patio is popular in summer.

1 Waverton Street, W1 · Map 12 A2
01–499 1307   *Owner* London Hosts   *Landlord* Mr David Butterfield
Credit Access, Amex, Diners, Visa
🍺 Webster's Yorkshire Bitter; Watneys Stag; Combes Bitter; Ruddle's
County; Guinness; Foster's; Holsten; cider.

Salisbury

A favourite meeting place before the play, with the lush decor of the 1890s and a clientele that is sometimes equally colourful. Moulded ceilings, engraved glass screens, gilded statuettes and red velvet summon up the right mood for an evening at the theatre.

90 St Martin's Lane, WC2 · Map 12 B2
01-836 5863   *Owner* Clifton Inns   *Landlord* Mr Gerry Wynne
Credit Access, Amex, Diners, Visa
🍺 Ind Coope Burton Ale; Taylor Walker Bitter; John Bull Bitter;
Guinness; Löwenbräu; Castlemaine; cider.

Samuel Pepys

A representation of a 17th-century inn, skilfully constructed in an old warehouse on the Thames opposite Bankside. Samuel Pepys was not only a diarist but also for some time Secretary to the Navy, and both facets are recalled in detail in the flagstoned cellar bar. Closed Bank Holidays.

Brooks Wharf, 48 Upper Thames Street, EC4 · Map 12 C2
01-248 3048   *Brewery* Charrington   *Landlord* Mr Spencer
Children welcome   *Credit* Access, Amex, Diners, Visa
🍺 Charrington's IPA, Bass; Stones Bitter; Guinness; Carling Black
Label; Tennent's Pilsner, Extra; cider. ♀

Seven Stars

First licensed in 1602, this delightful little pub situated between the Law Courts and Lincoln's Inn Fields is much loved by the legal profession. The busy bar features Spy cartoons of eminent judges and lawyers. Closed Saturday, Sunday and Bank Holidays.

53 Carey Street, WC2 · Map 12 B1
01-242 8521   *Brewery* Courage   *Landlord* Mr J. A. Crawley
🍺 Courage Best Bitter, Directors, JC; Guinness; Hofmeister;
Kronenbourg; cider.

Shepherd's Tavern

You can phone from a converted sedan chair (once the property of the Duke of Cumberland) in an upstairs room of this 300-year-old pub on a corner site in the heart of Shepherd Market. Downstairs, a large bow window and mellow pine panelling add to the traditional charms of the bar.

Hertford Street, W1 · Map 12 A2
01-499 3017   *Owner* London Hosts   *Landlord* Mr Lindley
Credit Access, Amex, Diners, Visa
🍺 Ruddle's County; Watney's Stag Bitter; Webster's Yorkshire Bitter;
Guinness; Holsten; cider.

Sherlock Holmes

Sherlock Holmes' creator Sir Arthur Conan Doyle was a regular here when it was the Northumberland Arms, and he mentions it in *The Hound of the Baskervilles*. It's now something of a mecca for fans of the indomitable detective, with its collection of Holmes memorabilia and early instruments of forensic science.

10 Northumberland Street, WC2 · Map 12 B2
01-930 2644   *Brewery* Whitbread   *Landlord* Mr E. C. Hardcastle
Credit Access, Amex, Diners, Visa
🍺 Whitbread, Flowers Original; Guinness; Stella Artois; Heineken.

Ship

Boat Race Day brings the crowds to the Thames towpath and to this pleasant pub right opposite the finishing post. In a history going back to the first Elizabeth it has borne several names, including the Hart's Horn and the Blue Anchor.

10 Thames Bank, Riverside, SW14 · Map 10 A3
01-876 1439   *Owner* Gateway Hosts   *Landlord* Mr A. G. Davidson
Children welcome   *Credit* Access, Visa
🍺 Combes Bitter; Ruddle's County; Webster's Yorkshire Bitter; Guinness; Carlsberg; Foster's; Budweiser; cider.

Slug & Lettuce   *(Food)*   **New Entry**

47 Hereford Road, W2 · Map 10 B2
01-229 1503

Brewery Watney, Combe & Reid
Landlord Mr Paul Hayles

Children welcome
🍺 Ruddle's County Bitter; Webster's Yorkshire Bitter; Combes Bitter; Guinness; Holsten; Budweiser; cider.

The philosophy in this smartened-up Victorian pub is to concentrate on the food side while retaining the pub atmosphere. The range is comprehensive, with everything cooked on the premises: a selection from the blackboard could include eggs Benedict, smoked mackerel, tagliatelle carbonara, sirloin steak Café de Paris, and ice cream with butterscotch sauce. *Typical prices:* Seafood pancakes £3.50   Country terrine £2 (Last bar food 10.15pm) ⊖

Slug & Lettuce   *(Food)*

1 Islington Green, N1 · Map 11 C1
01-226 3864

Brewery Watney Combe Reid
Landlord Mr Chris Bromley

Children welcome
🍺 Ruddle's County; Combes Bitter; Webster's Yorkshire Bitter; Guinness; Foster's; Holsten; cider.

The cooking is consistently enjoyable at this large, bustling Victorian pub very much geared towards food. The daily changing blackboard menu is imaginative, and has something for everyone: cream of lettuce soup, hot vegetable platter, tagliatelle napoletana, lamb's kidneys with a brandy sauce. A good selection of cheeses and sweets. Outside tables. *Typical prices:* Seafood pancakes £4.25   Orange & lemon cheesecake £1.95 (Last bar food 10.15pm) ⊖

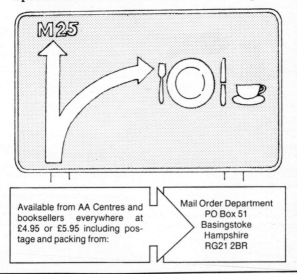

Slug & Lettuce *(Food)*

11 Warwick Way · SW1 · Map 13 C1
01–834 3313

Brewery Watney Combe Reid
Landlord Mr Hugh Corbett

🍺 Ruddle's County; Webster's Yorkshire Bitter;
Combes Bitter; Guinness; Holsten; Carlsberg;
Budweiser; cider.

The blackboard menu changes daily at this attractive pub-cum-bistro with a lively atmosphere. Light bites range from soup and garlic mushrooms to bacon and egg baps, while more substantial fare includes a tasty tagliatelle, honey-baked ham salad, rack of lamb, and a chicken, apricot and mozzarella pie. Yummy sweets. *Typical prices:* Chicken breast with avocado & garlic £4.50 Baked cheesy ratatouille £2.50 (Last bar food 10.15pm) ✍

Spaniards Inn

A famous old pub near Hampstead Heath, with a weatherboarded frontage and mellow beamed bars. Its garden was used as the setting for the tea party in Dickens' *Pickwick Papers*. Other literary connections abound, but the pub's best known links are with the highwayman Dick Turpin.

Spaniards Road, NW3 · Map 10 B1
01–455 3276   *Owner* Vintage Inns   *Landlord* David Roper
Children welcome   *Credit* Access, Amex, Visa
🍺 Charrington's IPA; Bass; Stones Bitter; Guinness; Carling Black Label; Tennent's Extra; cider.

Sun Inn

This popular pub dating from the 18th century overlooks Barnes Pond and the common. The bowling green in front of the pub has a much longer history, and the story goes it was there that Drake and Walsingham taught Elizabeth I to play bowls. Ground-floor rooms are traditional in style, the cellar bar modern.

7 Church Road, Barnes, SW13 · Map 10 A3
01–876 5893   *Brewery* Taylor Walker   *Landlords* Len & John Harris
🍺 Taylor Walker Bitter; Ind Coope Burton Ale; John Bull; Tetley's Bitter; Guinness; Löwenbräu; Castlemaine; cider.

Swan Tavern   *(Food)*   `New Entry`

66 Bayswater Road, W2 · Map 10 B2
01–262 5204

Free House
Landlord D. C. Stone

Children welcome
🍺 Tetley's Bitter; Webster's Yorkshire Bitter;
Friary Meux Bitter; Foster's; Carlsberg; cider.

A traditional, white-painted pub on busy Bayswater Road, its large terrace filled with tables, benches and parasols. The bar food is very decent, comprising an assortment of home-made pies, hot sausages and the very popular turkey casserole, plus quiches, cold turkey, ham and simple, well-made salads. Children are admitted to the back bar. *Typical prices:* Steak & kidney pie £2.50 Turkey casserole £2.50 (Last bar food 10pm) ✍

Tom Cribb

Originally called the Union Arms, this popular corner pub was renamed when barefist prize-fighter Tom Cribb became its landlord following his retirement from the ring in 1811. Prints and posters in the cosy panelled bar record his and others' pugilistic exploits. In fine weather, tables with parasols are set out on the pavement.

36 Panton Street, SW1 · Map 12 B2
01–839 6536   *Brewery* Charrington   *Landlord* P. Cook
🍺 Charrington's IPA, Bass; Worthington Best Bitter; Guinness; Carling Black Label; Tennent's Extra; cider.

Trafalgar Tavern

Originally built in the 1830s, this handsome Thames-side tavern was sympathetically restored in 1965. The decor is decidedly nautical, and the bars and restaurants take their names from Nelson's admirals. One bar is a representation of the forecastle of a ship of the line about 1730.

Park Row, SE10 · Map 11 D2
01–858 2437   *Owners* Gateway Hosts   *Landlord* Mr E. Thomas
🍺 Ruddle's County; Ben Truman Export; Webster's Yorkshire Bitter; Guinness; Carlsberg; Holsten; cider.

Two Chairmen

An authentic 18th-century tavern in a dignified Westminster street. A sign depicting two sedan chairmen hangs outside, and there's a similar theme in the panelled bar with its charming murals. Closed Saturday evening and all Sunday.

39 Dartmouth Street, SW1 · Map 12 B2
01-222 8694   *Owners* Clifton Inns   *Landlord* Miss Jenny Allcorn
🍺 King & Barnes Sussex Bitter; Webster's Yorkshire Bitter; Ruddle's County; Guinness; Foster's; Carlsberg; cider.

Two Chairmen

In a narrow street near Trafalgar Square, this pleasant little pub was built in 1683 and reconstructed 200 years later. Its name refers to the sedan chairmen who kept City folk on the move during the 17th and 18th centuries, and prints of London life line the walls of the welcoming bar.

Warwick House Street, off Cockspur Street, SW1 · Map 12 B2
01–930 1166   *Brewery* Courage   *Landlord* J. Lorking
🍺 Courage Best Bitter, Directors; Hofmeister; Kronenbourg; cider.

Victoria

Queen Victoria called in at this lovely old pub when she opened nearby Paddington Station. Perhaps she too admired the etched glass, mahogany panelling and ornate plaster ceiling, though she might not have been amused by the fittings from the Gaiety Theatre in the upstairs bar!

10a Strathearn Place, W2 · Map 10 B2
01-262 5696   *Brewery* Charrington   *Landlords* Mr & Mrs Bryne
🍺 Charrington's IPA, Bass; Stones Bitter; Guinness; Carling Black Label; Tennent's Extra; cider. ♀

White Horse on Parsons Green   (Food)

1 Parsons Green, SW6 · Map 10 A3
01-736 2115

Brewery Vintage Inns
Landlord Mrs Sally Cruickshank

Children welcome (lunchtime)
🍺 Bass; Springfield Bitter; Charrington's IPA; Highgate Mild Ale; Guinness; Carling Black Label; Tennent's Extra; cider. ♀

Hearty weekend breakfasts and wine tastings with Spanish tapas are typical of Sally Cruickshank's imaginative approach to food. She supplements favourites like quiche, jacket potatoes and salads with such appetising daily specials as chicken casserole and savoury cod. Traditional Sunday roast, and crêpes for dessert. *Typical prices:* Sweet & sour pork £2.85   Liver casserole & vegetables £2.50 (Last bar food 9pm. No bar food Sat & Sun eves) ☺

Windsor Castle

A young and lively crowd throngs this welcoming pub, which stands atop Campden Hill on the site of the now forgotten Kensington spa. Oak and elm panelling and old settles add to the period charm, and in summer there are lots of tables and chairs in the garden.

114 Campden Hill Road, W8 · Map 13 A1
01-727 8491   *Brewery* Charrington   *Landlord* A. J. Owen
Credit Visa
🍺 Charrington's IPA; Bass; Guinness; Carling Black Label; Tennent's Extra; cider. ♀

Yacht

There are splendid river views from the terrace of this popular Thames-side pub, which dates back to the 17th century but was rebuilt after World War II bomb damage. The watery theme continues in the mahogany-panelled bar with its portholes, nautical instruments, and yachting photographs.

Crane Street, SE10 · Map 11 D2
01-858 0175   *Owner* Gateway Hosts   *Landlord* Mr T. Ryan
Children welcome
🍺 Webster's Yorkshire Bitter; Watneys Stag; Guinness; Holsten; Foster's; cider.

Ye Grapes *(Food)*

16 Shepherd Market, W1 · Map 12 A2
01-629 4989

Free House
Landlords A. F. Wigram & P. I. Jacobs

🍺 Wethered's Bitter; Arkell's BBB; Ind Coope Burton Ale; Brakspear's Bitter; Guinness; Stella Artois; cider.

Popular, fine old Victorian pub, efficiently run by the smartly uniformed staff who serve an appetising selection of lunchtime dishes from one end of the bar. Regulars enjoy cold meats, traditional pork or turkey pie, smoked salmon, sandwiches or pâté, all with potato salad and coleslaw. There's also an excellent hot dish of the day. Just sandwiches in the evening. *Typical prices:* Lasagne with salad £2.60 Cottage pie with salad £2.25 (Last bar food 9.30. No bar food Sun) ⊖

Ye Old Dr Butler's Head

Dr William Butler, physician to James I and a great believer in the medicinal properties of ale, founded this City hostelry in 1610. Today, his spirit lives on in the form of a convivial crowd that throngs the sawdust-strewn bar with its blackened beams and old brewery mirrors. Closed Saturday, Sunday & Bank Holidays.

Mason's Avenue, Coleman Street, EC2 · Map 12 C1
01-606 3504 *Free House* *Landlords* Nigel & Caroline Field
Credit Access, Amex, Diners, Visa
🍺 Bass; Tolly Cobbold Original; Guinness; Tennent's Extra; Carling Black Label; cider.

Ye Olde Cheshire Cheese

Once a favourite tippling place of Dr Johnson's, this renowned Fleet Street pub now attracts journalists, lawyers and tourists. It was rebuilt in 1667 after the Great Fire of London, and the sawdust-strewn floors, panelled stairway and narrow courtyard contribute to its immense period charm. Closed Saturday & Sunday.

145 Fleet Street, EC4 · Map 12 C1
01-353 6170 *Owner* Mr L. Kerly *Landlord* Mr L. Kerly
🍺 Marston's Pedigree; Burton Bitter; Pilsner Lager.

Ye Olde Cock Tavern

Both the Great Fire of London and the Plague by-passed this venerable tavern right opposite the Law Courts and presided over by a fine gilded cock. Scribblers continue to outnumber barristers – in keeping with the strong literary and theatrical tradition – and a superb Tudor chimney piece dominates the beamed and galleried bar.

22 Fleet Street, EC4 · Map 12 B1
01-353 3454 *Owner* London Hosts *Landlord* Sarah Kelly
Credit Access, Amex, Diners, Visa
🍺 Truman's Best Bitter, Bitter, Mild; Guinness; Holsten; Carlsberg; Foster's.

Ye Olde Mitre Tavern

This little gem of a pub in a narrow passageway linking Hatton Garden and Ely Place was originally built in 1546 for the Bishop of Ely and later used as a prison and Civil War hospital. The present 18th-century building has considerable charm, with its beamed ceiling, darkwood panelling and handsome furnishings. Closed Sat, Sun, Bank Holidays & Christmas.

1 Ely Court, Ely Place, Holborn, EC1 · Map 12 C1
01–405 4751 *Brewery* Ind Coope *Landlord* M. M. Kennedy
🍺 Ind Coope Burton Ale, Double Diamond; Friary Meux Bitter; Guinness; Skol.

Ye Olde Watling

This gem of a pub in London's oldest street was once Sir Christopher Wren's office and provided lodgings for the workmen building St Paul's Cathedral. Little has changed over the centuries, and there are massive black beams, arched doorways and leaded windows in the bar. Closed Sat eve, all Sun, eves from about 8 & Bank Holidays.

29 Watling Street, EC4 · Map 12 C1
01–248 6252 *Brewery* Vintage Inns *Landlord* Mr D. Firth
Credit Access, Amex, Diners, Visa
🍺 Charrington's IPA, Bass; Guinness; Carling Black Label; Tennent's Extra; cider.

Ye Olde Windmill Inn *(B & B)*

South Side, Clapham Common, SW4 · Map 10 B3
01–673 4578
Brewery Young
Landlord Mr P. Nazer
Children welcome
Credit Access, Visa
🍺 Young's Bitter, Special Bitter, Winter Warmer (winter only); London Lager, Premier Lager; Guinness; cider. ♀
ACCOMMODATION 13 bedrooms £C (No dogs)
Check-in: all day

Once a prominent coaching inn, this sturdy pub by Clapham Common makes a convenient overnight stopping place for motorists. Bedrooms are smartly modern, with neat fitted furniture, colour TVs and tea-makers. One has a full bathroom, the rest shower units and washbasins. The spacious bars boast some fine wood panelling and stained glass, and there are two outside drinking areas. No children overnight.

ENGLAND

Abberley *(Food)* — *Bell at Pensax*

Near Worcester · *Hereford & Worcester*
Map 8 D1
Great Witley (029 921) 677

Free House
Landlords Robert & Pam Eaton

Children welcome
Hook Norton Bitter; Wadworth's 6X; Timothy Taylor's Bitter; Castlemaine; Stella Artois; cider.

Pam Eaton's good food and husband Robert's ready wit attract the customers to this out-of-the-way pub. Pam's speciality is her prize-winning lamb and apricot hot pot but her soups, pâtés, garlic mushrooms, casseroles and spaghetti bolognese are all firm favourites. Bumper helpings leave little room for tempting sweets. *Typical prices:* Garlic mushrooms £1.75 Lamb & apricot hot pot £3.75 (Last bar food 10pm)

Ainsworth *(Food)* — *Duke William Inn*

Well Street, near Bolton · *Greater Manchester* · Map 3 B3
Bolton (0204) 24726

Brewery Whitbread
Landlords Ann & Basil Coller-Brown

Whitbread Trophy; Dutton's Light; Chester's Best Mild; Heldenbrau; Stella Artois; Heineken; cider. *No real ale.*

Customers come from far and wide to enjoy the splendid lunchtime bar snacks that have made this cosy Georgian pub so popular. Home-made savoury pies are great favourites, along with pâté, grills and daily specials like roast lamb or poached halibut with shrimp sauce. Book, and remember that the early bird has the widest choice. *Typical prices:* Steak & mushroom pie £2.50 Mixed grill £4.95 (No bar food Sat, Sun or eves)

Alford Crossways *(Food)* — *Napoleon Arms*

Near Cranleigh · *Surrey* · Map 6 B3
Loxwood (0403) 752357

Free House
Landlords Wilf & Mary Forgham

Children welcome (except Sat eve)
Credit Access, Amex, Diners, Visa
Webster's Yorkshire Bitter; Fuller's London Pride; Carlsberg; cider. ♀

A pretty patio fronts this low, white-painted pub set back from the road. A good choice of bar food is available at lunchtime and in the evening, from light bites like sandwiches, filled jacket potatoes, omelettes and salads to full meals. The truly hungry can follow garlic mushrooms or French onion soup with, say, roast beef, fillet of cod or fried chicken – and profiteroles or apple pie for afters. *Typical prices:* Trout with almonds £3.40 Chicken curry £3 (Last bar food 10pm)

Alfriston *(B & B)* — *George Inn*

East Sussex · Map 6 C4

Owner Hotels of the Cinque Ports
Landlord Mrs Bond

Credit Access, Amex, Diners, Visa
King & Barnes Festive Bitter, Mild; Watneys Special; Ben Truman; Guinness; Carlsberg; cider.
ACCOMMODATION 8 bedrooms £B (No dogs)
Check-in: all day

Built of timber and flint, this lovely 16th-century inn was once the haunt of smugglers. Massive oak beams abound, from the entrance hall to the twin bars and in many of the bedrooms, too, which are modestly furnished in traditional style with a variety of freestanding pieces. Five have private facilities, the rest share two public bathrooms. No children under five overnight. Terrace and garden.

Alrewas   (B & B)   ### George & Dragon

Main Street, near Burton upon Trent
Staffordshire · Map 4 C4
Burton on Trent (0283) 790202
Brewery Marston, Thompson & Evershed
Landlords Ray & Mary Stanbrook
Children welcome
Credit Access, Visa
🍺 Marston's Pedigree, Burton Bitter, Pilsner;
Guinness; Heineken Lager; cider.
ACCOMMODATION   11 bedrooms   £C
Check-in: all day

A busy, popular inn standing in a village
between Lichfield and Burton upon Trent.
The accommodation is alongside in the
Claymar Motel. Rooms, though not very big,
are thoughtfully planned, and all have their
own bathrooms. There's no shortage of
accessories, either, with colour TVs, direct-
dial phones, radio-alarms, tea-makers and
trouser presses as standard. Amenities include a garden and a children's play area.
Accommodation closed 1 week Christmas.

Alsager   (Food, B & B)   ### Manor House

Audley Road, near Stoke-on-Trent · *Cheshire*
Map 3 B4
Alsager (093 63) 78013

Free House
Landlords Mr & Mrs A. Cottingham

Children welcome
Credit Access, Amex, Diners, Visa
🍺 Tetley's Bitter; Burton Ale; Skol; Löwenbräu;
Castlemaine; cider. ⚲

ACCOMMODATION 20 bedrooms £A (No dogs)
Check-in: all day

Just five minutes' drive from the M6, the
Manor House is an impressively refurbished
red-brick inn of handsome proportions.
There's a smart little cocktail bar, and the
spacious lounge bar allies period character
to modern comfort. Fish and seafood are a
speciality among the snacks, with lemon
sole, fillet of plaice and hot seafood platter
typical choices. There's also soup, sandwiches, pâté and a daily roast, plus good
salads and a lunchtime cold buffet. Fresh
fruit salad makes a refreshing finale. *Typical
prices:* Lemon sole £2.30   Steak & kidney
pie £2.05 (Last bar food 10pm) ⊖

Accommodation is a particular strength, all
rooms having handsome fitted units, well-
sprung beds and private bath or shower. TVs
and direct-dial phones. A new wing of 12
bedrooms has recently been added. Well-
trained, caring staff are a further plus.

Alswear   (B & B)   ### Butchers Arms

Near South Moulton · *Devon* · Map 9 C3
Bishop's Nympton (076 97) 477

Free House
Landlords Peter & Jean Gannon
Children welcome
🍺 Usher's Best Bitter, Triple Crown; Whitbread
Trophy, Best Bitter; Guinness; Carlsberg;
Tuborg Gold; cider.
ACCOMMODATION   3 bedrooms   £D
Check-in: restricted

The lounge bar at this 18th-century pebbledash pub is plush and cosy, with a real fire
that reflects the warm welcome of Peter and
Jean Gannon. Beams and brasses characterise the public bar, and there's a skittle
alley as well as a games room with a pool
table. Bedrooms are clean and bright, with
homely touches like books and dried flowers.
The pub stands on the A373 just south of
South Moulton. Garden.

Ansty   *(Food, B & B)*   *Fox Inn*

Near Dorchester · *Dorset* · Map 9 D3
Milton Abbas (0258) 880328

Free House
Landlord Peter Amey

Children welcome
Credit Access, Visa
🍺 Ansty Ale; Wadworth's 6X; Badger Best
Bitter; Hectors Bitter; Guinness; Carlsberg Hof;
cider. 🍷

A large village pub of brick and flint construction, with atmospheric bars that are full of
nooks and crannies; they also house two
notable collections, one of plates, the other
of Toby jugs. Chief among the bar fare is the
lavish cold buffet of cooked meats, quiches,
pies and up to 30 salads. This is best enjoyed
at lunchtime, when it's freshly made and very
appetising; it's liable to wilt a little in the
evening. Charcoal grills and filled jacket
potatoes are the main alternatives, and
home-made sweets include Black Forest
gâteau and mountainous meringues. *Typical
prices:* Cold buffet £4.50   Almond meringue
£1.10 (Last bar food 10pm) 🍽

ACCOMMODATION   11 bedrooms   £C
Check-in: all day

Seven bedrooms have en suite facilities, and
all are equipped with TVs. The comforts
provided are fairly modest, and several
aspects of both maintenance and housekeeping could do with attention. Staff, too,
are not always found at their most helpful.
Besides the bar, there's a large children's
room and a skittle alley.

Appleby   *(Food, B & B)*   *Royal Oak Inn*

Bongate · *Cumbria* · Map 3 B2
Appleby (0930) 51463

Free House
Landlords Colin & Hilary Cheyne

Children welcome
Credit Access, Amex, Diners, Visa
🍺 McEwan's 70/-, Lager; Webster's Yorkshire
Bitter; Guinness; Beck's Lager; cider. 🍷

The main bar of this long black and white
coaching inn is given old-world charm by oak
beams, mellow panelling, brassware and
antiques. Cooking here is honest and enjoyable, and the bar menu covers a fair span of
dishes, from soup and pâté to langoustines
with garlic butter, good-quality steaks and a
passable stab at the spicy South African dish
bobotie. Boodles fool is a nice sweet. *Typical
prices:* Langoustines with hot garlic butter
£3.95   Bobotie £2.95 (Last bar food 9pm) 🍽

ACCOMMODATION   7 bedrooms   £C
Check-in: all day

Bedrooms are of decent size, with tasteful
colour schemes and reassuringly solid furnishings. All now have TVs and tea-makers,
and nice home-from-home touches include a
selection of good books. Private facilities in
three rooms. Pleasant breakfasts, including
excellent kippers from Loch Fyne. As befits
the courteous Scots owners Colin and Hilary
Cheyne, there's a fine selection of malt
whiskies in the bar.

Appletreewick   *Craven Arms*

Standing among rolling hills between Burnsall and Bolton Abbey, this slate-roofed pub, some 300 years old, is a splendid spot to pause after a healthy walk. Copper kettles hang from beams in the bar, which is dominated by a huge fireplace. There's also a snug, as well as a garden.

Burnsall, Near Skipton · *North Yorkshire* · Map 4 C2
Burnsall (075 672) 270   *Free House*   Landlords Gordon & Linda Elsworth
Children welcome
🍺 Tetley's Bitter, Mild; Theakston's Old Peculier, Best Bitter; Younger's Scotch Bitter; Guinness; Carlsberg; cider. ♀

Armathwaite   *(B & B)*   *Duke's Head Hotel*

Front Street, Near Carlisle · *Cumbria* · Map 3 B1
Armathwaite (069 92) 226

Brewery Whitbread
Landlords Mr & Mrs Cuthbert

Children welcome
🍺 Whitbread Castle Eden Bitter, Trophy, Best Mild; Heineken; cider. ♀
ACCOMMODATION 7 bedrooms £C

Excellent salmon and trout fishing draws anglers to this homely inn, which stands near an imposing stone bridge over the picturesque river Eden. Overnight accommodation is neat and simple, and the seven bedrooms, which all have washbasins and tea-makers, share two public bathrooms. The public and lounge bars are relaxing spots for a drink and a chat, and the hotel has an attractive walled garden.

Ascot   *(Food)*   *Stag*

63 High Street · *Berkshire* · Map 7 C2
Ascot (0990) 21622

Brewery Friary Meux
Landlord Mr & Mrs T. McCarthy

Children welcome
🍺 Friary Meux Traditional Bitter; John Bull Bitter; Guinness; Castlemaine 4X; cider. ♀

Home-made wholemeal pasta is just one of many good things produced by Ann Mc-Carthy in this friendly high-street pub. Filled jacket potatoes are another popular choice, along with burgers, salads, made-to-order sandwiches and specials like chicken and ham pie. To round off a tasty meal there are homely sweets like apple and cherry crumble. Limited Sunday menu. Pavement tables. *Typical prices:* Chicken & ham pie £2.30 Vegetable lasagne £2 (Last bar food 10pm).

Ashburton   *Exeter Inn*

Francis Drake and Walter Raleigh are among past travellers who have refreshed themselves at this convivial 12th-century inn. Today, the low-beamed bar areas with their solid rustic furniture and old stone fireplaces make an atmospheric setting for a quiet drink. There's a pretty walled garden, too.

West Street · *Devon* · Map 9 C4
Ashburton (0364) 52559   *Free House*
Landlords Mr & Mrs Billington & Mr & Mrs McNichol
Children welcome
🍺 Bass; Hall & Woodhouse Badger; Flowers IPA; Tetley Bitter; Guinness; Carlsberg Export; cider.

Ashbury   *(Food, B & B)*   ## Rose & Crown

Near Swindon · *Oxfordshire* · Map 7 A2
Ashbury (079 371) 222

Free House
Landlord Mr Marcel Klein

Children welcome
Credit Access, Amex, Diners, Visa
🍺 Charrington's IPA; Worthington 'E'; Toby
Bitter; Stones Bitter; Guinness; Tennent's Extra;
Carling Black Label; cider. ⚲

Alsace-born owner Marcel Klein has established high standards for the bar snacks
offered at his sturdy whitewashed village pub
some four miles from junction 15 of the M4.
Our moist, rough pâté and flavoursome ham
baked slowly in white wine made excellent
eating: other favourites to look out for include
bangers with bubble and squeak, turkey
curry, casseroles and hot pots. Relax in the
comfortable lounge bar or join the locals in
the lively public bar. *Typical prices:* Beef &
Guinness pie £2.60 Pâté and toast £1.55
(Last bar food 10.30pm) ⊖

ACCOMMODATION   10 bedrooms   £C
Check-in: all day

The 10 centrally heated bedrooms (all with
TVs and tea-makers) have pretty floral bedspreads and simple modern furnishings. One
room boasts its own private bathroom, the
rest share three well-kept public ones.
There's a peaceful residents' lounge on the
first floor.

Ashcott   *(Food)*   ## Ashcott Inn

50 Bath Road · *Somerset* · Map 9 D3
Ashcott (0458) 210282

Free House
Landlords Mr & Mrs J. Mullet

Children welcome
🍺 Whitbread Trophy Bitter; Flowers; Butcombe
Bitter; Guinness; Stella Artois; cider.

The Mullets offer a wide variety of snacks at
this 17th-century roadside pub. Egg mayonnaise and Camembert-stuffed mushrooms
are typical starters, while main courses could
include chilli con carne, pasta shells with
chicken and rainbow trout with walnuts and
banana. Also charcoal grills and a good
choice for vegetarians. *Typical prices:* Mussels with seafood sauce £2.50 Lemon
cheesecake £1.25 (Last bar food 9.30pm.
Closed Sun lunchtime) ⊖

Ashwell   *(Food)*   ## Bushel & Strike Inn

Mill Street, near Baldock · *Hertfordshire*
Map 7 C1
Ashwell (046 274) 2394

Brewery Wells
Landlords Sandy & Tony Lynch

Children welcome
Credit Access, Amex, Diners, Visa
🍺 Wells Eagle Bitter, Bombardier, Silver Eagle;
Guinness; Red Stripe; Kellerbräu cider. ⚲

The friendly Lynches offer an amazing array
of different salads in their inviting cold buffet,
which is an attractive feature of their delightful
village pub. The menu changes frequently,
but you might catch venison pie, lamb curry,
Mexican beef or stir-fry chicken. Sweets, too,
are a real treat. *Typical prices:* Steak & kidney
pie £3.75 Red snapper with créole sauce
£3.30 (Last bar food 10pm) ⊖

Ashwell   *(Food, B & B)*   *Three Tuns Hotel*

High Street · *Hertfordshire* · Map 7 C1
Ashwell (046 274) 2387

Brewery Greene King
Landlord Mrs E. M. Harris

Children welcome
Credit Access, Amex, Diners
🍺 Greene King Abbot Ale, IPA, Light Mild;
Guinness; Kronenbourg; Harp; cider. ♀

A two-storey, brick-built inn with a large garden, standing in a pretty village a mile or so from the A505 Baldock–Royston road. Run by Liz Harris for the past 12 years, it's very much at the heart of village social life. The bar is warm and inviting, and both lunchtime and evening there are tasty snacks to enjoy. Go for the blackboard dishes of the day, which could include filled jacket potatoes, cream of celery soup, fish pie and a very good casserole of wood pigeon. Also ploughman's, salads and, for sweet, perhaps apple strudel. *Typical prices:* Celery soup 95p Wood pigeon in red wine £3.50 (Last bar food 10.30pm) ⏚

ACCOMMODATION   12 bedrooms   £C
Check-in: all day

Bedrooms, including four in a Victorian house along the street, are individually furnished to a high standard, and many feature interesting antiques. TVs and tea-makers in all rooms, shower cubicles in some.

Children welcome *indicates a pub with an area where children are allowed whether eating or not.*

Askham   *(Food, B & B)*   *Punch Bowl*

Penrith · *Cumbria* · Map 3 B2
Hackthorpe (093 12) 443

Brewery Whitbread
Landlord Aubrey Zalk

Children welcome
Credit Access
🍺 Whitbread Castle Eden Ale, Trophy, Mild;
Guinness; Heineken; Stella Artois; cider.

The M6 is only ten minutes away, but this 17th-century sporting inn enjoys a peaceful setting in a delightfully unspoilt village. The bar has lots of character, with beams and a log-burning stove, and it's a great favourite locally. Bar food spans an imaginative range, from subtly spiced curried apple soup and houmus with pitta bread to chicken Kiev, Chinese-style spare ribs and the very tasty minced beef cobbler with its dumpling-type crust. Sandwiches, salads and well-kept English cheeses are available for lighter bites, and there are some nice puddings such as peach meringue or lemon ice-cream cake. *Typical prices:* Spare ribs £2.95   Pâté £1.50 (Last bar food 9.30pm) ⏚

ACCOMMODATION   5 bedrooms   £C
Check-in: restricted

The five bedrooms, all decent-sized doubles or twins, are simply but tidily furnished; housekeeping is good, and there's always plenty of hot water for the washbasins. Tea-making facilities are provided. Patio.

Askham *(B & B)*

Queen's Head Inn

Near Penrith · *Cumbria* · Map 3 B2
Hackthorpe (093 12) 225

Brewery Vaux
Landlords Anne & John Askew
Children welcome
🍺 Ward's Bitter; Vaux Sunderland Bitter, Mild;
Lorimer's Scotch; Guinness; Tuborg; cider.
ACCOMMODATION 5 bedrooms £C (No dogs)
Check-in: all day

Dating back to 1682, this fine cottage inn is kept in tip-top condition by the caring Askews. Fresh flowers and pretty ornaments lend a homely air to the comfortable lounge and beamed main bar, a delightfully welcoming room with its gleaming oak furniture and open fire. Bright, appealing bedrooms share two equally well-kept bathrooms. Children under seven not accommodated overnight.

Askrigg *(B & B)*

King's Arms Hotel

Wensleydale · *North Yorkshire* · Map 4 C2
Wensleydale (0969) 50258
Free House
Landlords Mr & Mrs R. Hopwood
Children welcome
Credit Access, Diners, Visa
🍺 Younger's No 3 Bitter, Scotch Bitter;
Newcastle Exhibition Bitter; McEwan's 80/-
Bitter, Lager; cider. 🍷
ACCOMMODATION   10 bedrooms   £C
Check-in: all day

Askrigg was used as the setting for the television series 'All Creatures Great and Small', and some scenes were filmed in this charming 17th-century coaching inn. The main bar features a huge inglenook and some original saddle hooks, while the panelled lounge bar boasts handsome period furnishings. Bedrooms – with more fine pieces, including several splendid beds – are kept in excellent order, and each has its own en suite bathroom.

Aston Cantlow

King's Head

Shakespeare's parents held their wedding breakfast in 1557 at this lovely old black and white half-timbered inn, where today's hosts the Saunders are just as welcoming and hospitable. The heavily beamed main bar with its fresh flowers and old wooden settles and the cosy snug provide ample space for drinking. Garden.

Bearley Road, Near Stratford-upon-Avon · *Warwickshire* · Map 5 A2
Stratford-upon-Avon (078 981) 242   *Brewery* Whitbread/Flowers
Landlords Mr & Mrs Saunders   **Children welcome**
🍺 Flowers IPA, OB, Best Bitter; Whitbread Best Bitter; Stella Artois;
Heineken.

Aswarby *(B & B)*

Tally Ho

Near Sleaford · *Lincolnshire* · Map 4 D4
Culver Thorpe (052 95) 205

Free House
Landlords Rachel & Christopher Davies

🍺 Bateman's Best Bitter; Adnams Best Bitter;
Stella Artois; Ayinger Bräu; cider. 🍷
ACCOMMODATION   6 bedrooms   £C
Check-in: all day

Delightful owners and staff contribute to the pleasure of a stay in this 200-year-old pub, which lies south of Sleaford alongside the A15. The spacious bar is in the original building, while the former stable block houses the overnight accommodation. The bedrooms are smartly kept, and the beamed pair on the top floor are particularly attractive. All rooms have TVs, tea-makers and private bath or showers. Garden.

Axbridge   *(B & B)*   *Oak House*

Somerset · Map 9 D3
Axbridge (0934) 732444

Free House
Landlords Mr & Mrs Love

Children welcome
Credit Access, Amex, Diners, Visa
🍺 Wadworth's Northgate Bitter; Löwenbräu.
ACCOMMODATION 11 bedrooms £B (No dogs)
Check-in: all day

Right in the heart of the village, overlooking the pretty market square, this delightful 14th-century inn is full of charm and character. Blackened beams, an open fire and chintzy furnishings are features of the comfortably traditional bar-lounge, while simply appointed bedrooms are spacious and well kept. All have TVs and tea-makers, and all but two their own modern bath or shower room.

Axminster   *(Food)*   **New Entry**   *New Commercial Inn*

Trinity Square · *Devon ·* Map 9 C3
Axminster (0297) 33225

Brewery Palmer
Landlord W. Walden

Children welcome
Credit Visa
🍺 Palmer's IPA, Bridport Bitter, Tally Ho!; Shilthorn Bitter; cider.

The Walden family run this thriving little inn with its adjoining restaurant and baker's shop. Bar snacks are fresh and tasty; the choice includes soup and sandwiches, pasties, steak pies and a lunchtime cold table. There's also a lunchtime hot special each day, Thursday's fried cod with sauté potatoes being a particular favourite. *Typical prices:* Soup of the day 90p   Roast chicken with vegetables £2.95 (Last bar food 10pm) ⊖

Axmouth   *(Food)*   **New Entry**   *The Ship Inn*

Church Street, near Seaton · *Devon ·* Map 9 C3
Seaton (0297) 21838

Brewery Devenish
Landlords Jane & Christopher Chapman

🍺 Devenish Wessex Best Bitter, Cornish Original; cider.

The Chapmans have looked after this 14th-century pub for over 21 years, and among the many regulars who crowd the tiny bar can be found the local fishermen and gamekeepers who supply the produce for the tempting snack menu. Turbot, brill, bass and conger eel might feature from the morning's catch, along with wild duck casseroled in port. Also sandwiches, cheese and puddings. *Typical Prices:* Fresh fish from £1.75   Steak & vegetable pie £2 (Last bar food 9.30pm) ⊖

Bainbridge   *(B & B)*   *Rose & Crown Hotel*

Near Leyburn · *North Yorkshire ·* Map 4 C2
Wensleydale (0969) 50225

Free House
Landlord Mrs P. A. Thorpe
Children welcome
Credit Access, Visa
🍺 Younger's Scotch Bitter 80/-; John Smith's Bitter; Magnet.
ACCOMMODATION   13 bedrooms   £B
Check-in: all day

The famous Bainbridge horn – traditionally blown to guide lost travellers – adorns the panelled entrance hall of this fine old coaching inn that's still welcoming visitors today. The beamed main bar and cosy snug are full of atmosphere and there's a larger bar with pub games. Immaculate bedrooms, which are comfortably furnished in a variety of styles, offer TVs and tea-makers; most have private facilities. Patio.

Bamford *(B & B)*   *Rising Sun Hotel*

Hope Road, Hope Valley · *Derbyshire* · Map 4 C3
Hope Valley (0433) 51323

Free House
Landlords John & Theresa Ellis

Children welcome
Credit Access, Amex, Visa
🍺 Mansfield Bitter, Mild, Lager. *No real ale.* ♀
ACCOMMODATION 13 bedrooms £B
Check-in: all day

Outside Bamford on the A265, this cheerful half-timbered inn enjoys fine views of the surrounding Peak District. Comfortable bedrooms (including two new luxurious mini-suites) are all furnished with deep-pile carpets and pretty fabrics. All offer TVs, tea-makers, radio-alarms and direct-dial telephones. Six have en suite bathrooms, the rest shower cabinets. Beamed and traditional public rooms include a spacious popular main bar. Garden.

Bantham *(B & B)*   *Sloop Inn*

Near Kingsbridge · *Devon* · Map 9 C4
Kingsbridge (0548) 560489

Free House
Landlord Mr Neil Girling
Children welcome
🍺 Bass; Usher's Best; Webster's Yorkshire; Worthington; Whitbread Poachers; Stella Artois; cider. ♀
ACCOMMODATION 5 bedrooms £C
Check-in: restricted

It's only 300 yards across the dunes to the sea from this 16th-century inn, famous once as a smugglers' base. The several interconnecting bars have a good deal of old-world charm, and one area, with counters made from old rowing boats, has a distinctly nautical feel. Prettily decorated bedrooms equipped with TVs are kept neat and perfectly shipshape, and all have good, up-to-date bathrooms. Patio.

Barbon *(B & B)*   *Barbon Inn*

Near Kirby Lonsdale · *Cumbria* · Map 3 B2
Barbon (046 836) 233
Free House
Landlord Mr K. Whitlock
Children welcome
Credit Access, Visa
🍺 Theakston's Real Ale, Best Bitter, Old Peculier; Younger's Scotch Bitter; Carlsberg Hof; cider. ♀
ACCOMMODATION 9 bedrooms £C
Check-in: all day

Public rooms are spick-and-span at this homely old coaching inn in a scenic location between the Lakes and the Dales. The little bar with its carved settle and china plates is most appealing, and chintzy armchairs create a cosy atmosphere in the lounge areas. Pleasant bedrooms with pretty wallpaper have TVs and tea-makers. Good breakfasts.

Barnard Castle *(Food)*   *Red Well*

Harmire Road · *Co. Durham* · Map 4 C2
Teesdale (0833) 37002

Free House
Landlords Mr & Mrs M. J. Rudd & Mr & Mrs K. N. Thompson

Children welcome
Credit Access, Visa
🍺 John Smith's Bitter; Theakston's Best Bitter; Guinness; Hofmeister; Kronenbourg; cider.

There's no shortage of choice in the snacks served in the cheery lounge bar of this creeper-clad old pub on the Egglestone road. Fresh fish is much in evidence: mussels and a seafood rosette along with sole, salmon and trout. Also on the menu are salads, ploughman's, steaks, and a peppery fried beef and savoury rice. Delicious apple pie. *Typical prices:* Deep-fried mushrooms £1.95 Lemon sole with prawn butter £3.45 (Last bar food 9.30pm) ☺

Bartlow   (Food)   *Three Hills*

Near Linton · *Cambridgeshire* · Map 7 D1
Cambridge (0223) 891259

Brewery Greene King
Landlords Sue & Steve Dixon

🍺 Greene King IPA, Abbot Ale;
Kronenbourg. 🍷

Built early in the 16th century, this pretty
village pub has been lovingly maintained and
provides a cosy, bright bar with inglenook
fireplace and polished brasses. The snacks
are wholesome and varied. Try soup with
crusty bread, coarse pâté or peppered mackerel and then move on to a steak, seafood
platter, chilli or steak pie. *Typical prices:*
Home-made pies £3.60 Spaghetti bolognese £2.50 (Last bar food 9.30pm) ⊖

Bassenthwaite Lake   (Food, B & B)   *Pheasant Inn*

Near Cockermouth · *Cumbria* · Map 3 B1
Bassenthwaite Lake (059 681) 234

Free House
Landlords Mr & Mrs W. E. Barrington-Wilson

Children welcome (Mon–Sat)
🍺 Theakston's Best Bitter; Bass; Guinness;
Carlsberg Hof. 🍷

Picture a typical old English inn – long and
low with a rustic porch, whitewashed walls
and mossy slate roof. The Pheasant fits the
bill perfectly and is only a few minutes walk
away from picturesque Bassenthwaite Lake.
Inside, at lunchtime, you can order a pleasant
snack in the charmingly old-fashioned bar
that's hung with hunting prints. There are
potted shrimps, smoked salmon, game pâté,
soup, smoked trout or eel, Cumberland pork,
ham and egg pie and cold meat platter, to
name a few. Avocado vinaigrette and cottage
cheese and pineapple salad provide choice
for vegetarians. Breakfasts are carefully
cooked and served with strong hot tea and
there's also a restaurant. *Typical prices:*
Sweet smoked chicken £2.20 Ploughman's
lunch £1.70 (No bar food eves) ⊖

ACCOMMODATION 20 bedrooms £A
Check-in: all day

Bedrooms are excellent. Each one is furnished differently but they are all crisp, clean
and light and one has a half-tester bed. All
have private bathrooms. Service is excellent:
beds are turned down, shoes cleaned and
early morning tea served in rooms.

Bathampton   (Food)   `New Entry`   *George Inn*

Mill Lane, Bath · *Avon* · Map 8 D2
Bath (0225) 25079

Brewery Courage
Landlord Mr Walter John Hall

Children welcome
🍺 Courage Best Bitter, Directors; John Smith's
Yorkshire Bitter; Guinness; cider.

Cross the old tollbridge from the A4 to this
lovely 15th-century inn by the canal. The
many lounge areas do full justice to the
setting, and there's excellent eating to be
had: home-prepared ham and salt beef for
ploughman's or salads, garlic mushrooms,
salmon quiche, sautéed lamb, a really regal
queen of puddings. *Typical prices:* Baked
ham in cauliflower cheese sauce £3.25
Chocolate fudge pudding £1.25 (Last bar
food 9.30pm) ⊖

Beaulieu   *(Food, B & B)*   *Montagu Arms Hotel*

Hampshire · Map 6 A4
Beaulieu (0590) 612324

Free House
Landlord Mr Nicholas J. Walford

Credit Access, Amex, Diners, Visa
🍺 Wadworth's 6X; Flowers Original; Whitbread
Best; McEwan's Export; Guinness; Heineken;
cider. 🍷

A tempting range of home-cooked dishes,
from pizzas and steaks to cauliflower and
broccoli casserole, keeps up the tradition of
hospitality at this former monks' hostelry and
coaching inn near the abbey and the National
Motor Museum. Our potato-topped fish pie
was a tasty blackboard special, and there
are appetising cold meats, smoked fish and
salads, with crème brûlée and ginger mousse
among the sweets. Excellent dishes both
traditional and modern are on the menu in
the panelled restaurant. *Typical bar prices:*
Deep-fried monkfish £3.45   Desserts from
£1.20 (Last bar food 8pm) 🕑

ACCOMMODATION   26 bedrooms   £A
Check-in: all day

A very pleasant place to drop anchor, with
abundant English charm behind an attractive,
creeper-clad facade. Comfortable bedrooms
are sturdily furnished (some have four-
posters) and all offer TVs, direct-dial phones
and well-equipped bathrooms. There are two
inviting bars and a roomy lounge. Amenities
include laundry service and croquet.

Beauworth   *Milbury's*

Sympathetic restoration has returned much of its original charm to this
friendly old pub, with flagstones, beams and an inglenook fireplace. Pride
of place goes to a huge treadwheel – designed to be worked by a man –
which lowers a bucket into a 300-foot-deep well. But the real ales are a
more efficient way of quenching your thirst.

Near Cheriton · *Hampshire* · Map 6 B4
Bramdean (096 279) 248   *Free House*   *Landlords* Simon & Nicky Harris
Children welcome   *Credit* Access, Amex, Diners, Visa
🍺 Gales HSB; Flowers Original; Wadworth's 6X; Wethereds; Guinness;
Stella Artois; cider. 🍷

Beckley   *(Food)*   *Abingdon Arms*

Near Oxford · *Oxfordshire* · Map 7 B1
Stanton St John (086 735) 311

Free House
Landlords Mr & Mrs H. B. Greatbatch

🍺 Wadworth's 6X; Hall's Harvest Bitter; John
Bull Bitter; Guinness; Löwenbräu; Skol.

This handsome stone pub has comfortable,
traditional bars and a large, pretty garden.
Mrs Greatbatch's cooking is a big attraction,
and her summer menu concentrates on
tempting cold dishes like prawns creole or
poached salmon salad. Winter brings warming fare like fish soup, sweetbreads, game
pie and curry. Gâteau and tarts for pudding.
Typical prices: Cold poached salmon & salad
£2.95   Game pie £3.05 (Last bar food
9.30pm. No bar food Sun eve in summer) 🕑

Bedford *(B & B)*

Embankment Hotel

The Embankment · *Bedfordshire* · Map 7 C1
Bedford (0234) 61332

Owner Toby Restaurants
Landlord Mr Bradnam

Credit Access, Amex, Visa
🍺 Charrington's IPA, Worthington Best;
Tennent's Extra; Carling Black Label. ♀
ACCOMMODATION 20 bedrooms £B (No dogs)
Check-in: all day

A half-timbered building set at a discreet distance from the bustle of the town centre on a broad stretch of the Ouse. Overnight accommodation, already of a high standard, is being improved further. All rooms are fitted in pleasant contemporary style and equipped with a good range of extras including TVs, telephones, trouser presses and tea-makers. All rooms but two have up-to-date en-suite facilities.

Bedford *(Food)*

Park

98 Kimbolton Road · *Bedfordshire* · Map 7 C1
Bedford (0234) 54093

Brewery Charles Wells
Landlords Janet & Bob Broomhall

Credit Access, Amex, Diners, Visa
🍺 Wells Eagle Bitter, Bombardier, Noggin;
Guinness; Red Stripe; Ketterbräu; Talisman;
cider. ♀

Just the place to come if you want to sample English cheeses, this popular mock-Tudor pub with a fine collection of pewter tankards has several dozen splendid ones from which to choose your ploughman's platter. They also do tasty speciality pies and daily specials like Lancashire hot pot. Note the à la carte restaurant. *Typical prices:* Soup of the day 95p Beef stew with dumplings £1.65 (No bar food eves or Sun) ⊖

Beer *(B & B)*

Anchor Inn

Fore Street · *Devon* · Map 9 C3
Seaton (0297) 20386
Free House
Landlord David M. Boalch
Children welcome (lunchtime)
Credit Access, Visa
🍺 Samuel Whitbread; Flowers Original, IPA; Hall & Woodhouse Badgers; Guinness; Stella Artois;
cider. ♀
ACCOMMODATION 9 bedrooms £C (No dogs)
Check-in: restricted

At the sea end of a small fishing village, this white pebbledash pub is a pleasant place to drop anchor. Some of the bedrooms enjoy sea views, and all are neat and freshly decorated, with simple furnishings, TVs and tea-makers. There's an extensive bar area, a pleasant reception-lounge and a neat little garden that overlooks the beach. No under-tens overnight. Accommodation closed one week Christmas.

Beetham *(B & B)*

Wheatsheaf Hotel

Near Milnthorpe · *Cumbria* · Map 3 B2
Milnthorpe (044 82) 2123

Free House
Landlords Miller family

Children welcome
🍺 Thwaites Bitter; Younger's Bitter; Stones Bitter; Bass Mild; Guinness; Carlsberg; cider.
ACCOMMODATION 8 bedrooms £C
Check-in: all day

The Miller family's pub has long been a popular stopping off place for travellers on the A6. There's a choice of three bars, two cosily traditional in character, plus a panelled upstairs lounge with TV. Eight neatly furnished bedrooms all offer TVs and tea-makers; two have private facilities, and the rest share two neat simple public bathrooms.

Belford   *(B & B)*   *Blue Bell Hotel*

Market Square · *Northumberland* · Map 2 D4
Belford (066 83) 543
Free House
Landlord M. C. & J. Shirley
Children welcome
Credit Access, Amex, Diners, Visa
🍺 Drybrough Heavy; McEwan's Scotch Bitter,
Exhibition; Scottish & Newcastle Bitter; cider. *No
real ale.* ♀
ACCOMMODATION   15 bedrooms   £B
Check-in: all day

This pretty little 18th-century coaching inn
with a pretty garden is less than a mile from
the A1. It offers pleasant overnight accommodation in good-size bedrooms furnished
in traditional style and equipped with private
bathrooms, TVs, radio-alarms and tea-
makers. There's a comfortable residents'
lounge as an alternative to the smart bar with
its attractively upholstered seating and copper-topped tables.

Belsay   *(Food)*   *Highlander Inn*

Hygham Dykes · *Northumberland* · Map 4 C1
Belsay (066 181) 220

Brewery Newcastle
Landlord Barrie Dixon

Children welcome
Credit Access, Amex, Visa
🍺 Scottish & Newcastle Exhibition; Scotch
Bitter; Younger's Traditional Beer No 3; Harp;
Carlsberg Hof; cider. ♀

South of Belsay on the A696, this converted
farmhouse attracts the crowds for its appetising food, welcoming staff and convivial
atmosphere in the bright, jolly bar. Cooked
meats, pies and salads make up an attractive
cold display, while hot dishes might include
steaks or prawn curry. Soup, sandwiches
and home-made sweets complete the picture. Courtyard. *Typical prices:* Chicken
chasseur £3.50   Cumberland sausage with
chips £2 (Last bar food 9.30pm) ⊖

Benenden   *(Food)*   *King William IV*

The Street · *Kent* · Map 6 C3
Benenden (0580) 240636

Brewery Shepherd Neame
Landlords Nigel & Hilary Douglas

🍺 Shepherd Neame Masterbrew, Hurlimann;
Guinness; Steinbock Lager; cider.

Fresh flowers decorate the beamed bar of
this tile-hung village pub, making it a most
appealing setting for an ever-changing selection of food. Typical choices might include
duck liver pâté and chilli tacos, Senegalese
soup and toasted sandwiches, moussaka
and a splendid fish pie with a garlic crumb
topping. *Typical prices:* Red wine casserole
£3.25   Bananas with Kirsch and cream 95p
(Last bar food 9pm. No bar food Mon eve &
all Sun) ⊖

Berkeley Road   *(B & B)*   *Prince of Wales Hotel*

Near Berkeley · *Gloucestershire* · Map 8 D2
Dursley (0453) 810474
Free House
Landlords Mr & Mrs D. K. Taylor
Children welcome
Credit Access, Amex, Diners, Visa
🍺 Wadworth's 6X; Marston's Pedigree; Ansells
Bitter; Guinness; Castlemaine 4X; Löwenbräu;
cider.
ACCOMMODATION   9 bedrooms   £C
Check-in: all day

The Taylors ensure a warm welcome and a
restful stay at their well-run hotel, which was
named at the Prince's own suggestion in
about 1870. Bedrooms – all but two with
private bathrooms – are comfortably contemporary in style and are well equipped, with
thick carpets, effective double glazing, TVs
and direct-dial phones. Only the housekeeping can be a slight let-down. Day rooms
include an inviting, traditional bar lounge.

Bewdley *(Food, B & B)*   *Black Boy Hotel*

Kidderminster Road · *Hereford & Worcester*
Map 8 D1
Bewdley (0299) 402119

Free House
Landlord Mr A. R. Wilson

Children welcome
Credit Access, Amex, Visa
🍺 Mitchells & Butlers Bitter, Springfield Bitter;
Tennent's Pilsner; Carling Black Label; cider. *No
real ale.*

ACCOMMODATION 28 bedrooms £C
Check-in: all day

A quaint medieval building and a Georgian
town house combine in this fine inn, where
lunchtime snacks are served in the club-like
bars. Hot things include cottage pie and
deep-fried mushrooms, plus specials such
as fish pie and the very popular braised
oxtail. There are also sandwiches (white or
wholemeal bread), seafood platters and cold
meat salads. Sandwiches or restaurant
menus in the evening; three-course Sunday
lunch. *Typical prices:* Oxtail casserole £3.25
Cottage pie £1.60 (Last bar food 9pm) 🍴

Redecoration has made the whole place very
smart, and other improvements include central heating for the older bedrooms. Rooms
in the Georgian section are very spacious,
with some on the ground floor opening out
on to the garden. 15 rooms have private
bathrooms and there are abundant facilities
for the rest. Personal service includes an
early morning tea-tray with newspapers.
Besides the bars, there are two lounges with
TV, and a quiet reading room.

Bibury *(Food, B & B)*   *Catherine Wheel*

Gloucestershire · Map 7 A1
Bibury (028 574) 250

Brewery Courage
Landlord Mr Bill May

Children welcome
🍺 Courage Best; John Smith's Yorkshire Bitter;
Simonds Bitter; Guinness; Kronenbourg 1664;
Hofmeister; cider.

ACCOMMODATION 2 bedrooms £C
Check-in: all day

Heavy beams, massive stone walls, cheerful
log fires and old wooden benches create a
splendidly cosy feel in the bar of this charming
village inn. Families have the use of a
separate room, and there's a pretty garden.
Bar snacks are mostly of the hearty, traditional kind, well prepared and generously
served: home-made soup with crusty bread,
ploughman's and pâté, classic English sausages, cold meats, sirloin steak. Daily specials often include a good steak and
mushroom pie, and bread pudding is a
favourite sweet. *Typical prices:* Bibury trout
with chips & peas £4 Bread pudding £1
(Last bar food 10pm) 🍴

Upstairs are two delightful bedrooms featuring prettily patterned duvets, smart new white
wardrobes and remote-control TVs. They
share a large, well-equipped bathroom and
separate shower cubicle.

Biddenden *(Food)*   *Three Chimneys*

Kent · Map 6 C3
Biddenden (0580) 291472

Free House
Landlords Mr & Mrs C. F. Sayers

Children welcome
🍺 Adnams Best Bitter; Harvey's Best Bitter; Goachers Maidstone Ale; Godsons Black Horse; Fremlins Bitter; Marston's Pedigree; Stella Artois; cider. 🍷

Ancient beams, bare brick walls and a cheery fire in the grate characterise this friendly country pub. A blackboard lists the day's imaginative offerings – perhaps cauliflower tartlet, taramasalata or carrot and tarragon soup to start, lamb meatballs or sweet and sour pork to follow. Good cheeses, plus homely sweets like plum crumble and gooseberry fool. Garden. *Typical prices:* Rabbit casserole £3.80 Ginger pudding £1.25 (Last bar food 10pm) ⊝

Bidford-on-Avon *(B & B)*   *White Lion Hotel*

High Street · Warwickshire · Map 7 A1
Stratford-on-Avon (0789) 773309
Free House
Landlords Barry & Hilary Coomber
Children welcome
Credit Access, Amex
🍺 Everards Old Original Bitter; Newcastle Bitter; Sam Smith's Bitter; McEwan's Export Bitter; Beck's Bier; Tuborg; cider. 🍷
ACCOMMODATION 15 bedrooms £C
Check-in: all day

New owners Barry & Hilary Coomber personally run this sturdy white-painted hotel, which stands by an old stone bridge on the banks of the Avon. Bedrooms (eight with en suite shower/bathrooms) are of a decent size, with central heating, colour televisions and mainly modern furnishings. The honeymoon suite features a four-poster bed. The cosy bar is a popular place with locals, and there's a riverside terrace and mooring.

Bierton *(Food)*   *Red Lion*

Near Aylesbury · Buckinghamshire · Map 7 C1
Aylesbury (0296) 24453

Brewery Aylesbury
Landlords Mr & Mrs L. Bishop

🍺 Aylesbury Bitter; Ind Coope Pale Ale; Bass; Double Diamond; Guinness; Carlsberg; cider.

Run by successive generations of the Bishop family since 1918, this friendly pub offers a different menu in each of its beamed bars. Choose between a selection of snacks – shepherd's pie, jumbo sausages, savoury pancakes, smoked mackerel, sandwiches – or more elaborate dishes like trout with almonds and steak Stroganoff. Pleasant sweets. Patio. *Typical prices:* Steak & Guinness pie £1.30 Pork fillet in wine sauce £5 (Last bar food 9pm. No bar food Sat & Sun) ⊝

Binfield   *Stag & Hounds*

Elizabeth I is said to have watched maypole dancing on the green from this historic hunting lodge. Outside remains the stump of the ancient elm that marked the centre of Windsor Great Forest. Today's visitors can enjoy refreshment in the cosy lounge bar furnished with sturdy old settles and pews, or in one of the little beamed snugs.

Forest Road · *Berkshire* · Map 7 C2
Bracknell (0344) 483 553 *Brewery* Courage *Landlords* Mr & Mrs Howard
Credit Access
🍺 Courage Best Bitter, Directors, JC; Guinness; Kronenbourg 1664; Hofmeister; cider. 🍷

Bishop Wilton (B & B)
Fleece Inn

Near York · Humberside · Map 4 D2
Bishop Wilton (075 96) 251

Free House
Landlords Colin & Joan Hague

🍺 John Smith's Bitter; Tetley's Bitter, Mild;
Scottish & Newcastle Scotch Bitter; Guinness;
Skol; cider. ♀
ACCOMMODATION 4 bedrooms £D (No dogs)
Check-in: all day

Colin and Joan Hague are a very friendly couple who extend the warmest of welcomes to their peaceful inn in the centre of the village. Cosy overnight accommodation (no under-12s) is provided in four cheerful bedrooms furnished in various styles; all have washbasins and they share a single well-kept bathroom. Guests can watch television in the homely residents' lounge, and they'll enjoy a carefully cooked breakfast in the little dining area.

Bishop's Waltham (Food)
White Horse

Beeches Hill · Hampshire · Map 6 A4
Bishop's Waltham (048 93) 2532

Brewery Whitbread
Landlords Arthur & Carol Noot

🍺 Samuel Whitbread; Flowers Original;
Wethered's; Guinness; Stella Artois;
cider. ♀

Take the Beeches Hill turning off the B3035 on the edge of town to reach this cheerful little low-beamed inn. Choose the home-cooked rabbit pie, cheese bake or chilli con carne, with roly poly and custard to follow for the really famished. Snackers can opt for various ploughman's with crisp French or granary bread and salads. Garden with children's play area. *Typical prices:* Rabbit pie £1.85 Fisherman's lunch £1.25 (Last bar food 10pm. No bar food Mon eve) ⊖

Blackpool (Food)
Grosvenor Hotel

Cookson Street · Lancashire · Map 3 B3
Blackpool (0253) 25096

Brewery Bass
Landlords John & Jackie McKeown

🍺 Bass; Stones Bitter; Guinness; Carling Black Label; Tennent's Pils; cider. ♀

The McKeowns have built a smokehouse at the rear of their Victorian pub, so tasty smoked meats and fish now feature on their straightforward lunchtime menu. Regular items like soup, freshly cut sandwiches, omelettes and grills are supplemented by appetising daily offerings such as chicken and ham pie, roast beef and seafood pasta. Seasonal berries, fruit pies and ice cream to finish. *Typical prices:* Chicken curry £2 Sirloin steak £4.15 (No bar food eves).

Blakesley (B & B)
Bartholomew Arms

Near Towcester · Northamptonshire · Map 7 B1
Blakesley (0327) 860292

Free House
Landlord Mr K. Claridge
Children welcome (till 8pm)
🍺 Marston's Pedigree; Newcastle Bitter;
McEwan's Export; Guinness; Beck's Bier;
Carlsberg Export; cider.
ACCOMMODATION 6 bedrooms £D (No dogs)
Check-in: all day

Only about ten minutes' drive from Silverstone, this friendly pub is a popular pit stop on motor racing weekends, and the village is also a centre for soapbox racing, as shown by photographs in the public bar. The bars are filled with a variety of bric-à-brac, from model ships to firearms. Six well-kept bedrooms with TVs and washbasins include an annexe room with its own shower.

Bledington   *(Food, B & B)*   *King's Head*

The Green, Near Kingham · *Oxfordshire*
Map 7 A1
Kingham (060 871) 365

Free House
Landlords Mr & Mrs M. Royce

Children welcome
🍺 Wadworth's 6X; Hook Norton; Hall's Harvest
Bitter; Guinness; Löwenbräu; Castlemaine;
cider.

A friendly 15th-century pub of many attractions, not least the setting by the village green
with its brook and its sociable ducks. The
pub is rich in old-world charm, and the
traditional game of Aunt Sally is played in the
garden. The bar menu provides a fair choice
of enjoyable dishes, from garlic mushrooms,
ploughman's and vegetable soup (help yourself from a tureen) to Gloucester sausage,
devilled lamb cutlets and tasty chicken pie
with a light crusty top. The tempting selection
of sweets includes treacle tart and rum-
flavoured bread pudding. An interesting à la
carte restaurant menu is available in the
evening. *Typical bar prices:* Soup 95p Devilled lamb cutlets £4.25 (Last bar food
10.15pm. No bar food Sun eve) ☻

ACCOMMODATION 3 bedrooms £C (No dogs)
Check-in: all day

The three bedrooms, all with private facilities,
have a good deal of cottage charm, with
beams, sloping ceilings, pretty fabrics and
simple white furniture. TVs, trouser press,
tea-makers.

Bletchingley   *(B & B)*   *Whyte Hart*

High Street · *Surrey* · Map 6 C3
Godstone (0883) 843231

Brewery Allied
Landlord Geoff Parsons

Credit Access, Amex, Diners, Visa
🍺 Burton Ale; Friary Meux Bitter; John Bull
Bitter; Skol; Castlemaine 4X; cider. ♀
ACCOMMODATION 9 bedrooms £B (No dogs)
Check-in: restricted

Neatly done out in black and white, this 600-
year-old inn stands proudly on the main
street. Inside, everything has a delightfully
mellow patina, from the well-worn brick floor
in the entrance to the traditional furnishings
and burnished brass in the bar. Spick-and-
span little bedrooms have pretty matching
curtains and bedcovers; four functionally
fitted rooms have en suite facilities, whereas
traditionally furnished rooms share two public bathrooms. There's a tiny TV lounge.

Blickling   *(B & B)*   *Buckinghamshire Arms*

Near Aylsham · *Norfolk* · Map 5 D1
Aylsham (0263) 732133
Free House
Landlord Nigel Elliott
Children welcome
Credit Access, Amex, Diners, Visa
🍺 Adnams Bitter; Greene King Abbot Ale, IPA;
Ind Coope Burton Ale; John Bull Bitter;
Guinness; Löwenbräu; Carlsberg; cider. ♀
ACCOMMODATION 3 bedrooms £B
Check-in: all day

The gates of Blickling Hall are only a stone's
throw from this fine 17th-century pub, and
two bedrooms look out across the old
orchard to the hall. Each spacious room has
a four-poster bed and pine or period furnishings. Books, magazines and Perrier are
among the comforts, which also include tea-
makers and cosy armchairs in which to watch
TV. The two bars – one tiny – are homely and
friendly. Garden.

Bollington (Food)

Church House Inn

24 Church Street · Cheshire · Map 4 C3
Bollington (0625) 74014

Free House
Landlords Mr & Mrs R. Gray

Children welcome
🍺 Tetley's Bitter, Mild; Winkles Saxon Cross;
Ruddle's County; Guinness; Castlemaine;
Carlsberg Export Hof; cider. ♀

Warming coal fires make the open-plan bar
of this hospitable little pub a cosy setting for
Mrs Gray's delicious food. Soup or mushrooms in garlic butter might precede such
hearty main courses as hot pot, curry and
richly flavoured steak and kidney pie. Salads,
lunchtime sandwiches and super sweets like
apricot and mincemeat plait. Garden. *Typical
prices: Steak & kidney pie £2.90 Vegetarian
crêpes £2.95 (Last bar food 9.30pm)* ☕

Boot (B & B)

Woolpack Inn

Eskdale, Holmbrook · Cumbria · Map 3 B2
Eskdale (09403) 230

Free House
Landlords Mr & Mrs G. F. Fox
Children welcome
Credit Visa
🍺 Younger's Scotch, IPA; Carlsberg; Harp;
cider.
ACCOMMODATION 7 bedrooms £C
Check-in: all day

This friendly inn nestling in the Eskdale Valley
is just the place to recover from the tortuous
gradients of the Hardknott Pass. Thirsty
hikers tend to annexe the main bar, but the
lounge with its open fire is very cosy, and
there's a chintzy residents' lounge. Delightfully old-fashioned bedrooms have tea-
makers and electric blankets. Four have
shower cubicles; the rest share a spotless
bathroom. Garden.

Boston (B & B)

New England Hotel

Wide Bargate · Lincolnshire · Map 5 C1
Boston (0205) 65255

Free House
Landlord Mr Chris Dyson
Children welcome
Credit Access, Amex, Diners, Visa
🍺 John Smith's Bitter, Old Tom; Courage Bitter;
Hofmeister. ♀
ACCOMMODATION 25 bedrooms £A
Check-in: all day

Step inside this red-brick hotel in the town
centre and you're immediately in the spacious, panelled lounge bar with its handsome
plaster ceiling. Overnight accommodation is
a strong point, all rooms having smartly fitted
units and being equipped with telephones,
remote-control TVs, clock-radios and plenty
of writing space. En suite facilities, fully tiled
and of a decent size, are a further plus.
Manager and staff are friendly and helpful.

Bourton-on-the-Hill (B & B)

Horse & Groom Inn

Near Moreton-in-Marsh · Gloucestershire
Map 7 A1
Blockley (0386) 700413

Brewery Bass
Landlords Mr & Mrs J. L. Aizpuru
🍺 Carling Black Label; Bass; Toby Bitter;
Worthington Best Bitter.
ACCOMMODATION 3 bedrooms £D (No dogs)
Check-in: all day

An attractive sandstone pub with a pretty
garden and views of the Cotswolds. The
outside is hung with colourful flower baskets,
while inside the stone-walled public and
lounge bars abound in horsy prints, reflecting
the Basque landlord's enthusiasm for English
racing. Well-kept bedrooms, all with shower
cubicles and washbasins, offer space and
simple comforts (no children under seven).
Accommodation is closed from December to
February.

Bowdon *(Food)*   *Griffin Tavern*

Stamford Road, Near Altrincham · *Cheshire*
Map 3 B3
061-928 1211

Brewery Pennine Hosts
Landlords Tony & June Lee

Credit Access, Amex, Diners, Visa
🍺 Wilsons Great Northern Bitter, Mild;
Guinness; Carlsberg; Foster's; cider.

A tradition of hospitality dates back over 200 years at this former church meeting house, run today in efficient and welcoming fashion by Tony and June Lee. There's a simple choice of soup and pâté, ploughman's, toasted sandwiches and traditional barm-cake (try one with hot roast beef), supple-mented by daily specials like lamb casserole and quiche. *Typical prices:* Hot beef barm-cake £1.50   Prawn & coleslaw open sand-wich £1.75 (No bar food eves or Sun) ☺

Bowland Bridge *(B & B)*   *Hare & Hounds*

Grange-over-Sands · *Cumbria* · Map 3 B2
Crosthwaite (044 88) 333

Free House
Landlords Peter & Barbara Thompson

Children welcome
🍺 Tetley's Bitter, Mild; Guinness; Skol; cider.
ACCOMMODATION 9 bedrooms £C
Check-in: all day

Dating back to 1600, this fine old inn enjoys a peaceful valley setting. The spacious, softly lit main bar makes an atmospheric spot for a quiet drink, and prettily decorated bedrooms in the original building also have considerable appeal. They share two modern bathrooms, while remaining rooms – located above the pool room bar – have en suite showers. Colour TVs and tea-makers are standard throughout. Garden.

Box *(Food, B & B)*   *Chequers Inn*

Market Place · *Wiltshire* · Map 8 D2
Box (0225) 742383

Brewery Usher
Landlords Kenneth & Jackie Martin

Children welcome
🍺 Usher's Country Bitter, PA, Best Bitter, Founders Ale; Guinness; Carlsberg; cider.

In the market place of a largely unspoilt village, this stone-built pub was around in Cromwell's day and was an important chang-ing post in coaching days. The present landlords couldn't be more charming and hospitable, Kenneth dispensing bonhomie in the bar and Jackie producing snacks to delight one and all. Ploughman's, burgers and lasagne are popular quickies, while other choices might include moussaka and a super game pie. Simply prepared trout and a vegetarian special show a trend towards healthy eating. Sweets range from ice cream to apple flan. Best choice in the evenings. *Typical prices:* Steak & kidney in Guinness £2.95   Apple flan £1.30 (Last bar food 9.30pm) ☺

ACCOMMODATION 1 bedroom £C (No dogs)
Check-in: restricted

Heavy beams and a sloping floor characterise the single bedroom, where floral prints brighten the decor and home comforts in-clude television and a tea-maker. There's a well-kept en suite bathroom.

Boxford *(Food)*

Fleece

Near Colchester · *Suffolk* · Map 5 D2
Boxford (0787) 210247

Brewery Tollemache & Cobbold
Landlord Mr Franco Crocco

🍺 Tolly Cobbold Best Bitter, Original; Hansa.

Franco Crocco's Italian specialities add zest to the bill of fare offered at this charming, 15th-century pub. Seafood plays a prominent part, with choices like fish soup, plaice meunière and haddock San Remo, and there's also appetising sauced pasta, plus meaty dishes such as sirloin steak with green peppercorns. Nice fresh fruit pies to finish. *Typical prices:* Spaghetti alla bolognese £2.25 Seafood pancake £4.95 (Last bar food 10pm).

Branscombe *(Food, B & B)*

Masons Arms

Near Seaton · *Devon* · Map 9 C3
Branscombe (029 780) 300

Free House
Landlord Mrs J. B. Inglis

Credit Access, Visa
🍺 Bass; Hall & Woodhouse Badger Best Bitter; Guinness; Carlsberg; cider. ♀

Run with care and pride by Janet Inglis, this charming creeper-clad inn enjoys an idyllic setting amidst attractive terraced gardens in an unspoilt Devon village. A huge central fire warms the beamed and slate-floored bar, making it a particularly appealing setting for some excellent snacks. The range extends from soup and sandwiches, salads and omelettes to kebabs, steaks, fresh local fish and some delicious sweets. *Typical prices:* Seafood platter £3.80 Apfel strudel 80p (Last bar food 9.45pm).

ACCOMMODATION 21 bedrooms £B
Check-in: all day

Guests staying overnight sleep in neat, prettily furnished bedrooms (some in nearby cottages), most of which have private facilities. Residents can also relax in the peaceful upstairs lounge or TV room – and a smashing breakfast awaits in the morning. Housekeeping and maintenance throughout are exemplary and service is of the old school, with beds turned down at night.

Bratton *(B & B)*

The Duke

Near Westbury · *Wiltshire* · Map 9 D3
Bratton (0380) 830242
Brewery Usher's
Landlords Mr & Mrs Snelgrove
Children welcome
Credit Amex, Visa
🍺 Usher's Founder's Bitter, Best Bitter, Pale Ale; Guinness; Budweiser; Carlsberg Pilsner; cider. ♀
ACCOMMODATION 5 bedrooms £C (No dogs)
Check-in: all day

A kindly Wiltshire couple have taken over the running of this pleasant village pub, which stands on the B3098 between Westbury and West Lavington. Overnight accommodation consists of five good-sized, well-kept bedrooms all with modern fitted units, TVs, radio-alarms and very efficient central heating. The open-plan bar and lounge offer ample comfort and space, and for summer sipping there's a nice patio and garden.

Bray *(Food)*   *Crown Inn*

High Street · *Berkshire* · Map 7 C2
Maidenhead (0628) 36725

Brewery Courage
Landlords Mr H. Whitton & Mr M. Ashcroft

Children welcome
Credit Access, Amex
🍺 Courage Best Bitter; Guinness; Hofmeister;
Kronenbourg. ♀

Old-world charm and tasty lunchtime bar
snacks prove an irresistible combination at
this smart black and white high street pub.
Highlights of the changing blackboard menu
include pâté, roast lamb, cottage pie and
lovely home-made flans like prawn and
tomato. Splendid treacle tart for afters. On
Saturday filled rolls only, and a barbecue
in the garden for Sunday lunch (if fine).
Typical prices: Steak & mushroom pie
£3.20 Cheese & asparagus pie £2.85 (No
bar food eves) ☺

Breage *(B & B)*   *Queen's Arms*

Near Helston · *Cornwall* · Map 9 A4
Helston (032 65) 3485

Brewery Devenish
Landlords Mr & Mrs V. M. Graves
Children welcome
🍺 Devenish Cornish Bitter, Falmouth; Mild,
John Devenish Bitter; Guinness; Heineken;
Gunhalle; cider.
ACCOMMODATION 3 bedrooms £D
Check-in: all day

The Graveses are friendly and welcoming
hosts at this tiny village pub opposite the
village church. The two homely adjoining
bars are decorated with photos of the Fleet
Air Arm, and upstairs there are three quite
spacious bedrooms with simple modern
furnishings and tea-making facilities. They
share a large carpeted bathroom equipped
with a shower cubicle and lots of thoughtful
extras. Garden.

Bredwardine *(B & B)*   *Red Lion*

Hereford & Worcester · Map 8 D1
Moccas (098 17) 303

Free House
Landlord Mr M. Taylor
Children welcome
Credit Access, Amex, Diners, Visa
🍺 Bass, Allbright; Mitchells & Butlers DPA;
Carling Black Label; cider. ♀
ACCOMMODATION 10 bedrooms £D
Check-in: all day

Shooting parties and fishermen swap yarns
in the homely lounge and beamed bar of this
17th-century red-brick inn overlooking one
of the most beautiful parts of the Wye valley.
Main-house bedrooms have old-world
charm, but modernists will prefer those in the
outbuildings, which have central heating,
practical whitewood furniture and modern
bathrooms. Accommodation closed end
October–March except for party bookings.

Brendon *(B & B)*   *Stag Hunters*

Near Lynton · *Devon* · Map 9 C3
Brendon (059 87) 222
Free House
Landlords Mr & Mrs J. Parffrey
Children welcome
Credit Access, Amex, Diners, Visa
🍺 Usher's Best Bitter, Triple Crown; Exmoor
Ale; Webster's Yorkshire Bitter; Guinness;
Carlsberg; cider.
ACCOMMODATION 22 bedrooms £C
Check-in: all day

Lorna Doone country is within exploring
distance of this sturdy inn in an idyllic riverside
setting. Residents have the run of two cosy
chintzy lounges (one with TV) and two
spacious bars, and the well-kept bedrooms
offer simple comforts. Four have their own
bathrooms, and one has a nice fourposter.
Accommodation closed January–end March.
Garden.

Brendon Hills *(B & B)*   *Ralegh's Cross Inn*

Near Watchet · *Somerset* · Map 9 C3
Washford (0984) 40343
Free House
Landlords Mr & Mrs P. N. Nash
Children welcome
Credit Access, Visa
🍺 Golden Hill Exmoor Ale; Flowers Original
Bitter, Best Bitter; Whitbread Best Bitter,
Trophy; Guinness; Heineken; cider.
ACCOMMODATION 9 bedrooms £C
Check-in: all day

An ideal base from which to explore Exmoor's
rugged charms, this isolated 17th-century inn
provides comfortable overnight accommodation for intrepid visitors to the area. Choose
from three traditionally furnished bedrooms
in the main house (no dogs) and six in a
bungalow annexe (closed in winter). All have
TVs, tea-makers and smart modern bathrooms. A log fire warms the long, narrow bar
that's hung with old photographs. Garden.

Brereton Green *(B & B)* **New Entry**   *Bears Head Hotel*

Near Sandbach · *Cheshire* · Map 3 B4
Holmes Chapel (0477) 35251

Free House
Landlord Mr Tarquinie

Credit Access, Amex, Diners, visa
🍺 Bass; Burtonwood; Guinness; Carlsberg;
Black Label; cider.
ACCOMMODATION 21 bedrooms £B (No dogs)
Check-in: all day

On the edge of a hamlet just a few miles from
the M6, this 17th-century pub has a classic
appeal: little bars arranged higgledy-pig-
gledy, doorways of different heights, beams,
brassware, even a section of wattle and
daub. Fifteen of the brightly decorated bedrooms are in the main building, six in a recent
annexe; furnishings are modern, and all
rooms have TVs, telephones and private bath
or shower. The welcome is not always the
warmest.

Bridestowe *(Food)*   *White Hart*

Fore Street · *Devon* · Map 9 B3
Bridestowe (083 786) 318

Free House
Landlords Owen & Millard families

Credit Access, Amex, Diners, Visa
🍺 Palmer's IPA; Worthington Best Bitter; St
Austell Duchy; Guinness; Carling Black Label.

Simple, wholesome food is provided at this
17th-century pub in a village just off the A30.
Gnarled black beams, natural stone and an
open fire make the bar a welcoming spot to
relax and enjoy tasty snacks ranging from
home-made soup, omelettes and salads with
ham or prawns to steak on toast and lemon
sole. Patio and garden. *Typical prices:* Blue
trout £3.40   Gammon & pineapple £4.50
(Last bar food 10pm)

Bridgnorth *(B & B)*   *Falcon Hotel*

St John Street, Lowtown · *Shropshire* · Map 8 D1
Bridgnorth (074 62) 3134

Brewery Mitchells & Butlers
Landlord Mr A. R. Owen
Children welcome
Credit Access, Amex, Diners, Visa
🍺 Mitchells & Butlers Brew XI, Mild, Springfield
Bitter; Carling Black Label; cider. ♀
ACCOMMODATION 17 bedrooms £C
Check-in: all day

The spacious, elegantly appointed bar with
deep, well-upholstered seating is an attraction of this 16th-century coaching inn not far
from the Severn bridge in the lower part of
the town. Warm, comfortable bedrooms with
practical fitted units and colour TVs offer
pleasant overnight accommodation. Three
rooms have private facilities, while the rest
share well-maintained public bathrooms.

Bridgwater *(Food)*   *Admirals Landing*

Admirals Court, The Docks, Northgate
Somerset · Map 9 C3
Bridgwater (0278) 422515

Free House
Landlord Mr P. Wood

Children welcome
🍺 Tetley's Bitter; Halls Harvest Bitter; Burton
IPA; Guinness; Castlemaine; Löwenbräu; Skol;
cider.

Very much in the new-style pub tradition, this
large and lively pub in a converted dockside
warehouse has tables for outside eating and
a heavily beamed interior supported by cast-
iron pillars. Dishes like lamb stew, fried plaice
and gammon are robust and satisfying, while
filled rolls, salads and omelettes provide
lighter bites. *Typical prices:* Braised beef &
vegetables £2.95   Ham & leek in cheese
sauce £2.45 (Last bar food 9.30pm. No bar
food Sun eve) ☺

Bridport *(B & B)*   *Bull Hotel*

34 East Street · *Dorset* · Map 9 D3
Bridport (0308) 22878
Free House
Landlords Terleski family
Children welcome
Credit Access, Visa
🍺 Bass; Badger Best Bitter; Hector's Bitter;
Royal Oak Bitter; Carlsberg Hof; Carling Black
Label. ⚥
ACCOMMODATION   16 bedrooms   £D
Check-in: all day

Once a posting house on the coach run from
Hendon to the south-west, this solidly built
hotel in the town centre continues to provide
travellers with a convenient overnight stopping place. Simply furnished bedrooms all
offer TVs and tea-makers, and seven rooms
have their own smart bathrooms. Downstairs, there's a cosy, welcoming bar and a
homely family room. Courtyard.

Bridport *(Food, B & B)*   *George Hotel*

4 South Street · *Dorset* · Map 9 D3
Bridport (0308) 23187

Brewery Palmer
Landlord Mr John Mander

Children welcome
🍺 Palmer's IPA, Best Bitter, Tally Ho; Faust;
Guinness; Shilthorn.

Behind a formal Georgian facade, this is a
really delightful pub with a happy blend of
tradition and flair, very civilised and relaxed.
Two cosy bars with open fires and rustic
decor provide the setting for some very
enjoyable eating. Sandwiches, hot sausages
and quiche are popular light bites, with
omelettes and cold meat salads for interme-
diate appetites; heartier fare could include
moussaka, curry and the day's pie – perhaps
rabbit, pigeon or steak and kidney. Traditional
tarts and puddings feature among the
sweets, and there's a good selection of well-
kept English cheeses. *Typical prices:* Pigeon
pie £2.25   Bread & butter pudding 85p (Last
bar food 10pm. No bar food Sun except eves
July & Aug) ☺

ACCOMMODATION   3 bedrooms   £C
Check-in: restricted

The three bedrooms, which share a homely
modern bathroom, are furnished with some
splendidly old-fashioned pieces. TVs and
magazines entertain, and guests can look
forward to a super breakfast. Accommodation closed 1 week Christmas.

Brightling *(Food)* — *Fullers Arms*

Oxley Green, Near Robertsbridge · *East Sussex* · Map 6 C4
Brightling (042 482) 212   *Free House*
Landlords John & Sheila Mitchell-Sadd   **Children welcome**
Flowers Best; Fuller's London Pride; Wethered's Winter Royal (winter only); Guinness; Stella Artois; Heineken; cider.

Wholesome cooking of star quality finds a home in this attractive country pub named after an eccentric local MP, gambler and folly builder. On the long list of main courses are superb wholemeal pastry pies (steak and kidney, turkey and ham, prawn and halibut), plus quiches and vegetarian lasagne. Side dishes are equally appealing – try ratatouille, cheesy spinach and brown rice or the crisp salads. And leave room for one of the scrumptious sweets such as old-fashioned spotted dick, chocolate pudding or lovely blackcurrant and apple crumble with oats, brown sugar and spices. English wines available by the bottle or glass. *Typical prices:* Vegetarian lasagne £2.50   Chocolate brandy cake £1.20 (Last bar food 10pm) Closed Mon except Bank Holidays.

---

*Prices given are as at the time of our research
and thus may change.*

Brighton *(B & B)* — *Black Lion Hotel*

London Road, Patcham · *East Sussex*
Map 6 C4
Brighton (0273) 501220
Brewery Beard
Landlords Mr & Mrs Colin Patey Johns
Children welcome
Credit Access, Amex, Diners, Visa
Harvey's Bitter, Old Ale, Mild; King & Barnes Festive; Flowers Bitter; Carlsberg; cider.
ACCOMMODATION   15 bedrooms   £B
Check-in: all day

A very spruce brick, stone and pebbledash pub in a village on the A23, a few miles from Brighton. It's a pleasant place for an overnight stop and, with central heating in every room, a warm one. Large colour TVs, radios and telephones are also provided, and only two rooms lack private facilities. There are two plush bars and a big garden (spot the giant play animals).

Brighton *(Food)* — *Cricketers*

15 Black Lion Street · *East Sussex* · Map 6 C4
Brighton (0273) 24620

Brewery Watneys
Landlord Miss W. Sexton

King & Barnes Festive Bitter; Watneys Special; Ben Truman; Guinness; Foster's; Holsten; cider.

Lively landlady Winnie Sexton has made this friendly old pub with its gilded mirrors and red velvet seating almost as popular as she is. Regulars and visitors alike will also testify to the excellence of her home-made savoury pies, stars of a menu that also includes smashing sausages and jacket potatoes, tasty sandwiches and hot specials like steak, scampi and chicken curry. *Typical prices:* Fisherman's platter £3   Grilled sirloin steak garni £4.50 (Last bar food 10.45pm).

Brighton *(Food)* *The Greys*

105 Southover Street, off Lewes Road · *East Sussex* · Map 6 C4
Brighton (0273) 680734

Brewery Whitbread
Landlords Jackie Fitzgerald & Michael Lance

Credit Visa
🍺 Whitbread Strong Country Bitter; Wethered's Bitter; Flowers Bitter; Guinness; Heineken; Stella Artois; cider. ♀

Poached trout with garlic mayonnaise, pepper steak and chicken baked with honey and ginger are just some of the treats from Jackie Fitzgerald's imaginative menu at this friendly modern pub. Lighter bites include soups, ploughman's and jacket potatoes, plus super chocolate brownies. *Typical prices:* Fish kebab & salad £3.25   Tagliatelle with pesto & mixed salad £2.25 (Last bar food 9pm. No bar food Sat–Tues except Sat eve) ⊖

Brightwell Baldwin *(Food)* *Lord Nelson*

Near Watlington · *Oxfordshire* · Map 7 B2
Watlington (049 161) 2497

Free House
Landlords Barry Allen & David & Muriel Gomm

Credit Amex
🍺 Brakspear's Pale Ale; Webster's Yorkshire Bitter; Carlsberg; cider.

You can eat extremely well at this pretty stone-built pub opposite the church. Co-owner-cum-chef Barry Allen offers a nicely varied menu, from ample starters like garlicky scampi meunière and seafood pancake to main courses such as chicken in prawn and asparagus sauce, lemon sole and roast beef. Salads and good sweets, too; less choice at night. *Typical prices:* Maritime chicken £5.75 Lemon sole meunière £5.50 (Last bar food 10pm) Closed Mons except Bank Hols. ⊖

Bristol *(Food)* *Jolly Cobblers*

20 King Street · *Avon* · Map 8 D2
Bristol (0272) 28672

Free House
Landlords C. L. Giorgione & A. B. Jacobs

Children welcome
Credit Access, Amex, Diners, Visa
🍺 Wadworth's 6X; Bass; Courage Best Bitter; Theakston's Best Bitter; Kronenbourg; Carlsberg.

Full of beamed character, this old ale house near Bristol's floating harbour draws the lunchtime crowds with a tempting range of hearty dishes. Savoury pies, casseroles and curries are served in generous helpings, along with the day's roast with lashings of gravy and all the traditional trimmings. Also cold meats and salads, plus conventional sweets. The upstairs restaurant provides further choice. *Typical bar prices:* Roast beef £5.60   Trifle 95p (No bar food eves).

Broad Chalke *(B & B)* *Queen's Head*

Near Salisbury · *Wiltshire* · Map 6 A4
Salisbury (0722) 780344

Free House
Landlord Mr R. Grier
Credit Visa
🍺 Webster's Yorkshire Bitter; Wadworth's 6X; Ringwood Best Bitter; John Smith's Yorkshire Bitter; Guinness; Hofmeister; cider. ♀
ACCOMMODATION 4 bedrooms £B (No dogs)
Check-in: restricted

Set among the peace and beauty of the Chalke Valley, this immaculate little inn has a history that spans six centuries. The main house, containing bars and restaurant, oozes old-world atmosphere with its heavy beams and rough stone walls. Accommodation, in a separate block, is contrastingly modern, and all rooms offer abundant space, warmth and amenities (phones, remote-control TVs, smart private bathrooms). No children overnight.

Broadwell *(Food, B & B)*

Fox Inn

Moreton-in-Marsh · *Gloucestershire* · Map 7 A1
Cotswold (0451) 30212

Brewery Donnington
Landlords Denis & Debbie Harding

Credit Access, Visa
🍺 Donnington's BB, SBA; Carlsberg;
cider. ♀

Everything is splendidly traditional at this cosy old stone pub on the village green. A collection of snuff boxes adorns the rustic, beamed bar, where the blackboard menu sets the mouth watering. Soup or perhaps crab pâté can be followed by a hearty main course such as Nepalese lamb, cassoulet or seafood noodles, while winter casseroles of jugged hare or beef, Guinness and walnuts would warm the cockles of anyone's heart. Delicious sweets like syllabub and an almondy Bakewell tart. Good wines. Booking is essential in the evenings. *Typical prices:* Roast pork with apple & perry sauce £2.80 Bakewell tart £1 (Last bar food 8.45pm. No bar food Tues and Sun eves) ⊖

ACCOMMODATION 2 bedrooms £D (No dogs)
Check-in: restricted

The two delightfully homely bedrooms offer a most inviting prospect. Equally comfortable and charming, they have tea-makers and TV, and share a spotless bathroom. Garden. No under-14s overnight.

We publish annually so make sure you use the current edition.

Brockton

Feathers Inn

Dating back to the 14th-century, this charming roadside pub of wattle and daub construction is run by super hosts, the Robinsons. Local farmers make up much of their custom, and the bar area is full of interest with its fine inglenook fireplace and six-foot-long pair of blacksmith's bellows, used today as a drinks table. Patio.

Near Much Wenlock · *Shropshire* · Map 8 D1
Brockton (074 636) 202   *Free House* *Landlords* Mr & Mrs Robinson
Children welcome *Credit* Access, Amex, Diners, Visa
🍺 Holden's Black Country Bitter; Mitchells & Butlers Springfield Bitter, Mild; Carlsberg Pilsner; cider. ♀

Brome   (Food, B & B)   *Oaksmere*

Near Eye · *Suffolk* · Map 5 D2
Diss (0379) 870326

Free House
Landlords W. J. & M. P. Hasted

Children welcome
Credit Access, Amex, Diners, Visa
🍺 Courage Directors Bitter, Mild; Adnams
Bitter, Winter Old; Guinness; Kronenbourg;
cider. ♀

Built in 1550, this delightful country mansion
stands in 200 acres of parkland that feature
some fine topiary. Ancient beams, log fires
and a brick-lined well in the splendid bar
create an atmospheric setting for some
imaginative snacks. The choice ranges from
taramasalata and pitta or avocado, blue
cheese and walnut salad among starters to
chargrilled steaks, chicken casserole and
daily specials such as locally caught eel in
red wine sauce. There are sandwiches,
salads and ploughman's, too, as well as
enjoyable sweets like plum pie or apple
pancakes. *Typical prices:* Chicken pie
£3.50   Devilled lamb's kidneys £2.75 (Last
bar food 10pm) ❧

ACCOMMODATION   5 bedrooms   £A
Check-in: all day

Spacious bedrooms are splendidly appointed – traditional furnishings, tea-makers,
clock-radios and carpeted modern bathrooms. The Victorian conservatory with its
leafy grapevine is a perfect spot for summer
breakfasts.

Bromham   (Food)   *Greyhound Inn*

High Street, near Chippenham · *Wiltshire*
Map 7 A2
Bromham (0380) 850241

Free House
Landlords Mo & George Todd

Children welcome
🍺 Wadworth's 6X, IPA; Mole's Mouse's Ear;
Guinness; Carlsberg Hof; Carling Black Label;
cider.

Former diver George Todd makes this village
pub a cheerful place to stop for a good bar
meal. His menu reflects his travels with
choices like taramasalata, clam fries, swordfish steaks and Malaysian pork with chilli
sauce. Simple sweets like moist lemon
gâteau. Generous portions will satisfy the
hungriest. *Typical prices:* Pork spare ribs
£3.30   Sambal udang £4.60 (Last bar food
10pm) ❧

Brook   (Food)   `New Entry`   *Dog & Pheasant*

Surrey · Map 6 B3
Wormley (042 879) 3364

Brewery Allied Lyons
Landlord John Keary

Credit Access, Visa
🍺 Burton Ale; Friary Meux; Benskins; Tetley;
Castlemaine 4X; Löwenbräu; cider.

Excellent bar snacks keep business brisk at
this friendly old pub on the A286, and the
customers regularly spill over from the
beamed bars into the garden. Traditional pub
grub includes ploughman's, burgers and
super shepherd's pie. A little more unusual,
and equally delicious: deep-fried calamari
rings with a garlicky mayonnaise dip. Full
dinner menu also available. *Typical prices:*
Cheesy fish pie £2.25   Beef & blue cheese
jacket potato £2.25 (Last bar food 10pm) ❧

Broom *(Food)* `New Entry`

Broom Tavern

High Street, Near Alcester · *Warwickshire*
Map 7 A1
Stratford-upon-Avon (0789) 773656

Brewery Whitbread
Landlords Gieniek & Liz Zdanko
Children welcome
Credit Visa
🍺 Flowers Original Bitter, Best Bitter; Whitbread Best Bitter; Guinness; Heineken; Stella Artois; cider.

The long regular menu and daily specials provide abundant choice at this attractive village pub between Bidford and Alcester. Dutch pâté or garlic mushrooms could precede gammon, a seafood platter or chicken in an excellent cream and prawn sauce. French bread sandwiches and salad platter are also popular. Children's portions available on some items. Garden. *Typical prices:* Steak & kidney pie £3.30 Apple pie 95p (Last bar food 10pm) ⊖

Our inspectors are our full-time employees; they are professionally trained by us.

Buckler's Hard

Master Builders House Hotel

The beamed bars are all that remains now of master shipbuilder Henry Adams' original home overlooking the Beaulieu River. A miniature cannon stands on the mantelpiece, and there are numerous pictures of sailing ships, plus a list of over 50 ships built here on the river between 1698 and 1822. Patio and garden.

Near Beaulieu · *Hampshire* · Map 6 A4
Buckler's Hard (059 063) 253 *Brewery* Allied Lyons *Landlord* Mr James Doland
Children welcome *Credit* Access, Amex, Diners, Visa
🍺 Ind Coope Burton Ale; Halls Harvest Bitter; John Bull Bitter; Tetley's Bitter; Guinness; Skol; Löwenbräu; cider.

Burcot *(Food)*

Chequers

Near Abingdon · *Oxfordshire* · Map 7 B2
Clifton Hampden (086 730) 7771

Brewery Usher
Landlords Michael & Mary Weeks

Credit Access, Visa
🍺 Usher's PA, Founders Ale; Webster's Yorkshire Bitter; Guinness; Carlsberg; Holsten. ♀

This attractive thatched pub on the A415 is run in charming, convivial style by Michael and Mary Weeks. Blackboards in the bar proclaim an extensive selection, from tasty soups and pâtés to steaks, casseroles and excellent tarragon chicken with spinach pasta. Quiche, ham and smoked mackerel for salads, Mary's Disaster cake to finish. *Typical prices:* Lamb & vegetable curry £3.95 Tarragon chicken £4.95 (Last bar food 10pm. No bar food Sun eve) ⊖

Burford *(B & B)*   *Bull Hotel*

High Street · *Oxfordshire* · Map 7 A1
Burford (099 382) 2220

Free House
Landlords Mr & Mrs Clive Nicholls
Children welcome
Credit Access, Amex, Diners, Visa
🍺 Wadworth's 6X, IPA, Farmers Glory;
Guinness; Löwenbräu; Heineken.
ACCOMMODATION 14 bedrooms £C
Check-in: all day

Steeped in history, this ancient hostelry enjoys a prominent position on the High Street. Mr & Mrs Nicholls have put a lot of work into upgrading the bedrooms, where period furnishings and plush upholstery take the eye. Two rooms have four-poster beds, and nine offer private facilities. All have tea/coffee makers. Housekeeping is really excellent. The bar is full of Cotswold character, with exposed stonework and original beams. Good breakfasts.

*We neither seek nor accept hospitality
and we pay for all food and drinks in full.*

Burford *(B & B)*   *Inn for All Seasons*

The Barringtons · *Oxfordshire* · Map 7 A1
Windrush (045 14) 324

Free House
Landlord John Sharp
Children welcome
Credit Access, Amex, Visa
🍺 Hall & Woodhouse Badger Bitter; Raker
Bitter; Wadworth's 6X; Löwenbräu. ♀
ACCOMMODATION 9 bedrooms £A (No dogs)
Check-in: all day

Homely comforts are combined with rustic charm at this sturdy 17th-century coaching inn three miles west of Burford on the A40. Public areas are splendidly ancient, with beams, stone walls, original flagstones, and open fires. Pretty, cottage bedrooms (front ones double-glazed) have quality units, TVs, tea-makers, and well-kept modern bathrooms. No children under ten accommodated. Attractive garden.

Burham *(Food)*   *Golden Eagle*

80 Church Street, near Rochester · *Kent* · Map 6 C3
Medway (0634) 668975 *Free House* *Landlords* Chris & Chiu Blackmore
Credit Access, Visa
🍺 Wadworth's 6X; Goachers Maidstone Ale; Shepherd Neame Master
Brew; Guinness; Hurlimann; cider.

To find Malaysian food in a pub is rare enough, but the quality of Chiu Blackmore's cooking makes this a really exceptional place. The choice changes according to the availability of ingredients, and dishes are notable for their fresh, spicy flavours – some pungent, others comparatively gentle. Nasi goreng, egg noodles, chicken with mixed nuts, beef and peppers with chilli in black bean sauce – these are typical of the delights that bring in the crowds from near and far. Familiar pub snacks are also available, but this is a place where you really should take advantage of the fine speciality cooking. *Typical prices:* Egg noodles £2.85 Malaysian fried rice £2.85 (Last bar food 10.15pm. No bar food Sun. No Malaysian food Mon eve)

★   ★

Burnham-on-Crouch   *(B & B)*   *Ye Olde White Harte Hotel*

The Quay · *Essex* · Map 6 D3
Maldon (0621) 82106

Free House
Landlords Lewis family
Children welcome
🍺 Southwold; Adnams Bitter; Tolly Cobbold Bitter; Stones Bitter; McEwan's Export; Carling Black Label; Guinness; cider. 🍷
ACCOMMODATION   15 bedrooms   £C
Check-in: all day

This 400-year-old free house has its own jetty where visitors can enjoy a pint while watching the yachts in the estuary. A nautical theme runs through the bars, where open fireplaces, old settees and shiny brass paint a canvas of mellow charm. Homely bedrooms – top ones with sloping ceilings and dormer windows – include three with private bathrooms. There's a simple lounge with TV.

Burton   *(Food, B & B)*   ★   *Plume of Feathers*

Near Chippenham · *Wiltshire* · Map 8 D2
Badminton (045 421) 251   *Brewery* Usher   *Landlords* Mr & Mrs Bolin
Children welcome
🍺 Usher's Best Bitter, Founder's Ale, Triple Crown; Guinness; Carlsberg; cider. 🍷

★ A conventional village pub, but with a real surprise in store! The Bolins' years in the Far East taught them the joys of oriental cuisine, which they now pass on to a gleeful public. The Sinhalese chicken curry is a subtle delight with just the right amount of spices, accompanied by perfect white rice and splendid side dishes. Indonesian lamb curry is another winner, and Sunday lunchtime brings an Indonesian-style buffet. Occidental palates are also catered for, with dishes like grilled trout, seafood lasagne and sachertorte (the last bought in but delicious). *Typical prices:* Indonesian lamb curry £2.95   Chicken Stroganoff £4.85 (Last bar food 9.45pm) ★

ACCOMMODATION   2 bedrooms   £D
Check-in: restricted

For guests staying overnight there are two spacious double bedrooms, restfully decorated in pastel shades and fully carpeted, with pretty duvets, curtains and practical modern furnishings. Each has a good tiled shower room with generous soft towels.

Burton upon Trent   *(B & B)*   *Riverside Inn*

Riverside Drive, Branston · *Staffordshire*
Map 5 A1
Burton upon Trent (0283) 63117

Free House
Landlords Mr & Mrs D. J. Martindale
Credit Access, Amex, Visa
🍺 Marston's Pedigree, Premium Bitter; Bass Special Bitter; Löwenbräu; Stella Artois.
ACCOMMODATION   22 bedrooms   £B
Check-in: all day

A peaceful setting on the banks of the Trent is enjoyed by this extended old inn just half a mile from the A38. Pleasant overnight accommodation is in a 1970s wing, and the nicest rooms are front ones with river views. All rooms have TVs, direct-dial phones, fitted wardrobes and little writing desks, plus spotless tiled bathrooms with lots of towels. New executive bedrooms are among major developments planned or happening.

Burtonwood *(Food)*

Fiddle i'th Bag Inn

Alder Lane, Near Warrington · Cheshire
Map 3 B3
Newton-le-Willows (092 52) 5442

Brewery Greenall Whitley
Landlords Don & Jean Roy

Children welcome
Credit Access, Amex, Visa
🍺 Greenall Whitley Bitter, Festival, Mild;
Guinness; Grünhalle; cider. ♀

Named after the old seed-sowing fiddle hung
up on the wall of its cosy bar, this smart pub
offers a wide choice of tasty fare. Juicy
steaks, fried plaice and traditional North
Country hot pot provide man-size meals;
sandwiches, filled barmcakes and ploughman's for lighter bites, and there's also a
lunchtime cold buffet (except Sat). *Typical
prices:* Chicken & mushroom pie £2.95
Lamb creole £3.25 (Last bar food 10pm) ©

*Any person using our
name to obtain free
hospitality is a fraud.
Proprietors, please inform
the police and us.*

RECEPTION

Burwash *(B & B)*

Bell Inn

High Street · *East Sussex* · Map 6 C4
Burwash (0435) 882304

Brewery Beard
Landlords Maureen & Bruce Townend
Children welcome
Credit Access, Visa
🍺 Harvey's 4X, Best Bitter; Fremlins;
Hurlimann; Carlsberg Pilsner; cider. ♀
ACCOMMODATION 5 bedrooms £C
Check-in: restricted

The cheerful bar of this attractive 17th-
century inn is a meeting point for many locals,
with darts and quiz games on the weekly
agenda. Overnight accommodation is simple,
but comfortable enough, and all bedrooms
have washbasins and tea-makers. Two
rooms have recently been redecorated and
recarpeted, and further improvements are
planned. Low oak beams and sloping floors
make the oldest room in the building especially appealing. Nice views from the patio.

Calderbridge *(B & B)*

Stanley Arms

Near Egremont · *Cumbria* · Map 3 B2
Beckermet (094 684) 235

Brewery Younger
Landlord Mr I. W. Robinson

Children welcome
Credit Access, Visa
🍺 Younger's XXPS Scotch, Bitter, Lager; cider.
ACCOMMODATION 9 bedrooms £D
Check-in: all day

This modernised 18th-century roadside pub
stands in extensive grounds reaching to the
river Calder, on which it has fishing rights.
The garden is a popular spot in summer,
while in cooler weather the spacious panelled
bar comes into its own. Decently furnished
bedrooms sharing four bathrooms offer simple overnight comforts, and there's a modest
little TV room.

Callington (Food)

Newport Square · *Cornwall* · Map 9 B4
Liskeard (0579) 82567

Free House
Landlords Sandy & Jon Dale

Credit Access, Visa
🍺 Bass; Stones Bitter; Worthington Best Bitter,
'E', Mild; Guinness; Tennent's Pilsner; cider.

Coachmakers Arms

Good honest home cooking is served up at
this 300-year-old pub in the middle of the
town. Salmon pâté is one of the favourites,
and main dishes could be anything from fresh
fish to fillet of pork or a very tasty lamb
casserole. Sweets like apple pie and sherry
trifle maintain the reliable standards of the
amiable new landlords. *Typical prices:* Pork
in cider £5.50   Salmon pâté £2 (last bar food
9.30pm) 🍵

Calstock (B & B)

Fore Street · *Cornwall* · Map 9 B4
Tavistock (0822) 832331

Free House
Landlords Mr & Mrs R. W. Slack
Credit Access, Amex, Diners, Visa
🍺 Flowers Original, IPA; Whitbread Best Bitter,
Poacher; Guinness; Stella Artois; Heineken;
cider. 🍷
ACCOMMODATION   3 bedrooms   £D
Check-in: all day

Boot Inn

A 300-year-old cobbler's shop and grocers
have joined hands to form the Slacks'
delightful inn in a quiet little village. The cosy
beamed bar houses rustic furniture and a bar
billiards table. Overnight accommodation is
available in a spacious double room with
private bathroom and two smaller rooms with
shower cubicles. Two have colour TVs and
all three tea-makers. Patio.

*We welcome complaints
and bona fide
recommendations on the
tear-out pages for readers'
comments. They are
followed up by our
professional team. Please
also complain to the
management instantly.*

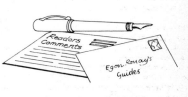

Cambridge (Food)

Gloucestershire · Map 8 D2
Cambridge (045 389) 270

Brewery Whitbread
Landlords Ray & Annette Whiteley

Children welcome
Credit Access, Amex, Diners, Visa
🍺 Flowers Original, IPA; Whitbread Best Bitter;
Guinness; Heineken; Stella Artois; cider. 🍷

George Inn

A canalside terrace, splendid garden (complete with childrens' playground) and numerous bars provide ample eating space at this
much-modernised inn. Crunchy tuna bake,
garlicky mushrooms and whitebait are typically tempting snacks, and for larger appetites, there are omelettes and vegetarian
specials, chicken curry, fisherman's pie, and
a summer cold table. Children's menu. *Typical prices:* Lasagne £3.25   Stuffed bacon
chop £3.50 (Last bar food 10pm) 🍵

Carey *(Food, B & B)*

Cottage of Content

Hereford & Worcester · Map 8 D2
Carey (043 270) 242

Free House
Landlords Mike Wainford & Glyn Johns

Children welcome
Credit Access, Visa
🍺 Hook Norton Best Bitter, Old Hookey;
Hereford Traditional; Flowers Original;
Worthington Best Bitter; Löwenbräu 1051; cider.

New owners are intent on restoring the reputation of this delightful 500-year-old inn in the depths of the country. The young chef's well-balanced menus include soups, pâtés and sandwiches as well as more substantial snacks like beef and an appealing vegetable hotpot with a tasty cheese topping, and there are fruit puds such as a kiwi Pavlova, and a well-chosen wine list. Winter brings traditional Sunday lunches. There's also a restaurant. *Typical bar prices:* Pork chops in cider £2.85 Fruit cheesecake £1.50 (Last bar food 10pm) ☕

ACCOMMODATION 3 bedrooms £C
Check-in: restricted

Improvements to the three bedrooms include attractive chintz furnishings, tea-makers and colour TVs; two or them also have private bathrooms. The slate-floored public bar and beamed lounge with its cosy stove are full of character.

Carthorpe *(Food)*

Fox & Hounds

Near Bedale · North Yorkshire · Map 4 C2
Thirsk (0845) 576433

Free House
Landlords Bernie & Howard Fitzgerald

Children welcome
🍺 Cameron's Lion Bitter, Strong Arm;
Younger's Scotch Bitter, Hansa; McEwan's
Lager; Guinness; cider. ♀

The village blacksmith's forge survives intact as part of this welcoming pub convenient for the A1. The enthusiastic Fitzgeralds offer some super food, with market-fresh fish a firm favourite, closely followed by such delights as creamy Stilton and onion soup, succulent steaks and chops – and lovely boozy trifle. *Typical prices:* Avocado pear with herb cheese £2.25 Fresh salmon and prawn pancake £3.95 (Last bar food 10pm. No bar food Mon). Closed Mon lunch. ☕

Cartmel Fell *(Food)*

Mason's Arms

Strawberry Bank, Near Grange-over-Sands
Cumbria · Map 3 B2
Crosthwaite (044 88) 486

Free House
Landlord Mrs Helen Stevenson

Children welcome
🍺 McEwan's 70/-, 80/-; Wadworth's 6X;
Guinness; Kronenbourg; Beck's Bier;
cider. ♀

The excellent bar food and range of specialist and guest beers draw an appreciative crowd to this fine old converted farmhouse. In the beamed bars you can enjoy an exotic collection of dishes, from tandoori chicken and stuffed vine leaves to gravlax and hearty rabbit and prune pie. Salads and sandwiches provide lighter bites, and there are some memorable desserts. *Typical dishes:* Chinese-style chicken wings £1.95 Nut roast en croûte £3.25 (Last bar food 8.45pm) ☕

Casterton   (B & B)   *Pheasant Inn*

Near Kirkby Lonsdale · *Cumbria* · Map 3 B2
Kirkby Lonsdale (0468) 71230

Free House
Landlord Mr D. Hesmondhalgh

Children welcome
🍺 Thwaites Traditional, Mild; Younger's Scotch
Bitter; Tuborg; Becks Bier; cider. ♀
ACCOMMODATION   10 bedrooms   £C
Check-in: all day

All is commendably neat and tidy at this nice-looking pebbledash pub, which has a pleasant little patio for summer drinking. Four of the ten bedrooms are traditionally furnished (one has a four-poster), while the rest use decent white fitted units. There are TVs and tea-makers in every room, and en suite bathrooms are smart and modern. Residents have their own comfortable lounge.

Castleton   (B & B)   **New Entry**   *Castle Hotel*

Castle Street · *Derbyshire* · Map 4 C3
Hope Valley (0433) 20578

Brewery Bass North
Landlord Mr Peter Nicholls
Children welcome
Credit Access, Amex, Diners, Visa
🍺 Stones Bitter; Guinness; Carling Black Label;
Tennent's Pilsner lager; cider
ACCOMMODATION   11 bedrooms   £B
Check-in: all day

A coaching inn of 17th-century origins, this welcoming pub stands in the centre of an attractive Peak District village, below the hilltop ruins of Peveril Castle. A major refurbishment programme is due to increase the bedrooms to 11, with six rooms being created out of an adjacent cottage. Furnishings are traditional (some four-posters), while accessories are modern (remote-control TVs, good tiled bathrooms). There are three pleasant, comfortable bars.

Castleton   (Food, B & B)   *Ye Olde Nag's Head*

Cross Street · *Derbyshire* · Map 4 C3
Hope Valley (0433) 20248

Free House
Landlords Mr & Mrs G. Walker

Credit Access, Amex, Diners, Visa
🍺 Stones Bitter, Mild; Tennent's Pilsner Extra;
Carling Black Label; cider.

Situated in a delightful village at the heart of the Peak District, this well-kept former coaching inn has a friendly, welcoming feel. In the comfortable bar, heated by a cheerful open fire in winter, there's a fair selection of wholesome snacks, from hearty home-made soup and fresh dressed crab to salads, sandwiches on white or rye bread, prawn-stuffed cod, steaks and the joint of the day. Ice creams, sorbets and things like fresh cream gâteau round things off. Decent, reliable cooking with flavours to the fore. There's also a restaurant. *Typical bar prices:* Joint of the day & vegetables £3.25   Soup 75p (Last bar food 10.30pm) ⏰

ACCOMMODATION 8 bedrooms £C (No dogs)
Check-in: all day

Housekeeping is immaculate and bedrooms have recently seen improvements in the shape of new deep-pile carpets and handsome darkwood reproduction furniture. Direct-dial phones, TVs and tea-makers are standard, and three rooms have their own gleaming bathrooms. Good breakfasts. Friendly staff.

Castleton *(B & B)*   *Moorlands Hotel*

Near Whitby · *North Yorkshire* · Map 4 D2
Castleton (0287) 60206

Free House
Landlords Mr & Mrs K. Gowland

Children welcome
🍺 John Smith's Magnet Bitter; Guinness;
Hofmeister; cider. *No real ale.* ♀
ACCOMMODATION   10 bedrooms   £C
Check-in: all day

Both business people and holidaymakers
are well catered for at this small family-run
hotel at the heart of the North Yorkshire
moors. There are lovely views from the neat
cheerful bedrooms, with pretty floral curtains
and practical fitted units. Six have their own
shower rooms, while the others share two
well-maintained showers. Downstairs there
is a homely lounge, a small TV room, and a
simple, friendly bar. Decent breakfasts.

*We publish annually
so make sure you use
the current edition.*

Cavendish *(Food, B & B)*   *Bull*

High Street · *Suffolk* · Map 5 C2
Glemsford (0787) 280245

Brewery Adnams
Landlords Lorna & Mike Sansome

🍺 Adnams Old (Oct–April), Bitter; Carling Black
Label; cider.

There's a friendly, homely atmosphere about
this pub, and the beamed bar has a very
mellow feel. Bar snacks are tasty and satisfying, with delicious home-cooked ham featuring in sandwiches, ploughman's platters
or salads. Lasagne and casseroled dishes
such as beef bourguignon are popular in
winter, along with soups like chicken with
vegetables or parsley and watercress. For
vegetarians there's usually a quiche, and
Sunday brings a traditional roast. For sweet
there may be apple crumble or treacle and
ginger tarts. *Typical prices:* Steak, kidney &
mushroom pie £2.30   Ham ploughman's
£1.20. (Last bar food 8.45pm. No bar food
Sun–Wed eves) ⊖

ACCOMMODATION 3 bedrooms £D (No dogs)
Check-in: restricted

The neatly kept bedrooms have beams and
simple white furnishings. They share a bathroom and a compact shower room. On the
ground floor is a resident's lounge with an
old-fashioned three-piece suite and a TV.

Cerne Abbas (B & B)   *New Inn*

14 Long Street, Dorchester · *Dorset* · Map 9 D3
Cerne Abbas (03003) 274

Brewery Eldridge Pope
Landlords Brian & Maria Chatham

Children welcome
🍺 Eldridge Royal Oak, Dorset IPA, Dorchester
Bitter; Faust Pils, Export; cider.
ACCOMMODATION 5 bedrooms £C
Check-in: restricted

Built in the 16th century, this slate-roofed
pub is a comparative newcomer in a village
with a thousand years of history. Originally
an abbot's home and later a courthouse and
coaching inn, it's a friendly, comfortable
place. The five bedrooms, all with TVs and
tea-makers, are neat and simple; they share
two public bathrooms full of greenery.
There's a cosy, many-nooked bar, along with
a family room and an attractive garden.

Chaddleworth (Food)   *Ibex*

Berkshire · Map 7 B2
Chaddleworth (048 82) 311

Brewery Courage
Landlords Mr & Mrs P. J. Houser

Children welcome
🍺 Courage Best Bitter, Directors; Guinness;
Hofmeister; cider. ♀

The talk is of horses and racing at this
picturesque little village inn in stables and
gallops country. Flavoursome soup can be
followed by a tasty steak and kidney pie,
grilled trout or home-made lasagne, or for
lighter appetites there are roast beef or
smoked salmon salads, ploughman's, rolls
and freshly made sandwiches. Hungry
horses can finish with apple pie or treacle
tart. Garden. *Typical prices:* Steak & kidney
pie £3.75   Home-cooked ham salad £3.50
(Last bar food 9.30pm) ⊖

Chagford (B & B)   *Globe Inn*

High Street · *Devon* · Map 9 C3
Chagford (064 73) 3485

Free House
Landlords Gerald & Polly Catterall

Children welcome
🍺 Whitbread Best Bitter, Trophy; Bass;
Guinness; Skol; Carlsberg; cider. ♀
ACCOMMODATION 4 bedrooms £C
Check-in: all day

The four bedrooms at this 18th-century
Dartmoor inn are large and comfortable, with
nice views of the church and the hills beyond.
Furnishings are traditional mixed with pine,
and all rooms have TVs and tea-makers
(fridge for milk), plus smart modern bathrooms. The lively public bar is home to
several darts teams, and there's a lounge
bar with horse-racing prints and photos.
Hearty breakfasts.

Chale (B & B)   *Clarendon Hotel*

Newport Road · *Isle of Wight* · Map 6 A4
Isle of Wight (0983) 730431

Free House
Landlords John & Jean Bradshaw
Children welcome
🍺 Burt's Bitter; Whitbread Strong County, Best
Bitter; Flowers Original; Samuel Whitbread;
Guinness; Stella Artois; cider. ♀
ACCOMMODATION 13 bedrooms £C
Check-in: all day

Lovely sea views towards the Needles are
an attraction of this delightful 17th-century
coaching inn. Pretty individually decorated
bedrooms, with some nice antique furniture,
are equipped with TV, tea-makers and mineral water. The smart modern bathrooms
have hairdryers. There's live music most
nights at the adjoining Wight Mouse Inn, a
spacious characterful old pub with a fine
collection of malt whiskies. Garden.

Charlbury *(B & B)*   *Bell at Charlbury*

Church Street · *Oxfordshire* · Map 7 A1
Charlbury (0608) 810278

Free House
Landlord David Jackson
Children welcome
Credit Access, Amex, Diners, Visa
🍺 Tadworth's 6X, IPA; Whitbread Best Bitter;
Guinness; Tuborg Gold, Pilsner. ♀
ACCOMMODATION   14 bedrooms   £B
Check-in: all day

Dating from 1700, this attractive honey-
coloured stone inn offers delightful accommodation in 14 individually decorated bedrooms (some housed in converted stables).
Most offer excellent private facilities and all
have stylish soft furnishings, nice antique
pieces and modern comforts like TVs, telephones and tea-makers. Public rooms include a flagstone bar with a fine inglenook
fireplace, a cosy little lounge and spacious
residents' lounge. Patio.

Charlton Village   *(Food)*   *Harrow*

142 Charlton Road, Shepperton · *Middlesex*
Map 7 C2
Sunbury (0932) 783122

Brewery Watney
Landlord Mr R. John

🍺 Watney's Stag Bitter; Webster's Yorkshire
Bitter; Ben Truman; Guinness; Carlsberg;
Foster's.

Reputedly the oldest inhabited building in
Middlesex, this lovely thatched cottage has
a lot of charm. It's busy at lunchtime, when
crowds throng the beamed bars to enjoy the
good food. A blackboard announces familiar
favourites like quiche, jacket potatoes, shepherd's pie and a roast. Simple starters and
sweets, plus sandwiches (the sole Saturday
choice). *Typical prices:* Shepherd's pie £2
Steak & kidney pie £2.75 (No bar food eves
or Sun) ⊖

Chedworth   *Seven Tuns*

Winding country lanes lead to this delightfully secluded little creeper-clad
pub some 300 years old. High-backed wooden settles furnish the cosy
beamed bars, and there's a family room and skittle alley next to the bright
public bar. The stone-walled garden complete with bubbling stream is a
favourite spot in summer.

Cheltenham · *Gloucestershire* · Map 7 A1
Fossebridge (028 572) 242   *Brewery* Courage   *Landlords* Mr & Mrs B.
Eacott
Children welcome
🍺 Courage Best Bitter, Directors; Simmonds Bitter; John Smith's
Yorkshire Bitter; Guinness; Hofmeister; cider.

Chelsworth   *(B & B)*   *Peacock Inn*

Near Hadleigh · *Suffolk* · Map 5 D2
Bildeston (0449) 740758
Free House
Landlords Mr Marsh & Mrs Bulgin
Children welcome
🍺 Adnams Bitter; Greene King IPA, Abbot Ale;
Mauldons Bitter; Norwich Bitter, Mild; Guinness;
Kronenbourg; Carlsberg; cider. ♀
ACCOMMODATION 5 bedrooms £C (No dogs)
Check-in: all day except Wed

Dating back to the 14th century, this oak-
timbered village inn with its inglenook fireplaces and comfortable seating is a particularly convivial spot on winter evenings, while
in summer the pretty garden is a real bonus.
The simple, cottage bedrooms (one single
and four doubles) all have tea-making facilities and share a carpeted public bathroom.

Chenies   *(Food, B & B)*

Bedford Arms Thistle Hotel

Near Rickmansworth · *Hertfordshire* · Map 7 C2
Chorleywood (092 78) 3301

Free House
Landlord Mr Gerard L. Virlombier

Children welcome
Credit Access, Amex, Diners, Visa
🍺 William Younger's No. 3 Ale, Scotch Bitter,
Tartan; Guinness; Beck's Bier. ⏰

It was the day of the local hunt when we
visited this Elizabethan-style roadside hotel,
but in spite of the throng the staff were very
efficient and friendly. Snacks may be enjoyed
in bars that abound in mellow country charm;
the menu is varied and imaginative, and
everything's served in more than ample
helpings. Sandwiches (over 30 varieties) are
favourite quick bites, and other choices run
from salade niçoise and garlicky grilled
sardines to sweetbreads, sole and braised
oxtail. Familiar desserts and an excellent
cheeseboard. Limited choice on Sunday.
There's also a very good restaurant serving
mainly classic French dishes. *Typical bar
prices:* Soft herring roes on toast £3   Hot
salt beef sandwich £4.90 (Last bar food
9.30pm) ⊖

ACCOMMODATION 10 bedrooms £A (No dogs)
Check-in: all day

A long panelled hall leads from the entrance
to the rear reception, passing the bars and
chintzy lounge. Bedrooms are of a good size,
smartly furnished and fully equipped (direct-
dial phones, TVs, trouser presses, hairdryers). All have splendidly fitted bathrooms
en suite.

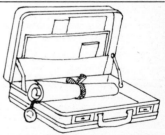

*Our inspectors are our
full-time employees; they
are professionally trained
by us.*

Chester   *(B & B)*

Ye Olde King's Head

48 Lower Bridge Street · *Cheshire* · Map 3 B4
Chester (0244) 24855

Brewery Greenall Whitley
Landlords Richard & Jane Casson
Children welcome
Credit Access, Amex, Diners, Visa
🍺 Greenall Whitley Local, Festival Keg;
Guinness; Grünhalle; cider.
ACCOMMODATION   7 bedrooms   £C
Check-in: all day

Built as a private house in 1520, this half-
timbered inn near the famous Rows is one of
the oldest in Chester. It changed hands quite
recently, and the new owners plan refurbish-
ments that will not detract from the character
of this listed building. Bedrooms are on the
small side, but cosy, beamed and homely; all
have TVs, radios and tea-makers.

Chichester   *(Food, B & B)*   *Nags*

3 St Pancras · *West Sussex* · Map 6 B4
Chichester (0243) 785823

Owner Mr John Speleers
Landlord Donald K. Hoare

Credit Access, Amex, Diners, Visa
🍺 Samuel Whitbread; Flowers Original, Strong
Country Bitter; Guinness; Stella Artois;
Heineken; cider. ♀

Food is a strong point at this handsome
timbered pub in the town centre. In the
Victorian-style bar each weekday lunchtime
there's an appetising cold buffet selection
that includes various quiches, salads and
home-made pies, together with hot specials
(soup in winter) and enjoyable puddings like
apple pie and chocolate mousse. At night
(and Sun lunchtime) it's the turn of a hot
carvery featuring succulent roasts served
with a selection of delicious seasonal vegetables. *Typical prices:* Steak & kidney pie £2
Quiche £2 (Last bar food 9.30pm. No bar
food Sun eve) ☉

ACCOMMODATION 11 bedrooms £B (No dogs)
Check-in: restricted

Attractively refurbished bedrooms of varying
size boast pretty soft furnishings, good
carpets and smart modern units. All have
colour TVs, tea-makers and excellent private facilities (three with shower cabinets).
Housekeeping throughout is consistently
high. No children under 16 overnight. Accommodation closed 2 weeks Christmas. Patio.

---

*We welcome complaints
and bona fide
recommendations on the
tear-out pages for readers'
comments. They are
followed up by our
professional team. Please
also complain to the
management instantly.*

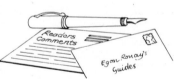

Chickerell   *(B & B)*   *Turk's Head*

6 East Street, Weymouth · *Dorset* · Map 9 D4
Weymouth (0305) 783093

Brewery Devenish
Landlords Tom & Heather Williams

Credit Access, Visa
🍺 Devenish Bitter, Wessex Bitter, John Grove;
Watneys Mild; Guinness; Carlsberg; cider. ♀
ACCOMMODATION 4 bedrooms £C
Check-in: restricted

Nestling at the heart of a pretty village near
the coast, this well-run inn (vintage 1769)
combines traditional charm and contemporary comfort. The well-furnished bedrooms
are kept in splendid order, and all have colour
TVs, tea-makers and gleaming, up-to-date
bathrooms. The stone-walled bar mingles
Tudor and seafaring themes, and there's a
popular skittles alley. Accommodation (no
under fives) closed 1 week Christmas.

Chiddingfold   *(Food, B & B)*   *Crown Inn*

The Green · *Surrey* · Map 6 B3
Wormley (042 879) 2255

Free House
Landlords Mr & Mrs M. Bosch

Children welcome
Credit Access, Amex, Diners, Visa
🍺 Adnams Bitter; Brakspear's Bitter; Young's
Special (summer); Carlsberg.

ACCOMMODATION   8 bedrooms   £A
Check-in: all day

One of the oldest recorded inns in the land,
the Crown began life as early as 1383. The
village-green setting is picture-postcard English, and the timber-framed building oozes
charm both outside and inn. Under oak
beams in the bar there are good simple
snacks to enjoy: home-baked ham in sandwiches and salads, croque monsieur, ploughman's and a hot dish of the day. The tiny
restaurant offers straightforward fixed-price
dinners every day except Sunday. *Typical
bar prices:* Croque monsieur £1.25   Baked
ham salad £1.25 (Last bar food 9pm) ☺

Records show that Edward VI (definitely) and
Elizabeth I (maybe) stayed here, and the
rooms bearing their names have oak beams
and four-poster beds. Other rooms, which
are located in a 1950s annexe, are of a more
modest nature, but both sorts offer TVs, tea-
makers, private bathrooms and ample storage space. Terrace.

Chiddingfold   *(Food)*   *Swan*

Petworth Road · *Surrey* · Map 6 B3
Wormley (042 879) 2073

Brewery Friary Meux
Landlords Jackie & Neil Bradford

Children welcome
🍺 John Bull; Friary Meux Bitter; Tetley's
Yorkshire Bitter; Guinness; Skol; Löwenbräu;
cider.

Fish and seasonal game feature strongly on
the menu of this attractive, tile-hung village
pub, which is run by angling enthusiast Neil
Bradford and his wife Jackie. Other popular
items might include home-cured smoked
beef, steak and lasagne, and treacle tart is a
favourite pud. Garden. *Typical prices:* Steak
& kidney pie £2.65   Brie, pâté & garlic
sausage with French bread £2.25 (Last bar
food 10pm. No bar food Sun eve) ☺

Chilgrove   *(Food)*   *White Horse Inn*

Near Chichester · *West Sussex* · Map 6 B4
East Marden (024 359) 219

Free House
Landlords Barry & Dorothea Phillips

🍺 Antelope Ale; Ben Truman; Guinness;
Carlsberg. ♀

In a pretty position beneath the South Downs,
this handsome old inn offers a short but
appealing selection of lunchtime bar fare. In
summer there are excellent smoked salmon
sandwiches, cold cuts and salads, in winter
some tasty hot dishes. There's also a good
restaurant (lunchtime and eve) with an outstanding cellar. *Typical prices:* Pigeon in wine
£2.95   Hot crab gratin £3.45 (No bar food
eves). Closed Mon, 3 weeks February & 10
days October.

Chilham (Food, B & B)   *Woolpack*

High Street · *Kent* · Map 6 D3
Canterbury (0227) 730208

Brewery Shepherd Neame
Landlord Mr John Durcan

Children welcome
Credit Access, Amex, Diners, Visa
🍺 Shepherd Neame Masterbrew; Hurlimann;
Guinness; Steinbock.

Once inside this former coaching inn you can really sense its 400-year-old history. Hops adorn the oak beamed bar, where a huge inglenook fireplace and pew seating add to the atmosphere. Here cooked meats served with plentiful vegetables from the adjacent Carvery restaurant can be enjoyed, or you can choose a snack from the blackboard menu. There are ploughman's, plus a few hot dishes such as beef pie and gammon steak. Round things off with a simple sweet like crème caramel, chocolate fudge cake or fresh fruit salad. *Typical prices:* Cottage pie £2.50 Ploughman's £1.75 (Last bar food 10pm) 🍴

ACCOMMODATION 13 bedrooms £C
Check-in: all day

Pleasant bedrooms, eight of which are in a separate building, have pretty fabrics and neat modern furniture (though one boasts a four-poster). All are equipped with TVs and tea-makers and most offer private facilities; those without share two functional public bathrooms. Courtyard.

Chipping   *Dog & Partridge*

Hesketh Lane, near Preston · *Lancashire*
Map 3 B3
Chipping (099 56) 201

Free House
Landlords John & Mary Barr

Children welcome
Credit Access, Amex
🍺 Tetley's Bitter, Mild; Skol. *No real ale.* ♀

A homely, stone-built pub with a large restaurant offering classic English fare. Home-cooked bar snacks are available as well. Among these are vegetable soup, steak, roast chicken or duck, scampi plus a changing daily special such as splendid steak and kidney pie with rich, tasty gravy. *Typical prices:* Roast chicken £2.30 Ploughman's lunch £1.80 (Last bar food 9.45pm. No food Sat eve or Sun lunch) 🍴

Chipping Norton (B & B)   *Crown & Cushion*

High Street · *Oxfordshire* · Map 7 A1
Chipping Norton (0608) 2533

Free House
Landlord Mr J. M. Frazer
Children welcome
Credit Access, Amex, Diners, Visa
🍺 Wadworth's 6X, IPA; Donnington's Best Bitter; Guinness; Kronenbourg; Kestrel. ♀
ACCOMMODATION 18 bedrooms £B
Check-in: all day

At the centre of a small Cotswold town, this handsome coaching inn dates back to 1497. The facade is a mellow honey colour, and there's a splendid bar with original stone walls and oak beams. Good-sized bedrooms, all very neat and tidy, offer TVs and radio-alarms, plus compact modern bathrooms. The residents' lounge has plenty of inviting armchairs and settees. Pleasant, smiling staff. Patio.

Chipping Norton *(B & B)*

Fox Hotel

Market Place · *Oxfordshire* · Map 7 A1
Chipping Norton (0608) 2658
Free House
Landlord Mr C. J. Finch
Children welcome
Credit Visa
🍺 Hook Norton Bitter, Best Bitter; Carlsberg;
Guinness; cider.
ACCOMMODATION 6 bedrooms £C (No dogs)
Check-in: all day

New owner Mr Finch is breathing fresh life into this old stone inn, which stands right at the heart of things in the market place. The public bar has been restyled and refurbished, and the walkway from the car park is lined with well-tended shrubs and rose bushes. The saloon bar is traditionally styled with darkwood panelling. Radio-alarms join TVs and tea-makers in the simple bedrooms, one of which has its own bathroom.

Chiseldon *(B & B)*

Patriots Arms

New Road, Near Swindon · *Wiltshire* · Map 7 A2
Swindon (0793) 740331

Brewery Courage
Landlords Mr & Mrs D. Day

Children welcome
🍺 Courage Directors Bitter, Best Bitter;
Guinness; Hofmeister; Kronenbourg; cider.
ACCOMMODATION 3 bedrooms £D
Check-in: all day

Ex-sailor Mr Day and his wife keep everything shipshape at their homely, welcoming pub. The three cheerfully decorated bedrooms, which have central heating, are pin-bright and share an equally spotless modern bathroom. Downstairs, pride of place in the attractive lounge bar is given to a huge collection of ships' crests. There's a simple public bar, and especially useful for families is the lounge overlooking the garden and children's play area.

Chorleywood *(B & B)*

Sportsman Hotel

Station Approach · *Hertfordshire* · Map 7 C2
Chorleywood (092 78) 5155
Brewery Bass
Landlord Mr S. Morgan
Children welcome
Credit Access, Amex, Diners, Visa
🍺 Bass, IPA; Stones Bitter; Guinness;
Tennent's Extra, Pilsner; Carling Black Label;
cider. ♀
ACCOMMODATION 18 bedrooms £A
Check-in: all day

Eighteen comfortable bedrooms are a great attraction of this handsome late 19th-century hotel close to Chorleywood underground. All have private bath/shower rooms and provide TVs, tea-makers, radio-alarms and trouser presses. The basement houses a traditional oak-panelled public bar and there's a second brightly decorated bar which leads to the patio and garden – the latter incorporating a children's play area.

Christow *(B & B)*

Artichoke Inn

Village Road, Near Moretonhampstead
Devon · Map 9 C4
Christow (0647) 52387
Brewery Heavitree
Landlords Mike & Sue Fox
Children welcome
🍺 Flowers Original, IPA; Whitbread Best Bitter,
Poacher; Guinness; Heineken; cider. ♀
ACCOMMODATION 3 bedrooms £C (No dogs)
Check-in: restricted

Tucked away in a small village not far from Exeter, this white-painted thatched pub has a modest charm. Flagstones, rustic panelling and an old stone fireplace give the bar its character, and a tiny fern-fringed stream runs by the little patio. The three cottage bedrooms upstairs are neat, fresh and pleasant, with traditional furnishings and black and white TVs. There is a single modern bathroom.

Church Enstone (B & B)

Crown Inn

Oxfordshire · Map 7 B1
Enstone (060 872) 262

Free House
Landlords Mr & Mrs G. Wolfe
Children welcome
Hook Norton Bitter; Flowers Best Bitter, Original; Whitbread Poacher; Guinness; Heineken; Stella Artois; cider.
ACCOMMODATION 5 bedrooms £C
Check-in: restricted

An attractive 17th-century pub of Cotswold stone in a lovely quiet village two miles from the A34. Spotlessly clean overnight accommodation is neat and attractive, with pretty duvets, pleasing velour-clad chairs and tea-making facilities; one double room has its own bathroom. The bar has a very good atmosphere and the handsome appearance that is typical of the area, with exposed stone walls and flagstone floors. Pretty garden.

Churchstow (Food)

Church House Inn

Near Kingsbridge · *Devon* · Map 9 C4
Kingsbridge (0548) 2237

Free House
Landlord Mr H. Nicholson

Children welcome
Usher's Best Bitter; Founder's Ale; Bass, Worthington Best Bitter; Guinness; Carlsberg; cider.

This heavily beamed roadside inn, which was once a haven for Benedictine monks, now provides visitors with plenty of atmosphere and a good range of bar snacks, from basket meals, grills and hearty fish pie to salads and sandwiches. Daily specials listed on the blackboard might include paella or bubble and squeak, with home-made fruit pie to follow. *Typical prices:* Fish pie £1.95 Trout with chips £2.90 (Last bar food 9pm)

Cirencester (Food)

Crown

17 West Market Place · *Gloucestershire*
Map 7 A2
Cirencester (0285) 3206

Brewery Courage
Landlord Graham Williams

Children welcome
Courage Best, Directors; John Smith's Yorkshire Bitter, Lager; Kronenbourg; cider.

Part of the expanding Slug & Lettuce group, this gleaming white pub attracts a lively crowd with its good atmosphere and good food. A blackboard spells out the wide variety of dishes available, from grilled sardines with lemon butter to beef casserole and lamb's kidneys Amontillado. Sweets include an indulgent but delicious chocolate and rum mousse. *Typical prices:* Chicken breast with avocado & garlic £5 Chocolate & rum mousse £1.25 (Last order 10pm)

Clanfield (Food, B & B)

Clanfield Tavern

Near Witney · *Oxfordshire* · Map 7 A2
Clanfield (036 781) 223

Free House
Landlords Keith & Susan Nadin

Children welcome
Credit Visa
Arkell's BBB; Hook Norton Best Bitter; Morland's Bitter; Carlsberg; cider.

An attractive old stone pub with a fine slate roof, thick walls, heavy beams and time-worn but well-preserved flagstones. Susan Nadin's bar snacks are well above average, and the choice is varied: beside the staples of sandwiches, salads and pâtés there are specials of the day such as carrot and orange soup or loin of lamb with a good tasty gravy. Chocolate and strawberry roulade could be your choice for dessert. The pub has a garden and a useful snug where children can sit. *Typical prices:* Chicken roulade £3.75 Smoked pigeon with pistachios £4 (Last bar food 9.45pm) ⏎

ACCOMMODATION 4 bedrooms £D (No dogs)
Check-in: all day

A steep staircase leads from the main bar to the simple but very civilised bedrooms, which are kept in apple pie order and have the ambience of a private home. Beds are comfortable, linen excellent, towels soft and generously sized, and there's a good supply of books. The largest room has its own bathroom. Very decent breakfasts.

Clare   *(B & B)*   *Bell Hotel*

Market Hill · *Suffolk* · Map 5 C2
Clare (078 727) 7741
Free House
Landlords Brian & Gloria Miles
Children welcome
Credit Access, Amex, Diners, Visa
🍺 Nethergate Bitter; Mauldon's Bitter, Special; Adnams Bitter; Younger's Tartan; Webster's Yorkshire Bitter; cider. 🍷
ACCOMMODATION 19 bedrooms £C
Check-in: all day

Right in the town centre, this fine half-timbered pub dates back to the 16th century. Heavy beams and rough plaster walls give a mellow, traditional feel to the public rooms, and the aquarium is a splendid new feature in the lounge bar. Eleven bedrooms, four of which have four-posters, are in an attractive courtyard block; these, and two of the simpler rooms in the main building, have private facilities. Garden.

Clearwell   *(Food, B & B)*   *Wyndham Arms*

Near Coleford · *Gloucestershire* · Map 8 D2
Dean (0594) 33666

Free House
Landlords John & Rosemary Stanford

Children welcome
Credit Access
🍺 Marston's Pedigree; Theakston's Bitter; Flowers Best Bitter; Guinness; Heineken, Stella Artois; cider. 🍷

Hanging baskets and an attractive garden add colour to this spotless whitewashed pub, built in 1340 and originally the manor house. The bar, with its beams, exposed stone and gleaming brass, is a pleasant place for enjoying a snack or light meal: there's a selection of sandwiches, along with pâté, ploughman's, snails and a number of fish dishes – perhaps grilled trout, Portuguese sardines, and smoked or fresh salmon. Home-made sweets could include almond flan, sherry trifle and a nice cherry and nectarine Pavlova. The pub also has a restaurant, and bar snacks are sometimes suspended at busy times. *Typical prices:* Grilled rainbow trout £2.75   Profiteroles £1.65 (Last bar food 10pm) ⏎

ACCOMMODATION 5 bedrooms £A
Check-in: all day

Accommodation comprises five spacious bedrooms, all with fully tiled bathrooms en suite. An impressive list of accessories includes colour TVs, telephones, trouser presses, hairdryers and tea-making facilities. Plans exist for an extension of 12 new rooms.

Clifton Hampden   (B & B)   *Barley Mow*

Near Abingdon · *Oxfordshire* · Map 7 B2
Clifton Hampden (086 730) 7847

Brewery Westward Hosts
Landlords Mr & Mrs P. Turner
Children welcome
Credit Access, Amex, Diners, Visa
🍺 Usher's PA Bitter, Best Bitter, Founders;
Guinness; Carlsberg. ♀
ACCOMMODATION 4 bedrooms   £C
Check-in: all day

Standing near the Thames in a quiet Oxfordshire village, this lovely thatched pub has a
history that spans seven centuries. Beams
and panelling capture a time long past in the
public areas, and the bedrooms, too, have
real character, with sloping ceilings, handsome darkwood furnishings and pretty floral
wall coverings. The four rooms, all with TVs,
share a modern bathroom. Accommodation
(no under-twos) closed 1 week Christmas.

Clun   (Food, B & B)   *Sun Inn*

Near Craven Arms · *Shropshire* · Map 8 C1
Clun (058 84) 559

Free House
Landlords Keith & Bunny Strong

🍺 Wood Special Bitter; Davenports Traditional
Bitter; Banks's Black Country Bitter; Guinness;
Carlsberg Hof; cider. ♀

Keith and Bunny Strong, former restaura-
teurs from Birmingham, do an excellent line
in bar snacks at their 15th-century village
pub. Skill and imagination get together on a
menu that always offers something different
– things like cashew nut paella, Mexican
bean pot or Brazilian beef with its flavourings
of coffee and ginger. Ploughman's and pâtés,
soups and steaks represent the more traditional side of things, and Bunny's sweets
include a splendid blackberry and apple pie.
The same menu is available in the 24-seat
restaurant area, and there's a neat little
suntrap patio for summer snacking. *Typical
prices:* Moroccan chicken £3.50   Seafood
lasagne £4 (Last bar food 9.30pm) ☺

ACCOMMODATION 7 bedrooms £C (No dogs)
Check-in: all day

Bedrooms are well, if simply, furnished, the
roomiest (with private bathrooms) being in a
modern annexe. Central heating and double
glazing add to the general comfort, and
accessories include tea-makers and hairdryers. There are two residents' lounges,
one with TV. No children overnight.

Clyst Hydon   (Food)   *Five Bells*

Near Cullompton · *Devon* · Map 9 C3
Plymtree (088 47) 288

Free House
Landlords Mr & Mrs J. A. Hayward

🍺 Hall & Woodhouse Badger Best; Toby; Bass;
Worthington Best; Carlsberg; cider. ♀

Rustic tranquillity abounds at this little
thatched pub set in a pretty garden. The bar
menu features sandwiches, salads and omelettes, and the local ham is excellent in all
three. You can also choose from the restaurant menu to eat in the bar. *Typical prices:*
Steak & kidney pie £2.75   Celery & stilton
soup 80p (Last bar food 9.45pm. No bar food
Sun night in winter.) Pub closed Monday in
winter ☺

Cobham *(Food)* — *Plough*

Plough Lane · *Surrey* · Map 7 C2
Cobham (0932) 62514

Brewery Courage
Landlords John & Irene Huetson

Children welcome
Credit Access, Visa
🍺 Courage Directors Bitter, Best Bitter; John
Smith's Bitter; Guinness; Hofmeister;
Kronenbourg; cider. 🍷

Whether you eat out in the garden or in the
beamed lounge of this mellow, brick-built pub
near Downside Bridge, you soon realise that
food is important here, especially at lunchtime. The choice ranges from a woodman's
lunch (with home-cooked gammon), through
sandwiches and salads to grills and basket
meals. Lunchtime extras include jacket potatoes and hot specials. *Typical prices:* Liver
& bacon casserole £2.10 Steak & kidney pie
£1.95 (Last bar food 9pm) 🍽

*Any person using our
name to obtain free
hospitality is a fraud.
Proprietors, please inform
the police and us.*

Cockwood *(Food)* — *Anchor Inn*

Starcross, near Exeter · *Devon* · Map 9 C4
Starcross (0626) 890203

Brewery Heavitree
Landlord Mr J. Endacott

Credit Access, Visa
🍺 Flowers IPA, Original; Eldridge Pope Royal
Oak; Guinness; Heineken; Stella Artois;
cider. 🍷

An inlet of the Dart estuary provides an
attractive setting for this well-run, atmospheric pub. Local fish is a feature of the bar
menu, with oysters, mussels and prawns
joined by specials like sole or grilled red
mullet. Hot pot and cottage pie for carnivores,
and some nice puds (apple crumble, sherry
trifle). Traditional Sunday lunch in winter.
Typical prices: Moules marinière £3.50 Pork
in cider with apples £2.95 (Last bar food
10pm) 🍽

Cockwood *(Food)* — *Ship Inn*

Near Exeter · *Devon* · Map 9 C4
Starcross (0626) 890373

Brewery Courage
Landlords Bert & Shirley Hoyle

Children welcome
Credit Amex
🍺 Courage Directors Bitter, Best Bitter; John
Smith's Yorkshire Bitter, Mild; Guinness;
Hofmeister; cider.

Seafarers used to obtain their provisions
here when this served as a victualler's house
in Cockwood's days as a ship-building
centre. Some 350 years later, it's the lovely
fresh seafood that attracts visitors to this
inviting waterside inn. Local oysters, mussels, crab and salmon all feature on the bar
menu, which also lists sandwiches and
salads, spicy chicken and steaks. *Typical
prices:* Cockwood special £6.25 Bouillabaisse £5.95 (Last bar food 10pm) 🍽

Coggeshall (Food, B & B)   Woolpack Inn

91 Church Street · *Essex* · Map 5 C2
Coggeshall (0376) 61235

Brewery Ind Coope
Landlords Bill & Judith Hutchinson

🍺 Ind Coope Bitter; Friary Meux Bitter;
Benskins Bitter; Taylor Walker Bitter;
Löwenbräu; Skol; cider. ♀

ACCOMMODATION 2 bedrooms £C (No dogs)
Check-in: restricted

Atmosphere in abundance is guaranteed at
this creeper-clad 15th-century pub, whose
cosy bars feature splendid oak beams, heavy
panelling and lovely lattice windows. Landlady Judith Hutchinson claims a resident
ghost, too, but a far more earthly attraction
is her range of excellent bar snacks. Consult
the blackboard for the day's choice of French
bread sandwiches, market-fresh fish, pâtés,
casseroles and tasty specials, plus a seasonal fruit crumble or winter warmer like
treacle pudding. *Typical prices:* Pâtés from
£1.25 Brunch £2.95 (Last orders 9.30pm.
No bar food Sun–Tues eves) ⊘

Upstairs, the two homely bedrooms are
comfortably old-fashioned and share a modern bathroom. Children under 14 not accommodated overnight.

Coleford (B & B)   Speech House Hotel

Forest of Dean · *Gloucestershire* · Map 8 D2
Cinderford (0594) 22607

Free House
Landlords Mr & Mrs R. Jones
Children welcome
Credit Access, Amex, Diners, Visa
🍺 Bass; Younger's Tartan; Ben Truman;
Flowers Best Bitter; Worthington 'E'; Carlsberg.
ACCOMMODATION   14 bedrooms   £B
Check-in: all day

Three huge, intricately carved antique four-
posters occupy pride of place in the bedrooms of this 17th-century hunting lodge on
the B4226 in the heart of the Forest of Dean.
Other rooms have more modest furniture,
and all are equipped with TV and tea-making
facilities. There are three private and four
public bathrooms. The beamed lounge-bar
areas have been attractively refurbished, and
central heating backs up a log fire. Garden.

Colesbourne (Food)   Colesbourne Inn

Near Cheltenham · *Gloucestershire* · Map 7 A1
Coberley (024 287) 376

Brewery Wadworth
Landlord Mr Eric Bird

Children welcome
Credit Access, Amex, Diners, Visa
🍺 Wadworth's 6X, IPA, Farmer's Glory, Old
Timer (winter only); Northgate; Guinness;
Heineken. ♀

New tenants Eric and Mary Bird are welcoming and enthusiastic, and plans for this 17th-
century roadside inn include the creation of
bedrooms in a stable block. Bar food is tasty
and wholesome: sandwiches and ploughman's for light snacks; sizzling platter steaks;
Cotswold sausages; a very good fish pie.
There's a cold buffet summer lunchtimes.
Roast Sunday lunch (otherwise restricted
choice). *Typical prices:* Fish pie £3.10 Fruit
crumble £1.25 (Last bar food 10pm) ⊘

Coleshill (B & B)   *Coleshill Hotel*

152 High Street, Near Birmingham
Warwickshire · Map 5 A2
Coleshill (0675) 65527
Brewery Whitbread
Landlords Mr & Mrs S. Kimbell
Children welcome
Credit Access, Amex, Diners, Visa
🍺 Flowers Best Bitter, Best Mild; Whitbread
Best Bitter; Stella Artois; Heineken. *No real ale.*
ACCOMMODATION 15 bedrooms £A
Check-in: all day

Conveniently close to the M6 and National
Exhibition Centre, this well-kept high-street
hotel provides excellent overnight accommodation. All rooms have smartly tiled bath
or shower rooms, along with quality built-in
units, TVs and tea-makers. Redecoration has
brightened public areas like the spacious,
relaxing main bar and lounge; there's a lively
basement disco bar, too. Accommodation
closed one week Christmas.

Coleshill (B & B)   *Swan Hotel*

High Street · *Warwickshire* · Map 5 A2
Coleshill (0675) 64107

Brewery Ansells
Landlords Mr Narey & Miss Wright
Children welcome
Credit Access, Amex, Diners, Visa
🍺 Tetley's Bitter; Ansells Bitter, Mild; Guinness;
Castlemaine 4X; cider. ♀
ACCOMMODATION 32 bedrooms £B
Check-in: all day

Handy for the National Exhibition Centre and
the motorways, this modernised 17th-cen-
tury inn is a popular place with businessmen
and motorists. The beamed main bar has a
pleasantly rustic feel, and there's another
smaller bar. Bedrooms are of a good standard, with modern fitted units, TVs, telephones, hairdryers and trouser presses; all
have functional private facilities (showers for
annexe rooms).

Collyweston (B & B)   *Cavalier Inn*

Near Stamford · *Northamptonshire* · Map 5 B1
Duddington (078 083) 288

Free House
Landlords Andrew & Noel Heigh
Children welcome
Credit Access, Amex, Diners, Visa
🍺 Ruddle's County, Bitter; Greene King IPA;
Guinness; Tetley's Bitter; cider. ♀
ACCOMMODATION 7 bedrooms £D (No dogs)
Check-in: all day

This friendly roadside inn still has its cavalier
– a life-size model who can be seen, tankard
in hand, perched on the beer barrels in the
cellar. He is protected by plate glass from the
bar above, which has three levels and plenty
of lounge seating. Pretty, simply furnished
bedrooms (five with carpeted bathrooms)
have restful colour schemes, TVs and tea-
makers. Terrace.

Coln St Aldwyns (B & B)   *New Inn*

Near Cirencester · *Gloucestershire* · Map 7 A1
Coln St Aldwyns (028 575) 202

Free House
Landlords Mr & Mrs R. Warren

Credit Visa
🍺 Morland's PA; Wadworth's 6X; Mitchells &
Butlers Brew XI; Guinness; Carling Black Label.
ACCOMMODATION 5 bedrooms £C
Check-in: restricted

Much of the original character survives at
this 16th-century village inn, both in the lively
public bar and in the lounge bar with its
flagstones, beams and huge inglenooks. A
narrow winding staircase climbs to the two
main-house bedrooms, decorated in modest,
homely style, which share a bathroom. In the
cottage annexe are three more modern
rooms with en suite facilities, plus a TV
lounge. Garden.

Congleton   *(Food, B & B)*   *Lion & Swan Hotel*

Swan Bank · *Cheshire* · Map 4 C4
Congleton (0260) 273115

Free House
Landlords Peter & Janet Hudson

Children welcome
Credit Access, Amex, Diners, Visa
🍺 Burtonwood Bitter; Marston's Pedigree,
Bitter; Guinness; Heineken, Stella Artois;
cider. ♀

ACCOMMODATION   13 bedrooms   £B
Check-in: all day

New owners Peter and Janet Hudson are
keeping up the high standards associated
with this handsome timbered coaching inn,
which dates back to the 16th century. The
bars exude character and charm, from the
cosy little tap room and relaxing cocktail bar
to the split-level lounge bar where a tempting
lunchtime cold table offers roast meats,
salmon mayonnaise, smoked trout and decent fresh salads. Other choices, available
both lunchtime and evening, include soup,
sandwiches, sirloin steak and grilled fillet of
plaice, plus pleasant sweets. *Typical prices:*
Grilled plaice £2.50   Sirloin steak £4.95 (Last
bar food 9.30pm) ☕

Bedrooms are smart, comfortable and well
appointed. A couple boast fine Jacobean
furnishings, while the rest have whitewood
pieces; TVs, tea-makers and direct-dial telephones in all rooms, private facilities in ten.
There's an inviting beamed residents' lounge
and a garden. Accommodation closed one
week at Christmas.

Constable Burton   *(Food)*   *Wyvill Arms*

Near Leyburn · *North Yorkshire* · Map 4 C2
Bedale (0677) 50581

Free House
Landlord P. B. Ingham

Children welcome
🍺 Theakston's Best Bitter; John Smith's Bitter;
Guinness; Carlsberg Hof; Hofmeister; cider. ♀

Once a farmhouse, this friendly North Yorkshire pub enjoys a peaceful country setting.
Good eating can be had in the stone-walled
bars, with baguette sandwiches a favourite
light bite. Other choices include soup, lasagne, deep-fried cod and roast pork with
crispy crackling and a decent stuffing. To
finish, there are gâteaux, ices, fresh fruit
salad and good cheeses. *Typical prices:*
Grilled gammon with chips £3.60   Lasagne
£2.90 (Last bar food 9.30pm) ☕

Corsham   *(B & B)*   *Methuen Arms Hotel*

High Street · *Wiltshire* · Map 8 D2
Corsham (0249) 714867
Brewery Gibbs Mew
Landlords Mike, Morwenna & Mark Long
Children welcome
Credit Access, Visa
🍺 Gibbs Mew Wiltshire, Salisbury, Bishop's
Tipple; Bass; Guinness; Harp, Carlsberg Pilsner,
Kronenbourg; cider. ♀
ACCOMMODATION   24 bedrooms   £B
Check-in: all day

The new incumbents are making dramatic
improvements at this fine old inn, whose
15th-century origins lurk behind a Georgian
facade. Stylish modern decor and fittings
have transformed the lounge and six of the
bedrooms; all rooms have colour TVs and
direct-dial telephones, and all but four quite
basic rooms offer private facilities. The oldest
area is the Long Bar with its stone walls and
splendid beams. The walled garden is also
being restored.

Corton *(Food)*

Dove at Corton

Near Warminster · *Wiltshire* · Map 9 D3
Warminster (0985) 50378

Brewery Usher
Landlords Jane & Michael Rowse

Credit Access, Visa
🍺 Usher's Best Bitter; Webster's Yorkshire
Bitter; Carlsberg. ⚲

Doves still flutter outside this charming
Victorian pub, where Jane Rowse's home-
cooked fare is a great attraction: hearty soup,
fresh salmon mayonnaise, salads, fish curry
and vegetarian dishes, and delectable
sweets. Excellent English cheeseboard, too.
Beyond the cosy bar is an equally cosy
restaurant. *Typical prices:* Veal véronique £3
Chocolate gunge £1.50 (Last bar food
9.30pm) Closed Sun eve, Mon (except Bank
Holidays) & 2 weeks Jan. ⊖

Cousley Wood *(Food)*

Old Vine

Near Wadhurst · *East Sussex* · Map 6 C3
Wadhurst (089 288) 2271

Brewery Whitbread
Landlords Mr & Mrs A. Peel

Children welcome
Credit Access, Diners, Visa
🍺 Wethered's Bitter; Fremlins Bitter; Whitbread
Best Bitter; Guinness; Stella Artois; Heineken;
cider. ⚲

Well known locally for its appetising food,
this cosy pub enjoys a pretty rural setting.
Interesting daily specials like moules marinière and minty lamb pie combine with
popular snacks like home-made soup and
pâté, sandwiches and ploughman's. Pleasant sweets. Garden. *Typical prices:* Peppered chicken in cream with vegetables £2.95
Pork loin in barbecue sauce with vegetables
£2.95 (Last bar food 9.30pm. No bar food
Sun & Mon eves).

Coxwold *(Food, B & B)*

Fauconberg Arms

North Yorkshire · Map 4 C2
Coxwold (034 76) 214

Free House
Landlords Richard & Tricia Goodall

Children welcome
🍺 Younger's Scotch Bitter; Tetley's Bitter;
Theakston's Best Bitter; Guinness; Harp;
Carlsberg. ⚲

Richard and Tricia Goodall generate a really
friendly atmosphere at their delightful 17th-
century village pub. Fresh flowers throughout
add a homely touch and the bar is full of
character with its flagstoned floor, heavy
beams and old stone fireplace decked with
brass and copperware. The lunchtime selection couldn't be simpler – soup of the day;
pork pie with a salad garnish; and a small
range of very good sandwiches with fillings
like cheese and tomato, roast ham, crab or
the Fauconberg special with cottage cheese,
fruit and nuts. There's also an à la carte
restaurant. *Typical bar prices:* Smoked
salmon sandwich £1.50 Soup of the day
85p (No bar food eves)

ACCOMMODATION 4 bedrooms £C (No dogs)
Check-in: all day

The four charming bedrooms are individually
decorated with pretty co-ordinating papers
and soft furnishings. Thoughtful touches like
pot-pourri make them feel like home and they
share an attractive modern bathroom.

Cranborne (B & B) — Fleur-de-Lys

5 Wimborne Street · *Dorset* · Map 6 A4
Cranborne (072 54) 282
Brewery Hall & Woodhouse
Landlord Mr C. T. Hancock
Children welcome
Credit Access, Amex, Diners, Visa
🍺 Hall & Woodhouse Badger Best, Tanglefoot;
Stella Artois; Malthouse Bitter; Carlsberg Hof;
cider. ⚲
ACCOMMODATION 8 bedrooms £D
Check-in: restricted

Traces of the 11th century abound in this historic building, which records show as an inn as far back as the 1600s. Overnight accommodation is modest but more than adequate (functional fitted furniture, TVs, tea-makers), and half the rooms have private bath or shower. The public bar is now styled like the lounge bar with beams, stone walls and attractive bench seating. There's a very pleasant garden.

Crawley (Food) — Fox & Hounds

Near Winchester · *Hampshire* · Map 6 A3
Sparsholt (096 272) 285

Free House
Landlords Alan & Janet Silsbury

Credit Amex, Visa
🍺 Strong's Country Bitter; Wadworth's 6X;
Flowers Original; Ringwood Fortyniner;
Heineken; Stella Artois; cider.

A jolly, red-brick village pub offering dependably enjoyable snacks in its cosy, mellow bars. The daily-changing menu includes nourishing soups and sandwiches, pâtés and smokies, plus hot specials like spiced chicken or liver and bacon. Home-made apple pie or cheesecake to finish. Patio. *Typical prices:* Fish soufflé £1.95   Hot beef roll £1.80 (Last bar food 9.30pm. No bar food Sun eve) 🌀

Crazies Hill (Food) — Horns

Near Wargrave · *Berkshire* · Map 7 B2
Wargrave (073 522) 3226

Brewery Brakspear
Landlords Mr & Mrs A. Wheeler

🍺 Brakspear's PA Bitter, XXXX; Heineken. ⚲

Thai and Malaysian dishes are a popular feature of the daily menu at this black and white country pub. Mrs Wheeler's flavoursome touch also extends to moussaka, carbonnade of beef, lasagne and a tasty tender chicken basquaise, while her sweets – such as a superb rhubarb, orange and apple crumble – are not to be missed. Limited menu Sunday and Monday evenings. Garden. *Typical prices:* Thai fried rice £1.25 Lasagne £2.30 (Last bar food 9pm).

Croscombe (B & B) — Bull Terrier

Wells · *Somerset* · Map 9 D3
Shepton Mallet (0749) 3658

Free House
Landlords Stan & Pam Lea
Children welcome
Credit Access
🍺 Butcombe Bitter; Royal Oak; Palmers IPA;
Guinness; Faust; Stella Artois; cider. ⚲
ACCOMMODATION 2 bedrooms £D (No dogs)
Check-in: restricted

This village inn of great character, its oldest part dating from the 15th century, was first granted a licence to sell ale in 1612. The bars abound in rustic charm, and a steep flight of stairs climbs to the refurbished bedrooms. The double is large and tastefully traditional, with a spotless modern bathroom; the other, smaller, room is in similar style, with a shower cubicle. No children overnight.

Croyde *(B & B)*
Thatched Barn Inn

Hobbs Hill, Braunton · *Devon* · Map 9 B3
Croyde (0271) 890349

Free House
Landlords Mr T. Pickersgill & Miss E. Barough

🍺 Courage Best Bitter, Directors; John Smith's;
Simmonds Bitter; Hofmeister; cider. ♀
ACCOMMODATION 6 bedrooms £D
Check-in: all day

Dating back many centuries and once used for storage by the monks of the nearby St Helen's Priory, this thatched barn has a great deal of charm and character. Beams and bare stone walls feature in the spacious bars, and there's a pretty flagstoned patio as well as a garden. The six bedrooms, including a double with TV, offer simple comforts for an overnight stay. Garden.

Croydon *(B & B)*
Windsor Castle

415 Brighton Road · *Surrey* · Map 7 D2
01-680 4559

Brewery Bass
Landlords Mr & Mrs Wenham
Credit Access, Amex, Diners, Visa
🍺 Charrington's IPA, Bass; Stones Bitter; Toby Bitter; Guinness; Carling Black Label; Tennent's Extra, Pilsner. ♀
ACCOMMODATION 30 bedrooms £A (No dogs)
Check-in: all day

The three pleasant bars of this former coaching inn on the A235 Brighton Road include an Edwardian-style one for residents. Bedrooms, housed in a modern, purpose-built block at the rear, offer hotel comforts, with fitted units and an impressive range of facilities from trouser presses to TVs and radio-alarms with bedside controls. Compact tiled bathrooms have plenty of towels.

Damerham *(Food, B & B)*
Compasses Inn

Near Fordingbridge · *Hampshire* · Map 6 A4
Rockbourne (072 53) 231

Free House
Landlords Mr & Mrs Reilly

Children welcome
🍺 Ind Coope Burton Ale, John Bull Bitter; Wadworth's 6X; Guinness; Skol; Löwenbräu; cider. ♀

ACCOMMODATION 4 bedrooms £D
Check-in: restricted

The friendly Reillys have created a very pleasant atmosphere at their homely red-brick pub, which is a popular haunt of fishermen. June Reilly's tasty home-made fare is a real attraction, and ranges from hearty soups, sandwiches and ploughman's to local trout, gammon steaks and a savoury cottage pie, with simple favourites like baked apple and cream for afters. *Typical prices:* Grilled trout £4.50   Farmer's lunch £2 (Last bar food 9.30pm) 🍽

A good breakfast is the bonus for guests staying overnight in one of the neat, chintzy bedrooms, which have well-polished period furnishings and share a spotless, old-fashioned bathroom. Garden.

*Prices given are as at the time of our research
and thus may change.*

Darrington *(B & B)*   *Darrington Hotel*

Great North Road, Near Pontefract · *West Yorkshire* · Map 4 C3
Pontefract (0977) 791458
Brewery Younger
Landlords Robert & Mavis Kerry
Children welcome
Credit Access, Amex, Diners, Visa
🍺 Younger's Scotch Bitter; Newcastle Bitter; Kestrel; Harp; Beck's Bier; cider. 🍷
ACCOMMODATION 31 bedrooms £B (No dogs)
Check-in: all day

A sauna and solarium, exercise facilities and conference rooms are extra attractions of this red-brick pub that's conveniently sited on the A1 near the M62. The racing fraternity are enthusiastic patrons of the Victorian-style bar with its horsy prints, and there's also a smart little cocktail bar. Well-furnished bedrooms, with TVs, tea-makers and telephones, have neat compact bathrooms. Even the garden is immaculate.

We welcome complaints and bona fide recommendations on the tear-out pages for readers' comments. They are followed up by our professional team. Please also complain to the management instantly.

Dartington *(Food, B & B)*   *Cott Inn*

Near Totnes · *Devon* · Map 9 C4
Totnes (0803) 863777

Free House
Landlords Mr & Mrs S. G. Culverhouse & Mrs M. C. Yeadon

Credit Access, Amex, Diners, Visa
🍺 Worthington 'E'; Ansells Best Bitter, Mild; Bass; Guinness; Carlsberg Export; Skol; cider. 🍷

High standards of comfort, hospitality and service are offered at this delightful thatched 14th-century inn. Daniel Defoe is said to have written *Robinson Crusoe* here in 1720, but it's definitely not a case of desert island rations in the cosily rustic beamed bar. A buffet displays generous ploughman's plus interesting salads and dishes like crab flan and galantine of chicken. Hot choices might include veal in cream and mushroom sauce, grilled lemon sole and calvados-flamed pork tenderloin. Finish with favourite treacle tart. *Typical prices:* Pork escalope & cheese in beer £5.95   Salmon coulibiac £4.95 (Last bar food 10pm) 🍴

ACCOMMODATION 6 bedrooms £B (No dogs)
Check-in: all day

The six pretty little bedrooms with simple modern furnishings all have tea-makers; they share two public bathrooms. Residents can watch TV in the comfortable lounge, or enjoy a quiet drink in the garden when it's fine. No under-tens overnight.

Dartmouth *(Food)* **New Entry**   *Cherub Inn*

13 Higher Street · *Devon* · Map 9 C4
Dartmouth (080 43) 2571   *Free House*   *Landlords* Milne family
Credit Access, Visa
🍺 Flowers Original; Black Awton; Whitbread Best, Poachers; Flowers
IPA; Stella Artois; cider.

★ The Milne family have moved from Ashcott to this splendid timber-framed
inn, the oldest building in Dartmouth. Super snacks can be enjoyed either
in the bar or at lunchtime in the dining room, which in the evening becomes
a restaurant. Local seafood, including scallops, oysters, crab and lobster,
is a feature, and other items on the tempting menu could be courgette and
watercress soup, celery hearts with ham and savoury mince pie.
Sandwiches and ploughman's for quick bites, and a mouthwatering
selection of sweets such as peach ice cream, elderflower syllabub and a
marvellous chocolate mocha gâteau. *Typical prices:* Smoked chicken,
ham and broccoli bake £2.85   Crab sandwich £1.30 (Last bar food 10pm.
No bar food Sun) Closed Sun lunch. ★

Children welcome *indicates a pub with an area
where children are allowed whether eating or not.*

Dedham *(Food, B & B)*   *Marlborough Head*

Mill Lane · *Essex* · Map 5 D2
Colchester (0208) 323124

Brewery Ind Coope
Landlords Brian & Jackie Wills

Children welcome
🍺 Ind Coope Best, Mild; Löwenbräu;
Oranjeboom; Skol; cider. 🍷

Dating back to the 15th century, this efficiently
run pub fits very well into the heart of this
picturesque Essex village. The decor is
delightful, with heavy beams and rough
plaster walls, wheelback chairs and polished
oak tables. The extensive range of bar snacks
changes daily: delicious thick soup, well-
filled sandwiches, ploughman's with cheese
or black pudding for quick snacks, plus more
substantial fare like moussaka, roast bacon
steak and rolled stuffed topside in a rich
gravy. Vegetarian dishes, too, and some nice
sweets. *Typical prices:* Ham, cream cheese,
walnut & onion sandwich £1.40   Moussaka
£3.40 (Last bar food 9.30pm)

ACCOMMODATION 4 bedrooms £C (No dogs)
Check-in: restricted

Upstairs are four simple but characterful
bedrooms with beams, old-fashioned furnishings, washbasins and TVs; one room is
a double with a comfortable furnished sitting
area. No children overnight. Accommodation
closed one week at Christmas. Garden.

Dersingham *(B & B)* — *Feathers Hotel*

Manor Road · *Norfolk* · Map 5 C1
Dersingham (0485) 40207

Brewery Charrington
Landlords Tony & Maxine Martin
Credit Access, Visa
🍺 Charrington's IPA; Adnams Southwold Bitter;
Stones Bitter; Guinness; Tennent's Extra;
Carling Black Label; cider.
ACCOMMODATION 6 bedrooms £C (No dogs)
Check-in: all day

The Sandringham Estate and lovely wood-
land walks are within easy reach of this
friendly, well-kept pub. Good-size bedrooms,
with modern freestanding furniture, colour
TVs and tea-makers, are cosy and comfortable, and share a single spacious bathroom.
The oak-panelled Sandringham Bar and the
mellow Saddle Bar are pleasantly traditional;
one overlooks the attractive garden.

Devizes *(Food, B & B)* — *Bear Hotel*

Market Place · *Wiltshire* · Map 7 A2
Devizes (0380) 2444

Brewery Wadworth
Landlords Jacqueline & Keith Dickenson

Children welcome
Credit Access, Amex, Visa
🍺 Wadworth's IPA, 6X; Guinness; Heineken;
Harp Extra; cider.

ACCOMMODATION 27 bedrooms £B
Check-in: all day

A prominent West country hostelry for over
three centuries, this handsome coaching inn
on the market square is rich in traditional
atmosphere. Nobly proportioned public
rooms include an elegant lounge and thoroughly traditional bar, the latter a favourite
local meeting place – especially at mealtimes,
when appetising snacks are served. There
are freshly cut sandwiches and giant meat
rolls, bacon-wrapped sausages stuffed with
cheese ('Bear Bait') and charcoal grills,
substantial salads and raised pies. *Typical
prices:* Meat pastie 65p   Hot dish of the day
£2.20 (Last bar food 11pm).

Charming bedrooms are sturdily furnished (a
couple boast four-posters) and all offer TVs,
tea-makers and direct-dial telephones, together with simple private bathrooms. Long-
serving tenants Jacqueline and Keith Dickenson are amiable and welcoming hosts.

Devizes *(B & B)* — *Moonrakers*

29 Nursteed Road · *Wiltshire* · Map 7 A2
Devizes (0380) 2909

Brewery Wadworth
Landlord Mr V. W. Gafney

🍺 Wadworth's IPA, 6X, Northgate; Guinness;
Heineken; Löwenbräu.
ACCOMMODATION 5 bedrooms £C (No
dogs)
Check-in: all day

Rose and Vic Gafney are the welcoming
hosts at this homely mock-Tudor pub standing just outside town. Locals enjoy a game of
pool or darts in the atmospheric public bar
and there's a comfortable, relaxing lounge
bar. Five spacious bedrooms offer TVs, tea-
makers and shower cubicles; a neatly kept
public bathroom is also available. Garden.

Doddiscombsleigh *(B & B)* *Nobody Inn*

Near Exeter · *Devon* · Map 9 C3
Christow (0647) 52394
Free House
Landlords Mr & Mrs Bolton & Mr Borst-Smith
Credit Access, Visa
🍺 Hall & Woodhouse Badger Bitter; Hancock's
Best Bitter; Bates Best Bitter; Stones Best
Bitter; Guinness; Carlsberg Export; Carling
Black Label; cider. ⚲
ACCOMMODATION 7 bedrooms £D (No dogs)
Check-in: all day

Guests can expect a more hospitable welcome than that provided by a long-ago landlord who locked the doors and pretended there was nobody in – hence the name. Today's bedrooms are comfortable and characterful, with some lovely antique pieces and thoughtful extras; five have private facilities (no children overnight). Look out for the impressive collection (over 120) of malt whiskies in the splendidly atmospheric beamed bar. Patio.

Dorchester-on-Thames *(Food, B & B)* *George Hotel*

High Street · *Oxfordshire* · Map 7 B2
Oxford (0865) 340404

Free House
Landlord Mr M. Kay

Credit Access, Amex, Diners, Visa
🍺 Morland's PA; Brakspear's Bitter; Guinness;
Heineken; Stella Artois. ⚲

Built some 800 years ago, this fine old inn has a spectacular medieval dining hall used for breakfasts and bar lunches. The bar itself boasts old beams, wooden settles and comfortable leather upholstered chairs. On the bar menu are mouthwatering dishes such as smoked haddock and lime omelette, a pint of langoustines and deep-fried mushroom caps filled with Stilton, as well as ploughman's, cold meat and fish with a refreshing selection of salads. Fresh or toasted sandwiches too and a cheese board. *Typical prices:* Steak & kidney pie £3.20 Chicken & pigeon terrine £2.75 (No bar food eves or Sun) ⊖

ACCOMMODATION 17 bedrooms £A
Check-in: all day

The comfortable bedrooms, mainly beamed and traditionally furnished (two have four-posters) are well fitted out – all have TVs and telephones – and nearly all have their own modern bathroom. Plainer rooms in the converted stable block open on to the courtyard. There's also a very civilised residents' lounge. Accommodation closed 1 week Christmas.

Dorney *(Food)* *Palmer Arms*

Village Road, Near Windsor
Buckinghamshire · Map 7 C2
Burnham (062 86) 666 12

Brewery Regent Inns
Landlord Mr M. Ismail
Children welcome
Credit Access, Visa
🍺 Bass, Charrington IPA, Toby Bitter; M&B
Mild; Guinness; Carling Black Label; Tennent's
Extra; cider. ⚲

Stylishly revamped, this friendly village pub offers enjoyable food in its smart pine-clad bar. Rich soups and flavoursome terrines make tasty snacks or starters. Follow, perhaps, with minty grilled lamb cutlets or lemon sole in a shrimp and mushroom sauce. Fresh fruits with liqueurs make a delicious finale. Garden. *Typical prices:* Chicken suprême in avocado & garlic sauce £3.95   Sirloin steak with herb butter £5.25 (Last bar food 10pm)

Dragons Green   *George & Dragon*

Surrounded by lovely Sussex countryside, this mellow, 17th-century inn boasts a splendid orchard-like garden where you can enjoy the excellent real ale on sunny days. Inside, the cosy low-ceilinged bar (mind your head!) is decorated with gleaming horse brasses and pewter mugs and old-world charm is much in evidence.

Near Shipley, Horsham · *West Sussex* · Map 6 B4
Coolham (040 387) 320   *Brewery* King & Barnes   *Landlord* Mr John Jenner
Children welcome
🍺 King & Barnes Sussex Bitter, Festive, Old Ale (winter); Guinness; Holsten; J.K. Lager; cider.

Driffield   *(B & B)*   *Bell Hotel*

Market Place · *Humberside* · Map 4 D2
Driffield (0377) 46661
Free House
Landlords Mr and Mrs G. Riggs
Children welcome
Credit Access, Amex, Diners, Visa
🍺 Younger's Scotch Bitter, No. 3 Bitter; Cameron's Strongarm; Webster's Yorkshire Bitter; Guinness; Carlsberg Hof; cider. 🍷
ACCOMMODATION 14 bedrooms £B (No dogs)
Check-in: all day

Mr and Mrs Riggs make guests feel welcome at their former coaching inn, whose amenities include squash, billiards and a laundry service. Bedrooms are very comfortable and tidy, with freestanding furniture and pretty fabrics, plus TVs, direct-dial phones, hairdryers and trouser presses. All rooms have private bathrooms with bidets. There's a pleasant panelled lounge bar and a glass-roofed courtyard. No under-12s overnight. Accommodation closed 24–30 December.

Dummer   *(Food)*   **New Entry**   *The Queen*

Near Basingstoke · *Hampshire* · Map 6 B3
Dummer (025675) 367

Free House
Landlords John & Jocelyn Holland

Children welcome
Credit Access, Diners, Visa
🍺 Courage Best; Fuller's ESB; Wadworth's 6X; John Smith's; Guinness; Miller Lite; Kronenbourg; cider.

Pleasant staff contribute to a cheerful atmosphere in this pebbledash pub in the Duchess of York's former home village. Bar food is above average, with starters like deep-fried crab claws or grilled grapefruit preceding kebabs, burgers, halibut steak or lasagne. Charcoal grills, too, plus salads. Super wholemeal bread sandwiches are especially noteworthy. *Typical prices:* Lasagne £4.95 Ham & Stilton sandwich £1.50 (Last bar food 10pm) 🍴

Dunsfold   *(Food)*   *Sun*

The Common · *Surrey* · Map 6 B3
Dunsfold (048 649) 242

Brewery Friary Meux
Landlord Mr J. Bundy

Children welcome (lunchtime)
🍺 Friary Meux Bitter, Mild; Ind Coope Burton Ale; John Bull Bitter; Guinness; Skol; Castlemaine; Löwenbräu; cider. 🍷

A nicely varied snack menu makes this village pub on the edge of the green a popular spot at mealtimes. You can enjoy soup, sandwiches and ploughman's, or a rather more exotic snack such as garlicky grilled sardines or pan-fried prawns. Main courses include haddock, roast chicken and daily specials plus appealing sweets. *Typical prices:* Spinach & mushroom pancake £1.65 Steak & kidney pie £2.55 (Last bar food 9.30pm. No bar food Sun eve) 🍴

Duxford *(Food)*   *John Barleycorn*

Moorfield Road · *Cambridgeshire* · Map 7 D1
Cambridge (0223) 832699

Brewery Greene King
Landlords Christina & Henry Sewell

🍺 Greene King Abbot, Mild, Bitter; Guinness;
Kronenbourg; Harp; cider.

This picture-postcard thatched pub (dated
1660) stands in a charming village not far
from the M11 (junction 10). In the low-beamed
bar, where a log fire burns in winter, a variety
of snacks is served, from pâté and tasty
cock-a-leekie to spiced beef, steak sandwiches and smoked cod with poached eggs.
Evening grills. Sweets are not a strong point.
Typical prices: French onion soup £1.60
Spiced beef £3 (Last bar food 10pm) ℮

Eartham *(Food)*   *George Inn*

Near Chichester · *West Sussex* · Map 6 B4
Slindon (024 365) 340

Free House
Landlord Mr Rex Colman

Children welcome (lunchtime)
Credit Access
🍺 Gale's HSB; Harvey's Bitter; Flowers Original
Bitter; Fuller's ESB; Hall & Woodhouse Badger
Best Bitter; Guinness; Stella Artois; cider. ♀

Bar food is available both sessions, seven
days a week, in this popular village pub on
the South Downs. Soup, sandwiches, pâté
and ploughman's are the staples, supplemented by blackboard specials such as
vegetarian lasagne, steaks, beef casseroles
and a nice creamy-mild chicken curry. Simple
sweets. The pretty garden is a favourite spot
when the sun shines. *Typical prices:* Vegetarian lasagne £2.65 Chicken provençale
£3.30 (Last bar food 10pm) ℮

East Clandon *(Food)* `New Entry`   *Queens Head*

The Street · *Surrey* · Map 7 C2
Guildford (0483) 222332

Brewery Friary Meux
Landlord Mr J. Miller

Credit Access, Diners, Visa
🍺 Friary Meux Bitter; Ind Coope Burton Ale;
John Bull Bitter; Guinness; Löwenbräu; Skol;
cider.

Eating is the big event at this modernised but
mellow 16th-century pub. The choice is
extremely varied, and many dishes bear
traditional names (pan haggerty, carpetbag
steak), whereas others are gimmicky. Savoury pies are particularly popular, and it's
nice to see bubble and squeak on the menu.
Sandwiches and ploughman's are lunchtime
extras (not Sun). *Typical prices:* Steak, kidney
& mushroom pie £4 Apple crumble £1.25
(Last bar food 10.15pm) ℮

East Dean   *Tiger Inn*

Summer visitors can take full advantage of this charming old pub's
peaceful position by the village green. Part of a cluster of little flint cottages,
it's just as appealing inside as out, with ancient beams and settles, shiny
horse brasses and pastoral pictures creating a homely scene in the cosy
bar. Patio.

East Sussex · Map 6 C4
East Dean (032 15) 3209   *Brewery* Courage   *Landlord* Mr James Conroy
🍺 Courage Directors, Best Bitter; John Smith's Yorkshire Bitter;
Guinness; Hofmeister; Kronenbourg; cider.

East Dereham *(B & B)*

King's Head Hotel

Norwich Street · *Norfolk* · Map 5 D1
East Dereham (0362) 3842
Brewery Norwich
Landlords Mr and Mrs R. Black
Children welcome
Credit Access, Amex, Diners, Visa
🍺 Norwich Bitter, S&P, Mild; Guinness;
Carlsberg; Foster's; cider.
ACCOMMODATION 15 bedrooms £C
Credit Access, Amex, Diners, Visa
Check-in: all day

Down a side street near the centre of town, this modernised 17th-century inn is run with pride and care by owners Mr and Mrs Black. The bar is roomy and inviting, with doors that open on to a flowery little terrace and the hotel's own bowling green. Comfortable, centrally heated bedrooms, all with colour TV, include five modern rooms in a converted stable block; ten have their own shower/bathrooms.

East End *(Food)*

Plough & Sail

Paglesham, Near Rochford · *Essex* · Map 6 D3
Canewdon (037 06) 242

Brewery Watneys
Landlord Mr Kenneth Oliver

Credit Access, Visa
🍺 Combes Bitter; John Smith's Yorkshire Bitter;
Ben Truman; Watneys IPA; Foster's; Carlsberg;
cider. ♀

This delightful old timbered pub stands just a short walk from the river Roach, source of the superb oysters that are a feature of the menu between September and April, along with mussels. Throughout the year there's a wide selection of sandwiches, salads and hot dishes such as prawn omelette, poached salmon and Barnsley lamb chop. Check directions carefully off the B1013. *Typical prices:* ½ dozen oysters £5   Steak & kidney pie £2.95 (Last bar food 9.30pm) ☙

East Haddon *(B & B)*

Red Lion

Near Northampton · *Northamptonshire*
Map 5 B2
Northampton (0604) 770223

Brewery Wells
Landlords Mr & Mrs Ian Kennedy
Credit Access, Amex, Diners, Visa
🍺 Wells Eagle Bitter, Noggin, Kellerbräu; Red
Stripe; cider.
ACCOMMODATION 6 bedrooms £C (No dogs)
Check-in: all day

Some 7 miles from junction 18 of the M1, this stone pub is a welcoming place for a quiet weekend. A wealth of antiques and curios, a flower-filled patio and fresh flower arrangements are typical of the care taken by the Kennedys. Bedrooms are delightfully cosy and cottagy, with pretty floral bedspreads and homely ornaments; they share two spotless bathrooms. Accommodation closed 1 week Christmas. Garden.

Eastergate *(Food)*

Wilkes Head

Near Chichester · *West Sussex* · Map 6 B4
Eastergate (024 368) 3380

Brewery Friary Meux
Landlords Brian and Kathy Goldsmith

🍺 Friary Meux Bitter; Burton Ale; Guinness;
Skol; Löwenbräu; cider.

A pleasant and relaxed village pub with rustic bars and a menu of wholesome fare prepared by Kathy Goldsmith. The pâté is smooth and moist, and from the daily specials you might choose a burger, lasagne or robust sausage and onion pie with crisp short crust pastry. Chocolate, rum and raisin truffle makes a nice calorific ending. The choice on Sunday is limited. *Typical prices:* Steak & kidney pie £2   Chicken liver pâté £1.40 (Last bar food 10pm) ☙

Eastling   *(Food, B & B)*   *Carpenter's Arms*

Near Faversham · *Kent* · Map 6 D3
Eastling (079 589) 234

Brewery Shepherd Neame
Landlord Mrs M. J. Wright

Credit Visa
🍺 Shepherd Neame Master Brew, Stock Ale
(winter only), Abbey Ale, Master Brew Mild,
Hurlimann; cider. ♀

The warm and welcoming personality of Mrs
Wright fills this delightfully mellow old pub
set deep in the Kent countryside. Hop vines
hang from heavy beams in the brick-walled
bar, where you can sit by the inglenook
fireplace and enjoy some excellent home-
cooked fare. The extensive menu (less choice
on Sunday) ranges from mushroom salad
and smoked trout among starters to chicken
casserole, Kentish ham and eggs, pizzas and
the splendid beef in ale and mustard – a richly
sauced, flavour-packed feast. There are
sandwiches and ploughman's, too, and lovely
sweets like spicy bread pudding and beautifully glazed apple flan. *Typical prices:* Hot
buttered crab £1.95   Chicken in red wine
£4.50 (Last bar food 10pm) ⊖

ACCOMMODATION   2 bedrooms   £D
Check-in: restricted

There are two homely bedrooms, one with
simple modern furniture, the other with
antique pieces and a full bookshelf. Both are
of good size and share a huge bathroom.

Easton   *(Food)*   *White Horse*

Near Woodbridge · *Suffolk* · Map 5 D2
Wickham Market (0728) 746456

Brewery Tollemache & Cobbold
Landlord David Grimwood

Credit Access
🍺 Tolly Cobbold Original Bitter, Mild; Guinness;
Hansa; cider.

Prime local ingredients are used as much as
possible throughout the enterprising menu
at this charming 17th-century pub. In the
homely bar you can tuck into such delicious
treats as leek and potato soup or flavoursome
taramasalata followed by, say, Cromer crab
or a casserole of local lamb. Sweets like
fresh peach meringue round the feast off
splendidly. *Typical prices:* Fisherman's pie
£2.95   Pheasant cobbler £2.75 (Last bar
food 9pm. No bar food Sun & Mon eves) ⊖

Edge   *(Food)*   *Edgemoor Inn*

Near Stroud · *Gloucestershire* · Map 8 D2
Painswick (0452) 813576

Free House
Landlords Mike & Pat Smith

Children welcome
Credit Access, Visa
🍺 Flowers, Original, IPA; Younger's Tartan;
Worthington Best Bitter; West Country Pale Ale;
Guinness; Stella Artois; cider. ♀

There are breathtaking views from the terrace
of this Cotswold-stone pub, where tasty food
in generous portions is an added attraction.
The dish of the day is very popular and its
price includes a sweet; other choices include
soup, sandwiches, pâtés and omelettes.
Garden. *Typical prices:* Savoury pancake
with vegetables & sweet £2.75   Gammon,
eggs & mushrooms £3.65 (Last bar food
10pm. No bar food Sun eve) ⊖

Effingham   *(Food)*   *Plough*

Orestan Lane · *Surrey* · Map 7 C2
Bookham (0372) 58121

Brewery Courage
Landlord Derek Sutherland

🍺 Courage Best Bitter, Directors; Guinness;
Hofmeister; cider. ⚲

Imaginative bar snacks are carefully prepared and full of flavour at this smartly white-
painted pub with a pretty rear garden. Regular
favourites like pâté, smoked mackerel, sandwiches and savoury pies are supplemented
by a blackboard menu offering daily specials
such as haddock pasta and liver and onions.
Nice sweets include a rather good treacle
tart. *Typical prices:* Stuffed courgettes £1.95
Prawn & asparagus pancake with salad £2
(Last bar food 8.30pm) ℮

Elkstone   *(Food)*   *Highwayman Inn*

Near Cheltenham · *Gloucestershire* · Map 8 D2
Miserden (028 582) 221

Brewery Arkell
Landlords Mr & Mrs Bucher

Children welcome
Credit Visa
🍺 Arkell's BB, BBB, Kingsdown, Keller Lager,
Premium Lager; Guinness. ⚲

Look for the black and yellow stagecoach in
the car park of this 16th-century hostelry on
the A417. In the cosy bar – all beams, nooks
and rustic stone – a varied menu offers
sandwiches, jacket potatoes and pizzas,
seafood platter, chilli and the popular Stagecoach pie (steak and mushroom). Simple
sweets, too, and a children's menu. *Typical
prices:* Beef & mushroom pie £3.50   Fruit
crumble £1 (Last bar food 10.15pm) ℮

Ellisfield   *(Food)*   `New Entry`   *Fox*

Green Lane, near Basingstoke · *Hampshire*
Map 6 B3
Herriard (025 683) 210

Free House
Landlords Nigel, Lucy & John Moore

🍺 Wadworth's 6X; Bishop's Best Bitter; Gale's
HSB; Marston's Pedigree; Guinness; Foster's;
cider.

Three 17th-century cottages form the core of
this pleasant country pub, whose bar snacks
are fresh, wholesome and appetising. Baked
potatoes come with a wide variety of fillings
(tuna mayonnaise, beef and horseradish,
Cheddar and spring onion) and there are
sandwiches, salads, and Greek dips with
pitta bread. Blackboard specials include
steak, casseroles and a vegetarian dish.
Typical prices: Beef casserole £2.65   Steak
sandwich £1.95 (Last bar food 10pm) ℮

Elslack   *(Food)*   *Tempest Arms*

Near Skipton · *North Yorkshire* · Map 4 C3
Earby (0282) 842450

Free House
Landlord Francis Pierre Boulongne

Children welcome
🍺 Tetley's Bitter, Mild; Thwaites Bitter, Mild;
Guinness; Castlemaine 4X; Carlsberg Hof;
cider. ⚲

An attractive little beck flows past this stone-
built pub, where the French landlord provides
bar snacks with a difference. Fresh fish is the
speciality, with moules marinière, grilled
halibut and baked tuna provençale among
the options. Meat-eaters can tuck into steaks
and meat pies, and there's always a vegetable lasagne. Sweets include a really tipsy
sherry trifle. *Typical prices:* Fish & mushroom
pie with vegetables £1.95   French onion
soup £1.25 (Last bar food 10pm) ℮

Elsted *(Food)*   *Three Horseshoes*

Near South Harting · *West Sussex* · Map 6 B4
Harting (073 085) 746

Free House
Landlords S. C. & E. A. Hawkins

🍺 Friary Meux Bitter; Ballard's Bitter; Ringwood
Old Thumper; Harvey's Bitter; Guinness;
Foster's; Dortmunder; cider. ♀

The views of the South Downs are really
splendid at this charming country pub, where
snacks may be enjoyed in the cosy bars, the
dining room or the garden. Jacket potatoes
and ploughman's platters come in many tasty
variants, and there's soup along with robust
main courses and super treacle tart. Sunday
lunch brings a buffet in summer and a roast
in winter. *Typical prices:* Steak & kidney pie
£3.95   Venison casserole £3.95 (Last bar
food 10pm) ☕

Elsworth   *George & Dragon*

The heavily beamed and panelled main bar of this large pub built in 1700
are crammed with a collection of top hats, copper kettles and numerous
curiosities. High-backed settles grouped around the huge inglenook
fireplace are the most popular seats in winter, and there's a comfortably
furnished lounge which opens on to the well-kept rear garden.

Boxworth Road · *Cambridgeshire* · Map 5 C2
Elsworth (095 47) 236   *Brewery* Tollemache & Cobbold   *Landlords* Mr &
Mrs Brownlie
Children welcome   *Credit* Access, Amex, Diners, Visa
🍺 Tolly Cobbold Bitter, Original; Camerons Strong Arm, Guinness;
Hansa; cider. ♀

Elterwater *(B & B)*   *Britannia Inn*

Near Ambleside · *Cumbria* · Map 3 B2
Langdale (096 67) 210
Free House
Landlord David Fry
Children welcome
Credit Access, Visa
🍺 Hartley's XB Bitter; Tetley's Bitter; Bass,
Bass Special; Guinness; Skol; Carling Black
Label; cider. ♀
ACCOMMODATION   10 bedrooms   £C
Check-in: all day

Overlooking the green of a picture-book
village at the entrance to the Langdale Valley,
this white-painted pub is a popular haunt of
locals and walkers alike. The cosy little
beamed bar with its attractive Lakeland stone
fireplace is often packed, but residents can
take refuge in the chintzy, book-stocked
lounge. Simple, cheerful bedrooms with tea-
makers share two well-kept bathrooms.
There's a terrace.

Eltisley *(B & B)*   *Leeds Arms*

The Green · *Cambridgeshire* · Map 5 C2
Croxten (048 087) 283

Free House
Landlord Mr G. W. Cottrell
Credit Access, Visa
🍺 Greene King IPA; Whitbread Best Bitter, Mild;
Stones Bitter; Paine's EG; Guinness; Carlsberg;
Harp.
ACCOMMODATION 9 bedrooms £C (No dogs)
Check-in: restricted

On the edge of the large village green, this
late 18th-century coaching house provides
comfortable motel-style accommodation in
two single-storey blocks. The twin-bedded
rooms have private bathrooms, while the six
singles offer showers; all rooms are equipped
with TVs and tea-makers. Some of the period
flavour remains in the bars with their beams
and inglenook. There's a children's outdoor
play area.

Empingham   *(Food, B & B)*   *White Horse*

2 Main Street, near Oakham
Leicestershire · Map 5 B1
Empingham (078 086) 221

Brewery John Smith
Landlords Robert, Andrew & Helen Reid

Children welcome
Credit Access, Amex, Diners, Visa
🍺 John Smith's Bitter; John Courage Bitter;
Chestnut Mild; Guinness; Hofmeister;
Kronenbourg; cider.

Customers come from miles around to eat at
this friendly, well-run pub in the town centre.
The main bar with its central stone fireplace
and comfortable banquette seating features
a fine cold display of cooked meats, hand-
raised pies and salads. Other light bites
include grilled sardines, vegetarian burgers,
pâtés and a varied choice of ploughman's –
Leicester, Lymeswold, Brie and others. For
something more substantial there's hearty
beef and beer casserole with Stilton dumplings, saddle of lamb and kidneys Turbigo.
Tempting sweets such as blackberry and
apple pancakes or crème brûlée make a
delicious finale. *Typical prices:* Ploughman's
£2.20   Steak & kidney pie £3.95 (Last bar
food 9.45pm) 🍴

ACCOMMODATION   11 bedrooms   £C
Check-in: all day

Eight new bedrooms in the converted stables
with pretty floral fabrics and pine furniture
are all equipped with TVs, tea-makers, direct-
dial telephones and excellent private facilities. The three large doubles in the original
building are more traditional in style and
share a shower-cum-bathroom. Garden.

Eskdale   *(Food, B & B)*   *Bower House Inn*

Holmrook · *Cumbria* · Map 3 B2
Eskdale (094 03) 244

Free House
Landlords Smith family

Children welcome
🍺 Hartley's Best Bitter; McEwan's Scotch
Bitter; Guinness; Carlsberg; Foster's; cider.

The friendly Smith family make everyone feel
thoroughly at home in this charming slate-
roofed inn. The setting, among the peace
and beauty of Eskdale, is really delightful,
and the beamed bar is warm and inviting. Bar
snacks are fresh and appetising: soup,
salads and sandwiches are always available
or for something more substantial you could
start with smoked mackerel pâté and go on
to rabbit cooked in ginger ale or succulent
poussin with a lemon sauce. Apple crumble
is a popular pud, and there are some good
English cheeses. *Typical prices:* Steak &
kidney crock pie £2.75   Venison in red wine
£3.25 (Last bar food 9pm) 🍴

ACCOMMODATION   21 bedrooms   £C
Check-in: all day

Bedrooms are of two types: six simply and
traditionally furnished in the main house and
15 in a converted stable annexe that offer a
higher standard of comfort: modern furnishings, colour TVs and good bathrooms.
There's a comfortable, chintzy residents'
lounge and a pleasant garden.

Eton   *(B & B)*   *Christopher Hotel*

High Street, Near Windsor · *Berkshire*
Map 7 C2
Windsor (0753) 852359
Free House
Landlords Ron & Barbara France
Credit Access, Amex, Diners, Visa
🍺 Brakspear Bitter; John Smith's Bitter;
Courage Best; Younger's Tartan; Guinness;
Kronenbourg; Hofmeister; cider. ⚲
ACCOMMODATION 21 bedrooms £B
Check-in: all day

Comfortable overnight accommodation is
provided at this high-street hotel that was
once a coaching inn. Bedrooms (mostly in a
block adjoining the main building) are neat,
roomy and modern with TVs and useful
extras like hairdryers, trouser presses and
pay phones, plus carpeted bath/shower
rooms. Six rooms are equipped for families.
There are two bars, one in Victorian style.

Ettington   *(Food, B & B)*   **New Entry**   *Houndshill*

Banbury Road · *Warwickshire* · Map 7 A1
Stratford-upon-Avon (0789) 740267

Free House
Landlords Mr & Mrs Martin & A. Martin

Children welcome
Credit Access, Visa
🍺 Wadworth's 6X, Davenports Bitter;
McEwan's Export, Lager: Guinness; Beck's Bier;
cider.

ACCOMMODATION 8 bedrooms £C
Check-in: all day

A mile outside Ettington, this family-run inn is
a good place to stop for refreshment. An
extensive bar snack menu features familiar
pub fare, cooked soundly and straightfor-
wardly and served in generous portions.
Soup, pâté or deep fried mushrooms could
be followed by lasagne, moussaka, steak
and kidney pie or sirloin steak, and you can
also get omelettes, salads and basket meals;
sandwiches for quick bites, children's dishes
and simple sweets are available. There's an
à la carte restaurant, too. *Typical prices:*
Lasagne £2.90 Apple pie 70p (Last bar food
10pm) ℮

Housekeeping is first class, both in the day
rooms and in the bedrooms, which are very
comfortable and spacious. Pretty floral fabrics blend well with pine bedside furniture
and wicker chairs. All rooms have private
bathrooms, and one particularly large room
is suitable for family occupation. Garden.

Evercreech Junction   *(Food)*   *Natterjack*

Shepton Mallet · *Somerset* · Map 9 D3
Ditcheat (074 986) 253

Free House
Landlords Richard Sensham & Nigel Lea

Children welcome (till 8pm)
Credit Access, Visa
🍺 Courage Best Bitter; Butcombe Bitter; Double
Diamond; John Smith's Bitter; Symmonds Bitter;
Guinness; Hofmeister; cider. ⚲

The roomy bar is a comfortable spot to take
time out for a tasty snack at this sturdy
roadside pub. The menu runs an appetising
gamut, from sustaining soups and fresh
salads to quiche, crab mornay and very
decent lasagne in both meat and vegetarian
versions. Nice puds, too, like apple flan or
fruit Pavlova. Sunday roasts. *Typical prices:*
Steak & mushroom pie £4 Lasagne £2.80
(Last bar food 10pm) ℮

Ewen   (B & B)   *Wild Duck Inn*

Near Cirencester · *Gloucestershire* · Map 7 A2
Kemble (028 577) 364

Free House
Landlord Mr Kevin Shales
Credit Access, Amex, Diners, Visa
🍺 Wadworth's 6X; Worthington Best Bitter;
Toby Bitter; Guinness; Tuborg; Carling Black
Label; cider. ♀
ACCOMMODATION   7 bedrooms   £B
Check-in: all day

Standing in peaceful surroundings amidst attractive gardens, this rambling 16th-century Cotswold-stone inn oozes period charm. The Post Horn Bar, with its rustic stone flags, heavy beams and open fire, is particularly charming, while the cosy residents' lounge (complete with original inglenook fireplace) doubles as a meeting room. A more recent extension houses the simply furnished bedrooms which are equipped with TVs and have smart modern bathrooms.

Ewhurst Green   (B & B)   *White Dog Inn*

Near Robertsbridge · *East Sussex* · Map 6 C4
Staplecross (058 083) 264

Free House
Landlords Tina & Richard Hayward
Children welcome
Credit Amex, Visa
🍺 Charrington's IPA, Best Bitter; Guinness;
Tennent's Lager; Carling Black Label; cider. ♀
ACCOMMODATION   5 bedrooms   £C
Check-in: restricted

Overnight guests open their curtains on to lovely views of the countryside at this agreeable, tile-hung pub. The five bedrooms are neat and bright, with plain white furnishings, louvred fitted wardrobes, colour TVs and tea-makers. Four have modern bathrooms (one not en suite), while the fifth has a compact shower room. Continental breakfast only. Beams, flagstones and pew seating create an agreeable ambience in the bar. Amenities include a swimming pool for summer use.

Exford   (Food, B & B)   *Crown Hotel*

Near Minehead · *Somerset* · Map 9 C3
Exford (064 383) 554

Brewery Usher
Landlords John & Marjorie Millward

Children welcome
Credit Access, Amex, Visa
🍺 Usher's Founders Ale, Countryman;
Webster's Yorkshire Bitter; Carlsberg Pilsner;
cider. ♀

ACCOMMODATION   18 bedrooms   £B
Check-in: all day

Sound, honest kitchencraft makes for enjoyable snacking in this modernised, but still characterful, Exmoor inn. Soup has a proper taste of the stockpot, sandwiches are freshly cut, steaks well hung, pies tasty and full of goodness. Home-made sweets include chocolate mousse served with clotted cream. The bar is pleasantly rustic, and there's an attractive garden. *Typical prices:* Steak & kidney pie £2.75   Cornish pasty £1.25 (Last bar food 10pm) ☺

Overnight guests enjoy a very high standard of comfort in bedrooms that vary in size and shape and are individually (and prettily) decorated. A glass of sherry is a nice welcoming touch, and there are many thoughtful little extras besides major accessories like colour TVs and direct-dial telephones. Well-equipped en suite bathrooms throughout. The two lounges offer the warmth of log fires, the fragrance of fresh flowers and the plush of velvet. Amenities include laundry service, riding and stabling.

Eyam   *(Food, B & B)*   *Miners Arms*

Near Bakewell · *Derbyshire* · Map 4 C3
Hope Valley (0433) 30853

Free House
Landlords Mr & Mrs Peter Cooke & Mr & Mrs
Paul Morris

Children welcome
🍺 Stones Bitter; Ward's Best Bitter; Vaux Mild,
Tennent's Lager; cider.

ACCOMMODATION 6 bedrooms £C (No dogs)
Check-in: all day

A warm North Country welcome awaits
visitors to this delightful pub set in an unspoilt
Derbyshire village and run with the same
friendliness by the Cookes for over 25 years.
The main bar is simple, traditional and cosy
– the perfect setting for wholesome lunchtime
snacks like home-made soup and sandwiches, fresh fish and a daily roast, plus the
ever-popular chicken in red wine sauce
served on a bed of rice. Dinner can be
enjoyed in the pub's excellent restaurant
from Tues to Sat. *Typical prices:* Soup 75p
Chicken in red wine sauce £1.50 (No bar food
eves) Pub closed Mon lunchtime. ⊖

Four snug, well-kept bedrooms in the original
inn share the family bathroom and offer
thoughtful extras like tissues and biscuits.
Two double rooms of superior standard in
the newly converted stable block have duvets
plus good modern private facilities. No under-
12s overnight. Terrace and garden.

Eyam   *(B & B)*   *Rose & Crown*

Main Road · *Derbyshire* · Map 4 C3
Hope Valley (0433) 30858

Free House
Landlords Mason family

Children welcome
🍺 Stones Bitter; Tetley's Bitter; Skol Lager;
Carling Black Label; cider.
ACCOMMODATION 3 bedrooms £D (No dogs)
Check-in: restricted

Three neatly kept bedrooms provide homely
overnight accommodation at this little stone
pub, taken over last autumn by the efficient
Mason family. There are shower cubicles
and washbasins in each room, plus TVs and
tea-makers; the shared bathroom is well
looked after. Day rooms include an inviting
lounge bar, a very cosy public bar warmed
by a coal fire and a games room with pool
table and darts. Pub closed Monday lunchtime. Patio.

Fairbourne Heath   *(Food)*   *Pepper Box*

Harrietsham, Near Ulcombe · *Kent* · Map 6 C3
Maidstone (0622) 842558

Brewery Shepherd Neame
Landlords Mr & Mrs J. D. Wood

🍺 Shepherd Neame Master Brew, Stock Ale
(winter only), Abbey; Hurlimann; cider.

Overlooking the Weald, this charming old
pub specialises in fish fresh from Dungeness.
In the friendly bar with its festoons of dried
hops you can enjoy delicious cod, plaice and
scampi, excellent salads and meaty alternatives like giant locally made sausages. Sandwiches and ploughman's, too, plus lovely
sweets like boozy chocolate sponge. *Typical
prices:* Cod & chips £2.60 Home-made chilli
£2.20 (Last bar food 10 pm. No bar food Sun
eve) ⊖

Fairford *(B & B)*   *Bull Hotel*

Market Place · *Gloucestershire* · Map 7 A2
Cirencester (0285) 712535

Brewery Arkell
Landlord Mark Gulenserion
Children welcome
Credit Access, Amex, Diners, Visa
🍺 Arkell's Kingsdown Ale, BBB, Bitter, 1843;
Guinness; Carling Black Label; cider. ⚲
ACCOMMODATION   18 bedrooms   £B
Check-in: all day

Standing right on the market place, near the river Coln (and with 1½ miles of fishing on it) this hospitable inn of Cotswold stone was a monk's chantry in the 15th century, and later became an important posting house. Ancient beams and flagstoned floors lend a traditional charm to the cosy bar, and there's an inviting residents' lounge. Traditionally decorated bedrooms (one with a four-poster) have TVs and tea-makers; most have private facilities.

Faringdon *(Food, B & B)*   *Bell Hotel*

Market Place · *Oxfordshire* · Map 7 A2
Faringdon (0367) 20534

Brewery Wadworth
Landlord Mr W. Dreyer

Children welcome
Credit Access, Amex, Diners, Visa
🍺 Wadworth's 6X, Old Timer (winter only);
Guinness; Harp.

Former shipbuilder William Dreyer runs a larger-than-life pub, a 16th-century posting house with a real ring of the past. The bar snacks are a popular feature, ranging from salads and sandwiches (traditional or open French) to lasagne, curried chicken and a daily changing special like minced beef pancake or Friday's fish. Nice home-made sweets, including fresh cream gâteau and lemon meringue pie. An interesting feature in the bar is a fine old bread oven. *Typical prices:* Steak & mushroom pie £2.85   Chicken curry £2.25 (Last bar food 9.30pm) ◉

ACCOMMODATION   11 bedrooms   £C
Check-in: all day

Overnight guests will find comfort allied to the character that comes from beams and sloping floors. The bedrooms are neatly kept, with pretty floral fabrics and the seven that have TVs also offer good-sized bathrooms. The remaining rooms have a more than adequate shared facility.

Farnham *(Food)*   *Spotted Cow*

3 Bourne Grove · *Surrey* · Map 6 B3
Farnham (0252) 726541

Brewery Courage
Landlords Barry & Jane Soulsby

Credit Access, Visa
🍺 Courage Best Bitter, Directors Bitter, JC;
Guinness; John Smith's Lager; Kronenbourg;
cider.

South of Farnham off the Tilford road, this red-brick pub is a useful place to stop for popular snacks like minestrone, steak and kidney pie and ploughman's as well as more unusual offerings such as taramasalata, cod and prawn mornay or vegetarian lasagne. Steaks and grills, too, plus a traditional Sunday lunch. *Typical prices:* Chicken with Stilton sauce £3.50   Moussaka £2.50 (Last bar food 10pm. No bar food Mon eve) ◉

Faugh   *(Food, B & B)*   *String of Horses*

Heads Hook, near Carlisle · *Cumbria* · Map 3 B1
Hayton (022 870) 297

Free House
Landlords Mr & Mrs E. Tasker

Children welcome
Credit Access, Amex, Diners, Visa
🍺 Theakston's Best Bitter; Younger's Scotch
Bitter; Murphy's Irish Stout; Webster's Yorkshire
Bitter; Carlsberg Hof; Foster's. 🍷

ACCOMMODATION   13 bedrooms   £A
Check-in: all day

Oak beams, open fires and antiques contribute to the fine period feel of this 17th-century hostelry set in a quiet village. In the lounge bar a good choice of soundly prepared food is served: lunchtime brings an extensive cold buffet (Mon to Fri), plus grills, curries and specials like tasty beef goulash. In the evenings, seafood and salads are popular orders, along with dishes like lamb cutlets or Cumberland sausage. Sandwiches are available both sessions, and sweets include a very good chocolate gâteau. There's also a restaurant. *Typical bar prices:* Beef goulash £3.25   Chicken suprême with lemon butter sauce £3.75 (Last bar food 10.15pm) ☺

The bedrooms, including three four-poster suites, are individually decorated and furnished in luxurious, flamboyant style; cosseting extras abound, and the ornate bathrooms would not look out of place in Hollywood.

Fawley   *(Food)*   *Walnut Tree*

Near Henley-on-Thames · *Buckinghamshire*
Map 7 B2
Turville Heath (049 163) 360

Brewery Brakspear
Landlords Mr & Mrs F. Harding

Children welcome
Credit Access, Visa
🍺 Brakspear's Ordinary, Special, Old (winter only), Mild; Stella Artois; Heineken. 🍷

Enthusiastic cook Mr Harding offers a remarkable choice at this modern red-brick pub: from smoked cheese and olive croûte and pheasant liver pâté to main courses like lamb cooked in hay and pork in Pernod with prawns. There are also salads, ploughman's and vegetarian dishes, as well as nice sweets like walnut-studded treacle tart. Garden. *Typical prices:* Pheasant liver pâté £1.95   Baked scallops in cream £6.75 (Last bar food 10 pm) ☺

Felixstowe   *(B & B)*   *Ordnance Hotel*

1 Undercliff Road West · *Suffolk* · Map 5 D2
Felixstowe (0394) 273427
Brewery Tollemache & Cobbold
Landlord Mr James Yeo
Children welcome
Credit Access, Amex, Diners, Visa
🍺 Tolly Cobbold Original, Bitter, Best Bitter; Guinness; DAB Premium lager; Hansa. 🍷
ACCOMMODATION 11 bedrooms £C (No dogs)
Check-in: all day

Comfortable overnight accommodation in light, spacious bedrooms is the order of the day at this substantial Victorian pub near both the seafront and the town centre. Attractively furnished in period style, all rooms have TVs, tea-makers, duvets and direct-dial telephones. Four rooms have their own bathrooms; the others share two public bath/shower rooms. The large, oak-panelled bar is particularly popular at night, and there's an attractive residents' lounge. Garden.

Fen Drayton   *Three Tuns*

An old blacksmith's shop and the former guildhall (note the ornately carved beams) flank a thatched 15th-century inn, forming a picturesque whole. Chairs clustered round two inglenook fireplaces make for cosy winter get-togethers, while in summer the beer garden with its small stream is an appealing spot.

High Street · *Cambridgeshire* · Map 5 C2
Swavesey (0954) 30242   *Brewery* Greene King   *Landlords* Michael & Eileen Nugent
Children welcome
🍺 Greene King IPA, Abbot Ale; Guinness; Harp; Kronenbourg; cider. ♀

Fenay Bridge   *(Food)*   *Star Hotel*

1 Penistone Road, Near Huddersfield · *West Yorkshire* · Map 4 C3
Huddersfield (0484) 602049

Brewery Bass
Landlords Mr & Mrs Robert Lee

🍺 Bass Extra Light, Dark Mild; Stones Bitter; Carling Black Label; Tennent's Pilsner; cider.

If you're looking for a hearty midday meal that won't break the bank, pull in at this friendly pub on the A629 and order the special businessman's lunch – a feast consisting of soup, a roast with lots of vegetables, and a home-made sweet from the tempting trolley. Lighter alternatives include salads, meat pies and curries. Sandwiches the only choice at night. Traditional Sunday lunches. *Typical prices:* Beef curry £2.35   Steak & kidney pie £2.95 (Last bar food 10pm) ⊝

Fenny Bentley   *(Food, B & B)*   *Bentley Brook Inn*

Near Ashbourne · *Derbyshire* · Map 4 C4
Thorpe Cloud (033 529) 278

Free House
Landlords David & Jeanne Allingham

Children welcome
🍺 Marston's Pedigree Bitter, Lager; Guinness; Carlsberg Export Lager; cider.

Two miles north of Ashbourne, at the junction of the A515 and B5056, this handsome black and white half-timbered inn stands in over two acres of garden within the Peak District National Park. The spacious, bay-windowed bars provide a comfortable setting for some enjoyable snacks available all day. Honest, straightforward cooking results in such appetising choices as hearty vegetable soup, excellent lasagne (the chef is Italian), hot pot and chicken casserole. There are filled rolls for lighter bites and nice puddings like sherry trifle and Dutch apple tart. *Typical prices:* Lasagne £2.50   Derbyshire lamb hot pot £3.50 (Last bar food 10pm. No bar food Sun lunch) ⊝

ACCOMMODATION 8 bedrooms £C
Check-in: all day

Characterful beamed bedrooms (three with private bathrooms, the rest sharing two well-kept public ones) all have duvets, tea-makers, televisions and telephones. A comfortable lounge is available for residents' use on the first floor.

Fiddleford   (B & B)

Fiddleford Inn

Sturminster Newton · *Dorset* · Map 9 D3
Sturminster Newton (0258) 72489

Free House
Landlords Joyce, Philip & Valerie Wilson

Children welcome
🍺 Fiddleford Ale; Wadworth's 6X; Gale's HSB;
Hook Norton Old Hookey; Wiltshire Brewery Old
Devil; Marston's Pedigree; cider. ♀
ACCOMMODATION   4 bedrooms   £C
Check-in: restricted

Once a brewery, this charming, creeper-clad inn keeps the links alive with an excellent selection of real ales. Fires crackle a welcome in the cosy beamed bars, while the four cottage bedrooms have much appeal with their jumble of furnishings, attractive fabrics and numerous thoughtful little extras; one has TV and its own bathroom. The pub is fronted by a pleasant garden with a children's play area. Excellent housekeeping.

Fingest   (Food)

Chequers Inn

Near Henley-on-Thames · *Buckinghamshire* ·
Map 7 B2
Turville Heath (049 163) 335

Brewery Brakspear
Landlords Mr & Mrs Bryan J. Henshaw

Children welcome
Credit Amex, Visa
🍺 Brakspear's Ordinary Bitter, Special Bitter,
Old Ale; Stella Artois. ♀

There's no shortage of old-world atmosphere in this 12th-century village pub facing a Norman church. There's a tempting display of cold meats and game pie with help-yourself salads, and a blackboard menu of attractive hot dishes such as grilled sole, prawn curry and a really flavoursome steak, kidney and mushroom pie, with delicious vegetables. *Typical prices:* Steak & kidney pie £3.95 Pâté £2.25 (Last bar food 10pm. No bar food Sun eve) ⊖

Fiskerton   (Food)

Bromley Arms

Near Southwell · *Nottinghamshire* · Map 5 B1
Newark (0636) 830789

Brewery Hardys & Hansons
Landlords Harold & Sheila Taylor

Children welcome
🍺 Hardys & Hansons Bitter, Mild; Guinness;
Heineken; cider.

Weigh anchor for one of Sheila Taylor's appetising lunches at this lively riverside pub, where you watch boaters and anglers from the smart, flower-festooned terrace. Choose from market fresh fish and tasty pies, fine roast beef salad and excellent sweets. The choice at night and mainly on Sunday is limited to sandwiches and salads. *Typical prices:* Poacher's pie £2.55 Fisherman's nest £2.55 (Last bar food 10pm)

Fittleworth   (B & B)

Swan

Lower Street · *West Sussex* · Map 6 B4
Fittleworth (079 882) 429
Owners Gateway Hosts
Landlord James Crossley
Children welcome
Credit Access, Amex, Diners, Visa
🍺 Webster's Yorkshire Bitter; Gale's HSB;
Watneys Special, Mild; Guinness; Holsten;
Carlsberg; cider.
ACCOMMODATION   7 bedrooms   £C
Check-in: all day

A fascinating collection of truncheons and bottle openers decorates the cosy beamed bar of this attractive old inn, which dates back to the 14th century. There are beams, too, in some of the bedrooms, which have pretty floral fabrics and pleasant oak furniture in keeping with the pub's traditional character. One room (with a fourposter) has its own bathroom; the rest have shower cubicles. TV in a tiny lounge. Garden.

Fletching *(Food)* — *Griffin Inn*

East Sussex · Map 6 C4
Newick (082 572) 2890

Free House
Landlords Mr & Mrs Rob Setchell

Children welcome
Credit Access, Amex, Visa
🍺 Hall & Woodhouse Badger Best Bitter,
Tanglefoot; King & Barnes Sussex Bitter;
Guinness; Carlsberg; cider. ♀

There's a welcoming air about this old village
pub. In the oak-panelled bar with its cheerful
fire you can enjoy an interesting variety of
snacks, including veal and pork roulade with
apple chutney, smoked mackerel pâté or
fresh pasta. There are filled jacket potatoes,
too, ploughman's and hot daily specials.
Typical prices: Stuffed mushrooms £2.25
Chicken breast with ham & ginger £4.50 (Last
bar food 9 pm) ⊖

Fonthill Bishop *(Food, B & B)* — *King's Arms*

Near Salisbury · Wiltshire · Map 9 D3
Hindon (074 789) 523

Free House
Landlords Andrew & Sarah McDonald & Audrey
Usherwood

Children welcome
🍺 Wadworth's 6X, Farmer's Glory, IPA;
Worthington Best Bitter; Guinness; Heineken;
Löwenbräu; cider.

Originally a farm building (vintage 1846), this
smart little red-brick pub stands by the
roadside with a trim garden to one side. The
bar is neat and plush, with old photographs
about the walls and a raised area where
decent home-prepared snacks may be enjoyed. Lasagne, served with a simple salad
garnish, is certainly above average for a pub,
and other offerings run from sandwiches,
ploughman's and pâté to steak, mushroom
and Guinness pie and daily specials like
fisherman's pie or full-flavoured tomato and
ham soup. Sweets are mainly ice cream
variants. *Typical prices:* Chicken Kiev £3.95
Lasagne £2.95 (Last bar food 10pm) ⊖

ACCOMMODATION 2 bedrooms £D
Check-in: all day

The two bedrooms are spacious and light,
fully carpeted, with white furnishings and
pretty wallpaper. Sheets are beautifully
ironed, and housekeeping is of high standard.
An equally well-kept bathroom serves the
two rooms.

Ford *(B & B)* — *White Hart at Ford*

Near Chippenham · Wiltshire · Map 8 D2
Castle Combe (0249) 782213

Free House
Landlord Mr W. K. Gardner
Children welcome
Credit Access
🍺 Wadworth's 6X; Marston's Pedigree; Fuller's
London Pride; Guinness; Stella Artois; cider.
ACCOMMODATION 11 bedrooms £B (No dogs)
Check-in: all day

Run in friendly fashion by the Gardner family,
this fine 16th-century inn enjoys a peaceful
situation beside a trout stream overlooking
the Weavern Valley. Log fires warm the
beamed bar, where a handsome collection
of armour is displayed. Pretty pine-furnished
bedrooms (six with four-posters) all have
TVs, tea-makers and writing desks. Excellent
private bathrooms – some even boasting
bidets. No children under three overnight.

Forty Green   *Royal Standard of England*

One of the oldest free houses in England, with parts dating back to the 11th-century. There's a great sense of history throughout – note the blackened beams, the uneven floors, a fine old fireplace (once in Edmund Burke's home) and the lovely stained glass rescued from blitzed London churches.

Beaconsfield · *Buckinghamshire* · Map 7 C2
Beaconsfield (049 46) 3382   *Free House   Landlord* Mr Philip Eldridge
Children welcome
🍺 Marston's Pedigree, Owd Roger; Eldridge Pope Royal Oak; Carlsberg; Foster's; Holsten; cider. ♀

Fossebridge   *(Food, B & B)*   *Fossebridge Inn*

Near Cheltenham · *Gloucestershire* · Map 7 A1
Fossebridge (028 572) 310   *Free House   Landlords* Hugh & Suzanne Roberts
Children welcome   *Credit* Access, Amex, Diners, Visa
🍺 Marston's Pedigree; Burton Bitter; Guinness; Carlsberg; Stella Artois; cider.

★ A fine Georgian house is at the heart of this large, comfortable inn on the river Coln. Many changes have taken place down the years, and the new owners are making commendable efforts to recapture past glories. They've certainly raised the quality and sophistication of the bar snacks, and the frequently changing menu offers diverse delights like potted Wiltshire ham, smoked pheasant and perfectly grilled Cornish mullet with plenty of herbs. To finish, there's fresh fruit, rich sweets (toffee pudding à la Sharrow Bay) and a selection of excellent English farmhouse cheeses. ★
Typical prices: Ragout of market fish £5.75   Toffee pudding £2.10 (Last bar food 9.30pm)

ACCOMMODATION   14 bedrooms   £A
Check-in: all day

Restful overnight accommodation is provided in both main house and annexe, and many rooms have delightful views over the garden. They're generally quite spacious, with cheerful colour schemes and a happy blend of traditional and contemporary furnishings. En suite bath/shower rooms throughout. Gradual improvements are being made.

Fotheringhay   *(Food)*   *Falcon Inn*

Near Peterborough · *Northamptonshire*
Map 5 B1
Cotterstock (083 26) 254

Free House
Landlord Mr Alan Stewart

Children welcome
🍺 Theakston's Bitter; Greene King IPA, Abbot Ale; Elgood's Bitter; Guinness; Carlsberg; cider. ♀

A cosy village pub serving excellent bar food. Customers come from miles around to enjoy dishes as diverse as pear with Stilton and walnut dressing, fresh mussels, veal chop provençale and braised venison with port and oranges. Sweets are just as tempting – the lemon and brandy syllabub is a real wow! Also a cold table summer and weekends. *Typical prices:* Steak & kidney pie £2.90 Roast duckling £4.20 (Last bar food 9.30pm. No bar food Mon) 🍴

Fovant (B & B) — *Cross Keys Hotel*

Near Salisbury · *Wiltshire* · Map 6 A4
Fovant (072 270) 284

Free House
Landlord Mrs Pauline Story
Children welcome
Credit Visa
🍺 Wadworth's 6X; Gibbs New Wiltshire;
Carlsberg Hof; Heineken; cider.
ACCOMMODATION 4 bedrooms £D
Check-in: all day

Old-fashioned charm is much in evidence at Pauline Story's delightful 15th-century coaching inn on the A30 between Salisbury and Shaftesbury. Hens range freely in the garden, and public rooms include a beamed bar and a cosy residents' lounge. The four cheerful bedrooms provide cottage overnight accommodation: they are brightly decorated in fresh colours and enlivened with corn dollies, and they share two neat bathrooms.

We publish annually so make sure you use the current edition.

Fovant *New Entry* — *Pembroke Arms*

Once the Earl of Pembroke's shooting lodge, this creeper-clad Georgian hostelry is now most notable for its collection of World War I memorabilia. It's also the HQ of the Fovant Badges Society, who ensure the upkeep of the remarkable regimental badges carved out of chalk. On the A30 between Salisbury and Shaftesbury. Garden.

Salisbury · *Wiltshire* · Map 6 A4
Fovant (072 270) 201   *Free House*   *Landlords* Robert & Norma Kemp
Children welcome
🍺 Marston's Pedigree; Wadworth's 6X; John Smith's Yorkshire Bitter;
Guinness; Carlsberg Hof; Holsten Export; cider.

Fowlmere (Food) — *Chequers Inn*

High Street · *Cambridgeshire* · Map 7 D1
Fowlmere (076 382) 369

Owners Poste Inns
Landlord Mr N. S. Rushton

Credit Access, Amex, Diners, Visa
🍺 Tolly Cobbold Bitter, Original; Guinness;
Hansa; cider. ♀

This attractive village inn, once a haunt of Samuel Pepys, is often busy, so get there early. Consult the blackboard for an imaginative range of dishes from soup and moussaka to calves' brains in black butter or herring fillets in sour cream with onion and apple. There's a cold buffet, too, with a selection of roasts and salads. Desserts include chocolate mousse. *Typical prices:* Mousse-filled courgette flowers £3.10 Gazpacho £1.80 (Last bar food 10pm) ©

Fownhope   *(Food, B & B)*   *Green Man Inn*

Near Hereford · *Hereford & Worcester*
Map 8 D2
Fownhope (043 277) 243

Free House
Landlords Mr & Mrs A. F. Williams

Children welcome
🍺 Hook Norton Best Bitter; Samuel Smith's Old
Brewery Bitter; Marston's Pedigree; Guinness;
Hofmeister; cider.

ACCOMMODATION   14 bedrooms   £C
Check-in: all day

In a peaceful village setting near the river
Wye, this friendly, black and white timbered
inn once housed the petty sessions court.
Welcoming log fires warm the cosy, oak-
beamed bars, where the menu ranges from
pâté and a cheese platter to sandwiches,
salads and hot dishes such as grilled trout,
lasagne and a gammon platter. *Typical
prices:* Steak sandwich £2.35   Chicken curry
£2.65 (Last bar food 10.30pm) ⊖

Pretty bedrooms – some with lovely views –
are simply furnished, apart from one room
with a four-poster. All have TVs, tea-makers
and compact bath/shower rooms. The Stable
Room across the courtyard has a sitting
area, and the former Judge's Room is of an
ideal size for families. Residents have their
own lounge, and there's a garden.

Framfield   *(Food)*   *Barley Mow*

Eastbourne Road · *East Sussex* · Map 6 C4
Framfield (082 582) 234

Brewery Phoenix
Landlords Derek & Val Gilbert

Children welcome
🍺 King & Barnes Festive Bitter; Webster's
Yorkshire Bitter; Watneys Special; Usher's
Triple Crown; Guinness; Budweiser; cider.

A welcoming whitewashed pub with two bars
and a pleasant garden. Derek Gilbert's a
great enthusiast for his beers, while Val looks
to culinary matters, producing real home
cooking in generous helpings: vegetable
broth, savoury and fruit pies, ham and eggs,
lasagne, chilli, salad platters. Also sandwiches, bangers and jacket potatoes. *Typical
prices:* Turkey & ham pie £2.95   Vegetable
broth £1 (Last bar food 9.45pm. No bar food
Mon eve) ⊖

Frampton Mansell   *(B & B)*   *Crown Inn*

Stroud · *Gloucestershire* · Map 8 D2
Frampton Mansell (028 576) 601
Free House
Landlord Mr E. W. Sykes
Children welcome
Credit Access, Visa
🍺 Wadworth's 6X; Archers Village Ale;
Younger's Scotch Bitter; Guinness; Beck's Bier;
cider.
ACCOMMODATION   12 bedrooms   £A
Check-in: all day

A smart new block of 12 bedrooms has
widened the scope of this pub that's built of
Cotswold stone. Space and comfort are the
keynotes, and all rooms feature luxurious
carpeting, high-grade modular furniture and
good accessories, including colour TVs and
direct-dial phones. Bathrooms, too, are stylish and well equipped. The beamed bar has
a deal of traditional appeal, but isn't always
particularly warm or brightly lit. Accommodation closed 2 weeks Christmas.

Frilford Heath *(B & B)* *Dog House*

Near Abingdon · *Oxfordshire* · Map 7 B2
Oxford (0865) 390830

Brewery Morland
Landlord Mr Hagger
Children welcome
Credit Access, Amex, Diners, Visa
🍺 Morland's PA Bitter, Best Bitter, Mild;
Guinness; Heineken; Stella Artois.
ACCOMMODATION 10 bedrooms £B
Check-in: all day

This modernised 17th-century hotel stands in lovely rural Oxfordshire with views over rich farming land and the Vale of the White Horse. The large bar area is warm and welcoming, and dog-lovers will lap up the canine posters, pictures and prints. Centrally heated bedrooms have simple white furnishings (one is in attractive period style), tea-makers and TVs. Private facilities now extend to all rooms. Garden.

Friskney *(B & B)* *Barley Mow*

Sea Lane, near Boston · *Lincolnshire* · Map 4 D4
Friskney (075 484) 483

Brewery Bateman
Landlords Jack & Eileen McCluskie

Children welcome
🍺 Bateman's Best Bitter, also Triple X and Mild in summer; Guinness; Heineken; cider.
ACCOMMODATION 3 bedrooms £D (No dogs)
Check-in: restricted

A friendly place for an overnight stop, this attractive old pub stands alongside the A52 Boston–Skegness road. Simple, homely comforts are the order of the day, and sloping ceilings add a touch of character to the bedrooms, which are equipped with duvets. Two have washbasins and all three share the landlords' well-kept bathroom. There are two unpretentious bars and an outside drinking area. No children under five overnight.

Our inspectors never book in the name of Egon Ronay's Guides;
they disclose their identity only after paying their bills.

Fulking *(Food)* *Shepherd & Dog*

Near Henfield · *West Sussex* · Map 6 C4
Poynings (079 156) 382 *Brewery* Phoenix
Landlord Antony Bradley-Hole *Credit* Access, Visa
🍺 King & Barnes Festive; Usher's Best Bitter; Webster's Yorkshire Bitter; Gale's HSB; Guinness; Holsten; cider.

★ Tucked into a valley beneath the steepest part of the Sussex Downs, this immensely popular pub is always swarming with people – in the delightful old bars, the garden or out on the terrace – who come to enjoy the simply splendid food. The menu changes daily and is full of interest, whether you choose the home-made taramasalata, a lovely seafood salad or hot special such as impeccably prepared lasagne. There are more hot dishes at night, including hearty beef and Guinness pie, together with delectable sweets like our perfect chocolate mousse. Friendly staff cope in efficient style with the crowds. *Typical prices:* Seafood gratin £2.75   Duck, apple & sage pancakes £4.25 (Last bar food 9.30pm. No bar food Sun eve) ★

Fyfield *(Food)*

White Hart

Near Abingdon · *Oxfordshire* · Map 7 B2
Frilford Heath (0865) 390 585

Free House
Landlord Edward Howard

Children welcome
Credit Access, Amex, Diners, Visa
🍺 Morland's Bitter; Adnams Extra Bitter;
Wadworth's 6X; Ruddle's County; Theakston's
Old Peculier; Guinness; Tennent's Lager; cider.

Flagstones, beams and a gallery are features of this fine old pub with much baronial appeal, and the lovely garden is another attraction. The snacks are a mixture of traditional and a little bit different, with soup, steak and lasagne alongside vegetarian dishes, pork tropicana and chicken breast with a tasty pâté and mushroom stuffing. Bread is home-baked, and sweets are appealing. *Typical prices:* Steak & kidney pie £3.15 Chicken Strasbourg £3.95 (Last bar food 10pm) ☺

Gestingthorpe *(Food)*

Pheasant

Near Halstead · *Essex* · Map 5 C2
Hedingham (0787) 61196

Free House
Landlords Jeanne & Mike Harwood

🍺 Pheasant Bitter; Greene King IPA, Abbot Ale;
Adnams Best Bitter; Guinness; Harp; cider.

Walkers out enjoying the country air near this delightful old pub often end up in the bar at mealtimes for some of Jeanne Harwood's hearty home cooking. She does a smashing chicken curry, as well as favourites like fish and cottage pies, sticky treacle tart and hot winter puddings. Generously-filled sandwiches, too, plus tasty soups and pâtés. Garden. *Typical prices:* Fish pie £2.80 Goulash £3 (Last bar food 10pm) ☺

Glastonbury *(Food, B & B)*

George & Pilgrims Hotel

1 High Street · *Somerset* · Map 9 D3
Glastonbury (0458) 31146

Free House
Landlords Jack & Elzebie Richardson

Children welcome
Credit Access, Amex, Diners, Visa
🍺 Bass, Toby; Worthington Best Bitter;
Guinness; Carling Black Label; Tennent's
Pilsner; cider. 🍷

ACCOMMODATION 14 bedrooms £C
Check-in: all day

The tradition of hospitality at this ancient inn goes back more than 500 years, and today's visitors can feast on a wealth of history and legend along with their bar snacks. The choice ranges from soup, salads, sandwiches and ploughman's to fish and chips and a daily special – perhaps risotto or the popular Somerset bacon bake – with cheesecake or chocolate crunch cake for afters. *Typical prices:* Coq au vin £3.65 Steak & kidney pie £2.95 (Last bar food 9.30pm) ☺

The old world charm of blackened beams and four-posters – a feature of many of the rooms – is backed up by modern comforts such as direct-dial telephones, radio-alarms and TVs. All bedrooms have their own bath or shower rooms, and those overlooking the high street are double glazed. There are also a couple of modern rooms (without ghosts) in an annexe. Patio.

Goldsborough *(B & B)*   *Bay Horse Inn*

Near Knaresborough · *North Yorkshire*
Map 4 C2
Harrogate (0423) 862212
Brewery Whitbread
Landlord Mrs June Manks
Children welcome
Credit Access, Visa
🍺 Whitbread Trophy Traditional Bitter; Castle Eden Bitter; Stella Artois; Heineken; cider. ♀
ACCOMMODATION 5 bedrooms £C (No dogs)
Check-in: all day

In a quiet village just off the busy A59, this friendly old inn offers comfortable overnight accommodation (no under-fives) in a rear extension. The five neat bedrooms with modern fitted units and hand washbasins all have tea-making facilities and share two well-kept public bathrooms. A collection of fearsome weapons adorns the heavily beamed bar and there's a peaceful lounge area overlooking the pretty garden.

Gomshall *(B & B)*   *Black Horse*

Station Road · *Surrey* · Map 6 B3
Shere (048 641) 2242
Brewery Young
Landlords Anne & Andrew Brown
Children welcome (lunchtime)
Credit Diners, Visa
🍺 Young's Best Bitter, Special Bitter, Premium Lager; Beamish; John Young's London Lager; cider. ♀
ACCOMMODATION   6 bedrooms   £C
Check-in: all day

There's a solid, dependable air about this late 17th-century inn, which stands on the A25 in an area of great natural beauty. Heavy carved antique chairs, sturdy tables and a coal fire give character and warmth to the bar, and bedrooms feature well-chosen fabrics, electric blankets and tea-makers. The residents' TV lounge is large, light and very comfortable. No under-12s overnight.

Goostrey *(Food)*   *Olde Red Lion Inn*

Main Road · *Cheshire* · Map 3 B4
Holmes Chapel (0477) 32033

Brewery Tetley
Landlords Mary & Peter Yorke

Children welcome
Credit Access, Amex, Visa
🍺 Tetley's Bitter, Mild; Walkers Best Bitter; Guinness; Castlemaine 4X; Oranjeboom; cider.

Log fires keep things cosy at this rambling pub, whose bars feature mock beams, unevenly plastered walls and copper-topped tables. The bar menu, available all sessions, offers some very enjoyable eating: cheesy-stuffed mushrooms or grilled sardines for starters or snacks, open and closed butties, home-cooked ham, beef bourguignon, even oysters when available. *Typical prices:* Pea & ham soup 80p   Cheesy-stuffed mushrooms £2.25 (Last bar food 10.30pm) ©

Gosberton *(B & B)*   **New Entry**   *Five Bells*

Spalding Road · *Lincolnshire* · Map 5 B1
Spalding (0775) 840348

Brewery Manns
Landlords Mr & Mrs Woodhouse

🍺 Webster's Yorkshire Bitter; Wilsons Bitter; Manns Best Bitter; Guinness; Foster's; Carlsberg.
ACCOMMODATION 3 bedrooms £D (No dogs)
Check-in: all day

Simple comforts are offered for an overnight stay in this solid white inn, which stands alongside the A16 Boston–Spalding Road. There are three bedrooms, very clean and well-maintained, with white walls and modern white furnishings, TVs and tea-makers. They all have washbasins and share a functional bathroom. Public rooms include two bars, one with a pool table. Garden.

Great Chishill — *Pheasant Inn*

Horsy bric-à-brac and racing memorabilia decorate the cosy beamed bar of this peaceful old village pub, where ex-jockey Denis Ryan is the exuberant host. A splendid inglenook fireplace, antique furniture and stuffed pheasants in display cases add to its charms. Garden.

Near Royston · *Hertfordshire* · Map 7 D1
Royston (0763) 838535   *Free House*   *Landlord* Denis Ryan
Children welcome (lunchtime)   *Credit* Access, Visa
■ Younger's IPA, Scotch Bitter, Tartan; Greene King IPA; McEwan's lager; Carlsberg. ♀

Great Ryburgh   *(B & B)* — *Boar Inn*

Near Fakenham · *Norfolk* · Map 5 D1
Great Ryburgh (032 878) 212

Free House
Landlords Jim & Margaret Corson
Children welcome
Credit Access, Visa
■ Tolly Cobbold Original Bitter; Adnams Bitter; Guinness; Carlsberg; Hansa; cider. ♀
ACCOMMODATION   4 bedrooms   £C
Check-in: all day

Tucked away in sleepy countryside this friendly village pub opposite a round-towered Saxon church is perfect for a quiet retreat – unless you're disturbed by the lively locals who crowd into the bustling bar, where in winter a log fire blazes in the huge inglenook fireplace. The four cottage bedrooms, with characterful furniture, colour TVs and tea-makers, share a modest shower room and separate WC. Patio and garden.

Great Stainton   *(Food)* — *Kings Arms*

Cleveland · Map 4 C1
Sedgefield (0740) 30361

Brewery Whitbread
Landlord Gordon Mitchell

Credit Visa
■ Whitbread Trophy, Castle Eden Ale; Guinness; Heineken; Stella Artois; cider.

Food rules the roost in the traditional lounge bar of this white-painted village pub. The yards-long blackboard menu offers a splendid choice, from generous portions of main dishes like kidneys turbigo, beef bourguignon and gammon with sherry and peach sauce to sandwiches and tasty buns filled with hot roasted meat. *Typical prices:* Beef Stroganoff £3.65   Smoked salmon & prawn sandwich £2.25 (Last bar food 9.45pm) ☙

Great Tew   **New Entry** — *Falkland Arms*

Beams of oak and elm, stone flags worn smooth and high-backed settles characterise this mellow creeper-covered inn in a delightful village setting. A vast collection of old beer mugs hangs from the bar ceiling, where country wines (including damson, parsnip, and mulled in winter) are also kept. Snuff fanciers will find 50 different varieties on sale. Garden.

Oxfordshire · Map 7 B1
Great Tew (060 893) 653   *Free House*   *Landlord* John Milligan
■ Donnington's Best Bitter; Wadworth's 6X; Hook Norton; Theakston's XB; cider.

Great Waltham *(Food)* *Windmill*

Essex · Map 7 D1
Chelmsford (0254) 360292   *Free House*   *Landlord* Martin Ridgewell
Credit Access, Visa
🍺 Adnams Bitter; Carling Black Label. ♀

★ Splendid food, expertly prepared and generously served, brings hungry crowds to this friendly, unassuming pub just off the A130. Seasonal delights such as pheasant, lobster and wild salmon share space on talented young chef Adrian Powell's menu with equally tasty but homelier treats like duck liver pâté with hot toast, ham off the bone and fried pork liver and bacon. There are freshly cut sandwiches and ploughman's, too, as well as super sweets – perhaps flavoursome fresh peach cheesecake or a winter pudding – and some fine cheeses. Garden. *Typical prices:* Steak, kidney & mushroom pie £3.95   Fish & chips £3.25 (Last orders 9.15pm. No bar food lunch Sat or Sun). Closed Sun eve and Bank Holidays. ★

Great Wolford *(B & B)* *Fox & Hounds*

Near Shipston-on-Stour · *Warwickshire*
Map 7 A1
Barton on the Heath (060 874) 220

Free House
Landlords Mr & Mrs C. Olcese
Credit Visa
🍺 Flowers IPA, Flowers Best Bitter; Guinness; Stella Artois; Heineken; cider.
ACCOMMODATION   4 bedrooms   £A
Check-in: all day

In a quiet village about two miles from the A34, this former coaching house is strong on country charm. The bar with its low ceiling, beams and handsome open fireplace is a very popular local meeting place. Four bedrooms in a converted stable block provide comfortable, smartly kept accommodation. Fabrics and furnishings are appealing, and each room has its own spacious, well-fitted bathroom. Garden.

*Prices given are as at the time of our research
and thus may change.*

Greenhalgh *(Food)* *Blues*

Fleetwood Road, near Kirkham,
Preston · *Lancashire* · Map 3 B3
Weeton (039 136) 283

Brewery Thwaites
Landlords Mr & Mrs R. G. Smith

Children welcome
Credit Access, Amex, Diners, Visa
🍺 Thwaites Bitter, Best Mild; Guinness; Stein; cider.

Appetising bar snacks, carefully prepared and courteously served, ensure that no one leaves this stylish modern pub near junction 3 of the M55 feeling the blues. You could snack lightly on a toasted steak sandwich, quiche or salad – or go for something more substantial like breaded haddock or Cumberland sausage. The large garden, with children's play area, is a great summer attraction. *Typical prices:* Ploughman's £1.95 Lasagne £2.25 (Last bar food 10.30 pm)

Greta Bridge   *(B & B)*   *Morritt Arms Hotel*

Near Barnard Castle · *Co. Durham* · Map 4 C2
Teesdale (0833) 27232

Free House
Landlords Mr & Mrs S. R. Waldron
Children welcome
Credit Access, Diners, Visa
🍺 Theakston's Best Bitter; Newcastle
Exhibition, Scotch Bitter; Carlsberg; cider. ⛲
ACCOMMODATION   23 bedrooms   £B
Check-in: all day

Charles Dickens stayed at this attractive,
stone-built hotel in 1838 while writing *Nicholas
Nickleby* – as visitors are reminded by
murals in the pleasant beamed bar. A welcoming
fire burns in the spacious lounge,
where a grandfather clock ticks slowly.
Homely bedrooms, which are furnished in
simple, traditional style, all have TVs. Most
offer private facilities. Garden.

*Our inspectors are our
full-time employees; they
are professionally trained
by us.*

Grimsthorpe   *(Food, B & B)* ★   *Black Horse Inn*

Near Bourne · *Lincolnshire* · Map 5 B1
Edenham (077 832) 247

Free House
Landlords Mr & Mrs K. S. Fisher

Children welcome
Credit Access, Amex, Visa
🍺 Samuel Smith's Tadcaster Bitter. ⛲

ACCOMMODATION   4 bedrooms   £A
Check-in: all day

Resident owners the Fishers have been
running this stone-built Georgian inn with
care and dedication for over 20 years. An
open fire warms the convivial buttery, where
a nicely varied menu with the emphasis on
English food is served. Follow vegetable
soup and lovely crusty bread with, say,
Lincolnshire sausages with tomato, fish hors
d'oeuvre or Grimsby plaice. Traditional
sweets like treacle tart or Queen of puddings
to finish. Well-kept cheeses. *Typical prices:*
Stilton and herb pâté £2.25 Mrs Beeton's
steak & kidney pie £3.95 (Last bar food
9.45pm. No bar food Sun) ☕

Prettily decorated bedrooms offer thoughtful
extras like books and biscuits, as well as tea-
makers and radios. Each has a key to its own
excellent carpeted bathroom. Residents can
relax in the cosy lounge bar with colour TV;
there's also a large, beamed main bar. Pub
closed one week Christmas.

Grindleford   *(Food, B & B)*   *Maynard Arms Hotel*

Near Sheffield · *Derbyshire* · Map 4 C3
Hope Valley (0433) 30321

Brewery Bass (North)
Landlord Robert Lindsay Graham

Credit Access, Amex, Diners, Visa
🍺 Stones Traditional Bitter, Bitter; Carling Black Label.

Tasty bar snacks are always available at this handsome Victorian hotel in the splendid setting of the Peak District National Park. The choice ranges from home-made soup and a breakfast-style grill to stir-fried prawns and chicken, aubergine and mushroom lasagne, and large Yorkshire puddings filled with roast meat or stew. Blackboard specials too, simple sweets and well-kept English cheeses. Nice garden. *Typical prices:* Steak & kidney pie £2.75   Yorkshireman £2.50 (Last bar food 9.45pm) 🍽

ACCOMMODATION   13 bedrooms   £B
Check-in: all day

Smart, comfortable bedrooms – some with lovely views – have tea-makers, direct-dial phones, and good bath/shower rooms. Public areas boast stained-glass windows, wood panelling, and a splendid oak staircase.

Guisborough   *(B & B)*   *Fox Inn*

10 Bow Street · *Cleveland* · Map 4 C2
Guisborough (0287) 32958
Brewery Scottish & Newcastle
Landlords Mr & Mrs Williamson
Children welcome
Credit Access, Amex, Visa
🍺 Scottish & Newcastle Exhibition; Younger's Scotch Bitter; McEwan's 80/-, Lager; Guinness; Harp. 🍷
ACCOMMODATION 7 bedrooms £C (No dogs)
Check-in: all day

In the centre of a relatively unspoilt market town, this pebbledash pub is run on welcoming lines by the Williamsons. The whole place is kept in apple pie order, and the bedrooms, all of a decent size, offer the comforts of central heating and double glazing, plus colour TVs and tea-makers. There are two bars – one smartly plush, the other with mock beams and a separate area where children may sit. Decent breakfasts.

Guisborough   *(B & B)*   *Moorcock Hotel*

West End · *Cleveland* · Map 4 C2
Guisborough (0287) 32342

Brewery Whitbread
Landlord Alan Mitchell

Children welcome
🍺 Whitbread Trophy; Guinness; Heineken; Stella Artois; cider. *No real ale.*
ACCOMMODATION   6 bedrooms   £D
Check-in: all day

A purpose-built public house on the outskirts of town offering practical comforts for an overnight stay. Bedrooms are centrally heated and each has a modern shower unit, functional fitted furniture and a black and white TV. There's a large bar, a residents' lounge (colour TV) and a family room where video cartoons are shown. The roomy beer garden has a well-equipped area where children may play.

Gunnislake *(B & B)* — *Cornish Inn*

The Square · *Cornwall* · Map 9 B4
Tavistock (0822) 832475

Free House
Landlords Brian & Dawn Marsh
Credit Access, Amex, Diners, Visa
🍺 St Austell Tinners, Hicks Special; Flowers
Best; Worthington Best; Guinness; Carlsberg
Hof.
ACCOMMODATION 9 bedrooms £C
Check-in: all day

Brian and Dawn Marsh are the friendly new
owners of this freshly painted pub right in the
centre of town. The whole place is neat and
tidy, and the bright bedrooms (six with en
suite private facilities) offer modest but
comfortable overnight accommodation. The
bar, with its rustic tables, pew seating and
horsy paraphernalia, is a nice spot for a drink,
and there's a relaxing residents' lounge.

Halford *(B & B)* **New Entry** — *Halford Bridge Inn*

Fosse Way · *Warwickshire* · Map 7 A1
Stratford-upon-Avon (0789) 740382
Brewery Northampton
Landlords Mr & Mrs Westwood
Children welcome
Credit Access
🍺 Ruddle's County; Wilsons Original Bitter;
Webster's Yorkshire Bitter; Guinness; Foster's;
Carlsberg; cider.
ACCOMMODATION 6 bedrooms £C
Check-in: all day

On the A429 Fosse Way, this 16th-century
coaching inn offers comfortable overnight
accommodation in six homely bedrooms. All
rooms are double-glazed and have TVs, and
residents have the use of a lounge where
tea-making facilities and an ironing board are
provided. There are two public bathrooms
with showers. Downstairs, an open fire
warms the simply furnished bar. Courtyard.

Hallaton *(Food)* **New Entry** — *Bewicke Arms*

1 Eastgate, Near Market Harborough
Leicestershire · Map 5 B1
Hallaton (085 889) 217

Free House
Landlords Mr & Mrs N. A. Spiers

Children welcome
🍺 Ruddle's County Bitter, Best Bitter;
Marston's Pedigree Bitter; Guinness; Carlsberg;
cider. ♀

Drive through rolling countryside to the pretty
village of Hallaton, famous for its Easter
Monday bottle kicking. The 400-year-old
Bewicke Arms has three cosy bars (one
bookable as a restaurant) where they serve
tasty snacks spanning sandwiches and pâté,
fillet of haddock, grilled gammon and steaks,
plus specials like seafood pancakes or gently
curried chicken. Garden. *Typical prices:* Lasagne £3.20 Pâté £1.65 (Last bar food
9.45pm) ☕

Hambleden   *(Food, B & B)*   *Stag & Huntsman Inn*

Near Henley-on-Thames
Buckinghamshire · Map 7 B2
Henley-on-Thames (0491) 571227

Free House
Landlords Mr & Mrs D. Vidgen & Mr N. Vidgen

Children welcome
Credit Access, Visa
🍺 Brakspear's PA Bitter, Flowers Original;
Wadworth's 6X; Huntsman Royal Oak;
Guinness; Stella Artois; cider. ♈

A menu dominated by Mexican dishes reflects the travels of the Vidgens, the enthusiastic owners of this 17th-century pub set in a picturesque village in the Chiltern Hills. The three bars are full of atmosphere, and if you want to catch up on local gossip, try the cosy snug. Nick Vidgen's bar food is justly popular, and our Mexican puerco verde – flavoursome pork on a bed of corn chips – was delicious. For the less adventurous there are salads (smoked trout and rare roast beef), a tasty pâté, ploughman's, chicken and mushroom pie, and tempting sweets such as orange cheesecake and a refreshing banana split with peach ice cream. *Typical prices:* Puerco verde £2.90   Chicken & mushroom pie £2.75 (Last bar food 10pm. No bar food Sun eve) ⊖

ACCOMMODATION 3 bedrooms £C (No dogs)
Check-in: all day

Bright, airy bedrooms – one with a shower cabinet – offer simple, spotless overnight accommodation. Good breakfasts. Garden.

Handcross   *(Food)*   *Royal Oak*

Horsham Road · *West Sussex* · Map 6 C4
Handcross (0444) 400703

Brewery Phoenix
Landlords Roz & Ted Field

Credit Access, Visa
🍺 King & Barnes Festive Bitter; Ben Truman;
Usher's Best Bitter; Webster's Yorkshire Bitter;
Guinness; Holsten; Carlsberg; cider. ♈

In a village just off the busy A23 London–Brighton road, this congenial pub offers a good selection of conventional bar fare. Freshly cut sandwiches, soup, salads and gammon steaks are supplemented by daily specials which could be anything from excellent grilled trout and mushroom-stuffed plaice to chicken pie and curry. The bar is neat and well kept, and it has a cheerful, relaxed air. *Typical prices:* Chicken pie £2.95   Ploughman's £1.50 (Last bar food 9.30pm) ⊖

Harome   *(Food)*   *Star Inn*

Near Helmsley · *North Yorkshire* · Map 4 C2
Helmsley (0439) 70397

Free House
Landlords Mr A. D. Bowron & P. Gasgoigne-Mullett

Credit Access, Amex, Diners, Visa
🍺 Cameron's Lion Bitter; Theakston's Bitter,
Old Peculier, Vaux Samson Bitter; Carlsberg
Hof.

Character and charm abound at this delightful thatched pub in a quiet village. The very popular lunchtime menu offers home-made soup and delicious sandwiches (white or brown bread) with tasty fillings ranging from roast beef and ham to curried chicken, smoked trout pâté and tuna mayonnaise. There's a pretty garden. *Typical prices:* Vegetable soup 75p   Prawn curry sandwich £2 (No bar food eves)

Harpenden   *(Food)*   *Silver Cup*

West Common, St Albans
Road · *Hertfordshire* · Map 7 C1
Harpenden (058 27) 3095

Brewery Wells
Landlords Roy & Rita Mills

Credit Access, Visa
Wells Bitter, Bombardier, Noggin, Kellerbräu,
Guinness; Red Stripe; cider.

We'll take a bet you enjoy your fodder at this
immensely popular pub whose name recalls
the horse races that used to be held on the
common opposite. Portions are generous,
so tuck into a warming casserole, steak pie,
a seafood platter, or a sizzling sausage
sandwich. Salads will leave you with plenty
of room for treacle tart or fresh plum pie.
Patio. *Typical prices:* Steak pie & vegetables
£2.50   Fish pie £2.50 (No bar food eves, Sun
& Bank Hols)

Harrietsham   *Ringlestone Inn*

Deep in the Kentish countryside, close to the Pilgrims Way, this splendid
old pub is an excellent place to enjoy a fine range of traditional beers,
country wines and ciders and soak up the history. Blackened beams, an
inglenook fireplace and stone floors are the perfect background for some
fine 17th-century furnishings.

Near Maidstone · *Kent* · Map 6 C3
Maidstone (0622) 859207   *Free House*   *Landlord* Michael Millington-
Buck
Children welcome   *Credit* Access, Amex, Diners, Visa
Adnams Bitter; Ringlestone Bitter; Fremlins Bitter; Heineken; cider.

Harrogate   *(B & B)*   *West Park Hotel*

19 West Park · *North Yorkshire* · Map 4 C2
Harrogate (0423) 524471

Brewery Tetleys
Landlords Mr & Mrs C. A. Gillis
Children welcome
Credit Access, Amex, Diners, Visa
Tetley's Bitter, Mild; Guinness; Skol;
Castlemaine 4X; cider.
ACCOMMODATION   18 bedrooms   £B
Check-in: all day

With its pleasant outlook over the green
expanses of the Stray and its proximity to the
town's amenities, this up-dated inn is a good
stopover for both business visitors and
tourists. Bedrooms are all of a decent size,
with modern furnishings, light colour
schemes and attractive units. Direct-dial
telephones and remote-control TVs are
standard, and most rooms have private
facilities. Note the splendid ornate ceiling in
the main bar.

Hartfield   *(Food)*   *Anchor*

Church Street · *East Sussex* · Map 6 C3
Hartfield (089 277) 424

Free House
Landlord Ken Thompson

Children welcome
Credit Access, Visa
King & Barnes Sussex Bitter, Festive;
Adnams Bitter; Fremlins Tusker; Guinness;
Heineken; Stella Artois; cider.

Built in the 15th-century as a farm dwelling,
this cheerful, red-brick pub offers an appetising selection of bar food. Deep-fried mushrooms or moules marinière give way to
enterprising main courses like curried crab
and prawns, jugged venison and chicken
gratinée. Salads, sandwiches and ploughman's, too, plus simple sweets and children's
dishes. There's also a restaurant. *Typical
prices:* Garlic prawns £3.85   Beef or lamb
kebabs £5.25 (Last bar food 10pm)

Haslemere *(Food)* *Crowns*

Weyhill · *Surrey* · Map 6 B3
Haslemere (0428) 3112

Brewery Friary Meux
Landlord Benjamin Heath

Children welcome (lunchtime)
Credit Access, Amex, Diners, Visa
🍺 Friary Meux Bitter; John Bull Bitter; Ind
Coope Burton Ale; Guinness; Löwenbräu; Skol;
cider.

A wide range of wholesome, home-cooked fare is the attraction of this smart, substantial pub. Spinach and bacon bake, steak and kidney pie, moussaka, are typical dishes, with seafood kebabs, local trout and squid in garlic on the seafood menu. A mammoth tureen of soup makes a warming starter, but save room for the delicious sweets. Garden. *Typical prices:* Peppered chicken in Dijon sauce £5.25   Prawn, haddock & courgette pie £3.45 (Last bar food 10.30pm) ℰ

Hastingwood Common *Rainbow & Dove*

Despite its proximity to junction 7 of the M11, this welcoming, 17th-century pub with its crooked roof and splendid garden enjoys a delightful rural setting. A rustic patio and putting green are further exterior assets, and inside the heavily beamed building, the snug little bars are crammed with assorted bric-à-brac.

Near Harlow · *Essex* · Map 7 D1
Harlow (0279) 415419   *Brewery* Ind Coope   *Landlords* Joyce & Tony Bird
🍺 John Bull Bitter; Double Diamond; Guinness; Löwenbräu; Skol. *No real ale.*

Hatherleigh *(Food, B & B)* *George Hotel*

Market Street · *Devon* · Map 9 B3
Okehampton (0837) 810454

Free House
Landlords Mr & Mrs Andrew Grubb

Children welcome
Credit Access, Visa
🍺 Courage Best Bitter; Devenish Cornish Bitter;
John Smith's Bitter; Simmonds Bitter; Guinness;
Hofmeister; cider.

This charming 15th-century building – a former coaching inn – makes the perfect English pub with its thatched roof, cobbled courtyard hung with gay flower baskets, scrubbed parquet floor and huge inglenook fireplace. The spacious, beamed lounge bar is well known for hearty, carefully prepared food. There are rich soups, salads, toasted sandwiches, ploughman's lunches or lunch-time fry-ups, together with a selection of savoury pies. There is always a dish of the day which could be a vegetarian special such as cauliflower cheese. Puddings, particularly the lemon meringue pie, and breakfasts are also highly recommended. *Typical prices:* Chicken pancakes with salad £2.70   Steak & kidney pie with vegetables £2.50 (Last bar food 10pm) ℰ

ACCOMMODATION 12 bedrooms £C
Check-in: all day

Bedrooms are full of character – one has a four-poster bed and the best have lovely old traditional furnishings. Most have en suite bathrooms stocked with good-quality toiletries. Courtyard.

Hawk Green *(Food)*
Crown Inn

Marple, Near Stockport · *Greater Manchester* · Map 4 C3
061-427 2678

Brewery Robinson
Landlord Mr T. Lane

Children welcome (lunchtime)
Credit Access, Amex, Diners, Visa
🍺 Robinson's Mild, Best Bitter; Guinness; Einhorn; Tennent's Export. ⟡

At this popular black and white pub opposite the green you can enjoy a wide variety of appetising fare. Follow French onion soup or crunchy mushrooms with a succulent steak, Chinese-style prawns or chicken sorpresa. There are daily specials like roast beef and fresh crab, also giant open sandwiches, salads and pleasant sweets. Food all day from noon on Sun. Terrace. *Typical prices:* Open prawn sandwich £3.20 Chicken tandoori £5.40 (Last bar food 9.45) ⊖

We welcome complaints and bona fide recommendations on the tear-out pages for readers' comments. They are followed up by our professional team. Please also complain to the management instantly.

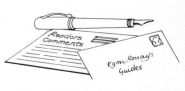

Hawkhurst *(Food, B & B)*
Tudor Arms Hotel

Rye Road · *Kent* · Map 6 C3
Hawkhurst (058 05) 2312

Free House
Landlord Barry Edwards

Children welcome
Credit Access, Amex, Diners, Visa
🍺 Fremlins Bitter; Whitbread Best Bitter; Stella Artois; cider. ⟡

ACCOMMODATION 13 bedrooms £A
Check-in: all day

On the A268 Rye road, this red-brick pub standing in pleasant grounds offers an appetising range of snacks in its handsome panelled bar. Flavoursome soups, sandwiches and crisp salads are always available, along with more substantial offerings such as cottage pie, chilli and an absolutely first-class lasagne. Delicious sweets from the restaurant menu might include fluffy lemon soufflé, fruit pies and coffee parfait. *Typical prices:* Lasagne with salad £2.75 Chilli con carne £2.50 (Last bar food 9.15pm) ⊖

Traditionally appointed bedrooms are of a good size and boast particularly comfortable beds (including two reproduction four-posters). Colour TVs, tea-makers and trouser presses are standard throughout and all but two rooms have modern carpeted bathrooms. Residents can also relax before an open fire in the inviting lounge furnished with leather sofas and armchairs. High standards of maintenance, housekeeping and personal service prevail. Garden.

Hawkshead   *(Food, B & B)*   *Queen's Head*

Cumbria · Map 3 B2
Hawkshead (096 66) 271

Brewery Hartley
Landlord Mr Allan Whitehead

Credit Access, Amex, Diners, Visa
🍺 Hartley's Best Bitter, Mild; Guinness; Stella
Artois; Heineken; cider. �

A popular and traditional pub in a very
attractive Lakeland village. The panelled
main bar and neighbouring snug provide a
fine setting for enjoying some very good bar
food, and the promise of the delicious smells
wafting from the kitchen is more than fulfilled.
Consistency is the keynote throughout the
range, from rich creamy mushroom soup and
venison pâté to casseroled pheasant, beef
curry and some excellent sweets like mocha
cheesecake with a super, penetrating coffee
taste. Sandwiches are an additional lunchtime offering. *Typical prices:* Beef & beer
casserole £3.95   Venison pâté £2.55 (Last
bar food 9pm) ☕

ACCOMMODATION 8 bedrooms £C (No dogs)
Check-in: all day

Beamed ceilings and simple furnishings be-
stow an old-world charm on the bedrooms,
which have neat private bathrooms notable
for their generous soft towels. There's a
plush, comfortable TV lounge for residents.
No under-tens overnight. Accommodation
closed 10 days Christmas.

---

*We neither seek nor accept hospitality
and we pay for all food and drinks in full.*

Haytor Vale   *(Food, B & B)*   *Rock Inn*

Near Newton Abbot · Devon · Map 9 C4
Haytor (036 46) 305

Free House
Landlord Mr Christopher Graves

Children welcome
🍺 Pope's 1880 Ale, Royal Oak Bitter; Bass;
Eldridge Pope IPA, Dorchester Bitter; Guinness;
Stella Artois; cider. ♵

Winding lanes lead to this attractive old pub
in a tiny village below Dartmoor's highest tor.
Its mellow, characterful rooms are a popular
eating place, and the long menu offers plenty
of choice. Hungry hikers can tuck into a
Cheddar or Stilton ploughman's platter or
warm up with a curry, rabbit or game pie,
venison casserole or mixed grill. There are
also sandwiches, jacket potatoes, soup, fish
and vegetarian dishes. *Typical prices:* Wide-
combe grill £4.25   Salcombe smokie £1.45
(Last bar food 9.45pm) ☕

ACCOMMODATION 9 bedrooms £B/C
Check-in: all day

Prettily decorated bedrooms – all with private
bathrooms – have TV, direct-dial telephones,
tea-makers and minibars. Landlord Christopher Graves is a very welcoming host. Don't
miss the pretty garden.

Maps

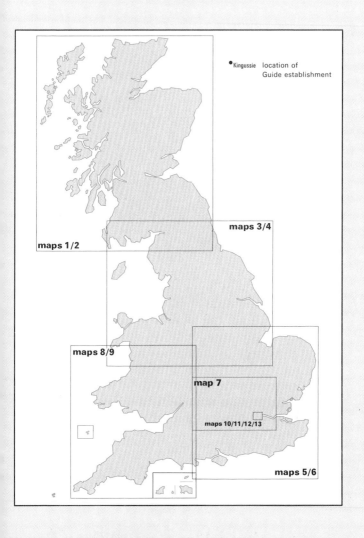

• Kingussie   location of
           Guide establishment

maps 3/4

maps 1/2

maps 8/9

map 7

maps 10/11/12/13

maps 5/6

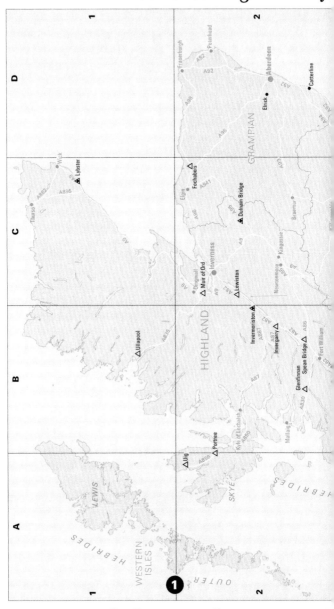

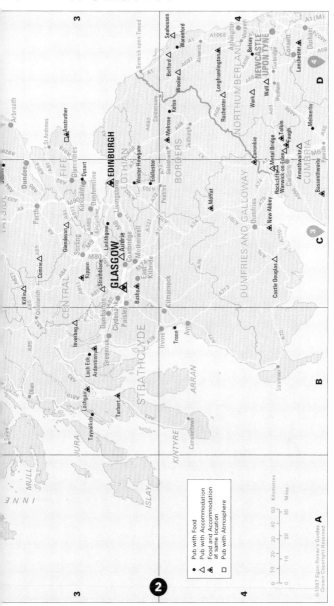

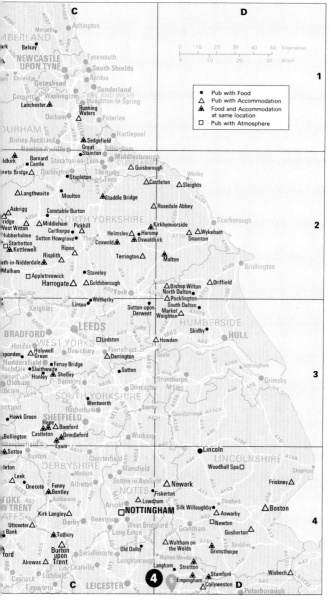

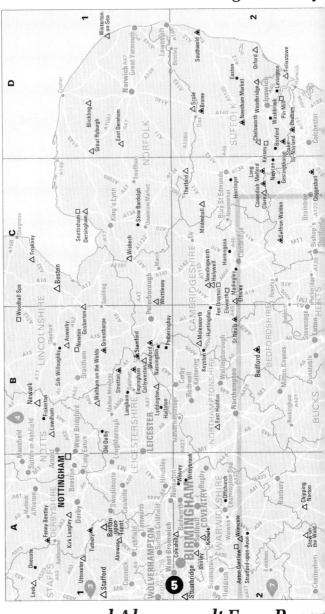

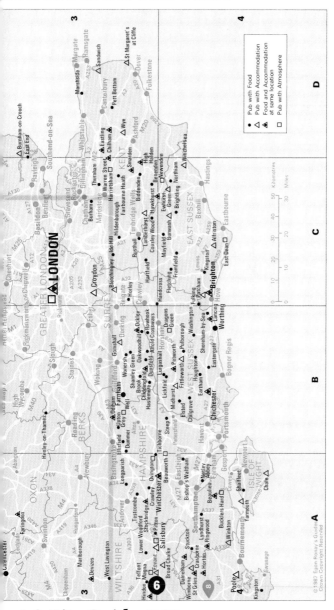

Also consult Egon Ronay's Guide 1987

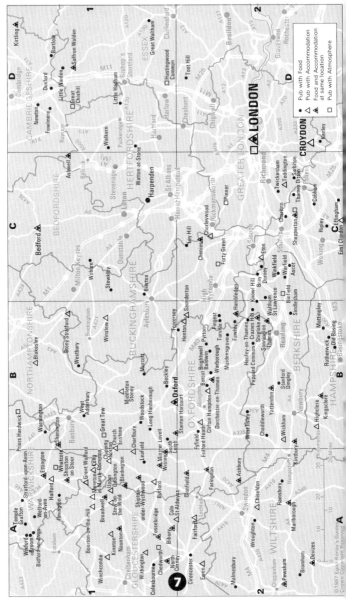

to the Lake District and Yorkshire Dales

Egon Ronay's
Minutes from the Motorway M25 AROUND LONDON GUIDE

Newly compiled for 1987, this colourful guide spotlights over 200 carefully selected eating places within easy reach of London's orbital motorway.

Everything from starred restaurants and country pubs to the best tearooms and wine bars.

Special features include detailed area maps.

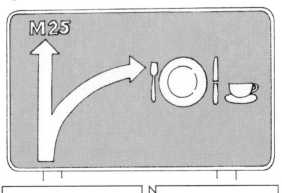

Available from AA Centres and booksellers everywhere at £4.95 or £5.95 including postage and packing from:

Mail Order Department
PO Box 51
Basingstoke
Hampshire
RG21 2BR

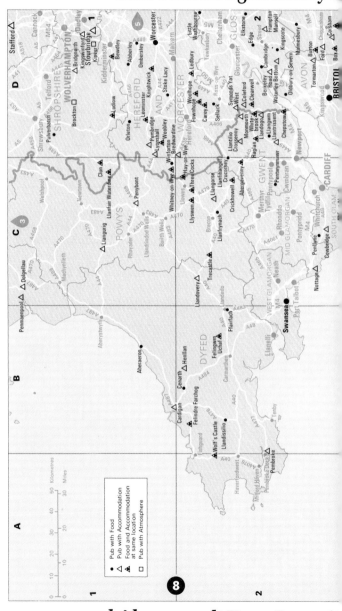

Just A Bite Guide 1987

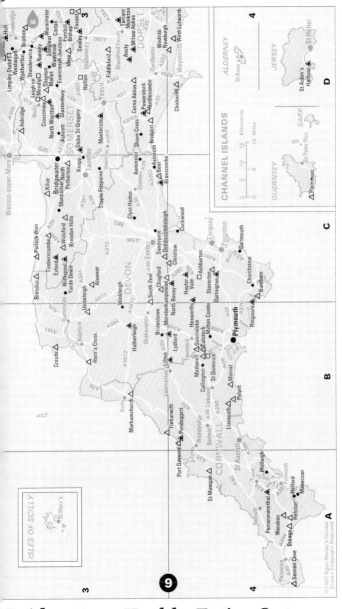

Guide 1987 to Healthy Eating Out

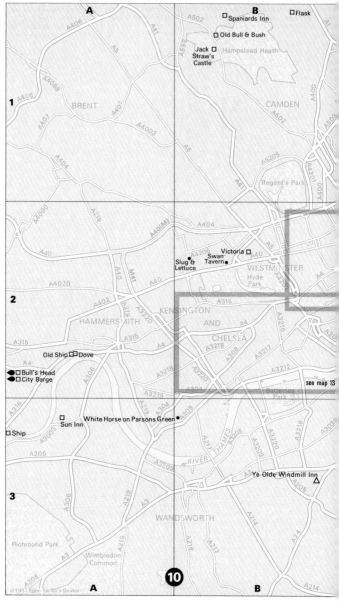

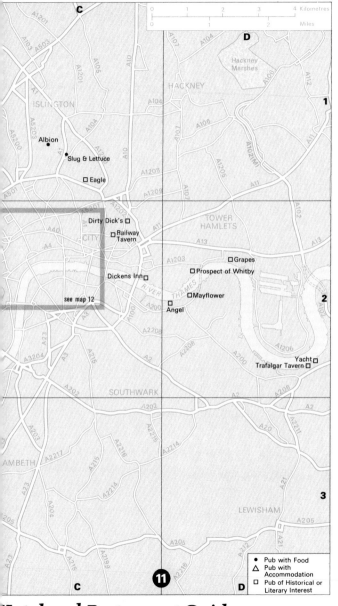

0   1   2   3   4 Kilometres

0   1   2 Miles

C

D

Hackney Marshes

HACKNEY

ISLINGTON

1

● Albion

● Slug & Lettuce

□ Eagle

TOWER HAMLETS

□ Dirty Dick's

□ Railway Tavern

CITY

□ Grapes

□ Prospect of Whitby

Dickens Inn □

see map 12

□ Mayflower

□ Angel

RIVER THAMES

2

Yacht □

Trafalgar Tavern □

SOUTHWARK

AMBETH

LEWISHAM

3

●	Pub with Food
△	Pub with Accommodation
□	Pub of Historical or Literary Interest

C   **⑪**   **D**

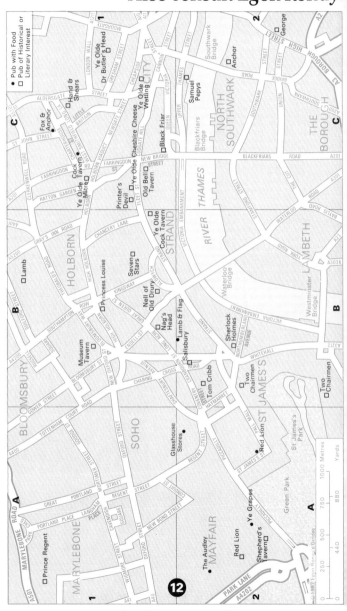

● Pub with Food
□ Pub of Historical or
   Literary Interest

1
Ye Olde Dr Butler's Head □

C
□ Hand & Shears
□ Fox & Anchor
● Cock Tavern
Ye Olde □ □ Mitre
Printer's □ Devil
Ye Olde Cheshire Cheese □
Olde □ Wetling
□ Black Friar
□ Old Bell Tavern

George □
Anchor □
Samuel □ Pepys
NORTH SOUTHWARK
THE BOROUGH

B
□ Lamb
HOLBORN
□ Princess Louise
□ Seven Stars
Nell of □ Old Drury
□ Nag's Head
● Lamb & Flag
● Salisbury
Ye Olde Cock Tavern □
STRAND
RIVER THAMES
LAMBETH
Sherlock □ Holmes
□ Two Chairmen
Two □ Chairmen

A
BLOOMSBURY
Museum □ Tavern
SOHO
● Glasshouse Stores
□ Tom Cribb
ST JAMES'S
St James's Park
● Red Lion
The Audley ●
Red Lion □
MAYFAIR
● Ye Grapes
Shepherd's □ Tavern
MARYLEBONE
□ Prince Regent
Green Park
PARK LANE

0 250 500 750 1000 Metres
0   440   880   Yards
©1987 Egon Ronay's Guides

12

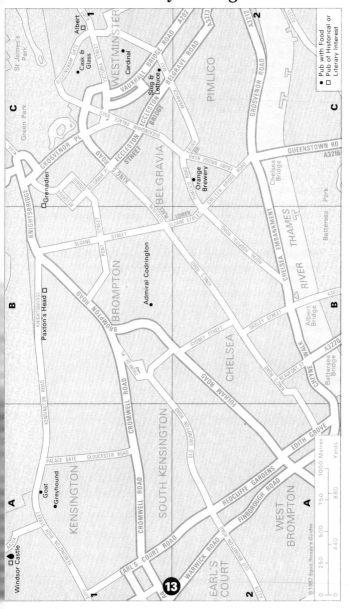

Egon Ronay's
BIRDS EYE *guide to*
HEALTHY EATING OUT

An essential guide containing detailed descriptions of over 500 eating places in Britain serving wholesome and healthy food. Whether you are in the mood for a bistro feast or a sophisticated dinner, this guide leads you there.

Introduction by leading health writer Miriam Polunin and a colour section including recipes from award-winning establishments.

A completely new source of reference for those who care about healthy eating.

Available from AA Centres and booksellers everywhere at £5.95 or £6.95 including postage and packing from:

Mail Order Department
PO Box 51
Basingstoke
Hampshire
RG21 2BR

Helford   (Food)

Shipwright's Arms

Near Helston · Cornwall · Map 9 A4
Manaccan (032 623) 235

Brewery Devenish
Landlord Mr Brandon Flynn

🍺 Devenish Cornish Bitter, Falmouth Bitter,
Mild, John Devenish Bitter; Guinness; Heineken;
Grünhalle; cider. ♀

Fresh seafood is a natural choice at this
delightful old thatched pub down by the river.
Crab is particularly popular, but there are
also grills, with soup, curries, and chilli among
the winter warmers. The lavish lunchtime
summer buffet tastes even better on the
waterside terrace. Tempting sweets. *Typical
prices:* Charcoal grilled steak £5.95   Local
scallops £5.95 (Last bar food 9pm). Closed 1
evening a week in winter. ⊘

Helmsley   (B & B)

Feathers Hotel

Market Place · North Yorkshire · Map 4 C2
Helmsley (0439) 70275
Free House
Landlords Feathers family
Children welcome
Credit Access, Amex, Diners, Visa
🍺 Younger's Bitter; Theakston's Bitter, XB;
Cameron's Bitter; Strong Arm; Guinness; Carling
Black Label; Carlsberg Hof. ♀
ACCOMMODATION   18 bedrooms   £C
Check-in: all day

A 15th-century cottage and an 18th-century
house make up this friendly, family-run inn
overlooking the market square. Comfortable
bedrooms are furnished and decorated in a
variety of styles; all offer TVs and tea-makers,
most have their own modern bathroom.
There's a popular, rustic public bar, relaxing
lounge bar and a homely residents' lounge.
Garden. Accommodation closed Christmas–
end January.

Helston   (B & B)

Angel Hotel

Coinagehall Street · Cornwall · Map 9 A4
Helston (0326) 572701
Free House
Landlords Mr & Mrs S. W. Hudson
Children welcome
Credit Access, Amex, Diners, Visa
🍺 Flowers Bitter; Whitbread Best, Poachers;
Worthington; Carling Black Label; Stella Artois;
cider. *No real ale* ♀
ACCOMMODATION   21 bedrooms   £C
Check-in: all day

The bedrooms at this old town-centre coaching inn have benefited from redecoration,
with pleasant wallpapers among the improvements. Most of the rooms have well-polished
antique or traditional furnishings, and all are
equipped with TVs and tea-makers. They
share the use of eight good shower rooms.
Public areas include the main lounge bar with
the unusual feature of a 30-foot well. Patio.

Henley-on-Thames   (Food)

Argyll

Market Place · Oxfordshire · Map 7 B2
Henley-on-Thames (0491) 573400

Brewery Morland
Landlord Mr R. K. Boswell

🍺 Morland's Best Bitter, Bitter, Mild, Artist;
Guinness; Heineken; Stella Artois.

A fine cold table attracts the lunchtime crowds
to this black and white pub in the town centre.
The wood-panelled bar makes a cosy setting
in which to enjoy succulent ribs of beef,
home-cooked gammon, pâtés and quiches –
all delicious with crisp, fresh salads. There's
usually a hot dish, too, like hearty beef stew,
and traditional puddings. Sunday brings a
roast lunch. *Typical prices:* Steak & kidney
pudding £3.50   Chicken & ham pie £2.90 (No
bar food eves) ⊘

Henley-on-Thames *(Food)* — *Little Angel*

Remenham Lane, Remenham · *Oxfordshire* ·
Map 7 B2
Henley-on-Thames (0491) 574165

Brewery Brakspear
Landlord Mr Paul Southwood

Children welcome
Credit Access, Amex, Diners, Visa
Brakspear's Bitter, 4X Old Ale; Guinness;
Heineken. ♀

Just over the bridge on the A423 Maidenhead road, this attractive old pub is full of charm and character. The bar food is a very popular feature, and the regularly changing menu tends towards the sea with dishes like pan-fried sardines, grilled plaice and seafood tagliatelle. Meat dishes, too, plus sandwiches, salads and sorbets. Limited choice Sunday evening and Monday. Terrace. *Typical prices:* Seafood symphony £4.50   Steak pie £4.50 (Last bar food 10pm) ℮

Henton *(B & B)* — *Peacock*

Near Chinnor · *Oxfordshire* · Map 7 B2
Kingston Blount (0844) 53519
Free House
Landlord Mr H. S. Good
Credit Access, Amex, Visa
Brakspear's Ordinary Bitter; Hook Norton
Bitter; Adnams Bitter; Hall & Woodhouse Badger
Bitter; Guinness; cider.
ACCOMMODATION 3 bedrooms £B (No dogs)
Check-in: all day

Peacocks and ducks roam the grounds of this black and white thatched pub, which dates back more than 600 years. Inside, there's a spacious bar with a comfortable country feel, and three attractive bedrooms with beams, sloping ceilings and pretty curtains. Fitted wardrobes provide storage space, and each room has TV and its own private bath or shower. Good breakfasts. Closed Mon and Tues lunchtime.

Hexworthy *(Food, B & B)* — *Forest Inn*

Near Princetown · *Devon* · Map 9 B4
Poundsgate (036 43) 211

Free House
Landlords Mrs O. Wise & Mr A. Oake

Children welcome
Credit Diners, Visa
Worthington Best; Bass; Guinness;
Tennent's Pilsner; cider.

Ideal for walking, fishing or pony trekking holidays, this sturdy Dartmoor inn is set high up in a landscape of rugged, desolate beauty. Plants bring a touch of colour to the spacious courtyard and the homely bars, where a blackboard menu lists daily specials featuring fresh local fish. Also on the menu are hearty soups to warm you after a day on the moors, sandwiches, ploughman's, cold platters, and delicious filling puds topped with clotted cream. *Typical prices:* Barbican plaice £3.25   Steamed sponge pudding £1.50 (Last bar food 8.30pm) ℮

ACCOMMODATION 15 bedrooms £C
Check-in: all day

Comfortable beds with crisply laundered sheets ensure a good night's sleep in the simply furnished bedrooms, which share four old-fashioned bathrooms. Good breakfasts. Accommodation closed January and February (when whole pub also closed in the evenings).

High Halden *(Food, B & B)* | *Chequers Inn*

Near Ashford · *Kent* · Map 6 C3
High Halden (023 385) 218

Brewery Whitbread
Landlords John & Pauline Shaw

🍺 Fremlin's Bitter, Mild; Guinness; Stella Artois;
Heineken; cider. ♀
ACCOMMODATION 3 bedrooms £D
Check-in: restricted

A friendly and convivial atmosphere per-
vades this fine old roadside pub in the heart
of the Kentish countryside. The saloon bar is
a suitably homely setting for some simple,
tasty snacks, which range from sandwiches
and hearty soups to curries, grills and basket
meals. Sweets like cheesecake and lemon
mousse are a strong point. Three modest
bedrooms share the family bathroom. *Typical
prices:* Shepherd's pie £1.45 Fish pie £1.55
(Last bar food 9pm). ☻

Highclere *(B & B)* | *Yew Tree Inn*

Andover Road, near Newbury · *Berkshire*
Map 7 B2
Newbury (0635) 253360
Free House
Landlords Mr & Mrs A. M. Greenwood
Children welcome
Credit Access, Diners, Visa
🍺 Wadworth's 6X; Arkell's; Guinness;
Carlsberg; cider. ♀
ACCOMMODATION 4 bedrooms £C (No dogs)
Check-in: restricted

Everything is kept in apple-pie order at this
comfortably refurbished 17th-century inn, a
warm and friendly spot for an overnight stop.
The bedrooms have very comfortable beds,
ample wardrobe space, TVs and modern
bath or shower rooms with big towels. The
spacious open-plan bar boasts two splendid
inglenook fireplaces. Patio.

*We publish annually
so make sure you use
the current edition.*

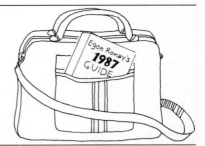

Hildenborough *(Food)* | *Gate Inn*

Rings Hill · *Kent* · Map 6 C3
Hildenborough (0732) 832103

Brewery Whitbread
Landlord Mr G. R. M. Sankey

Credit Amex, Visa
🍺 Fremlins Bitter; Flowers Original; Guinness;
Stella Artois; Heineken; cider. ♀

Seafood's the name of the game at this
substantial pub in Victorian style next to the
station. Mullet, conger eel and John Dory are
among the ingredients for the excellent fish
soup, and you'll also find crab and lobster,
mussels and oysters, sole and salmon on the
menu. The odd meaty special appears at
lunchtime, and there's a good cheeseboard.
Typical prices: Salmon en croûte £7 Avocado
vinaigrette £1.25 (Last bar food 10pm. No
bar food Sun or Bank Hol Mons) ☻

Hindon   (Food, B & B)   *Lamb at Hindon*

High Street, Near Salisbury · *Wiltshire* · Map 6 A3
Hindon (074 789) 225

Free House
Landlord E. W. Nell

Credit Access
🍺 Wadworth's 6X, IPA; Hook Norton Best
Bitter; Guinness; Heineken; Carlsberg Export;
cider. ⚲

A popular hostelry for over 300 years, this former coaching inn was once the headquarters of a notorious Wiltshire smuggler. Today's locals are more interested in the tasty snacks on offer in the comfortably traditional lounge bar. At the simpler end, there are sandwiches both plain and toasted, and ploughman's with good granary bread. Home-cooked ham and other cold meats or perhaps prawns and crab make good salads, while more substantial offerings include beef curry and a hot special like roast lamb or fried haddock. A few simple sweets or cheese to finish. There's less choice for Sunday lunch, when a traditional meal served in the restaurant is a favourite option. *Typical bar prices:* Beef curry £3.30 Fruit pie £1.15. (Last bar food 10pm) ☺

ACCOMMODATION 16 bedrooms £C (No dogs)
Check-in: all day

Bedrooms range from simply furnished traditional rooms (including one with a fine four-poster) to modern rooms with practical white units; nine have private facilities. Residents can make use of the simple little TV lounge and commendably good breakfasts are served by courteous, pleasant staff. Garden.

Holt   (Food, B & B)   *Old Ham Tree*

Near Trowbridge · *Wiltshire* · Map 9 D3
North Trowbridge (0225) 782581

Free House
Landlords John & Carol Francis

Children welcome
Credit Access, Diners, Visa
🍺 Usher's PA; Eldridge Pope Dorset IPA;
Wadworth's 6X; Marston's Pedigree; Carlsberg
Pilsner, Hof; cider. ⚲

Honest, satisfying home cooking is the order of the day at this pleasant 18th-century pub facing the village green. Eat in the main bar, which is adorned with old post horns; a blackboard displays daily-changing specials such as excellent home-made soup, lemon sole and fresh mackerel, tasty pies and sauced meat dishes. Alternative snacks include favourites like ploughman's, toasted sandwiches and ham salad, and there are fruit pies (apple, cherry and almond) to round things off. *Typical prices:* Lamb in spicy apricot sauce £2.50 Game pie £2.50 (Last bar food 10pm) ☺

ACCOMMODATION   4 bedrooms   £D
Check-in: restricted

Individually decorated bedrooms with pretty bedspreads all have tea-makers, washbasins and fitted wardrobes. They share a well-kept bathroom. Residents can also watch TV in the wicker-furnished lounge, or take the air in the secluded walled garden.

Holton
Old Inn

Once a coaching inn on the old London to Exeter road, this charming little village pub is now by-passed by the A303. Enjoy a drink with the locals round the fire in the homely panelled bar, where a collection of key-rings hanging from the beams is a striking feature. Patio and garden.

Near Wincanton · *Somerset* · Map 9 D3
Wincanton (0963) 32002   *Free House*   *Landlord* Mr Colin Davey
Children welcome   *Credit* Access, Visa
🍺 Wadworth's 6X, Marston's Pedigree Bitter; Butcombe's Best Bitter; Oakhill Farmers Ale; Guinness; Carlsberg Hof; cider. ♀

Holywell   *(B & B)*
Ye Olde Ferry Boat Inn

Near St Ives, Huntingdon
Cambridgeshire · Map 5 C2
St Ives (0480) 63227
Free House
Landlord Louis Vella
Children welcome
Credit Access, Amex, Diners, Visa
🍺 Greene King IPA, Abbot Ale; Adnams Bitter; Bass; Worthington Bitter; cider. ♀
ACCOMMODATION 6 bedrooms £C (No dogs)
Check-in: restricted

Records show that this ancient inn on the banks of the Ouse has been retailing drink since AD560, and its heavily beamed and pillared bar is certainly full of old-world character. Upstairs, the two best bedrooms have TVs and their own private facilities and one boasts a four-poster; the others are much more functionally equipped and share two public bathrooms. Terrace and garden.

Holywell Green   *(B & B)*
Rock Hotel

Near Halifax · *West Yorkshire* · Map 4 C3
Halifax (0422) 79721
Free House
Landlord Mr Robert Vinsen
Children welcome
Credit Access, Amex, Diners, Visa
🍺 Matthew Brown's John Peel, Lion Bitter; Theakston's Best Bitter, Old Peculier; Slalom; cider.
ACCOMMODATION   18 bedrooms   £B
Check-in: all day

Close to junction 24 of the M62 yet pleasantly rural in its setting, this comfortable old inn started life in the 17th century as a cluster of three cottages. Today, a modern extension houses the neatly fitted bedrooms, which all offer colour TVs, tea-makers, telephones and shower rooms. Traditional pub games are a popular feature of the bright and cheerful bars. Patio.

Honley   *(Food)*   `New Entry`
Coach & Horses

Eastgate, Honley, Huddersfield
West Yorkshire · Map 4 C3
Huddersfield (0484) 666135

Brewery Bass Yorkshire
Landlords Mr & Mrs Woodhead

Children welcome (lunchtime)
🍺 Bass, Light Bitter, Mild; Stones Keg; Guinness; Carling; cider.

A busy village pub offering a good choice of lunchtime bar snacks and a bistro-style menu on Mon eves. Tagliatelle with spicy meat sauce or crudités with garlic mayonnaise might precede chicken and vegetable crumble, a juicy steak or plaice stuffed with cheese and mushrooms. Super salads, sandwiches and sweets, too. *Typical prices:* Lasagne £2.75   Egg & prawn salad £2.85 (Last bar food 9.30pm. No bar food eves) ⊖

Hope *(Food, B & B)*   *Poachers Arms*

Castleton Road · *Derbyshire* · Map 4 C3
Hope Valley (0433) 20380

Free House
Landlords Anton & Barbara Singleton

Children welcome
Credit Access, Amex, Diners, Visa
🍺 Webster's Dark Mild, Bitter; Carlsberg;
Foster's; cider. ♀

Anton and Barbara Singleton keep things running smoothly and happily at this delightful little hotel by the A625. It's a popular place for bar food, and the menu is much more extensive than average. A mug of soup with a home-baked roll is a good warming starter, which you could follow with anything from cannelloni to curried prawns, from rabbit casserole to roast beef. Snackier items include hot smoked haddock and black pudding in mustard sauce. There's also a good span of vegetarian dishes, along with delicious sorbets, ice creams and sweets from the restaurant trolley. *Typical prices:* Rabbit casserole £3.95 Hot smokie £2.25 (Last bar food 10.30pm) ⊖

ACCOMMODATION 7 bedrooms £B
Check-in: all day

The seven bedrooms – each tenanted by a well-dressed teddy bear – are roomy and comfortable, and three of those facing south have the added attraction of large balconies. Direct-dial phones, TVs, clock-radios and tea-makers for all rooms, plus modern carpeted bathrooms.

Horley *(Food)*   *Ye Olde Six Bells*

Church Road · *Surrey* · Map 6 C3
Horley (0293) 782209

Brewery Vintage Inns
Landlords D. J. & K. E. Beaumont

Credit Access, Amex, Diners, Visa
🍺 Charrington's IPA; Bass; Worthington Bitter;
Guinness; Tennent's Extra; Carling Black Label;
cider. ♀

Nestling by the river Mole is this ancient tile-hung pub. Upstairs, among the splendid old roof timbers of the Monk's Pantry, some excellent bar snacks are served – succulent cold meats, crisp salads and hot dishes like steak and kidney pie at lunchtime, veal korma by candlelight at night. Sandwiches, good sweets and cheeses also available. Garden. *Typical prices:* Pasta tricolor £2.40 Veal korma £4.50 (Last bar food 9.30 pm) ⊖

Horningsea *(Food)*   *Plough & Fleece*

High Street · *Cambridgeshire* · Map 5 C2
Cambridge (0223) 860795

Brewery Greene King
Landlords Mr & Mrs K. Grimes

🍺 Greene King Abbot Ale, IPA; Guinness; Harp;
Kronenbourg; cider. ♀

Mr and Mrs Grimes offer a most appetising selection of snacks at this delightful 300-year-old pub. In the rustic beamed bar you can enjoy lunchtime treats like hot sausage and bacon flan, ploughman's and salads, with more elaborate evening choices such as beef Wellington or honey-roast guinea fowl. Lovely sweets include cherry cobbler. Garden. *Typical prices:* Suffolk ham hot pot £3 Fish pie £3.60 (Last bar food 9.30 pm. No bar food Sun & Mon eves) ⊖

Horn's Cross *(B & B)*   *Hoops Inn*

Near Bideford · *Devon* · Map 9 B3
Horn's Cross (023 75) 222

Free House
Landlords June & Jimmy Malcolm

🍺 Flowers Original, IPA; Whitbread Best,
Trophy; Guinness; Heineken; Stella Artois. ⅌
ACCOMMODATION 14 bedrooms £C
Check-in: all day

Picture-postcard material on the outside, this ancient thatched pub is no less appealing within. Beams, oak furnishings and winter fires give real atmosphere to the bar, and there's a cosy, chintzy lounge and pleasant TV room. Main-house bedrooms continue the period charm, while coach-house rooms are more modern, with well-fitted private bathrooms. No under-eights overnight. Accommodation closed last 2 weeks November.

Horringer *(Food)* `New Entry`   *Beehive*

The Street · *Suffolk* · Map 5 C2
Horringer (0284 88) 260

Brewery Greene King
Landlords Gary & Diane Kingshott

Children welcome
🍺 Greene King Abbot Ale, IPA; Kronenbourg
1664; Harp Lager.

An old beer house of mellow character, run by a young, enthusiastic couple. Bar food is good and varied, from sandwiches, salads and delicious soup to turkey and ham in a cream sauce with rice. Game is featured in season, and sweets include spotted dick and ewe's yoghurt with honey. *Typical prices:* Fresh sardines £3 Braised rabbit with smoked bacon £5.50 (Last bar food 10pm. No bar food Sun eve) ℮

Horton *(Food, B & B)*   *Horton Inn*

Cranborne, near Wimborne · *Dorset* · Map 6 A4
Witchampton (0258) 840252

Free House
Landlord Nicholas Caplan

Children welcome
Credit Access, Amex, Diner, Visa
🍺 Poole Bitter; New Forest; Ringwood;
Courage Directors; Whitbread Best; Ben
Truman; cider.

New owner Nicholas Caplan has set about restoring the splendour of former days to this handsome 18th-century inn on the B3078. Refurbished public areas include a roomy but cosy bar lounge and an attractive residents' bar that adjoins the restaurant. The regular bar menu offers a comprehensive variety of enjoyable fare, from sandwiches, ploughman's and salads to fish pie, jumbo sausages and home-cooked gammon. On the blackboard are daily specials like baked crab and succulent pork scallops in a tasty provençale sauce. Leave room for a sweet – hazelnut meringue with raspberry sauce is a winner. *Typical prices:* Fish pie £2.45 Hazelnut meringue £1.25 (Last bar food 10.30pm) ℮

ACCOMMODATION 6 bedrooms £B
Check-in: all day

The six good-sized bedrooms are furnished in traditional style, and a thoughtful list of accessories ranges from TVs to tissues. Two rooms have large, well-equipped bathrooms en suite, the rest share.

Horton in Ribblesdale *(B & B)* — *Crown Hotel*

Near Settle · *North Yorkshire* · Map 3 B2
Horton in Ribblesdale (072 96) 209

Brewery Theakston
Landlord Mr Richard Hargreaves
Children welcome
Credit Diners
🍺 Matthew Brown's John Peel Mild;
Theakston's Bitter, XB; Guinness; Slalom. ♀
ACCOMMODATION   10 bedrooms   £D
Check-in: all day

This whitewashed stone inn of uncertain but
considerable age stands right on the Pennine
Way. It's a popular place with walkers, who
can enjoy a spot of refreshment either in the
inviting bars or outside in the garden. For
residential guests there are ten simple, but
clean and bright bedrooms with a variety of
modernish furnishings. Most of them have
shower cabinets.

Houghton *(Food)* — *George & Dragon*

Near Arundel · *West Sussex* · Map 6 B4
Bury (079 681) 559

Free House
Landlord Mike Watson

Credit Access, Visa
🍺 King & Barnes; Young's Special; Harvey's
Best Bitter; Carlsberg; cider. ♀

Tradition has it that Charles II stopped here
for a quick drink whilst fleeing the country. A
slightly longer pause allows today's visitors
to relax over a tasty snack: there's always a
good soup, and other favourites range from
sandwiches (lunchtime only) and jacket potatoes to roast duck, steaks and the very
popular pan-fried local trout. Interesting
salads, good puds. *Typical prices:* Pan-fried
trout £5.35   Ploughman's £1.95 (Last bar
food 10pm) ☻

Howden *(B & B)* — *Bowmans Hotel*

Bridgegate · *Humberside* · Map 4 D3
Howden (0430) 30805

Owners Bowmans Hotel
Landlords Mr & Mrs M. Ucha
Credit Access, Amex, Diners, Visa
🍺 North Country Old Traditional, Ridings Bitter;
Guinness; Stella Artois; cider. ♀
ACCOMMODATION 13 bedrooms £B (No dogs)
Check-in: all day

A warm welcome awaits at this town-centre
hotel conveniently placed for the M62. Simple
overnight accommodation is provided in
neatly fitted bedrooms of varying sizes
(singles are quite small) equipped with TVs
and telephones; all but two have compact
tiled bathrooms. Downstairs, there's a comfortable main bar with banquette seating and
a smaller bar where you'll find a jukebox and
video games. Patio.

Hubberholme *(B & B)* — *George Inn*

Kirk Gill, Via Skipton · *North Yorkshire*
Map 4 C2
Kettlewell (075 676) 223

Free House
Landlords John Frederick & Marjorie Forster
Children welcome
Credit Access, Diners, Visa
🍺 Younger's IPA, Scotch Bitter; Harp; cider. ♀
ACCOMMODATION   4 bedrooms   £D
Check-in: all day

Old tree trunks act as beams in the flagstoned
bar of this charming village pub by the river
Wharfe. In summer, the patio is a particular
popular spot with thirsty hikers and cyclists.
Four neat little bedrooms (including one in an
attached cottage) share two public bathrooms and provide simple comforts. Children
under eight not accommodated overnight.

Huntingdon *(Food)*   *Old Bridge Hotel*

1 High Street · *Cambridgeshire* · Map 5 B2
Huntingdon (0480) 52681

Free House
Landlord Mr R. Waters

Children welcome
Credit Access, Amex, Diners, Visa
🍺 Ruddle's County; Paine's St Neots Bitter;
Tolly Cobbold Bitter; Younger's Newcastle
Bitter; Kestrel.

This attractive old inn on the banks of the
Ouse has a comfortable lounge bar where
bar meals are served. The cold buffet has
four different roasts, poached salmon and a
wide selection of varied salads. Hot dishes
on the menu include interesting soups, turkey
and mushroom pie, grilled gammon and
lamb's sweetbreads with garlic mayonnaise.
Typical prices: Smoked fish & cheese turn-
over £3.15 Pan-fried mushrooms with garlic
& wine £3.25 (Last bar food 10.30pm) ☕

Ide Hill *(Food)*   *Cock Inn*

Near Sevenoaks · *Kent* · Map 6 C3
Ide Hill (073 275) 310

Brewery Friary Meux
Landlords Jackie & Bob Arnett

🍺 Friary Meux Bitter; Ind Coope Burton Ale;
Guinness; Skol; cider.

Bring a hearty appetite along to this friendly
old pub on the village green. Bob Arnett's
wholesome snacks served in the two beamed
bars aren't for faint hearts: choose from
moist, chunky pâté and large baps filled with
hot salt beef, salads, herby sausages and
steaks. Seafood specials are worth looking
out for, too. Sandwiches only Sun lunchtime.
Terrace. *Typical prices:* Salt beef ploughman's £1.60 Sirloin with chips & salad £6
(Last bar food 8.30. No bar food Sun eve) ☕

Ilmington *(Food)* `New Entry`   *Howard Arms*

Near Shipston-on-Stour · *Warwickshire*
Map 7 A1
Ilmington (060 882) 226

Brewery Whitbread
Landlords David & Sarah Russon

Children welcome
Credit Access, Diners, Visa
🍺 Whitbread IPA, Original Bitter; Flowers Best
Bitter; Guinness; Stella Artois; Heineken; cider.

A spick-and-span village pub whose new
landlord David Russon is also the chef. The
blackboard bar menu changes regularly,
listing the likes of smoked trout and horseradish pâté, chicken curry or tasty kidneys in
red wine. Puds like nice gooey chocolate and
rum flan round things off. There's a restaurant, too. *Typical bar prices:* Game pie with
vegetables £3.75 Grilled swordfish steak
with vegetables £4.35 (Last bar food 9.30pm.
No bar food Sun eve) ☕

Kenley *(Food)*   *Wattenden Arms*

Old Lodge Lane · *Surrey* · Map 7 D2
01-660 8638

Brewery Charrington
Landlords Joan & Ron Coulston

🍺 Charrington IPA; Bass; Fuller's ESB (winter
only); Stones Bitter; Guinness; Tennents Extra;
cider.

The Coulstons offer a warm welcome at this
white-painted village pub, where tasty food
is served in the cosy panelled bar. Choose
from a tempting cold display of cooked
meats, seafood and salad, or go for a hot
dish like chicken curry, fried plaice or ham,
egg and chips. Nice traditional puds, and
sandwiches only on Sun. Garden. *Typical
prices:* Prawn curry £3 Beef salad £3 (Last
bar food 9pm) ☕

Kersey   *Bell Inn*

Attractive flower baskets festoon the timbered facade of this fine old inn in a village once renowned for its cloth industry, now known for its mainstreet watersplash and picture postcard prettiness. Open fires keep winter at bay in the brass-bedecked bars, while in summer the large garden comes into its own.

The Street, Near Ipswich · *Suffolk* · Map 5 D2
Hadleigh (0473) 823229   *Free House*   *Landlords* Mr & Mrs A. A. Fineman
Credit Access, Amex, Diners, Visa
🍺 Adnams Bitter; Flowers Original Bitter; Wethered's Spa; Whitbread Best Bitter; Guinness; Holsten; cider. ♀

Keswick   *(Food)*   **New Entry**   *Dog & Gun*

Lake Road · *Cumbria* · Map 3 B2
Keswick (07687) 73463

Brewery Theakston
Landlord Frank Hughes

🍺 Theakston's Old Peculier, XB, Best Bitter; Guinness; cider. ♀

Visitors to this characterful town-centre pub will enjoy hearty food in typical old-world surroundings. Cumberland sausage with fried onions in a hot brown loaf is a standing treat, and other favourites include goulash, beef curry and home-roast ham. Lunchtime brings more snack choices – sandwiches, jacket potatoes, ploughman's with excellent Cheddar. *Typical prices:* Goulash £3.25 Ploughman's £1.85 (Last bar food 9.30pm) ☕

Keswick   *(B & B)*   *Pheasant Inn*

Crosthwaite Road · *Cumbria* · Map 3 B2
Keswick (07687) 72219

Brewery Jennings
Landlords D. G. & M. Wright

Children welcome
🍺 Jennings Traditional Bitter, Mild; Tetley's Bitter; Guinness; Ayinger Bräu Lager; cider.
ACCOMMODATION 3 bedrooms £D
Check-in: all day

David and Marion Wright offer a warm North Country welcome at this homely old inn, which stands near the A66 about a mile from the centre of Keswick and thus is well located for touring the Lake District. Caricatures of local people liven up the bar, where a cheery fire burns in the hearth. Three modestly appointed bedrooms, all with tea-makers, washbasins and generous soft towels, share a modern bathroom. There's a patio for summer drinking.

Kettlewell   *(Food, B & B)*   *Racehorses Hotel*

Near Skipton · *North Yorkshire* · Map 4 C2
Kettlewell (075 676) 233

Free House
Landlords Mr & Mrs J. Rowbottom

Children welcome
Credit Access
🍺 Webster's Yorkshire Bitter; Tetley's Bitter; Carlsberg Pilsner, Hof; cider.

Dating back in part to the 17th-century, this hotel stands by the banks of the river Wharfe surrounded by the lovely Yorkshire Dales National Park and in a village that's a well-known centre for pot-holing. Bar snacks, prepared by Angela Rowbottom, are straightforward and satisfying. Delicious local trout is a standing treat, along with lasagne, ravioli and steak pie. Other favourites include robust soups, cold meats accompanied by fresh, crunchy salads and tasty puddings such as rhubarb crumble. *Typical prices:* Lasagne £2.50 Steak pie £3.10 (Last bar food 9pm) ⌒

ACCOMMODATION 15 bedrooms £C
Check-in: all day

The two bars, with their beams, brasses and open fires, have a good deal of traditional charm, and there's a cosy double lounge, one room with TV. Bedrooms are nearly all of a good size, smartly maintained and neatly decorated, with white-painted furniture and nice carpets. The eight without private bath or shower are served by adequate public bathrooms.

Keyston *(Food)*   *The Pheasant*

Near Huntingdon · *Cambridgeshire* · Map 5 B2
Bythorn (080 14) 241

Free House
Landlord Bill Bennett

Children welcome
Credit Access, Amex, Diners, Visa
🍺 Tolly Cobbold Bitter; Ruddle's County;
Younger's Tartan; Adnams Bitter; Stella Artois.

Enterprising chef-patron Bill Bennett provides an interesting and varied menu at this old thatched pub. Garlic bread accompanies good flavoursome soup, and other choices run from prawns and pâté to grilled plaice, Barnsley chop and bread and butter pudding. Free crudités on the bar, with chestnuts (in season) for roasting on the log fire. *Typical prices:* Rabbit & parsley dumpling soup £1.20 Barnsley chop with onion gravy £3.95 (Last bar food 10.30pm) ⌒

Kilve *(B & B)*   *Hood Arms*

Near Bridgwater · *Somerset* · Map 9 C3
Holford (027 874) 210

Free House
Landlords Robbie Rutt & Neville White

Credit Access, Visa
🍺 Flowers IPA, Original, Best; Whitbread
Trophy, Best; Stella Artois. 🍷
ACCOMMODATION 5 bedrooms £C
Check-in: all day

Robbie Rutt and Neville White continue to make improvements at their charming 17th-century pub, whose landscaped gardens and patio are delightful fair-weather alternatives to the pleasant bars. Smartly furnished bedrooms have lots of extras, from iced water to TVs and trouser presses; all now boast carpeted private bathrooms (one not en suite). No under-sevens overnight. Accommodation closed one week Christmas.

Kineton *(B & B)*   *Halfway House*

Near Guiting Power,
Cheltenham · *Gloucestershire* · Map 7 A1
Guiting Power (045 15) 344
Brewery Donnington
Landlords Mr & Mrs D. Marshall
Children welcome (lunchtime)
🍺 Donnington's Best Bitter, Special; Carlsberg;
cider. 🍷
ACCOMMODATION 3 bedrooms £D (No dogs)
Check-in: restricted

In an area abundant in history and natural beauty, this 17th-century stone inn stands in a little village overlooking the Windrush valley. The roomy bar is a popular local rendezvous, and there's a pretty garden for sipping in the sun. Three bedrooms offering modest comforts are kept in excellent order, as is the main guests' bathroom. No children overnight. Accommodation closed 4 days Christmas.

Kingsclere   (Food, B & B) — Crown

Near Newbury · *Hampshire* · Map 7 B2
Kingsclere (0635) 298956

Brewery Courage
Landlord Mrs Mary May

🍺 Courage Directors, Best; Simonds Bitter; Guinness; Hofmeister; cider.

A wide variety of homely food, much of it cooked by landlady Mary May, can be enjoyed in the cheerful bar of this friendly pub in the heart of the village. The blackboard menu choice ranges from very garlicky mushrooms, pizzas, pâté, ravioli and fried sardines to a generous rare beef salad, with more substantial dishes such as roast guinea fowl and pheasant casserole in the evenings. Simple puds include fruit pie, cheesecake and sorbets. Sunday lunch is a traditional roast or a ploughman's. *Typical prices:* Ploughman's £2   Guinea fowl £4.95 (Last bar food 9.30pm. No bar food Sun eve) ℮

ACCOMMODATION 2 bedrooms £C (No dogs)
Check-in: all day

The two modest bedrooms, which share a bathroom, are fine for overnight stays. Patio. Closed one week at Christmas.

Kingscote   (Food) — Hunters Hall Inn

Near Tetbury · *Gloucestershire* · Map 8 D2
Dursley (0453) 860393

Free House
Landlords David & Sandra Barnett-Roberts

Children welcome
Credit Access, Amex, Diners, Visa
🍺 Bass; Fussell's Best Bitter; Toby Bitter; Guinness; Tennent's Extra; Carling Black Label; cider.

A traditional country inn with reputedly the highest bar in the West Country. Enjoy bar snacks from a buffet laid with platters of cold meat, flans, pâtés and exquisitely prepared salads. Order hot blackboard-listed dishes such as steak pie, curry, chops or fish, and do leave room for a pud. Summer barbecues (Fri & Sat eves, Sun lunch) in the garden. *Typical prices:* Seafood pancakes £3.25 Steak & Guinness pie £3.15 (Last bar food 9.45pm) ℮

Kingston   (Food) — Scott Arms

Near Corfe Castle · *Dorset* · Map 6 A4
Corfe Castle (0929) 480270

Brewery Devenish
Landlords Phillip & Marcelle Stansfield

Children welcome
🍺 Devenish Wessex Bitter; Weymouth Bitter; Guinness; Grünhalle; cider. ♀

Perched high above Corfe Castle, with fine views from its garden, this friendly pub is a magnet for visitors. A blackboard menu offers simple home-cooked fare – hearty vegetable soup, a proper steak and kidney pudding, everybody's favourite jam roly-poly and custard. Lighter alternatives include Dorset pâté and peppered mackerel quiche. *Typical prices:* Steak & kidney pudding £2.80 Vegetable lasagne £2.60 (Last bar food 8.50 pm. No bar food Sun eve in winter) ℮

Kingston   *(Food)*   *Juggs*

Near Lewes · *East Sussex* · Map 6 C4
Brighton (0273) 472523

Free House
Landlords Andrew & Peta Browne

Children welcome
🏴 Harvey's Best Bitter, King & Barnes Festive
Bitter; Guinness; Tennent's Extra; Carling Black
Label; cider.

This 15th-century, tile-hung pub makes a
wonderfully atmospheric setting for some
highly enjoyable bar food. Blackened beams
and burnished brass are the background for
a menu that ranges from taramasalata and
smoked mackerel, salads and sandwiches to
fried haddock, steak and the house speciality
of toasted pitta with a savoury topping. Super
puds. Garden. *Typical prices:* Toasted pitta
with topping £2.10   Brownie with hot chocolate sauce 85p (Last bar food 9.30 pm) 🎧

Kingswinford   *(B & B)*   *Summerhill House Hotel*

Swindon Road · *West Midlands* · Map 8 D1
Kingswinford (0384) 295254

Brewery Ansells
Landlord Mr R. H. Beatty
Credit Access, Amex, Diners, Visa
🏴 Ansells Traditional Bitter, Mild; Guinness;
Skol; Löwenbräu; Castlemaine; Double
Diamond.
ACCOMMODATION   10 bedrooms   £C
Check-in: all day

Surrounded by pleasant grounds and trees,
this converted Georgian house stands on a
hilltop just outside the town centre. The bar
is very much in keeping with the building's
age, with plenty of space and a fine traditional
atmosphere. Bedrooms have a more contemporary feel, with plain colour schemes and
furniture of a simple, practical type. All are
equipped with TVs, telephones and tea-
making facilities.

Kintbury   *(Food, B & B)*   *Dundas Arms*

Berkshire · Map 7 B2
Kintbury (0488) 58263

Free House
Landlords Dalzell-Piper family

Children welcome
Credit Access, Amex, Diners, Visa
🏴 Morland's Bitter; Usher's Best Bitter; Arkell's
Best Bitter; Webster's Yorkshire Bitter;
Guinness; Carlsberg Hof; cider. ♀

This friendly, comfortable pub enjoys an
attractive setting by the banks of the Kennet
and Avon Canal. The Dalzell-Piper family are
not only welcoming and obliging hosts but
are very good cooks, and the snacks served
in the lounge are a major lunchtime draw.
Sandwiches, ploughman's platters and thick
nourishing soups are backed up by delights
like crab au gratin, smoked salmon quiche
and a richly sauced casserole of guinea fowl
served with abundant fresh vegetables.
There's also a small choice of delicious
sweets, such as pear charlotte. *Typical
prices:* Smoked salmon quiche £2.75
Guinea fowl casserole £3.45 (No bar food
eve or Sun)

ACCOMMODATION 5 bedrooms £B (No dogs)
Check-in: restricted

All bedrooms open out on to a canal-side
terrace; furnishings are chosen with taste,
and accessories include tea-makers, colour
TVs and drinks fridges. Bathrooms, all en
suite, are smartly equipped, too. Good breakfasts are a plus. Accommodation closed 24–
28 December.

Kinver — *Whittington Inn*

History seems to have stood still at this grand old pub, built in 1310 and the home of Dick Whittington's grandfather. Many original features have survived, and a welcoming open fire warms the splendid lounge with its blackened beams and panelled walls. Outside is a neat Tudor-style walled garden with fishpond.

Near Stourbridge, West Midlands · *Staffordshire* · Map 8 D1
Kinver (0384) 872496 *Free House Landlord* Miss J. Pike
Children welcome
🍺 Flowers IPA; Courage Directors; Marston's Pedigree, Owd Roger (winter only); Guinness; Stella Artois; cider. ♀

Kirk Langley *(B & B)* — *Meynell Arms Hotel*

Near Derby · *Derbyshire* · Map 4 C4
Kirk Langley (033 124) 515

Brewery Bass
Landlord John Richards
Children welcome
Credit Access, Amex, Diners, Visa
🍺 Bass; Worthington Bitter; Mitchells & Butlers Mild; Tennent's Lager; Carling; cider. ♀
ACCOMMODATION 10 bedrooms £C
Check-in: all day

Four miles out of Derby on the A52 Ashbourne Road, this well-run hotel is a converted Georgian farmhouse. It's a good place for an overnight stay, as all the attractively decorated bedrooms have central heating, colour TVs, telephones and tea-makers, and a decent breakfast is served. There are two lounge bars, a simple public bar and a pleasant garden for sipping in summer. Friendly staff.

Kirkby Stephen *(Food, B & B)* — *King's Arms Hotel*

Market Street · *Cumbria* · Map 3 B2
Kirkby Stephen (0930) 71378 *Brewery* Whitbread *Landlords* Mrs J. F. Reed & Mr K. Simpson
Children welcome *Credit* Access, Visa
🍺 Whitbread Trophy Cask, Trophy; Heineken; cider. ♀

 An attractive and very traditional inn standing at the heart of an unspoilt market town. Chef-partner Keith Simpson is responsible for the bar snacks that are such an outstanding attraction: subtly flavoured cucumber and cheese mousse; home-baked ham; an exemplary steak, kidney and mushroom pie; lovely pear tart served with whipped cream and tiny ratafias. In the evening the food is served in a simple restaurant; the range is similar but includes one or two specials such as game pie or a fresh fish dish. *Typical prices:* Cumberland hot pot £2.15 Game pie £5.75 (Last bar food 8.45pm) ☺

ACCOMMODATION 9 bedrooms £C
Check-in: all day

Entrance to this fine old hostelry is by a cosy, old-fashioned hall; there are two bars, including an intimate panelled cocktail bar, and a pleasant lounge where residents can watch TV. Bedrooms are plainish and unpretentious, but with the virtues of sturdy furnishings, soft mattresses and crisply laundered sheets. Two rooms have private facilities.

Kirkbymoorside *(Food, B & B)*   *George & Dragon*

Market Place · *North Yorkshire* · Map 4 C2
Kirkbymoorside (0751) 31637

Free House
Landlords Mr & Mrs Curtis & Mr & Mrs Austin

Credit Access, Visa
🍺 Theakston's Best Bitter; Younger's Scotch
Bitter; Newcastle Bitter; Guinness; Carlsberg;
cider. *No real ale.* 💰

This large 13th-century coaching inn facing
the market square makes a pleasant place to
stop for a simple wholesome lunchtime
snack. In the traditional beamed bar you will
find soup of the day plus a good range of
open or closed sandwiches packed with a
variety of fillings including prawns, mackerel,
ham, turkey or pâté. There are more substantial dishes such as steak and kidney pie or
roast beef with Yorkshire pudding, along with
a selection of delicious sweets – perhaps
excellent chocolate rum log or refreshing
mandarin cheesecake. *Typical prices:* Steak
& kidney pie £2.85   Lasagne £2.85 (No bar
food eves or Sun) 🍽

ACCOMMODATION 23 bedrooms £B (No dogs)
Check-in: all day

The bedrooms are situated in a converted
granary and old vicarage at the back of the
inn. Aside from varying in size, they are fairly
standard, with white units, pretty curtains,
TVs and direct-dial telephones, as well as
tea- and coffee-making facilities. All but three
have bath or shower room en suite. No under-
fives overnight.

Kirtling *(Food, B & B)*   *Queen's Head*

Near Newmarket · *Cambridgeshire* · Map 7 D1
Newmarket (0638) 730253

Brewery Tolly Cobbold
Landlord Ann Bailey

🍺 Tolly Cobbold Original, Ordinary, Best Bitter,
Mild; Guinness; Hansa; cider. 💰
ACCOMMODATION 3 bedrooms £D
Check-in: restricted

Built during the reign of Elizabeth I, this
attractive inn is run with energy and charm
by horse-loving Ann Bailey. Snacks served
in the cosy bars range from ploughman's
platters and spicy crab pâté to omelettes,
fried plaice and flavour-packed savoury pies.
Overnight guests climb a winding staircase
to reach the simply fitted bedrooms. *Typical
prices:* Ham, apple & onion pie £3.50 Fillet
steak £6.50 (Last bar food 9.30pm. No bar
food Thurs eve) 🍽

Knapp *(Food)*   *Rising Sun*

North Curry · *Somerset* · Map 9 C3
Taunton (0823) 490436

Free House
Landlords Mr & Mrs J. Ord Watt

Children welcome
Credit Access, Visa
🍺 Flowers Original, IPA; Whitbread Trophy;
Guinness; Heineken; cider.

The rustic charms of this quietly situated
former cider house are as strong as ever. An
agreeable Scottish couple now run it, and it's
Mrs Ord Watt who's in charge of the kitchen.
Her menu covers a good range, from sandwiches and salads to grills, curries, fish pie
and braised duck. Also vegetarian dishes
and nice sweets. *Typical prices:* Stuffed
plaice £4.50 Steak & kidney pie £3.50 (Last
bar food 10pm). The pub is closed Monday
lunchtime. 🍽

Knightwick   *(Food, B & B)*   *Talbot Hotel*

Near Worcester · *Hereford & Worcester*
Map 8 D1
Knightwick (0886) 21235

Free House
Landlords Mr D. Hiles & Mrs J. B. Clift

Children welcome
Credit Access, Visa
🍺 Wadworth's 6X; Bass; Flowers IPA; Banks
Bitter; Manns Best Bitter; Tennent's Lager;
Heineken; cider. ♀

ACCOMMODATION   10 bedrooms   £D
Check-in: all day

A vast and imaginative blackboard menu and
a huge wood-burning stove in the bar make
for cosy eating at this friendly, informal pub
with a picturesque riverside garden. Fish
comes direct from Billingsgate, and if you
don't fancy sole, plaice, monkfish or mullet,
there are steaks, delicious pasta and ever-
changing specials (always a vegetarian
choice), as well as sandwiches and ploughman's. Home-made sweets include a super
strawberry Pavlova. *Typical prices:* Chicken
& sweetcorn pie £3.25   Pork gasconne £4.50
(Last bar food 9.30pm) ⊖

Plump for the simply furnished bedrooms in
the old building if you value character, though
those in the modern annexe have the bonus
of en suite showers. All rooms are equipped
with tea-makers, clock-radios and the like.
Prepare to tackle a massive breakfast!

Knowl Hill   *(Food)*   *Bird in Hand*

Bath Road · *Berkshire* · Map 7 B2
Littlewick Green (062 882) 2781

Free House
Landlords Mr E. N. Shone & Company
Children welcome
Credit Access, Amex, Diners, Visa
🍺 Brakspear's Pale Ale, Old Ale; Courage
Directors Bitter; Young's Special Bitter; John
Smith's Yorkshire Bitter; Guinness; Carlsberg
Hof. ♀

A mouthwatering cold buffet is the main
lunchtime attraction at this popular 15th-
century pub by the A4. Salt beef, ham, tongue,
turkey, sausages and salmon are well
matched by imaginative salads. There's
soup, too, plus a daily special like steak and
kidney pudding. Toasted sandwiches, jacket
potatoes and savoury flans expand the
choice at night. *Typical prices:* Steak & kidney
pudding £3.75   Braised ham shank £3.75
(Last bar food 10.30 pm) ⊖

Knowle   *(B & B)*   **New Entry**   *Greswolde Arms*

High Street, Near Solihull · *West Midlands*
Map 5 A2
Knowle (056 45) 2711

Brewery Ansells
Landlord Mr I. P. Hartley
Credit Access, Amex, Diners, Visa
🍺 Ansells Traditional Bitter, Mild; Burton Ale;
Guinness; Skol; Castlemaine; cider.
ACCOMMODATION   18 bedrooms   £B (No dogs)
Check-in: all day

Named in 1858 after a prominent Warwickshire family, this high-street hotel had previously been a busy coaching inn. It is just 10
minutes' drive from the NEC and comfortable
overnight accommodation is its forte. The
bedrooms – modern in decor and furnishings
– offer a good range of accessories, including
TVs, radios, trouser presses and direct-dial
telephones. Some have their own shower
rooms. There are two bars, one a local
favourite. Patio.

Lacock   *(Food, B & B)*

Red Lion at Lacock

Near Chippenham · *Wiltshire* · Map 8 D2
Lacock (024 973) 456

Brewery Wadworth
Landlord Mr J. S. Levis

Children welcome
🍺 Wadworth's 6X, IPA, Farmer's Glory,
Northgate Bitter; Guinness; Heineken;
cider. ⅌

A fine old coaching inn set in the centre of
the National Trust village of Lacock. The bars
have a good deal of character, to which
beams, bare wooden floors, open fires and
stuffed game birds all make a contribution.
Another undoubted attraction is the bar food,
the product of a combination of sound skills
and a touch of imagination. Beef broth with
mushrooms and celery makes a tasty starter,
to be followed by lamb in mint and orange
sauce or a very good turkey and apricot pie.
Puddings include home-made ice creams
and a really delicious fruit and nut bread
pudding. *Typical prices:* Beef pie £3.45
Meringue with fresh cream & chocolate sauce
£1.40 (Last bar food 10pm) ℮

ACCOMMODATION   3 bedrooms   £C
Check-in: all day

A staircase lined with antiquarian bric-à-brac
leads to three spacious bedrooms with high
ceilings and antique wardrobes. There's a
splendid walnut-headed brass bed in one.
No children under ten overnight.

Lamberhurst   *(B & B)*

Chequers Inn

The Broadway · *Kent* · Map 6 C3
Lamberhurst (0892) 890260
Brewery Whitbread
Landlords Keith & Pam Smith
Children welcome
Credit Amex, Diners, Visa
🍺 Fremlins Bitter; Flowers Original; Whitbread
Best Bitter, Mild; Guinness; Heineken; Stella
Artois; cider.
ACCOMMODATION   4 bedrooms   £C
Check-in: restricted

In the heart of the village, this attractive, tile-
hung coaching inn has a warm and friendly
atmosphere. Winter fires in the inglenook
make the beamed lounge bar a particularly
cosy spot, and you can play pool in the simple
public bar. The four good-sized bedrooms,
each with private bathroom, offer colour TVs
and tea/coffee-making facilities. Excellent
breakfasts. Garden.

Lamberhurst   *(B & B)*

George & Dragon Inn

High Street · *Kent* · Map 6 C3
Lamberhurst (0892) 890277

Free House
Landlord Reg Godward
Children welcome
Credit Access
🍺 Charrington's IPA; Bass; Guinness;
Tennent's Lager; Carlsberg; cider.
ACCOMMODATION 4 bedrooms £C (No dogs)
Check-in: restricted

A garden running down to the river Teise is
an attractive feature of this friendly old black
and white inn on the A21. There's a pleasant
beamed bar and a recently completed games
room extension. Homely overnight accommodation is provided by four neat, simply
furnished bedrooms with candlewick bedspreads and tea-makers. Two have private
facilities (one bath, one shower) and TVs; the
others share a public bathroom.

Lancaster   *(B & B)*   *Farmers Arms Hotel*

Penny Street · *Lancashire* · Map 3 B2
Lancaster (0524) 36368

Brewery Thwaites
Landlord T. J. Baxter
Children welcome (lunchtime)
Credit Access, Visa
🍺 Thwaites Bitter, Mild; Guinness; Tuborg;
Carlsberg Hof.
ACCOMMODATION   14 bedrooms   £C
Check-in: all day

Today it's business travellers rather than
farmers who frequent this solidly built turn-
of-the-century hotel on a corner site not far
from the city centre. There's a spacious bar,
and upstairs on the second floor all the
attractively fitted bedrooms offer easy chairs,
colour TVs and tea-makers. The majority are
efficiently double-glazed and five have private modern bedrooms, the rest sharing
three public ones. Patio.

Lanchester   *(Food, B & B)*   *Kings Head*

Station Road · *Co. Durham* · Map 4 C1
Lanchester (0207) 520054

Brewery Scottish & Newcastle
Landlord Mr H. Bainbridge

Children welcome
Credit Access, Amex, Diners, Visa
🍺 Scottish & Newcastle Exhibition; McEwan's
Scotch; Harp; cider. *No real ale.*

A substantial stone-built pub on the edge of
the village green, opposite the parish church.
The interior is modernised, and in the bar
rough plaster walls and mock beams combine with darkwood furniture and plush
banquettes. There's a straightforward choice
of lunchtime bar food, the best things being
the roasts, the pies (steak and kidney with a
good meaty gravy, served with creamed
potatoes and mashed swede) and casserole-
style dishes such as moussaka. Salads and
sandwiches are available for lighter bites. A
traditional roast lunch is served in the restaurant on Sunday. *Typical prices:* Steak &
kidney pie £1.85   Roast of the day £2.20 (No
bar food eves or all Sun) ✆

ACCOMMODATION   5 bedrooms   £C
Check-in: all day

The bedrooms, compact without being
cramped, are neat, bright and cheerful, with
modern furnishings, tea-makers and large
colour TVs. Central heating keeps things
snug, and each room has a washbasin; there
are two spotlessly kept public bathrooms.
Accommodation closed 1 week Christmas.

Lancing   *(Food, B & B)*   *Sussex Pad*

Old Shoreham Road · *West Sussex* · Map 6 B4
Shoreham-by-Sea (0273) 454647

Free House
Landlord Mr Wally Pack

Children welcome
Credit Access, Amex, Diners, Visa

Wally Pack continues to make things go with
a swing at his substantial pebbledash pub on
the A27, within sight of Lancing College. Fish
is a notable feature of the snacks available in
his Edwardian-style bar, with fresh salmon,
locally caught crab, lobster and Atlantic
prawns all on the menu, along with soup,
sandwiches, attractive salads and hot dishes

Tetley's Bitter; Ind Coope John Bull; Guinness; Oranjeboom; Löwenbräu; cider. ♀

ACCOMMODATION 6 bedrooms £B
Check-in: all day

like spaghetti bolognese and shepherd's pie. The generous double deckers of cold meat and crisp salad make excellent light bites. *Typical prices:* Ham double decker sandwich £1.85 Crab salad £2.25 (Last bar food 10pm) ⊖

Spacious, comfortable bedrooms – all with carpeted bathrooms – have colour TVs, telephones, and tea-makers. Patio.

Langdale *(Food)*   *Pillar Hotel, Hobson's Pub*

Near Ambleside · *Cumbria* · Map 3 B2
Langdale (096 67) 302

Free House
Landlord Yvonne Lee

Children welcome
Hartley's Best Bitter, Mild; Theakston's Old Peculier; Marston's Merrie Monk; Guinness; Castlemaine 4X; cider.

Bar food spans a good choice at this modern pub, part of an impressive hotel and country club complex. Cumberland sausage with apple makes a tasty dish, and there's soup, open sandwiches, seafood platters and hot offerings like lamb goulash. Eat in the stone-floored bar or out on the terrace overlooking the waterfall. Live entertainment Saturday night. *Typical prices:* Cumberland sausage with apple £3.10 Game casserole £3.90 (Last bar food 9.30pm) ⊖

Langham *(Food)*   *Noel Arms*

Near Oakham · *Leicestershire* · Map 5 B1
Oakham (0572) 2931

Free House
Landlords Mr & Mrs A. M. Eacott

Children welcome
Credit Access, Amex, Diners, Visa
Ruddle's County Bitter, Best Bitter; Marston's Pedigree Bitter; Guinness; Stella Artois; Castlemaine 4X; cider. ♀

North of Oakham on the A606, this handsome converted farmhouse offers good food in friendly surroundings. Cold meats and salads make an eye-catching buffet, and other dishes, indicated on a blackboard, include pâté, grilled trout, steaks and specials like lasagne or an excellent turkey and ham fricassee. Also sandwiches, burgers, desserts. *Typical prices:* Steak & kidney pie £3.25 Ham, egg & chips £3.10 (Last bar food 10pm) ⊖

Langthwaite *(B & B)*   *C. B. Hotel*

Near Reeth · *North Yorkshire* · Map 4 C2
Richmond (0748) 84265

Free House
Landlords Mr & Mrs Gilbraithe & Mr & Mrs Dixon

Children welcome
Webster's Pennine Bitter, Yorkshire Bitter; Guinness; Carlsberg; Foster's; cider. ♀
ACCOMMODATION 8 bedrooms £D (No dogs)
Check-in: all day

A friendly welcome greets all who make it to this simple little 17th-century inn high up in picturesque Arkengarthdale, a mile from Langthwaite. The cheerful beamed bar with its barrel tables and the homely residents' lounge have a relaxing atmosphere, while the modest bedrooms – all of which are equipped with tea-makers – are bright and clean. One has its own bathroom and two have shower cubicles. Patio.

Lanreath *(B & B)*   *Punch Bowl Inn*

Near Looe · *Cornwall* · Map 9 B4
Lanreath (0503) 20218

Free House
Landlords Mr & Mrs Frith

Credit Access, Visa
🍺 Bass; Hicks Special; Worthington Best Bitter,
Dark; Toby Bitter; Guinness; cider.
ACCOMMODATION 17 bedrooms £C
Check-in: all day

Old-world charm and modern comforts blend
happily at this ancient hostelry with various
characterful bars and a residents' lounge
that overlooks the pretty garden. Bedrooms
vary from period rooms with four-posters to
modern style in the annexe. Most have
private facilities and all have TVs and tea-
makers. Friendly, welcoming staff. Accommodation closed end October to Easter.

Leafield *(Food)*   *Old George Inn*

Near Witney · *Oxfordshire* · Map 7 A1
Asthall Leigh (099 387) 288

Free House
Landlords Christine Seymour & Stephen
Duckworth

Children welcome
🍺 Marston's Pedigree; Hook Norton Best;
Glenny's Wychwood Best; Adnams Old Ale;
Guinness; Tennent's Pilsner; cider. ♀

Christine Seymour does the cooking at this
fine old village inn, using choice ingredients
for favourites like chunky terrine, lamb chops
and steaks. Chicken Maryland and moules
marinière are typical evening specials, and
puds could include peach melba and lemon
soufflé. Sandwiches and toasties for lighter
bites (restricted choice Mon & Tues lunch).
Typical prices: Tournedos rossini £6.75
Pork escalopes with cream & brandy £5.75
(Last bar food 9pm) 🍴

Ledbury *(Food, B & B)*   *Feathers Hotel*

High Street · *Hereford & Worcester* · Map 8 D2
Ledbury (0531) 2600

Brewery Mitchells & Butlers
Landlord Mr Michael Hester

Children welcome
Credit Access, Amex, Diners
🍺 Mitchells & Butlers Brew XI, Springfield Best
Bitter; Bass; Guinness; Carling Black Label;
cider. ♀

This splendid, half-timbered hotel in the
centre of the town was once famous as a
coaching inn; the original building dates back
to Elizabethan times, which explains the
heavy oak beams, panelling and open fireplaces. These are further enhanced by antique furniture and fine hanging tapestries.
Needless to say, the bar is brimming with
atmosphere and is a popular place for a drink
or excellent meal. The cold table has pride of
place and offers a selection of cold meats,
salads and a slimmer's special, together with
sweets. For those who prefer more hearty
fare, there are rich meat pies, warming soups,
club sandwiches and a fine cheeseboard.
Typical prices: Guinness pie £3.15 Quiche
£2.75 (No bar food eves or Sun) 🍴

ACCOMMODATION 11 bedrooms £A
Check-in: all day

Charming, large, old-fashioned bedrooms
have well-fitted en suite bathrooms, direct-
dial telephones, colour TVs, radio alarms and
tea-making facilities.

Ledbury   *(Food, B & B)*   *Verzons Country House Hotel*

Trumpet · *Hereford & Worcester* · Map 8 D2
Trumpet (053 183) 381

Free House
Landlords Carolyn & Edward Henson & Robin
Pollock

Children welcome
Credit Access, Amex, Diners, Visa
🍺 Marston's Burton Bitter, Premium Bitter;
Hook Norton Bitter; Guinness; Carlsberg; Stella
Artois; cider. ♀

ACCOMMODATION   7 bedrooms   £C
Check-in: all day

Three miles from Ledbury on the A438
Hereford road, this handsome Georgian
house set in ample grounds commands fine
views of the nearby Malvern Hills. Bar snacks
are simple but appetising, with a choice of
soup, pâté and ploughman's, various salads
and hot dishes such as pork chops normande, scampi, plaice and chips and a
favourite treacle tart. An open log fire,
exposed brickwork and lots of beams make
the bar an atmospheric setting for a quiet
drink or meal. *Typical prices:* French mustard
chicken £4   Pork chops normande £3.80
(Last bar food 9.30pm) ⊖

A splendid wooden staircase leads to the
seven centrally heated bedrooms, which all
provide comfortable seating, colour TVs and
tea-makers-cum-radios. Three rooms have
private facilities and there is a simple resident's lounge. Garden.

Ledbury   *(B & B)*   *Ye Olde Talbot Hotel*

New Street · *Hereford & Worcester* · Map 8 D2
Ledbury (0531) 2963

Free House
Landlords Mr & Mrs Morris

Children welcome
🍺 Ansells Bitter; Castlemaine; Ind Coope;
Guinness; Skol; cider.
ACCOMMODATION 6 bedrooms £C (No dogs)
Check-in: all day

The splendidly panelled dining room of this
fine half-timbered pub was once the setting
for a bloody Civil War struggle, and evidence
of the fight can still be seen. Today's visitors
can relax in one of the beamed bars or climb
the creaky staircase to the cosy TV lounge.
Low-beamed bedroom with sturdy furnishings share a public bathroom and shower
room. The accommodation is closed 5 days
over Christmas.

Ledsham   *(Food)*   *Tudor Rose*

Two Mills, South Wirral · *Cheshire* · Map 3 B3
051–339 2399

Brewery Higson
Landlord Mr F. Fairclough

Credit Access, Visa
🍺 Higson's Bitter, Special Bitter, Mild;
Guinness; Pilsner Lager; cider.

Built as a flying club in the 1930s, this smart
pub at the junction of the A540 and A550
does a tasty line in generously served bar
snacks. Hot favourites such as steak pie,
curry and chicken casserole always please,
while for a quick bite there are well-filled
baps, salads, omelettes and English
cheeses. Garden. *Typical prices:* Lasagne
£2.10   Chicken Kiev £2.30 (Last bar food
9.45pm) ⊖

Ledston — *White Horse*

A colourful little garden fronts this attractively modernised old stone pub, where Graham Bedford is an amiable host. The bar is a spotlessly kept room, where the brass plates and copper-topped tables gleam and a red carpet and open fires in winter add to the cosy atmosphere.

Main Street, Near Castleford · *West Yorkshire* · Map 4 C3
Castleford (0977) 553069   *Brewery* Whitbread   *Landlords* Graham & Mabel Bedford
Children welcome (lunchtime)
🍺 Whitbread Castle Eden Ale, Trophy, Light; Guinness; Heineken; Stella Artois; cider. ♀

Leek   *(B & B)* — *Three Horseshoes Inn*

Blackshaw Moor · *Staffordshire* · Map 4 C4
Blackshaw (053 834) 296

Free House
Landlord Mr W. R. Kirk
Children welcome
Credit Access, Amex, Diners, Visa
🍺 McEwan's Scotch, 80/-, Export, Lager; Guinness; cider.
ACCOMMODATION 7 bedrooms £D
Check-in: all day

In a beautiful setting on the A53 north of Leek, this spruce former farmhouse dates back some 300 years. Soft lighting makes the beamed lounge bar more intimate than the lively public bar. Cottagy-style bedrooms feature pine furniture and colour TVs, and those at the back have lovely moorland views. All but one have shower cabinets and there are two bathrooms. Garden. Accommodation closed 1 week at Christmas.

Leigh on Mendip — *Bell Inn*

There's a cosy welcoming feel about this attractive 17th-century inn, whose stone-walled bar is warmed by a wood-burning stove and lit by carriage lamps. Other features include black beams, brassware and ornamental plates, and the pub has its own skittle alley. Closed Monday lunchtime.

Near Bath · *Somerset* · Map 9 D3
Mells (0373) 812316   *Free House*   *Landlord* Mr S. Taylor
Children welcome   *Credit* Access, Visa
🍺 Bass; Wadworth's 6X; Worthington Best Bitter; Devenish Wessex Best Bitter; Guinness; Stella Artois; Carling Black Label; cider.

Leominster   *(Food, B & B)* — *Royal Oak Hotel*

South Street · *Hereford & Worcester* · Map 8 D1
Leominster (0568) 2610

Free House
Landlords Eden & Surrey families

Children welcome
Credit Access, Amex, Diners, Visa

This Georgian coaching house situated in the centre of the town has been extensively renovated and redecorated during the past year or two. While the cellar bar is ideal for a glass of wine or pint of real ale, it is the lounge bar where snacks are served. This warm and pleasant room with its original oak panelling and two open fires has a choice selection of bar snacks ranging from soup

Greenall's Bitter; John Smith's Yorkshire Bitter; Hook Norton Best Bitter; Wood's Parish Bitter; Guinness; Carling Black Label; cider. ♀

or pâté to omelettes or well-filled sandwiches to spit roast chicken, fried or grilled fish or farmhouse sausages. Sweets can be ordered from the trolley in the restaurant and include a very creamy trifle. *Typical prices:* Ploughman's from £2 Quiche £3.50 (Last bar food 9.30pm) ☺

ACCOMMODATION 18 bedrooms £C
Check-in: all day

Bedrooms are simply and traditionally furnished and all have bathrooms en suite, colour TVs, drinkmaster machines and electric blankets, radios and tea-makers.

Levington *(Food)*   *Ship*

Near Ipswich · *Suffolk* · Map 5 D2
Nacton (047 388) 573

Brewery Tollemache & Cobbold
Landlords Len & Jo Wenham

Tolly Cobbold Bitter, Original; Guinness; Hansa. ♀

Overlooking the Orwell estuary, this old thatched pub is rich in atmosphere. The beamed bar makes a cosy setting for some appetising lunchtime snacks – perhaps a roast beef or smoked mackerel salad, savoury pie or a nut roast. There's a good selection of English cheeses (the only Sunday choice), and enjoyable sweets like spicy lemon cake. Terrace. *Typical prices:* Steak & kidney pie with salad £2.95   Bread pudding £1.10 No bar food eves except occasionally. ☺

Ley Hill *(Food)*   *Swan Inn*

Near Chesham · *Buckinghamshire* · Map 7 C2
Chesham (0494) 783075

Brewery Benskins
Landlords Mr & Mrs Brian Williams

Benskins Bitter; Inde Coope Bitter; Burton Ale; Guinness; Skol; Löwenbräu; cider. ♀

Walk into the inviting bar of this attractive one-time hunting lodge and choose from a small selection of tasty snacks. Rolls, ploughman's and jacket potatoes are popular light bites, while more robust choices could include chilli or roast lamb, with a splendid Bakewell tart to finish. Garden. *Typical prices:* Steak pie £2.25   Smoked trout salad £2.40 (Last bar food 9pm. No bar food Sun eve. Limited choice Sun lunch) ☺

Lickfold *(Food)*   *Lickfold Inn*

Near Petworth · *West Sussex* · Map 6 B4
Lodsworth (079 85) 285
Free House
Landlords Roger Turner & Vivien Moyise
Children welcome
Credit Visa
Theakston's Old Peculier; Fuller's ESB, London Pride; Hall & Woodhouse Badger Best Bitter; Tangleroot; Eldridge Pope Royal Oak; Marston's Pedigree; Guinness; Fosters; Carlsberg; cider.

Built in 1460 of timber-frame construction, this friendly rural pub serves some reliably good snacks in its comfortable panelled bars warmed by lovely log fires. Traditional favourites such as salads and sandwiches, ploughman's and omelettes are supplemented by more elaborate daily specials like trout with tarragon and banoffee pie. Garden. *Typical prices:* Steak & kidney pie £3.25 Vegetable pie £2.95 (Last bar food 10pm. No bar food Mon eve) ☺

Lifton   *(Food, B & B)*   *Arundell Arms*

Devon · Map 9 B3
Lifton (0566) 84666

Free House
Landlord Anne Voss-Bark

Children welcome
Credit Access, Amex, Diners, Visa
🍺 Ushers County Bitter, Triple Crown,
Founders; Ben Truman; Guinness;
Carlsberg. ⚲

With 20 miles of water on the Tamar and
tributaries, Anne Voss-Bark's creeper-clad
hotel is a great favourite with fishermen. In
the pleasingly decorated Courthouse bar,
snacks comprise sandwiches and various
things with chips, available both sessions; in
the cocktail bar the lunchtime-only menu
offers rather more choice, including soup,
ploughman's, an attractive cold buffet and a
hot dish of the day like our excellent steak,
kidney and Guinness pie. Sweets such as
pineapple and kiwi fruit flan come with a little
dollop of clotted cream. Prime local produce
features on the restaurant menu. *Typical bar
prices:* Cold buffet £4.50   Chicken & pork
pâté £2.25 (Last bar food 9.30pm) ☕

ACCOMMODATION   29 bedrooms   £A
Check-in: all day

Comfortable, centrally heated bedrooms,
some in an annexe, have colour TVs, direct-
dial phones and, apart from two, private bath
or shower. The bars have considerable
period charm, and the lounge has been
handsomely refurbished in traditional style.
Amenities include game fishing, shooting, a
games room and skittle alley. Garden.

Limpley Stoke   *Hop Pole Inn*

Built of Bath stone many centuries ago, this characterful inn started life as
a monks' wine lodge. It takes its present name from the hop plant still
growing outside and reputedly planted in 1750. The two cosy bars are
reached through a handsome stone porch. Patio and garden.

Wood Hill, Near Bath · *Wiltshire* · Map 8 D3
Limpley Stoke (022 122) 3134   *Brewery* Courage   *Landlords* Mr & Mrs
G. C. Titcombe   **Children welcome**
🍺 Courage Bitter, Best Bitter, Directors; Guinness; Kronenbourg 1664;
Hofmeister; cider. ⚲

Lincoln   *(Food)*   *Wig & Mitre*

29 Steep Hill · *Lincolnshire* · Map 4 D4
Lincoln (0522) 35190

Brewery Samuel Smith
Landlords Valerie & Michael Hope

Children welcome
Credit Access, Amex, Diners, Visa
🍺 Samuel Smith's Old Brewery Bitter; Ayinger
Bräu; Pils. ⚲

Whatever your timetable the Hopes are
happy to feed you from 8am onwards at their
cosy pub-cum-wine bar in a medieval setting.
High-quality fare ranges from delicious
soups, pâtés, sandwiches and ploughman's
to vegetarian specialities, warming casseroles, macaroni cheese and chilli con carne,
with delectable puds. *Typical prices:* Leek &
tomato pie £3.25   Steak & mushroom pie
£2.95 (Last bar food 11pm) ☕

Linton   *(Food)*   *Windmill Inn*

Near Wetherby · *West Yorkshire* · Map 4 C3
Wetherby (0937) 62938

Brewery Younger
Landlords Mr & Mrs Toomey

Children welcome
🍺 Younger's Scotch Bitter, No. 3; McEwan's
Lager; Beck's Bier; cider.

An 18th-century farmhouse has been converted into this really super pub, with oodles
of rustic charm and a convivial bunch of
regulars. The bar snacks are a great draw,
being well prepared and full of interest:
creamed prawns and mushrooms, spicy
tomato soup, pasta, seafood pancakes,
steak Diane. Also sandwiches, ploughman's
and simple sweets. *Typical prices:* Chicken
strips in cream & mushroom sauce with rice
£3.85   Pâté £1.60 (Last bar food 10pm. No
bar food Sun & Mon eves) 🍽

Little Hadham   *(Food)*   *Nag's Head*

The Ford, Near Ware · *Hertfordshire* · Map 7 D1
Albury (027 974) 555

Brewery Rayment
Landlord Mr Michael Robinson

🍺 Greene King Abbot Ale; Rayment's BBA;
Guinness; Kronenbourg; cider. ♀

Market-fresh fish and marvellous sweets are
just two of the reasons for visiting this
smashing 16th-century village pub. Beneath
the blackened beams and hanging copper
kettles you can tuck into dishes like Dover
sole, grilled sardines and salmon mayonnaise, followed by seasonal fruit pie or
heavenly cheesecake. Book for the traditional   Sunday   lunch   roast.   *Typical
prices:* Hot dish of the day £1.60   Blackberry
cheesecake £1.25 (Last bar food 9.30 pm) 🍽

Little Langdale   *(Food, B & B)*   *Three Shires Inn*

Near Ambleside · *Cumbria* · Map 3 B2
Langdale (096 67) 215

Free House
Landlords Mr & Mrs Neil Stephenson

Children welcome
🍺 Webster's Yorkshire Bitter; Wilsons Original,
Special Mild; Guinness; Carlsberg; cider. *No real
ale.* ♀

Everything gleams at this immaculately kept
Lakeland pub, whose peaceful beer garden
with its own delightful stream is the perfect
place to appreciate the idyllic setting. Eat
here or by the fire in the slate-walled bar,
selecting from an interesting menu (more
choice at night) that includes substantial
dishes and Cumberland pie as well as soups,
sandwiches and salads. Tempting sweets,
too, and fine cheeses. *Typical prices:* Haddock bonne femme £3.95   Chocolate roulade £1 (Last bar food 8.30pm) 🍽

ACCOMMODATION 10 bedrooms £C (No dogs)
Check-in: all day

Pretty fabrics and modern white furniture
give bedrooms a light, airy appeal – enhanced
by the bonus of breathtaking views. One has
an excellent en suite shower, the rest share
three spotless bathrooms. There is a chintzy
TV lounge for residents' use. Accommodation closed Mon–Thurs Nov & Dec and the
month of Jan.

Little Walden *(Food)* *Crown Inn*

Saffron Walden · *Essex* · Map 7 D1
Saffron Walden (0799) 27175 *Free House Landlords* Chris & Gillian
Oliver *Credit* Access, Visa
🍺 Ruddle's County, Bitter; Courage Bitter, Directors; Adnams; Mauldon
Bitter; cider.

★ Dating from 1748, this delightful little white-panelled village pub has a ★
single cosily rustic bar where beer is drawn from the wood and the
atmosphere is warm and friendly. A positive feast of superbly fresh
seafood heads the enterprising menu, with choices like mussels poached
in garlic butter, local trout stuffed with prawns and mushrooms, grilled
Dover sole and beautifully dressed Cromer crab salad. Pâté and steaks
are also popular, while daily specials might include venison casserole,
game pie, oysters and sea bass. To finish, try homely damson crumble or
chocolate roulade. Garden. *Typical prices:* Stilton & curry soup £1.75
Seafood platter £8.50 (Last bar food 10pm. No bar food Sun) ℮

*We neither seek nor accept hospitality
and we pay for all food and drinks in full.*

Little Washbourne *(Food)* *Hobnails Inn*

Near Tewkesbury · *Gloucestershire* · Map 8 D2
Alderton (024 262) 237

Brewery Whitbread
Landlords Fletcher & Farbrother families

Children welcome
Credit Access, Visa
🍺 Whitbread IPA, Pale Ale, Best Bitter; Flowers
Original; Guinness; Heineken; Stella Artois;
cider. ♀

Speciality baps draw the crowds to this
popular roadside inn, built in 1474 as a manor
house. You can fill your fresh round roll with
anything from toasted cheese to steak and
onions or home-baked ham. Portions are
generous, but leave room for one of the
tempting desserts: perhaps Tyrolean chocolate gâteau or rum-laced mince tart. *Typical
prices:* Steak burger and mushroom bap
£1.65 French fruit flan £1.15 (Last bar food
10.30 pm) ℮

Liverpool *Philharmonic Dining Rooms*

High on everyone's list of Liverpool landmarks must be this late-Victorian
extravaganza. Ornate ceilings, rosewood panelling, stained and engraved
glass and intricate mosaics combine to splendid effect – even the fittings
in the gents are made of pink marble! Choose from three large bars and
two little snugs ('Brahms' and 'Liszt').

36 Hope Street · *Merseyside* · Map 3 B3
051–709 1163 *Brewery* Tetley Walker *Landlords* Mr & Mrs Smithwick
Children welcome (lunchtime)
🍺 Tetley's Bitter, Mild; Guinness; Skol; Castlemaine; cider.

Llanfair Waterdine   (Food, B & B)   Red Lion

Knighton · *Shropshire* · Map 8 C1
Knighton (0547) 528214

Free House
Landlords Jim & Joan Rhodes

🍺 John Smith's Yorkshire Bitter; Ansells PA;
Wrexham Lager; cider. *No real ale.* 🍷

In hilly border country on the banks of the river Teme, the Rhodes' welcoming pub makes a peaceful and relaxing place to stay. Local farmers like to congregate in the convivial little quarry-tiled public bar and there's a delightful lounge bar with blackened beams and a huge inglenook where appetising snacks are served. Flavoursome soups (perhaps creamy lettuce and cucumber or mushroom), home-made pâté and egg mayonnaise make tasty snacks or starters, while main courses range from juicy steaks to guinea fowl in red wine sauce and turkey stuffed with asparagus and ham. Joan Rhodes also does full meals by bookings at least 24 hours in advance. *Typical bar prices:* Steak & chips £5.50   Chicken & chips £1.90 (Last bar food 10pm) 🍴

ACCOMMODATION 3 bedrooms £C (No dogs)
Check-in: restricted

The sturdily furnished bedrooms have a cosy, cottage appeal, and all the beds have duvets. They share a neatly kept bathroom. No children under 15 overnight.

Long Compton   (B & B)   **New Entry**   Red Lion

Warwickshire · Map 7 A1
Long Compton (060 884) 221
Brewery Mitchells & Butlers
Landlord Mrs Sara McCall
Children welcome
Credit Access, Amex, Diners, Visa
🍺 Mitchells & Butlers Brew XI; Bass;
Worthington Bitter; Guinness; Carling Black Label; cider.
ACCOMMODATION   5 bedrooms   £C
Check-in: all day

Flagstoned floors, a low beamed ceiling and cheery open fires add to the charms of the long bar at this friendly pub on the busy A34 Oxford to Stratford road. Five cosy bedrooms with pretty floral wallpaper and attractive period-style furnishings provide comfortable overnight accommodation. All offer radio-alarms and magazines, and they share a bathroom and shower room. Housekeeping is excellent. Patio.

Long Hanborough   (Food)   Bell

Near Oxford · *Oxfordshire* · Map 7 B1
Freeland (0993) 881324

Brewery Morrell
Landlord Mr Graham Laer

🍺 Morrell's Varsity; Guinness; Harp;
Kronenbourg; cider. 🍷

A warm welcome and honest home cooking at old-fashioned prices await at this attractive stone pub. Berkshire broth, vegetarian pasty and a jumbo sausage in a wholemeal roll are typically tasty hot choices, and there's also dressed crab, ploughman's platters and smoked mackerel. Finish with a tempting sweet like hot treacle pudding or rum baba. Patio. *Typical prices:* Grilled red mullet 95p   Chicken & turkey pie £1.45 (No bar food eves) 🍴

Long Melford *(Food, B & B)* **New Entry** *Black Lion*

The Green · *Suffolk* · Map 5 C2
Sudbury (0787) 312356

Free House
Landlords Mr & Mrs L. J. Brady

Children welcome
Credit Access, Amex, Diners, Visa
🍺 Mauldon's Bitter; Nethergate Bitter;
Carlsberg. ⚥

ACCOMMODATION 8 bedrooms £B
Check-in: all day

Luke and Amelia Brady's attractively restored coaching inn has a smart bar featuring
fine old prints, and a pleasant walled garden
for summer use. The daily-changing bar
snacks menu is interesting if not extensive,
and often features some of the lighter dishes
from the restaurant's bill of fare. A typical
span could include salmon terrine (dainty but
delicious), bookmaker's sandwich and individual leek and bacon quiche. Bread and
butter pudding or prune posset among the
sweets. *Typical prices:* Soup £1 Poached
salmon £3.50 (Last bar food 10pm) ⊖

Bedrooms are not only spacious and attractive (soft pastel shades, nicely coordinated
fabrics, good-quality traditional furnishings)
but are also very well equipped, with extras
ranging from TVs and direct-dial phones to
flowers and pot-pourris. Bathrooms, too, are
excellent, and everything is splendidly maintained. The whole place is closed for 10 days
January/February.

Long Melford *(B & B)* *Crown Inn Hotel*

Hall Street, Near Sudbury · *Suffolk* · Map 5 C2
Sudbury (0787) 77666

Free House
Landlords M. J. Wright & A. A. F. Frampton
Children welcome
Credit Access, Amex, Diners, Visa
🍺 Adnams Bitter; Mauldon's Bitter, Special;
Greene King IPA; Guinness; cider.
ACCOMMODATION 13 bedrooms £C
Check-in: all day

Tudor cellars, oak beams, log fires and
antique furniture create an atmosphere of
traditional cosiness at this historic inn, especially in the comfortable little bars. Main
building bedrooms are full of character; those
in the converted stable block are modern and
functional, with fitted units. All have tea-
makers and colour TVs, and seven have
simple carpeted bathrooms. Garden.

Long Melford *(Food)* **New Entry** *Hare Inn*

High Street · *Suffolk* · Map 5 C2
Sudbury (0787) 310379

Brewery Greene King
Landlords John & Jill Pipe

Children welcome
Credit Access, Visa
🍺 Greene King Abbot Ale, IPA, Double X Dark;
Guinness; Kronenbourg 1664; cider.

The open fires and the friendly staff create an
atmosphere of warmth and cheer in this
traditional inn by the A134. The most interesting choice among the bar snacks is
provided by the blackboard specials: tomato,
leek and almond soup, moules marinière with
garlic bread, stir-fried chicken with bean
sprouts, peppers and rice. *Typical prices:*
Moules marinière with garlic bread £2.80
Game casserole £3.50 (Last bar food
10.30pm) ⊖

Longframlington   *(Food, B & B)*   *Granby Inn*

Near Morpeth · *Northumberland* · Map 2 D4
Longframlington (066 570) 228

Brewery Bass
Landlord Mr Gilbert Hall

Credit Access, Amex, Visa
🍺 Stones Bitter; Guinness; Worthington E;
Carling Black Label; cider. 🍷

ACCOMMODATION 6 bedrooms £C (No dogs)
Check-in: restricted

This former coaching inn, where you'll get a real Geordie welcome, makes a comfortable base for exploring Northumbria. The beamed bar with its gleaming brassware is usually packed with locals who are appreciative of the enjoyable bar snacks. Both sessions offer salads, sandwiches, grills, seafood and roasts, with the popular home-made steak and kidney pie available at lunchtime only. Pride of the cream and sundae sweets is the hot black cherries with Kirsch and cream. *Typical prices:* Steak & kidney pie £2.75   Cod & chips £2.75 (Last bar food 9.30pm) ☕

Accommodation is first class. Main house rooms are attractively traditional, while the three compact chalet rooms are neatly modern. All have TVs and tea-makers, and four have spotless bath/shower rooms. No children under five. Patio. Accommodation closed 24 December–1 January.

Children welcome *indicates a pub with an area where children are allowed whether eating or not.*

Longleat   *(Food, B & B)*   *Bath Arms*

Warminster · *Wiltshire* · Map 9 D3
Maiden Bradley (098 53) 308

Free House
Landlords Joe, Beryl & Paul Lovatt

Credit Access, Diners
🍺 Wadworth's 6X; Usher's Founder's Ale;
Bass; Eldridge Pope Dorchester Bitter;
Guinness; Holsten; Carlsberg Pilsner; cider.

ACCOMMODATION   6 bedrooms   £B
Check-in: all day

Tucked away in the heart of the Longleat estate, this mellow 18th-century priory house is a particular favourite with visitors to Longleat House. Fresh fish and seasonal game feature on the enterprising bar menu, and there are also curries and casseroles, quiches and kebabs, plus soups, sandwiches and an excellent home-made cheesecake among enjoyable desserts. Roaring fires in the three rustic bars aid the digestion wonderfully. *Typical prices:* Steak & kidney pie with vegetables £3.50   Lasagne and salad £2.95 (Last bar food 10pm) ☕

Good-sized bedrooms (some with lovely views of the estate) have a simple, cottage appeal with their sturdy freestanding furniture and candlewick bedspreads. All are equipped with TVs and tea-makers and five offer nicely kept private bathrooms. The peaceful lounge for residents' use is also to be found upstairs.

Longparish *(Food)* — *Plough Inn*

Near Andover · *Hampshire* · Map 6 A3
Longparish (026 472) 358   *Brewery* Whitbread   *Landlord* Mr Trevor
Colgate
Credit Access, Amex, Diners, Visa
🍺 Whitbread Best Bitter, Strong Country Bitter; Flowers Original;
Guinness; Heineken; cider. ♀

Wisteria outside and hops inside festoon this popular red-brick pub in a
picturesque little village about a mile from the A303. The rustic thatched
bar is matched by wholesome country fare such as hearty soup and a
range of ploughman's (excellent cheese, and their own succulent ham is
served with the most delicious apple chutney), which can be rounded off
★ with a chocolate roulade that just melts in the mouth. There are also ★
various tasty pâtés, smoked trout, prawns, and smoked salmon, and hot
dishes like grills, spicy venison sausages and fried fish can be ordered
from the restaurant menu. Sunday lunch is a roast. *Typical prices:* Ham
ploughman's £1.85   Venison sausages with egg £3.25 (Last bar food
10pm. No bar food Sun night)

Prices given are as at the time of our research
and thus may change.

Lowdham *(B & B)* — *Springfield Inn*

Old Epperstone Road · *Nottinghamshire*
Map 5 B1
Nottingham (0602) 663387
Free House
Landlords Gordon & Mavis Ferriman
Children welcome
Credit Access, Amex
🍺 Mansfield Bitter; Home Brewery Bitter, Mild;
Marston's Pedigree; Castlemaine; cider.
ACCOMMODATION 10 bedrooms £B
Check-in: all day

There's parking for helicopters – and excellent accommodation – at flying enthusiast
Gordon Ferriman's converted private house
in a picturesque country setting. Neat bedrooms, with cheerful decor, have compact
bath/shower rooms as well as colour TVs,
tea-makers, radio-alarms, and direct-dial
telephones. A parrot rules the roost in the
beamed bar, but if you're not feeling talkative
try the lounge bar. Well-kept gardens.

Lower Peover *(Food)* — *Bells of Peover*

Near Knutsford · *Cheshire* · Map 3 B4
Lower Peover (056 581) 2269

Brewery Greenall Whitley
Landlord Mr Goodier Fischer

Credit Diners
🍺 Greenall Whitley Local Bitter, Mild; Guinness;
Grünhalle; cider.

A monks hospice in the 13th century, this
ancient pub hides at the end of a cobbled
lane off the B5081. Persistence is rewarded
by excellent bar snacks enjoyed in the cosy
snug or lounge, or out by the stream on fine
days. Choose from generously filled sandwiches, salads and hot dishes like vegetable
soup, mussels and chunky meat pies. *Typical
prices:* Meat & potato pie £1.95   Fresh crab
salad £3 (No bar food eves or Sun)

Lower Woodford   *(Food)*   *Wheatsheaf*

Near Salisbury · *Wiltshire* · Map 6 A3
Middle Woodford (072 273) 203

Brewery Hall & Woodhouse
Landlord Peter Charlton

Children welcome
Credit Amex
🍺 Hall & Woodhouse Badger Best Bitter,
Tanglefoot; Guinness; Carlsberg Hof; Stella
Artois; cider. ♀

Families love this charming village pub, which
not only has a children's play area in the
garden but also offers a special menu, too.
Mum and Dad can tuck into home-made soup
or smoked mackerel pâté followed, perhaps,
by chicken curry, a steak or veal cordon bleu.
Lighter bites include salads, ploughman's
and filled jacket potatoes. *Typical prices:*
Lasagne verde £3.20   Ham, chips & salad
£3.75 (Last bar food 10pm) ⊖

Loweswater   *(B & B)*   *Kirkstile Inn*

Near Cockermouth · *Cumbria* · Map 3 B2
Lorton (090 085) 219
Free House
Landlord Mr Kenneth Gorley
Children welcome
Credit Access
🍺 Jennings Best Bitter; Younger's Scotch
Bitter, Tartan; Guinness; Ayinger Bräu Lager;
cider.
ACCOMMODATION   10 bedrooms   £C
Check-in: all day

The lakes and woods of Cumbria provide a
stunning setting for this agreeable 16th-
century inn, which has the village church as
a neighbour. Beams, wooden settles and a
hearth hewn from local stone give character
to the bars, and overnight guests will find
adequate if unremarkable comforts in the
functionally appointed bedrooms. Many
rooms enjoy lovely views, and all but two
have private bathrooms.

Lowick Green   *(Food, B & B)*   *Farmer's Arms*

Near Ulverston · *Cumbria* · Map 3 B2
Greenodd (022 986) 376

Brewery Younger
Landlord Mr Philip Broadley

Children welcome
Credit Access, Amex, Visa
🍺 Younger's No. 3, Scotch Bitter; McEwan's
80/-; Guinness; Harp; Beck's Bier; cider. ♀

A very pleasant old inn, built about the middle
of the 14th century, and originally a farmhouse that brewed its own beer. The bars
have a good deal of character, comprising a
warren of different rooms, nooks and crannies on several levels. The choice of bar
snacks is fairly standard, consisting mainly
of things like sandwiches (good ham),
smoked mackerel, pâté and steak and kidney
pie. Sweets could include lemon torte, fruit
pie and sherry trifle. There's an agreeable
patio for outdoor eating. *Typical prices:*
Cheese & onion pie £2   Cold roast Cumberland ham £2.55 (Last bar food 10pm) ⊖

ACCOMMODATION   11 bedrooms   £C
Check-in: all day

The bedrooms, all clean and well cared for,
provide adequate comforts for a short stay.
Furnishings are simple and traditional in
style, and seven rooms have functional
private facilities. There are televisions in all
rooms, and also a set in the comfortable
residents' lounge.

Ludlow   *(Food, B & B)*   Angel Hotel

8 Broad Street · *Shropshire* · Map 8 D1
Ludlow (0584) 2581

Free House
Landlord Mr D. Edwards

Children welcome
Credit Access, Amex, Diners, Visa
🍺 Flowers Original, IPA; Whitbread Best Bitter;
Guinness; Stella Artois; Heineken; cider.

ACCOMMODATION   17 bedrooms   £A
Check-in: all day

The handsome bow windows of this old half-timbered inn overlook a street of renowned elegance. Nelson may well have raised his elbow in the large, relaxing bar, where simple bar snacks are readily available. Soups, jacket potatoes and sandwiches are buttressed by specials like spaghetti bolognese and ham in parsley sauce, with puds from the restaurant menu. *Typical bar prices:* Jacket potato with cheese £1.30   Steak & kidney pie £3 (Last bar food 9.30 pm) ☺

Traditional furnishings combine with smart modern decor in the beautifully warm bedrooms, all of which have colour TVs, hairdryers, tea-makers, and carpeted bathrooms with a goodly supply of towels.

Our inspectors never book in the name of Egon Ronay's Guides;
they disclose their identity only after paying their bills.

Lurgashall   *(Food)*   Noah's Ark

The Green, Near Petworth · *West Sussex*
Map 6 B4
Northchapel (042 878) 346

Brewery Friary Meux
Landlord Mr Barton Edward Swannell

Children welcome
Credit Diners
🍺 Friary Meux Best Bitter; Burton Ale; John Bull
Bitter; Löwenbräu; cider. ♀

In a peaceful setting overlooking the village green, this attractive old pub is relaxed, civilised and sparkling clean. Ted Swannell has a welcome for one and all, and his wife prepares tasty, conventional bar snacks, from sandwiches and soup to fresh salads, lasagne and chicken Kiev, plus a few simple sweets. *Typical prices:* Steak & kidney pudding £2.20   Moussaka £2.20 (Last bar food 10pm. No bar food Sun) ☺

Lyddington   *(B & B)*   Marquess of Exeter

Near Uppingham · *Leicestershire* · Map 5 B1
Uppingham (0572) 822477

Free House
Landlords Evitt family
Children welcome
Credit Access, Amex, Diners, Visa
🍺 Ruddle's County, Bitter; Adnams Bitter;
Guinness; Stella Artois; cider. ♀
ACCOMMODATION   17 bedrooms   £B
Check-in: all day

Olde-worlde charm is still much in evidence at this 16th-century thatched coaching inn, which has been sympathetically modernised. Inglenook fireplaces and a fine collection of ornaments emphasise the traditional character of the beamed bars. The spacious bedrooms – all in a modern annexe – have quality furniture and furnishings, with colour TVs, direct-dial telephones, tea-makers, and excellent bathrooms. Terrace.

Lydford *(Food, B & B)*   *Castle Inn*

Near Okehampton · Devon · Map 9 B4
Lydford (082 282) 242

Free House
Landlords David & Susan Grey

Children welcome
🍺 Usher's Best Bitter, Founder's Ale, Triple
Crown; Webster's Yorkshire Bitter; Guinness;
Carlsberg. ♀

A secluded village setting for this most
attractive pink-coloured pub. The bars have
enormous character with their high-backed
settles, roaring log fires, the walls lined with
prints, daguerreotypes and decorative
plates; note, too, the charming little snug
where children may sit. Grills and basket
meals are the staples on the menu, and the
regularly appearing steak and kidney pie with
suet crust is a sure winner. Daily specials
could include leek and potato soup, cheese-
topped shepherd's pie and a rich, gooey
treacle tart. In summer a lunchtime cold table
offers further choice. *Typical prices:* Steak &
kidney pie £2.75 Beef curry £2.95 (Last bar
food 9pm) ☺

ACCOMMODATION 7 bedrooms £C
Check-in: all day

Four of the bedrooms have fine old beds and
solid period furnishings, with decent reproduction pieces for the others. All rooms are
of a good size, warm and well maintained.
Above average breakfast. Garden.

Lyndhurst *(Food)* **New Entry**   *Waterloo Arms*

Pikes Hill · Hampshire · Map 6 A4
Lyndhurst (042 128) 3333

Brewery Whitbread
Landlords Nick & Sue Wateridge

🍺 Whitbread Best, Strong Country; Flowers
Original; Guest Beer; Guinness; Stella Artois;
cider.

Much of this 300-year-old pub's character
comes from an extraordinary collection of
antiques that includes guns, boomerangs,
fishing rods and stuffed crocodiles. Lunchtime (Mon–Sat) brings hearty soup and tasty
hot dishes like liver and bacon casserole,
plus ploughman's, toasties and jacket potatoes. Just steaks evenings and Sunday lunch.
Typical prices: Sirloin steak £4.50 Liver &
bacon casserole £1.95 (Last bar food 9pm.
No bar food Sun eve) ☺

Lyonshall *(B & B)*   *Royal George Inn*

Near Kington · Hereford & Worcester · Map 8 D1
Lyonshall (05448) 210

Brewery Whitbread
Landlords Elaine & John Allen

Children welcome
🍺 Flowers Best, Original, IPA; Whitbread Best
Bitter; Guinness; Heineken; cider. ♀
ACCOMMODATION 3 bedrooms £D
Check-in: restricted

This charming black and white inn dating
from the 16th century takes its name from
the sailing ship whose timbers were used in
its construction. It's something of a centre
for gliding enthusiasts, and photographs in
the rustic bars highlight the sporting theme.
There are some attractive period pieces
among the assortment of furniture in the
bedrooms, which have TVs and tea-makers
and share a very basic bathroom and shower
room. Garden.

Madingley *(Food)* — *Three Horseshoes*

Cambridgeshire · Map 5 C2
Madingley (0954) 210221

Free House
Landlord Dominic Rowsell

Children welcome
Credit Access, Amex, Diners, Visa
🍺 Tolly Cobbold Original, Bitter; Hansa Lager; cider.

Whitewashed walls and a thatched roof give this village inn an attractive and very traditional appearance, and the bar is a comfortable spot for a snack. The interesting menu features a good selection of seafood – oysters, Cromer crab, flounder, Dover sole – and meat dishes include steak and kidney pie and succulent, spicy beefburgers. Also baguette sandwiches. *Typical prices:* Grilled red gurnet £3.95 Half-pound beefburger £3.65 (Last bar food 10pm)

Our inspectors never book in the name of Egon Ronay's Guides; they disclose their identity only after paying their bills.

Maidensgrove *(Food)* — *Five Horseshoes*

Near Henley-on-Thames · Oxfordshire · Map 7 B2
Nettlebed (0491) 641282 *Brewery* Brakspear *Landlords* Graham & Mary Cromack
🍺 Brakspear's Ordinary Bitter, Special Bitter; Guinness; Heineken; cider. ♀

★ New landlords Graham and Mary Cromack are maintaining high culinary standards at this friendly pub, which stands in lovely Oxfordshire countryside near Henley. The appetising choice includes Stilton soup, deep-fried mushrooms and a range of five pâtés for starters, and main dishes like sweet and sour pork, grilled prawns or the speciality fillet steak, sliced and served with a sauce of cream, mustard and brandy. Pancakes, ploughman's and baked potatoes make tasty quick snacks, and things like cherry flan and nutty treacle tart will delight pudding fanciers. The food selection is limited Saturday and Sunday lunchtimes and all day Monday. There are two characterful bars and an attractive garden. *Typical prices:* Lamb fricassee £3.50 Avocado pâté £2.30 (Last bar food 10pm. No bar food Sun Eve) ★

Malham *(B & B)* — *Buck Inn*

Near Skipton · North Yorkshire · Map 4 C2
Airton (072 93) 317

Free House
Landlord Mrs R. M. Robinson
Children welcome
🍺 Theakston's Bitter, XB, Old Peculier; Younger's Scotch Bitter; Guinness; Kestrel; cider. ♀
ACCOMMODATION 4 bedrooms £C
Check-in: all day

Walkers and tourists in the lovely Yorkshire Dales find this sturdy stone inn a good place to pause, whether for a refreshing drink or an overnight stay. Day rooms include a delightful main bar with a real feel of the area, a busy walkers' bar and a TV lounge. Some handsome pieces of period furniture may be found in the bedrooms, four of which have private bath or shower.

Malmesbury *(Food)*

Suffolk Arms

Tetbury Hill · *Wiltshire* · Map 8 D2
Malmesbury (066 62) 2271

Free House
Landlords John & Julia Evans

Credit Access, Amex, Diners, Visa
Wadworth's 6X, IPA, Farmer's Glory, Old
Timer (winter only); Guinness; Stella Artois;
Heineken; cider.

Wholesome home cooking is on the menu at
this handsome, ivy-covered inn on the Tetbury road. In the appealing lounge bar – even
supplied with magazines – the Evanses serve
their tasty fare, which ranges from thick
soups and local sausages to cottage pie and
hot, spicy chicken. Salads, sandwiches, and
jacket potatoes, too. Children are welcome
in the restaurant. Garden. *Typical prices:*
Smoked salmon salad £4   Steak & kidney
pie £2.25 (Last bar food 10pm)

Malton *(Food, B & B)*

Green Man Hotel

Market Street · *North Yorkshire* · Map 4 D2
Malton (0653) 2662

Free House
Landlords John & Liz Barwick

Children welcome
Credit Access, Amex, Visa
Cameron's Lion Bitter, Russel & Wranghams;
Guinness; Hansa; cider.

The staff seem particularly friendly and
helpful at this town-centre hostelry, where
both food and accommodation are thoroughly recommendable. Lunchtime in the
comfortable main bar brings a popular buffet
of cold meats, quiches and salads; there's
also a daily roast and a variety of other
dishes, from Yorkshire pudding with onion
gravy to filled jacket potatoes, grilled gammon and fried Whitby fish. Sandwiches
provide lighter bites, and home-made sweets
include a nice jam sponge. It's sandwiches
only in the evening except on Friday and
Saturday, when hot meals (steak, roast
chicken, curry) are also available. *Typical
prices:* Yorkshire pudding with onion gravy
80p   Steak & kidney pie £2.65 (Last bar food
10pm)

ACCOMMODATION   25 bedrooms   £C
Check-in: all day

Bedrooms are modestly fitted (candlewick
bedspreads, simple wooden bedheads). Several have recently been redecorated, and all
are kept in apple-pie order. Colour TVs and
tea-makers are standard, and most rooms
have their own shower or bathroom.

Manaccan *(Food)*

New Inn

Near Helston · *Cornwall* · Map 9 A4
Manaccan (032 623) 323

Brewery Cornish Brewery Company
Landlord Mr Patrick Cullinan

Children welcome
Devenish Cornish Original, John Devenish;
Guinness; Grünhalle; Stella Artois.

The very model of a country pub, with
thatched roof, low beams and simple pine
furnishings. A constantly changing blackboard menu offers a splendid variety of tasty
home-prepared food, from soup and sandwiches to crab salad, lamb chop à la grecque
and gooseberry crumble. More main dishes,
particularly fish, in the evening. Garden.
Typical prices: Seafood lasagne £4   Crab
sandwich £1.50 (Last bar food 9.30pm. No
bar food Tues eve in winter)

Manchester   *(Food)*   *Sinclairs*

Shambles Square · *Greater Manchester*
Map 3 B3
061-834 0430

Brewery Samuel Smith
Landlords Mr & Mrs Mitchell

Credit Access, Amex, Visa
🍺 Samuel Smith's Old Brewery Bitter, 4X, Mild;
Ayinger Bräu.

The low-beamed bars of this restored old pub provide a cosy setting for the Mitchells' appetising bar snacks. The lunchtime menu includes favourites like beef and oyster pie, home-made quiche and a seafood platter, as well as salads. From 5.30 choose from jacket potatoes and hot dishes like lasagne, moussaka or chilli with French bread. *Typical prices:* Beef & oyster pie £3.25 Quiche £2.25 (Last bar food 8pm. No bar food Sat & Sun eves) ☺

Marhamchurch   *(B & B)*   *Bullers Arms*

Near Bude · *Cornwall* · Map 9 B3
Widemouth Bay (028 885) 277

Free House
Landlords Bill & Liz Kneebone
Children welcome
Credit Access, Visa
🍺 St Austell HSD; Whitbread Best Bitter;
Cornish Original; Guinness; Grünhalle; cider.
ACCOMMODATION 7 bedrooms £D
Check-in: all day

Bill and Liz Kneebone offer excellent accommodation at their whitewashed pub in a peaceful village setting just two miles from the coast. Spacious bedrooms are furnished in simple modern style and all offer colour TVs and private bathrooms. Five have their own lounge areas and kitchens. The rustic beamed Hunter's Bar with its cheerful winter fire is the favourite spot for a convivial drink. Patio and garden.

Market Drayton   *(B & B)*   *Corbet Arms Hotel*

High Street · *Shropshire* · Map 3 B4
Market Drayton (0630) 2037

Free House
Landlord Mr J. Beckett
Children welcome
Credit Access, Amex, Diners, Visa
🍺 Springfield Bitter; Guinness; Tennent's
Pilsner, Extra; cider. ♀
ACCOMMODATION 12 bedrooms £C
Check-in: all day

Cheerful locals throng the bars of this town-centre coaching inn with a splendid bowling inn, but less sociable residents can take refuge in a quiet lounge. Spacious bedrooms – all but two with private facilities – have comfortable modern furnishings, colour TVs and direct-dial phones. Room 7 offers enterprising bachelors the spectral attentions of an amorous ghost.

Market Weighton   *(B & B)*   *Londesborough Arms*

High Road · *Humberside* · Map 4 D3
Market Weighton (0696) 72219

Brewery Camerons
Landlord Mr David Cuckston
Children welcome
Credit Access, Amex, Diners, Visa
🍺 Cameron's Lion Bitter, Strongarm; Everards
Traditional Bitter; Hansa, Export.
ACCOMMODATION 14 bedrooms £C
Check-in: all day

A handsome Georgian hotel providing good comfort for an overnight stay. Each bedroom is attractively done out in a different colour with white fitted furniture blending well. All rooms have TVs, telephones and compact bathrooms. A celebrated local giant of the 18th-century is commemorated in the Bradley's Bar, and you can still see his enormous chair. There's a second, plusher bar.

Marlborough   *(Food, B & B)*   **New Entry**   *Sun Inn*

High Street · *Wiltshire* · Map 7 A2
Marlborough (0672) 52081

Brewery Usher
Landlords Mr & Mrs Giles & Mr Culver

Children welcome
🍺 Usher's Best, Founders Ale, Country Bitter;
Guinness; Carlsberg; Holsten.

Notable as a survivor of the Great Fire of
1653, this whitewashed inn is today building
quite a hot reputation for food. Favourites on
the regular menu include open and toasted
sandwiches, herby sausages with Cumberland sauce and tagliatelle alla carbonara for
snacks; and main courses like Barnsley lamb
chop or the simple but delicious breast of
chicken baked with avocado and garlic.
Blackboard specials could be anything from
local trout with boulangère potatoes to beef
in ale and a morish banana fudge pie. *Typical
prices:* Breast of chicken with avocado £4.50
Baked bananas with rum & cream £1.75 (Last
bar food 9.30pm) ☺

ACCOMMODATION 7 bedrooms   £D
Check-in: all day

Narrow stairs wind up to five cottage bedrooms with washbasins, TVs and tea-makers. There are two larger rooms in the
converted coach house, and all share two
well-equipped modern bathrooms and a
shower room. Good breakfasts. Friendly
hosts. Patio and garden.

Marshside   *(Food)*   *Gate Inn*

Near Canterbury · *Kent* · Map 6 D3
Chislet (022 786) 498

Brewery Shepherd Neame
Landlord Christopher John Smith

Children welcome
🍺 Shepherd Neame Invicta Best Bitter,
Masterbrew, Mild, 6X; cider. ♀

Christopher Smith runs this smashing village
local with great enthusiasm, offering no-
nonsense food in a quarry-tiled bar lined with
photos of the Marshside cricket team. Tuck
into man-sized sandwiches filled with black
pudding, bacon, even a home-made burger.
Supplemented by lots of ploughman's and
salads in summer and winter soups. *Typical
prices:* Black pudding ploughman's £1.40
Burgers from 85p (Last bar food 10pm) ☺

Mattingley   *(Food)*   **New Entry**   *Leather Bottle*

Near Basingstoke · *Hampshire* · Map 7 B2
Heckfield (073 583) 371

Brewery Courage
Landlord Richard Moore

Credit Access, Amex, Diners, Visa
🍺 Courage Best, Directors; John Smith's;
Guinness; Hofmeister; Kronenbourg; cider.

Quite an attractive old pub, partly creeper
clad, and with a pretty little garden. Inside it's
warm and comfortable, a good spot in which
to enjoy a sandwich, a salad or something
more serious like ham, egg and chips,
chicken curry or a steak. Spicy sausages are
a popular choice, and there are pleasant
sweets. *Typical prices:* Chicken curry £3.60
Ploughman's with beef, ham, sausage &
cheese £3 (Last bar food 10.15pm) ☺

Mayfield *(Food)*

Rose & Crown

Fletching Street · *East Sussex* · Map 6 C4
Mayfield (0435) 872200

Free House
Landlords Richard & Claudette Leet

Children welcome
🍺 Everard's Tiger; Adnams Best Bitter;
Guinness; Faust; Tennent's Lager; cider. ♀

Log fires and beamed ceilings contribute to
the convivial atmosphere generated by landlord Richard Leet at this charming white-
painted pub. His wife Claudette supplies
delicious bar snacks – nourishing soups and
seafood pancakes, juicy steaks and chicken
mayonnaise, vegetarian specials and rich
puddings like peach and Drambuie cream
slice. *Typical prices:* Seafood pancakes
£2.50 Avocado & prawn aïoli £2.20 (Last
bar food 9.45pm) ☺

Mellor *(B & B)*

Millstone Hotel

Church Lane, Near Blackburn · *Lancashire*
Map 3 B3
Mellor (025 481) 3333
Owner Shire Inns
Landlords Mr & Mrs John Langford
Children welcome
Credit Access, Amex, Diners, Visa
🍺 Thwaites Bitter, Mild; Guinness; Tuborg;
Carlsberg Hof. ♀
ACCOMMODATION   16 bedrooms   £A
Check-in: all day

Conveniently placed for junction 31 of the
M6, this modernised stone inn is popular with
both business people and holiday makers.
Comfortable overnight accommodation is
provided in handsomely furnished bedrooms
equipped with TVs, tea-makers, radio-alarms
and trouser presses; all have fully tiled bath
or shower rooms maintained to the same
high standard. The bar is a relaxing room.

Melmerby *(Food)*

Shepherds Inn

Near Penrith · *Cumbria* · Map 3 B1
Langwathby (076 881) 217

Brewery Marston
Landlords Martin & Christine Baucutt

Credit Access
🍺 Marston's Pedigree; Ind Coope Burton Ale;
Merrie Monk, Mild; Old Roger Draught Barley
Wine; Marston's Pilsner; cider. ♀

Very good snacks are served in the cheerful
open-plan bar of this well-kept village pub.
Daily specials like barbecued spare ribs or
delicious ham and mushroom pie are a
popular choice, supplementing soups, filled
rolls, home-made pastries and good fresh
salads. Nice puds and an excellent cheeseboard including Wensleydale, smoked Cumberland and Yorkshire goat's cheese. *Typical
prices:* Spare ribs £3.60 Cumberland sausage hot pot £3 (Last bar food 9.45pm) ☺

Mere *(B & B)*

Old Ship Hotel

Castle Street · *Wiltshire* · Map 9 D3
Mere (0747) 860258
Brewery Hall & Woodhouse
Landlord Mr Philip Johnson
Children welcome
Credit Access, Visa
🍺 Hall & Woodhouse Badger Best Bitter, Export
Bitter; Worthington Dark; Guinness; Brock;
Carlsberg Hof; cider. ♀
ACCOMMODATION   24 bedrooms   £B
Check-in: all day

Log fires make things really snug at this
sturdy 17th-century coaching inn near the
town centre. The bars offer panelled walls,
beamed ceilings and log fires in winter, or
residents can sample the charm of the cosy
traditional lounge. The ten annexe bedrooms
have practical units and modern bathrooms,
while those in the main building have old-
fashioned furnishings (one boasts a four-
poster) and are being given much-needed
redecoration. All have tea-makers and TVs.

Metal Bridge (B & B)   *Metal Bridge Inn*

Near Gretna · *Cumbria* · Map 3 B1
Rockcliffe (022 874) 206

Brewery Younger
Landlord Mr D. O'Brien
Children welcome
Credit Access, Amex, Visa
🍺 Younger's Export, Tartan, IPA, Scotch Bitter;
McEwan's Export; Harp.
ACCOMMODATION 5 bedrooms £C
Check-in: restricted

This pleasant pub alongside the A74 makes a useful overnight stopping place for motorists travelling between England and Scotland. Four out of the five roomy, attractively furnished bedrooms have private facilities, and colour TVs and tea-makers are common to all. There is one well-kept public bathroom. Visitors can enjoy a drink in the split-level bar whose cane-furnished conservatory overlooks the river Esk.

Metherell (B & B)   *Carpenters Arms*

Near Callington · *Cornwall* · Map 9 B4
Liskeard (0579) 50242

Free House
Landlords Douglas & Jill Brace

Children welcome
🍺 Worthington Best; Bass; Wadworth's 6X; Ben Truman; Guinness; cider. ♀
ACCOMMODATION 3 bedrooms £D
Check-in: restricted

Look just south of the A390 Gunnislake – Liskeard road for this delightfully unspoilt old inn. The interconnecting bars offer the charm of rough stone walls and a wealth of black beams in contrast to the three neat bedrooms in a modern extension. Simply furnished, with cheerful decor and tea-makers, they share a spacious carpeted shower room. Terrace.

Middleham (B & B)   *Black Swan*

Market Place · *North Yorkshire* · Map 4 C2
Wensleydale (0969) 22221

Free House
Landlords Kenneth & Margaret Burton
Children welcome
🍺 Theakston's Best Bitter, Old Peculier; John Smith's Bitter, Lager; Guinness; Carlsberg; cider.
ACCOMMODATION 7 bedrooms £C
Check-in: all day

Middleham is a long-established centre of racehorse training, so the pictures and paraphernalia in the bar of this 17th-century inn are appropriately horsy. The bar itself is full of country charm, and summer sipping can be enjoyed in a pleasant garden. Bedrooms are very neat and tidy; four have original beams, and furnishings vary from traditional to modern. Private facilities throughout. No under-fives overnight.

Middleton Stoney (B & B)   *Jersey Arms*

Near Bicester · *Oxfordshire* · Map 7 B1
Middleton Stoney (086 989) 234

Free House
Landlords Don & Helen Livingstone

Children welcome
Credit Access, Amex, Diners, Visa
🍺 Courage Best Bitter, Directors. ♀
ACCOMMODATION 14 bedrooms £B (No dogs)
Check-in: all day

Overnight accommodation is a strong point at this 16th-century Cotswold-stone inn, which stands at the junction of the A43 and B4030. Bedrooms are very comfortable, with en suite bathrooms, direct-dial telephones and colour TVs; some have been smartly refurnished in pine. Four spacious suites in the courtyard boast stained-glass windows and heavy oak doors. There's a delightful beamed bar and an elegant lounge. Good breakfasts. Garden.

Midhurst (B & B)   *Angel Hotel*

North Street · *West Sussex* · Map 6 B4
Midhurst (073 081) 2421

Owner Lyons Catering Ltd
Landlord Mr N. Gibson
Children welcome
Credit Access, Amex, Diners, Visa
🍺 Gale's HSB, BBB; Guinness; Carlsberg;
cider.
ACCOMMODATION   17 bedrooms   £B
Check-in: all day

The rose garden is a really charming feature
of this former coaching inn. Bedrooms have
seen major improvements, and about half
boast smart pine furnishings; a few larger
rooms have handsome antiques. Colour TVs
and direct-dial phones are standard, and all
rooms except one have en suite facilities.
There are two fine beamed bars and a
comfortable residents' lounge. Staff are exceptionally friendly and efficient. Nice breakfasts are a plus.

Mildenhall (B & B)   *Bell Hotel*

High Street · *Suffolk* · Map 5 C2
Mildenhall (0638) 717272
Free House
Landlords Carolyn & John Child
Children welcome
Credit Access, Amex, Diners, Visa
🍺 Younger's Scotch Bitter; Greene King Abbot;
Adnams Bitter; Webster's Yorkshire Bitter;
Guinness; Carlsberg; cider. ⌇
ACCOMMODATION   13 bedrooms   £B
Check-in: all day

Black beams and cottage furniture in the
reception-lounge greet newcomers to this
busy town-centre inn that has retained much
of its coaching inn character. The spacious
L-shaped bar is in traditional style, while well-
appointed bedrooms are bright and pretty,
with TVs, tea-makers and direct-dial telephones. Most have modern carpeted bathrooms. Patio.

Milton Abbas   (Food, B & B)   *Hambro Arms*

Near Blandford Forum · *Dorset* · Map 9 D3
Milton Abbas (0258) 880233

Brewery Devenish
Landlord Mr Ken Baines

Children welcome
Credit Diners, Visa
🍺 John Devenish Bitter, Devenish Wessex
Stud; Guinness; Holsten Export; Carlsberg
Pilsner; cider.

Built around 1780, this fine thatched pub
stands at the top of an exceptionally pretty
Dorset village. The bar snacks stay in good
form under new landlord Ken Baines, and a
blackboard declares the day's choice. Sandwiches, ploughman's and slices of quiche
provide good light bites, and main courses
run from lasagne and lamb cutlets to sautéed
chicken and a very enjoyable pork curry with
rice and poppadoms. Traditional puds include apple pie and baked jam roll with
custard, and a popular Sunday extra is the
roast beef lunch served in the restaurant
(book for this). *Typical prices:* Steak &
mushroom pie £3.95   Lasagne £2.95 (Last
bar food 9.30pm) ⊖

ACCOMMODATION 2 bedrooms £C (No dogs)
Check-in: all day

There are but two bedrooms, both with plenty
of space and plenty of character: one has a
four-poster, the other a handsome period
wardrobe and Victorian spoonback chairs.
Comfortable, smartly kept and well heated,
they have little shower cubicles in the corner.

Milton Combe   (Food)

Near Yelverton · *Devon* · Map 9 B4
Yelverton (0822) 853313

Free House
Landlords Gary Rager & Keith Yeo

🍺 Wadworth's 6X; Flowers Best; Golden Hill
Exmoor Ale; Eldridge Pope Royal Oak; Foster's;
Heineken; cider. ⓨ

Who'd Have Thought It

The good bar food brings customers from
miles around to this unpretentious pebbledash pub. Almost all the snacks are home-
produced, and the list is quite extensive, from
chunky sandwiches and cold platters to
basket meals (super chips), steaks and
specials like sweet and sour pork or meaty
pies. Apple and blackberry crumble's a nice
pud. *Typical prices:* Steak & kidney pie
£3.15 Cornish pasty 60p (Last bar food
9.45pm) ⊖

*Our inspectors are our
full-time employees; they
are professionally trained
by us.*

Minster Lovell   (Food, B & B)

Near Witney · *Oxfordshire* · Map 7 A1
Minster Lovell (0993) 75614

Brewery Hall's
Landlords Mr & Mrs Tim Turner

Children welcome
Credit Access, Amex, Diners, Visa
🍺 Hall's Harvest Bitter; Ind Coope Burton Ale;
Löwenbräu; cider. ⓨ

ACCOMMODATION   10 bedrooms   £A
Check-in: all day

Old Swan Hotel

Cotswold stone and half-timbering blend
happily in this 600-year-old creeper-covered
inn with plenty of period charm. The flagstoned bars, warmed by log fires, make a
relaxing setting in which to enjoy tasty
lunchtime snacks. The choice includes soup,
sandwiches, kipper pâté, fish pie and a platter
of smoked sausages. *Typical prices:* Sausage ploughman's £2   Hot smoked chicken
legs with salad £2.25 (No bar food eves or
Sun) ⊖

Modern comforts are much in evidence in the
smartly furnished bedrooms, which have
everything from direct-dial phones and remote-control TVs to hairdryers, trouser
presses and tea-makers. All have excellent
bathrooms with thoughtful extras. One room
has elaborate carved furniture including a
splendid four-poster. There is a choice of
several comfortable lounges. Garden. No
children under 12 overnight.

Molesworth *(B & B)*   *Cross Keys*

Near Huntingdon · *Cambridgeshire* · Map 5 B2
Bythorn (080 14) 283

Free House
Landlord Frances Mary Bettsworth
Children welcome
🍺 Adnams Bitter; Stones Bitter; Younger's
Tartan; McEwan's Export; Guinness; Carlsberg;
cider.
ACCOMMODATION 10 bedrooms £D
Check-in: restricted

There's a friendly feel about this unpretentious pub, and the accommodation side is
doing very well. Four rooms are in the pub
itself, while a further six are in a well-designed
single-storey block to the rear. All rooms are
centrally heated, ʌnd tea-making facilities
are provided. In the ʌr there's a local version
of skittles, or you cɑ y your hand at billiards
in an adjoining roorɪ. Garden.

Monksilver *(Food)*   *Notley Arms*

Taunton · *Somerset* · Map 9 C3
Stogumber (0984) 56217 *Brewery* Ushers
Landlords Alistair & Sarah Cade **Children welcome**
🍺 Usher's Triple Crown, Founder's Ale, Best Bitter, Country Bitter;
Guinness; Carlsberg; cider. ⅋

★ A welcoming pub where the dedicated Cades and their talented young
chef Sally Wardell form a splendid team. The emphasis is on fresh, top-
quality produce and tempting menus really spoil you for choice – superbly
flavoured vegetable soup, wholewheat pitta stuffed with hot garlic lamb or
beef and cheesy courgette flan are just some of the treats in store. Daily
hot specials range from such tasty lunchtime options as seafood pasta
and chicken breast in pastry to evening steaks and local trout. There's a
traditional roast every winter Sun lunchtime, and lovely sweets like our
faultless lemon meringue pie. Eat in the beamed bar or stream-bordered
garden. *Typical prices:* Pasta with ham & mushrooms £2.25 Treacle tart
£1 (Last bar food 9.30pm) ⊖ ★

*Prices given are as at the time of our research
and thus may change.*

Monkton Combe *(B & B)* `New Entry`   *Wheelwrights Arms*

Near Bath · *Avon* · Map 9 D3
Limpley Stoke (022 122) 2287

Free House
Landlords Mr & Mrs R. J. Gillespie

🍺 Wadworth's 6X; Whitbread West Country PA;
Butcombe Bitter; Flowers IPA; Guinness; Stella
Artois; cider.
ACCOMMODATION 8 bedrooms £C (No dogs)
Check-in: restricted

A rustic stone hostelry lying three miles from
Bath in the lovely Midford Valley. The beamed
bar has period charm to spare, and there's a
quaint snug. A converted stone barn houses
the compact but very comfortable bedrooms,
which offer all the mod. cons. from TVs and
direct-dial telephones to shower rooms and
hairdryers. (Note that the Gillespies like
guests to pay for everything when ordering.)
No under-tens overnight; accommodation
closed 2 weeks January.

Montacute   (Food, B & B)   King's Arms Inn

Somerset · Map 9 D3
Martock (0935) 822513

Free House
Landlords Jean & Roger Skipper

Credit Access, Amex, Diners, Visa
🍺 Worthington Best Bitter, Bass, Toby;
Salisbury Best Bitter; Guinness; Carlsberg;
cider. 𝖄

You'll find this delightful 16th-century inn of
honey-coloured stone next to the village
church. A cheerful log fire, comfortable
seating and mullioned windows are a welcoming sight in the open-plan bar area,
where the cold buffet is a popular lunchtime
attraction. Other choices include soup and
daily specials such as chilli con carne and
chicken à la king, together with a tempting
array of sweets from the trolley. The range of
hot food is increased at night with the addition
of items like filled jacket potatoes, steaks
and scampi. *Typical prices:* Steak & kidney
pie £3.45   Chicken chasseur £3.95 (Last bar
food 10pm) 🄴

ACCOMMODATION   11 bedrooms   £A
Check-in: all day

Most of the bedrooms are in a converted
outbuilding and boast smart fitted units and
excellent private bathrooms, as well as TVs,
telephones, radio-alarms and a drinks tray.
Rooms in the original building are larger and
traditional in style. Patio.

Moreton-in-Marsh   (B & B)   Redesdale Arms Hotel

High Street · *Gloucestershire* · Map 7 A1
Moreton-in-Marsh (0608) 50308
Free House
Landlords Michael Elvis & Patricia Seedhouse
Children welcome
Credit Access, Amex
🍺 Courage Best Bitter, Directors Bitter; Bass;
John Smith's Bitter; Guinness; Tennent's;
Carlsberg; cider. 𝖄
ACCOMMODATION 17 bedrooms £B (No dogs)
Check-in: all day

This fine old coaching inn of Cotswold stone
stands in the high street. It boasts an
attractive beamed and panelled bar. Best of
the bedrooms, with quality furnishings and
smart bathrooms, are in the annexe, but
main-building rooms too are equipped with
colour TVs, tea/coffee-making facilities and
trouser presses. Patio.

Moretonhampstead   (B & B)   White Hart Hotel

The Square · *Devon* · Map 9 C3
Moretonhampstead (0647) 40406
Free House
Landlord Mr Peter Morgan
Children welcome
Credit Access, Amex, Diners, Visa
🍺 Bass; Flowers IPA; Whitbread Trophy;
Tetley's Bitter; Ansells Bitter; Guinness; Skol;
Carlsberg; cider. 𝖄
ACCOMMODATION   22 bedrooms   £B
Check-in: all day

A flowery courtyard, cosy beamed bar and
relaxing lounge set the tone of this well-
maintained Georgian posting house, run with
professionalism by landlord Peter Morgan.
Bedrooms, which differ in size and style, are
most appealing, with quality furniture and
many thoughtful extras including TVs and
tea-makers. All but two have their own
smartly decorated bathrooms.

Morval

Morval *(B & B)*   *Snooty Fox Hotel*

Near Looe · *Cornwall* · Map 9 B4
Widegates (050 34) 233

Free House
Landlords Tony & Lyn Hayward
Children welcome
Credit Access, Visa
🍺 Whitbread Best, Poacher; Flowers Original,
Best; Guinness; Stella Artois; cider.
ACCOMMODATION 8 bedrooms £B
Check-in: restricted

New owner Tony Hayward is landscaping the
gardens that surround this tile-hung hotel,
and plans include a waterfall and a children's
play park with a rustic climbing frame. The
games room, with snooker, pool table and
jukebox, provides indoor entertainment, and
the large, comfortable bar is an agreeable
place for relaxing with a drink. Overnight
accommodation is pleasantly practical, all
rooms offering colour TVs, tea-makers and
en suite modern bathrooms.

Moulton *(Food)*   *Black Bull Inn*

Near Richmond · *North Yorkshire* · Map 4 C2
Barton (032 577) 289   *Free House*   *Landlords* Mr & Mrs Pagendam
Children welcome   *Credit* Access, Amex, Visa
🍺 Theakston's Best Bitter; Carlsberg Hof. ♀

★ People come from miles around to enjoy the excellent lunchtime snacks ★
at this modest but welcoming pub with its pew-seated, beamed bar. There
are numerous small dining rooms, including a conservatory and even a
Pullman coach! Tuck into home-made soups (our asparagus was
excellent), jumbo sausages, Welsh rarebit, spare ribs, or a dish of super
gnocchi provençale. There are salads and sandwiches (prawns and
smoked salmon are popular ingredients), pâté, and for afters, excellent
cheeses and the famous cream-filled brandy snaps. *Typical prices:* Prawn
salad £2.75   Spare ribs £3 (No bar food eves or Sun) Closed 1 week
Christmas. 🥐

Murcott *(Food)*   *Nut Tree Inn*

Near Islip · *Oxfordshire* · Map 7 B1
Charlton-on-Otmoor (086 733) 253

Free House
Landlords Gordon & Diane Evans

🍺 Wadworth's 6X; Wychwood Bitter; Farmer's
Glory Bitter; Guinness; Löwenbräu; Burton Ale;
cider. ♀

Stone walls, low ceilings and original beams
create a cosy atmosphere at this delightful
thatched 15th-century inn with a veritable
zoo in the garden. Bar meals are popular;
follow pâté or garlic mushrooms with, say, a
large, juicy steak or locally made sausages.
Sandwiches, substantial salads and ploughman's are also available, plus cheeses and
gooey treacle tart to finish. *Typical prices:*
Ham salad £4.50   Sirloin steak £6.75 (Last
bar food 9.30pm. No bar food Sun) 🥐

Nantwich (Food, B & B)   *Lamb Hotel*

Hospital Street · *Cheshire* · Map 3 B4
Nantwich (0270) 625286

Brewery Greenall Whitley
Landlord Ronald Jones

Children welcome
Credit Access, Visa
🍺 Greenall Whitley Bitter, Mild; Wem Bitter;
Guinness; Grünhalle Gold, Lager; cider. ♀

ACCOMMODATION 16 bedrooms £C (No dogs)
Check-in: all day

The church clock nearby chimes the hours at this town-centre coaching inn, which has comfortable, old-fashioned bars. Lunchtime and evening snacks range from soup, sandwiches and pâté to favourites like cottage pie and stuffed mushrooms. Other choices include a tasty turkey and ham pie, chilli con carne and deep-fried clams. *Typical prices:* Cottage pie £1.50   Stuffed mushrooms £1.95 (Last bar food 10pm. No bar food Sun eve) ☺

Spacious bedrooms – some in need of a lick of paint – have sturdy freestanding furniture. Half have private facilities and TVs.

Any person using our name to obtain free hospitality is a fraud. Proprietors, please inform the police and us.

Nassington (Food)   *Black Horse Inn*

Near Peterborough · *Northamptonshire*
Map 5 B1
Stamford (0780) 782324

Free House
Landlord Mr Tom Guy

Children welcome
Credit Access, Amex, Diners, Visa
🍺 Greene King IPA; Adnams Bitter; John Smith's Bitter; Guinness; Harp; Kronenbourg; cider. ♀

Excellent cooking in an attractive 17th-century village inn just two miles from the A1. Devilled scallops or fritters of spinach and Gruyère could start your meal, with home-made pasta, grilled gammon or turkey, ham and mushroom pie to follow. Steak sandwiches and seafood pancakes are other popular choices, and there are some delicious desserts. Traditional Sunday lunch. *Typical prices:* Poacher's pie £5.95   Fish bake £3.85 (Last bar food 10pm) ☺

Children welcome *indicates a pub with an area where children are allowed whether eating or not.*

205

Naunton (Food, B & B)   *Black Horse*

Near Cheltenham · *Gloucestershire* · Map 7 A1
Guiting Power (045 15) 378

Brewery Donnington
Landlords Adrian & Jennie Bowen-Jones

🍺 Donnington's SBA, BB; Carlsberg; cider. ♀

Half a mile from the B4068, this unspoilt 17th-century inn hosted by jolly Adrian Bowen-Jones is the best kind of village pub. The cottage lounge bar makes a cosy setting for interesting, well-prepared snacks ranging from a robust vegetable soup and chicken liver pâté to salads, deep-fried duck, a tasty seafood platter, and blackboard specials such as beef casseroled in Guinness or an excellent steak. There are also things like cold meat and cheese ploughman's at lunchtime. Sweets include an irresistible chocolate roulade. *Typical prices:* Carbonnade of beef £3.50   Pork in cider £3 (Last bar food 10pm) ㊒

ACCOMMODATION 3 bedrooms £D (No dogs)
Check-in: restricted

Homely, brightly painted bedrooms, equipped with tea-makers and a good supply of books, share a neatly kept bathroom. No children under 14. Jennie Bowen-Jones, a most capable cook, sends you off with a good breakfast. Patio.

Needham Market (Food, B & B)   *Limes Hotel*

High Street · *Suffolk* · Map 5 D2
Needham Market (0449) 720305

Free House
Landlords Mr & Mrs T. W. Watts

Children welcome
Credit Access, Amex, Diners, Visa

🍺 Adnams Best Bitter; Webster's Yorkshire Bitter; Guinness; Carlsberg; Foster's; Holsten Export; cider. ♀

This handsome building with a creeper-clad Georgian facade stands in the centre of town. Inside are two traditionally furnished bars, one of which is tastefully oak-panelled and velour-upholstered while the other is more rustically decorated. Lunchtime bar meals are served from a buffet offering a selection of hot or cold dishes such as steak pie and chilli con carne, along with cold roast beef, turkey or ham and a selection of various salads. In the evening there's a short menu listing such things as seafood pancake, pizza and macaroni cheese. *Typical prices:* Scampi with chips £3.95   Chilli & pitta bread £2.75 (Last bar food 10pm) ㊒

ACCOMMODATION   11 bedrooms   £A
Check-in: all day

Standards of accommodation are excellent. There are 11 spacious bedrooms, all with modern bathrooms, some with sloping beamed ceilings. All are well decorated and equipped with good-quality furniture and particularly comfortable armchairs. All rooms have tea/coffee-making facilities, colour TVs, bedside radios and telephones.

Needingworth   *(B & B)*   *Pike & Eel*

Overcote Ferry, Near St Ives
Cambridgeshire · Map 5 C2
St Ives (0480) 63336
Free House
Landlord Peter Gunn
Children welcome
Credit Access, Amex, Diners, Visa
🍺 Bass; Adnams Bitter; Greene King IPA, Abbot
Ale; Stones Bitter; Toby Bitter; cider.
ACCOMMODATION   10 bedrooms   £C
Check-in: all day

Extensions have added over the years to the
scope of this fine old inn, whose position on
the banks of the Great Ouse makes it a
favourite with both anglers and boaters. Best
bedrooms are the three with private facilities,
but all are neat and tidy, with traditionally
styled furnishings. There's a spacious main
bar, two cosy, old-fashioned lounge bars and
a quiet residents' sitting room. Garden.

Netley Abbey   *(Food)*   **New Entry**   *Prince Consort*

Victoria Road, Near Southampton
Hampshire · Map 6 A4
Southampton (0703) 452676

Brewery Whitbread
Landlord Mr K. Lockstone

Credit Access, Amex, Visa
🍺 Whitbread Best Bitter, Samuel Whitbread;
Flowers Original; Guinness; Gold Label; Stella
Artois; cider.

Plush redecoration has breathed new life into
this busy turn-of-the-century pub with smart,
efficient staff. Excellent fresh seafood –
salmon, cockles, mussels, crab – tops the
menu, but there are also grills, home-made
pies, tasty quiches and lighter bites. Vegetarians are well catered for, and so are children
(who might choose a thunderburger washed
down by a Terror Hawks milk shake). Patio.
Typical prices: Mussels in white wine
£2.25   Mushroom & asparagus quiche £2.45
(Last order 10.15pm) ☺

Nettlecombe   *(B & B)*   *Marquis of Lorne*

Near Bridport · *Dorset* · Map 9 D3
Powerstock (030 885) 236

Brewery Palmer
Landlords Mr & Mrs R. W. Bone

Children welcome
🍺 Palmer's Bridport Bitter, IPA; Guinness;
Faust.
ACCOMMODATION 8 bedrooms £C (No dogs)
Check-in: restricted

Rolling green hills and a large garden (with a
children's play area) provide a picturesque
setting for this 16th-century stone-built inn,
which is popular for family holidays. Half the
brightly modern bedrooms have an extra bed
and private facilities, the rest share a spotless
public bathroom. The cosy residents' lounge
is equipped with TV and video, and there is a
comfortable relaxing bar.

Newark   *(B & B)*   *Robin Hood Hotel*

Lombard Street · *Nottinghamshire* · Map 4 D4
Newark (0636) 703858

Free House
Landlord Mr Gatenby
Children welcome
Credit Access, Amex, Diners, Visa
🍺 John Smith's Bitter, Lager; Old Tom Mild;
Guinness; cider. *No real ale.* ♀
ACCOMMODATION   21 bedrooms   £A
Check-in: all day

Friendly, efficient staff are a bonus at this
modernised town-centre coaching inn, a
popular overnight stop with business visitors.
Comfortable accommodation is provided in
21 spacious bedrooms, a number of which
have been attractively refurbished. All offer
private facilities as well as TVs, telephones
and tea-makers. The main bar, resplendent
with its oak beams, plush red seating and
gleaming copper tables, has a warmly convivial atmosphere.

Newenden   *White Hart*

Affable host Mr Faulkner presides behind the bar of this 16th-century clapperboard pub, where mellow beams, burnished brass and a fine old inglenook give a homely, traditional feel. Another fireplace is surrounded by swags of hop stalks, in classic Kentish fashion. Outside, there's a beer garden that runs down to a little river.

Kent · Map 6 C4
Northiam (079 74) 2166   *Brewery* Courage   *Landlord* Mr A. E. Faulkner
Credit Access
🍺 Courage Best Bitter, Directors, John Courage; Guinness; Hofmeister; Kronenbourg; cider. ♀

Newton   *(Food)*   *Queen's Head*

Near Cambridge · *Cambridgeshire* · Map 7 D1
Cambridge (0223) 870436

Free House
Landlord David Short

Children welcome
🍺 Adnams Bitter, Old (winter only); Guinness; Tuborg Gold; cider.

A real gem of a village pub, with bare brick walls, beams and a large open fireplace in the bar. The snacks are simple but delicious: at lunchtime there's a thick, nourishing soup and excellent wholemeal sandwiches generously filled with cheese, pâté, smoked salmon or top-quality home-cooked meats. In the evening they offer cold platters with chunks of granary bread. *Typical prices:* Soup 90p   Beef sandwich 90p (Last bar food 10.30pm).

Newton   *Red Lion Inn*

Dating from 1660, this attractive little pub in a remote rural setting off the A52 is kept in spotless order by long-standing owners the Powers. Two rooms make up the bar – one has antiques and rough brick walls hung with prints, the other features Bill Power's collection of nautical objects. There's an immaculate garden, too.

Near Sleaford · *Lincolnshire* · Map 4 D4
Folkingham (052 97) 256   *Free House*   *Landlords* Bill & Gaenor Power
Children welcome
🍺 Bateman's XB; Webster's Yorkshire Bitter; Guinness; Carlsberg; Holsten; cider.

Newton   *(B & B)*   *Saracen's Head*

Near Sudbury · *Suffolk* · Map 5 C2
Sudbury (0787) 79036

Brewery Tollemache & Cobbold
Landlord Mr J. Eglin
Children welcome
Credit Access, Visa
🍺 Tollemache & Cobbold Original Best Bitter; Guinness; Hansa; cider. ♀
ACCOMMODATION 2 bedrooms £D
Check-in: restricted

Overlooking the village green and golf course, this 16th-century roadside inn has a friendly, homely appeal generated by welcoming hosts the Eglins. The two prettily decorated bedrooms, each with TV and tea-making facilities, share a well-maintained public bathroom. Downstairs, the low-beamed bar with its solid oak settles is a convivial spot for a drink. Accommodation closed 1 week Christmas. Garden.

Newton-in-Bowland *(Food, B & B)*   *Parkers Arms Hotel*

Near Clitheroe · *Lancashire* · Map 3 B3
Slaidburn (020 06) 236

Brewery Whitbread
Landlord Mr H. Rhodes

Children welcome
🍺 Whitbread Trophy, Best Mild; Guinness;
Heineken; cider. *No real ale.*

A village setting in the heart of the lovely Hodder Valley for this former deer-keeper's house. Henry Rhodes is the warmest and friendliest of hosts, with a ready welcome for regulars and strangers alike. The lounge bar is mellow, traditional and comfortable, a good spot for enjoying simple, honest bar snacks headed by the excellent fresh local salmon. Other choices include hearty home-made soup, steak and kidney pie and sandwiches, plus decent English cheeses and some fairly conventional sweets. *Typical prices:* Fresh salmon salad £4.75 Steak & kidney pie £2.55 (Last bar food 10.30pm) 🥨

ACCOMMODATION 3 bedrooms £C (No dogs)
Check-in: all day

There are three simple but adequately comfortable bedrooms, neatly kept and fully carpeted, which share a well-equipped bathroom. There's a cosy residents' lounge with TV, and overnight guests can look forward to a very decent breakfast.

Prices given are as at the time of our research and thus may change.

North Bovey *(Food, B & B)*   *Ring of Bells*

Newton Abbot · *Devon* · Map 9 C4
Moretonhampstead (0647) 40375

Free House
Landlords Mr & Mrs Batcock

Children welcome
🍺 Wadworth's 6X; Flowers Original, IPA;
Exmoor Bitter; Bass; Heineken; cider. 🍷

Some of Dartmoor's prettiest scenery provides the background for this charming thatched inn with three characterful bars offering an excellent choice of real ales and wholesome snacks. The summer cold table gives place in winter to warming soup, curries and hearty casseroles. There are no sandwiches, but salads are supplemented by various ploughman's, and the sweets are a real treat, with a superb Bakewell tart served with thick clotted cream. *Typical prices:* Moussaka £3.55 Roast beef salad £3.75 (Last bar food 10pm) 🥨

ACCOMMODATION 4 bedrooms £C
Check-in: all day

Tortuously winding stairs lead to four spacious, attractively furnished bedrooms, two with four-posters. All have spotless en suite bathrooms and lovely moorland views. Garden with swimming pool. Accommodation closed in January.

North Cerney   *(Food, B & B)*   *Bathurst Arms*

Near Cirencester · Gloucestershire · Map 7 A1
North Cerney (028 583) 281

Free House
Landlords Freddie & Caroline Seward

Children welcome
Credit Visa
🍺 Gibbs Mew Bishop's Tipple; Hook Norton;
Wadworth's 6X; Archer's Best Bitter; Flowers
Original; Guinness; Beck's; cider. ♀

A former British Airways steward and his
young family are the new owners of this 17th-
century pinkwashed former farmhouse,
which has three characterful bars and a most
attractive riverside garden. Bar food includes
quiche, ploughman's and chicken in a basket,
along with Arbroath smokies, lasagne and
filled hot croissants. It's worth going for one
of the daily-changing blackboard specials, at
lunchtime with an oriental slant (satay, nasi
goreng), in the evening with more of a
traditional English ring (beef Wellington, casseroles, juicy lamb cutlets with mint butter).
Good puds, summer cold table, roast Sunday
lunch. *Typical prices:* Filled croissant £1.65
Pavlova 95p (Last bar food 9.30pm) ☺

ACCOMMODATION 5 bedrooms £C (No dogs)
Check-in: all day

Upstairs, five delightful bedrooms provide
excellent overnight accommodation: double
glazing, attractive cane furniture, prints, pas-
tels and duvets. Bathrooms, all en suite, are
modern and immaculate.

North Dalton   *(Food)*   **New Entry**   *Star Inn*

Near Driffield · Humberside · Map 4 D2
Middleton-on-the-Wolds (037 781) 688

Free House
Landlords Marie & Nick Cragg

Credit Access, Visa
🍺 Tetley's Bitter; John Smith's Bitter, Mild,
Tawny; Carlsberg; Hofmeister; cider.

In their four years of ownership the Craggs
have achieved great improvements at this
friendly pub by the village pond. Staff are
marvellously friendly, and bar food has
become a very popular feature, thanks to
delights like creamy fish pie, burgers and
salads, lamb with garlic and yoghurt, and a
scrumptious apple and pear sponge. *Typical
prices:* Steak & kidney pie £2.95 Vegetarian
curry £2.95 (Last bar food 10pm. No bar food
Mon & Tues until May 1987) ☺

North Petherton   *(B & B)*   *Walnut Tree Inn*

Fore Street, Near Bridgwater · Somerset
Map 9 C3
North Petherton (0278) 662255
Free House
Landlords Mr & Mrs Goulden
Children welcome
Credit Access, Amex, Diners, Visa
🍺 Wadworth's 6X, Northgate; John Smith's
Yorkshire Bitter; Heineken; Tuborg Gold. ♀
ACCOMMODATION 20 bedrooms £B
Check-in: all day

On the A38 close to junction 24 of the M5,
this much-extended coaching inn is a de-
servedly popular overnight stopping place.
Beautifully kept bedrooms with solid darkwood units all have TVs, tea-makers and
ample writing space, as well as tiled and
carpeted bathrooms with colourful modern
suites. The bars are smart and welcoming,
the housekeeping excellent, the staff courteous and friendly.

North Wootton *(Food, B & B)*   *Crossways Inn*

Near Shepton Mallet · *Somerset* · Map 9 D3
Pilton (074 989) 237

Free House
Landlords John & Cynthia Kirkham

Children welcome
Credit Access, Visa
🍺 Wadworth's 6X; Bass; Usher's Triple Crown;
Courage Best Bitter; Guinness; Löwenbräu;
cider. ⚲

The setting for this pleasant inn is a peaceful stretch of Somerset countryside between Shepton Mallet and Wells. Owners John and Cynthia Kirkham are very friendly and put visitors at ease in double-quick time. Bar snacks are mainly familiar pub favourites, but none the worse for that: beef, ham and turkey are prepared on the premises for good salads and sandwiches, and jacket potatoes come with a variety of hot and cold fillings. Home-made hot dishes include steak and kidney pie, chicken curry and a daily vegetarian special. Simple sweets (also home-made) like cheesecake or apple pie. *Typical prices:* Roast turkey salad £2.90   Lasagne £2.35 (Last bar food 10.45pm) ⊖

ACCOMMODATION 7 bedrooms £D (No dogs)
Check-in: all day

Decent-sized bedrooms (all with TV) are centrally heated and fully carpeted; two have compact shower rooms, the rest share a well-kept bathroom. There's a cosy, homely residents' lounge.

Northiam *(Food)* **New Entry**   *Six Bells*

East Sussex · Map 6 C4
Northiam (079 74) 2570

Free House
Landlords Mr W. S. Tipples & Miss J. A. Lilley

Children welcome
Credit Access, Amex, Diners, Visa
🍺 Fremlins Bitter; Shepherd Neame
Masterbrew; Flowers OB; King & Barnes
Festive; Heineken; Stella Artois; cider.

A welcoming old pub in the centre of the village, very much the hub of local life and usually filled with a cheerful young crowd. The bar food is appetising, imaginative and well prepared, with staples like soup, salads and steaks joined by daily-changing specials: favourites include pasta, scallops and pan-fried plaice. *Typical prices:* Moules marinière £2.75   Liver & bacon with onion gravy £3.50 (Last bar food 10pm. No bar food Sun eve, also Mon in winter) ⊖

Nottingham   *Ye Olde Trip to Jerusalem Inn*

Said to be the oldest pub in the land, this ancient inn whose records date back to 1189 is certainly one of the most unusual. Its 16th-century facade conceals a warren of cellars, rooms and passages literally carved out of the rock above which Nottingham Castle stands and today forming a most dramatic setting for a drink.

Brewhouse Yard, Castle Road · *Nottinghamshire* · Map 4 C4
Nottingham (0602) 473171   *Free House*   *Landlord* Mr & Mrs E. Marshall
🍺 Samuel Smith's Old Brewery Bitter; Marston's Pedigree; Ruddle's
County; Castlemaine 6X; Carling Black Label; cider.

Nunney *(Food, B & B)*   *George Inn*

11 Church Street, near Frome · *Somerset*
Map 9 D3
Nunney (037 384) 458

Free House
Landlord Mr J. S. B. Lewis

Children welcome
Credit Access, Amex, Diners, Visa
🍺 Butcombe Bitter; Oakhill Farmer's Bitter Ale; Bass; Guinness; Holsten; Carling Black Label; cider. ♀

ACCOMMODATION 14 bedrooms £C
Check-in: all day

Rustic character abounds in the bars of this white-painted 14th-century inn, which stands in a picturesque village opposite the ruins of a Norman castle. Bar snacks are based on good fresh ingredients and cover a span from soup, pâté and sandwiches to seafood pancakes and the always popular steak and kidney pie. Daily specials such as moules marinière and sautéed kidneys introduce further choice, and there are some nice puds like apple pie or chocolate brandy mousse. *Typical prices:* Moules marinière £2.50 Lasagne £2.75 (Last bar food 9.30pm) 🍽

Overnight accommodation ranges from a fine four-poster room with a commodious bathroom through charming rooms under the eaves to smartly modernised ones featuring much natural wood (these are in a converted skittles alley). Almost all rooms have bath or shower en suite. There's a pleasant residents' lounge, and a stone-walled dining room where a decent breakfast may be had.

*We neither seek nor accept hospitality
and we pay for all food and drinks in full.*

Oakwoodhill *(Food)*   *Punchbowl Inn*

Near Ockley · *Surrey* · Map 6 B3
Oakwoodhill (030 679) 249   *Free House*   *Landlords* Rob & Shirley Chambers
Children welcome   *Credit* Diners, Visa
🍺 King & Barnes Sussex Bitter; Young's Special; Hall & Woodhouse Badger Bitter; Guinness; cider. ♀

★   A country cottage 600 years ago, today a delightful, tile-hung pub where the number one attraction is Shirley Chambers' super cooking. T-bone steaks, sweet and sour crispy duck and fried fillet of plaice are just a few of the many delights listed on the blackboard menu; ploughman's platters and well-filled sandwiches are excellent for quicker snacks, and a small but select choice of sweets includes a lovely boozy sherry trifle. Weekday lunchtime visitors have an additional treat in the form of the splendid cold buffet, and the weekend barbecues are very popular. On Sunday a traditional roast is a lunchtime option (limited choice Sunday evening). *Typical prices:* Steak & kidney pie £3.50   Chicken curry £3 (Last bar food 10pm)   ★

Ockley *(Food, B & B)* — *King's Arms*

Stane Street · *Surrey* · Map 6 B3
Dorking (0306) 711224

Free House
Landlords Mrs Mary Doyle & family

Children welcome
Credit Access, Amex, Visa
🍺 King & Barnes Sussex Bitter; Hall &
Woodhouse Badger Bitter; Fuller's ESB;
Ruddle's Rutland Bitter; Guinness; Carlsberg;
Foster's; cider. ♀

ACCOMMODATION 6 bedrooms £B (No dogs)
Check-in: all day

Mary Doyle and her family offer the warmest
of welcomes at their 300-year-old tile-hung
pub. Wholesome, honest fare is served
among the polished copperware and fresh
flower displays of the convivial bar – soups
and sandwiches, cold meat, salads and
home-made pâté, hearty casseroles, and
apple pie for afters. In fine weather, the pretty
garden has plenty of seating for alfresco
diners, and there is a restaurant, too, offering
more elaborate dishes. *Typical prices:*
Smoked mackerel fillet £1.80   Chicken Kiev
£4.80 (Last bar food 10pm) ⊖

The six well-kept bedrooms (three in a recent
extension with private facilities) are furnished
in traditional style and all have radio-alarms.
The older rooms share a pretty little public
bathroom. No children overnight. Accommodation closed 1 week Christmas.

Odiham *(Food, B & B)* **New Entry** — *George Hotel*

High Street · *Hampshire* · Map 6 B3
Odiham (025 671) 2081

Brewery Courage
Landlords Peter & Moira Kelsey

Children welcome
Credit Access, Diners, Visa
🍺 Courage Best Bitter, Directors; John Smith's;
Guinness; Hofmeister; Kronenbourg.

ACCOMMODATION 8 bedrooms £B
Check-in: all day

The new management have completed a
major renovation programme that preserves
and enhances the best features of this lovely
village pub. The original building is late 14th
century, while the annexe (now an attractive
restaurant) is 16th century. In the comfortable
bars the choice of dishes is straightforward,
and everything bears the stamp of care in the
kitchen: well-flavoured chicken liver pâté,
super ham for sandwiches, tender steak with
Guinness and mushrooms in a really satisfying pie. Puddings are usually available.
Typical prices: Chicken curry £2.95   Prawn
& asparagus sandwich £2 (Last bar food
10.30pm) ⊖

The bedrooms are solidly furnished with
good-quality pieces and display many of the
original beams (mind your head in some
places!). Colour TVs and direct-dial telephones meet modern requirements, and
effective central heating and double glazing
make for a very comfortable stay. Private
facilities throughout. There's a splendid residents' lounge with exposed stonework and
old wooden furniture.

Offchurch *(Food)* **New Entry** — *Stag's Head*

Near Leamington Spa · *Warwickshire* · Map 5 A2
Leamington (0926) 25801

Brewery Ansells
Landlords Mr & Mrs Owen

Tetley's Bitter; Ind Coope Burton Ale; Ansells Bitter; Guinness; Skol; Löwenbräu; cider.

In the heart of the village, this attractive black and white inn with its low-beamed bars makes a cheerful setting for the landlord's robust, reliable cooking. Try crispy mushrooms or flavoursome taramasalata and houmus to start, followed perhaps by herby beef casserole, vegetarian moussaka or a speciality steak. Ploughman's and salads, too, plus simple sweets. Garden. *Typical prices:* Steak & kidney pie £3.45   Fillet Luigi £5.95 (Last bar food 10pm)

Old Basing *(Food)* **New Entry** — *Bolton Arms*

The Street · *Hampshire* · Map 7 B2
Basingstoke (0256) 22085

Brewery Courage
Landlord Mr Peter Kent

Courage Best, Directors, John Courage; Guinness; Hofmeister; Kronenbourg; cider.

A pleasant and popular 16th-century timbered inn with beams in abundance and a cosy rustic feel. The menu offers a choice of a dozen or so dishes such as chicken pancakes, steak in pitta bread or an excellent fisherman's hot pot. Also sandwiches and ploughman's, which are the only things available on Tuesday evening and all day Sunday. No starters or sweets. *Typical prices:* Fisherman's hot pot £2.95   Pâté ploughman's £1.45 (Last bar food 9pm)

*We neither seek nor accept hospitality
and we pay for all food and drinks in full.*

Old Dalby *(Food)* — *Crown Inn*

Near Melton Mowbray · *Leicestershire* · Map 5 B1
Melton Mowbray (0664) 823134   *Free House*
Landlords Salvatore Inguanta & Lynne Bryan   **Children welcome**
Marston's Pedigree Bitter; Ruddle's County Bitter, Best Bitter; Kimberley Bitter; Theakston's XB; Carlsberg.

★ Converted from a 200-year-old farmhouse in the heart of the village (check directions), this friendly inn is full of character and atmosphere. Seasonally changing menus offer a delicious selection of expertly prepared dishes, from blue Stilton dip with crudités and stuffed mushrooms served with horseradish sauce to beautifully tender chicken brochettes, halibut in a creamy wine sauce and juicy steak. Ploughman's, sandwiches and filled rolls are also available, and tempting sweets include rich rum trifle cake. The low-ceilinged, cottage bars are delightfully cosy and there's a large garden. *Typical prices:* Baked avocado £3.75   Black pudding and fried apple £3.75 (Last bar food 9.45pm. No bar food Sun & Mon eves) ★

Oldbury-on-Severn *(Food)* — *Anchor Inn*

Near Thornbury · *Avon* · Map 8 D2
Thornbury (0454) 413331

Free House
Landlord Mr Michael J. Dowdeswell

🍺 Theakston's Best Bitter, Old Peculier; Marston's Pedigree; Butcombe Bitter; Boddington's Bitter; Guinness; cider.

Food plays an important part in the life of this attractive converted mill house with a strong local following. The appetising cold selection includes Severn salmon salad and garlic prawns, or (up to 9.30) you might tuck into something hot like chilli tacos, seafood chowder or exotic Persian lamb. Excellent cheeseboard, plus super sweets like figs in cream and Pernod sauce. Garden. *Typical dishes:* Steak & kidney pie £1.75 Lasagne £1.75 (Last bar food 11pm) 🍴

Ollerton *(Food)* `New Entry` — *Dun Cow*

Chelford Road, Near Knutsford · *Cheshire*
Map 3 B3
Knutsford (0565) 3093

Brewery Greenall Whitley
Landlord Mr G. Tilling

Children welcome
🍺 Greenall's Local Bitter, Export Gold Lager; Guinness; Grünhalle; cider. 🍷

An unassuming little pub, its pebbledash exterior hiding a 300-year history that includes long service as an assize court. A pleasant, homely atmosphere is fostered by the kindly landlord, and tasty, home-cooked snacks are served on attractive floral china. Cauliflower soup, Cornish pasty, meatloaf and damson crumble show the range. Roast Sunday lunch. *Typical prices:* Steak & kidney pie £1.70 Damson crumble 80p (Last bar food 9.30pm) 🍴

We publish annually so make sure you use the current edition.

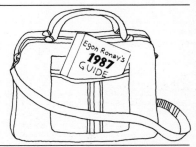

Ombersley *(Food)* — *Kings Arms*

Near Worcester · *Hereford & Worcester*
Map 8 D1
Worcester (0905) 620142

Brewery Mitchells & Butlers
Landlords Judy & Chris Blundell

Children welcome (lunchtime)
🍺 Bass; Mitchells & Butlers Brew X1, Springfield Bitter; Guinness; Carling Black Label; Tennent's Export; cider. 🍷

Built around 1411, there's a marvellous atmosphere at this crooked black and white inn, whose cosy beamed bars are filled with bric-a-brac. All the excellent snacks are home made, generously served and beautifully presented: try smokies in a creamy fish sauce, chilli beef chowder, the super cold meat salads and tempting sweets. Garden. *Typical prices:* Chicken & leek pie £3.45 Chilli beef chowder £3.45 (Last bar food 9 pm. No bar food Sun) 🍴

Onecote *(Food)*   *Jervis Arms*

Near Leek · Staffordshire · Map 4 C4
Onecote (053 88) 206

Free House
Landlords Peter & Julie Elizabeth Wilkinson

Children welcome
🍺 Theakston's Best, Old Peculier; Bass Bitter; Marston's pedigree; McEwan's 70/-; Ruddle's County; cider.

Access from the car park to this popular family pub is via a picturesque wooden bridge and the riverside garden. Inside, it's bright, warm and cosy, just right for enjoying some very decent cooking. Roasts, grills and shepherd's pie are favourite meat dishes, and there's a vegetarian menu. *Typical prices:* Vegetarian burgers with salad £2.50 Three-cheese ploughman's £1.60 (Last bar food 10pm) Pub closed lunchtime Mon–Fri end October–Easter. ⊖

Orford *(B & B)*   *King's Head Inn*

Front Street · Suffolk · Map 5 D2
Orford (0394) 450271

Brewery Adnams
Landlords Alistair & Phyl Shaw

Credit Diners
🍺 Adnams Bitter; Skol; cider. ♀
ACCOMMODATION 5 bedrooms £C
Check-in: restricted

Expect to find visitors packing the beamed bar of this remarkable 13th-century village inn, once the haunt of smugglers. Gleaming brassware, old prints and a handsome fireplace add to the characterful charm, while upstairs simple bedrooms with homely furniture nestle beneath low, sloping ceilings and share two neat bathrooms. Accommodation closed January.

Orleton *(Food)*   *Boot Inn*

Near Ludlow · Hereford & Worcester · Map 8 D1
Yarpole (056 885) 228

Free House

Children welcome
🍺 Marston's Pedigree; Burton Bitter; Davenport's Bitter; Guinness; Carlsberg; Heineken; cider. ♀

A splendid half-timbered 16th-century inn with a marvellous inglenook and collection of boots among its interesting features. Super food is served in the characterful bar – game pie, fresh fish, steaks, ploughman's, a cold summer buffet and some mouthwatering sweets like rich, dark chocolate and hazelnut mousse. Garden. *Typical prices:* Steak pie £2.95 Steak au poivre £5.15 (Last bar food 10pm. No bar food Mon eve in winter) ⊖

Oswaldkirk *(Food, B & B)*   *Malt Shovel Inn*

Near Helmsley · North Yorkshire · Map 4 C2
Ampleforth (043 93) 461

Brewery Samuel Smith
Landlords Ian & Carol Pickering

Children welcome
🍺 Samuel Smith's Old Brewery Bitter. ♀
Accommodation 3 bedrooms £D (No dogs)
Check-in: restricted

An interesting menu really gets the taste buds tingling at this fine old 17th-century manor house. Spinach roulade makes a lovely light snack, while more substantial offerings include cold meat salads, lamb cutlets, game pie and delicious little curried chicken buns. Three homely bedrooms share a well-maintained bathroom. Garden. *Typical prices:* Lemon sole £6 Cheese & spinach roulade £2.40 (Last bar food 9.30pm. No bar food Mon eves except Bank Hols) ⊖

Ovington
Bush Inn

A tree-lined lane leads from the A31 to this charming rose-covered pub, whose garden runs down to the river Itchen that's well-known to trout fishermen. A crackling fire and much gleaming brass and copperware add to the convivial atmosphere in the cosy bars.

Near Alresford · *Hampshire* · Map 6 A3
Alresford (096 273) 2764   *Free House*   Landlords Mr & Mrs G. M. Draper
Children welcome (lunchtime)   *Credit* Access, Amex, Visa
🍺 Strong's Country Bitter; Flowers Original Bitter; Wadworth's 6X; Guinness; Stella Artois; cider. ♀

Oxford   *(Food)*
Perch

Binsey · *Oxfordshire* · Map 7 B1
Oxford (0865) 240386

Brewery Halls
Landlords Vaughan & Sue Jagger

Children welcome
🍺 Hall's Harvest Bitter; Ind Coope Burton Ale; John Bull Bitter; Guinness; Skol; Löwenbräu; cider.

Tucked away down a turning off the A420, this attractive old thatched pub near the river Thames has plenty of atmosphere in its beamed and flagstoned bars. Consult the blackboard for appetising dishes like tender beef in ale, vegetarian harvest pie and Cumberland sausages in French bread. Also jacket potatoes at lunchtime. *Typical prices:* Beef curry £2.75   Cream of chicken soup 85p (Last bar food 9pm. No bar food Sun & Mon eves) ⊖

Oxford   *(Food, B & B)*
Turf Tavern

5 Bath Place, Holywell Street · *Oxfordshire*
Map 7 B1
Oxford (0865) 243235

Free House
Landlord Miss Midgley

Children welcome
🍺 Hook Norton Best Bitter, Old Hookey; Theakston's Old Peculier (winter only); Young's Special; Guinness; Stella Artois; Turf Tavern Lager; cider.

ACCOMMODATION 9 bedrooms £C
Check-in: all day

New College tower overshadows this ancient beamed tavern where Hardy's Jude courted Arabella. Popular with town and gown, it offers appetising bar food in two tiny bars and a number of courtyards (huge blue parasols are a colourful feature in a couple of them). Pastas and generously filled home-made pies of beef in wine, Cotswold rabbit or vegetables are very popular, as are filled jacket potatoes, spare ribs and spit-roast chicken. There's also a cold buffet of meat pies and salads. Nice puds, too. *Typical prices:* Lasagne £2.95   Beef & wine pie £3.25 (Last bar food 11pm) ⊖

Charming beamed bedrooms in adjacent cottages have spotless period furniture and share three bathrooms.

Parkgate   *(Food, B & B)*   *Ship Hotel*

The Parade, Near Neston, Wirral · *Cheshire*
Map 3 B3
051-336 3931

Owner Anchor Hotels (THF)
Landlord Mr Michael Kaiser

Children welcome
Credit Access, Amex, Diners, Visa
🍺 John Smith's Yorkshire Bitter, Chestnut Mild;
Guinness; Hofmeister.

Very good snacks are served in the main bar
of this sturdy, white-painted inn, and picture
windows afford excellent views of the Dee
estuary. Tables are smartly set and it's
waitress service. The choice is wide: starters
include soup, shrimps and pâté; and for light
meals there are burgers, toasted sandwiches
and ploughman's platters. Pies and pizzas
are popular, too, along with salads and grills.
Nice home-made sweets (sherry trifle, fresh
cream gâteau). *Typical prices:* Avocado pear
with shrimps £2.90 Beef steak and stout pie
£3.55 (Last bar food 10.30pm. No bar food
Sun & Mon eves) ☕

ACCOMMODATION 26 bedrooms £A
Check-in: all day

Bedrooms, all very comfortable and shipshape, range from standard, with fitted units,
to superior, with smart natural wood furnishings, and a couple of de-luxe ones with four-
posters and mini-bars. All rooms have colour
TVs, direct-dial phones and tea-makers, plus
well-equipped bathrooms. Overnight guests
start the day with a super cooked breakfast.

*Our inspectors are our
full-time employees; they
are professionally trained
by us.*

Pelynt   *(B & B)*   *Jubilee Inn*

Near Looe · *Cornwall* · Map 9 B4
Lanreath (0503) 20312

Free House
Landlord Mr F. E. Williams
Children welcome
Credit Access, Visa
🍺 Flowers Original; Whitbread Best, Poachers;
Guinness; Stella Artois; Heineken; cider.
ACCOMMODATION 10 bedrooms £C
Check-in: all day

There's a genuinely warm and friendly air
about this pink-washed pub, whose present
name was acquired in 1887. This was the
fiftieth year of Queen Victoria's reign, and
there's a commemorative display of china in
the appealing lounge bar. Good-sized bedrooms, six with spick-and-span private bathrooms, are mostly furnished in traditional
style, though a couple are more modern.
There's an attractive residents' lounge.

Pembridge *(Food, B & B)*   *New Inn*

Market Square · *Hereford & Worcester*
Map 8 D1
Pembridge (054 47) 427

Brewery Whitbread
Landlord Jane Melvin

Children welcome
🍺 Flowers Original, IPA, Best Bitter, PA;
Guinness; Stella Artois; cider. 🍷

Built in 1311, this black and white inn has been a regular stop for travellers down the centuries. It's a good place to choose for a snack in traditional surroundings, and Jane Melvin's menu changes with the seasons. She manages to offer something to suit everyone, from garlic mushrooms and variants on ploughman's to seafood vol-au-vent, chicken pancakes, crunchy aubergine bake and succulent pork fillet in a deliciously creamy sauce flavoured with apples, pears and cider. Treacle tart and cider-baked bananas are tasty sweets. The bars are agreeably rustic, and a little cobbled terrace overlooks the market place. *Typical prices:* Pork fillet £3 Meringue with hazelnut ice cream 90p (last bar food 9.45pm) 🥄

ACCOMMODATION 6 bedrooms £D
Check-in: restricted

Modest but comfortable bedrooms (one with TV) have plenty of character, with traditional furnishings, good old-fashioned beds and a notable lack of right angles. They share an adequate bathroom and separate shower.

---

*We neither seek nor accept hospitality
and we pay for all food and drinks in full.*

Pendoggett *(Food, B & B)*   *Cornish Arms*

Near St Kew · *Cornwall* · Map 9 B4
Bodmin (0208) 880623

Free House
Landlords Nigel Pickstone & Alan Wainwright

Credit Access, Amex, Diners, Visa
🍺 Pendoggett SB; Bass; Worthington Best; St Austell Duchy; Carlsberg Hof; cider.

Virginia creeper adorns the walls of this fine late 17th-century inn in a hamlet a mile from the coast. The lunchtime buffet – set up in one of the nest of beamed bars – looks most appetising, with cold meats carved to order and a selection of fresh, help-yourself salads. There is also a hot dish, with soup and sandwiches as evening additions, while Sunday lunch is limited to sandwiches, pâté and ploughman's. Simple puds include a nice crunchy cheesecake. *Typical prices:* Beef salad £2.75 Ploughman's platter £1.30 (Last bar food 10pm) 🥄

ACCOMMODATION 7 bedrooms £B
Check-in: all day

Immaculate bedrooms are pretty and comfortable, with floral furnishings and quality carpeting that extends to the five spotless en suite bathrooms. The split-level TV lounge is delightfully chintzy. No children under 14.

Peppard Common   (Food)   Red Lion

Near Henley · Oxfordshire · Map 7 B2
Rotherfield Greys (049 17) 329

Brewery Brakspear
Landlords Ian & Pauline Wadhams

Children welcome
🍺 Brakspear's Mild, Bitter, Special Bitter;
Guinness; Heineken; Stella Artois; cider. ♀

Standing on the edge of the common, this
welcoming pub has a plain, old-fashioned
public bar, a snug lounge bar and a third
room where children are admitted. The
speciality among the snacks is the jacket
potatoes with a choice of nine fillings, from
prawns in garlic to beef goulash; there's also
soup, sandwiches and pot meals like chicken
curry. Garden. *Typical prices:* Seafood au
gratin £2.50   Jacket potato with prawns in
cream £2.75 (Last bar food 10pm).

Perranarworthal   (Food, B & B)   Norway Inn

Truro · Cornwall · Map 9 A4
Truro (0872) 862081

Brewery Devenish
Landlord Mr William Herbert

Children welcome
Credit Access, Amex, Diners, Visa
🍺 Devenish Bitter, Cornish Best Bitter,
Falmouth Bitter; Guinness; Stella Artois;
Grünhalle; cider. ♀

Named to commemorate the Norwegian
ships that once unloaded their timber in a
nearby creek, this hospitable old roadside
inn has a lovely garden where the weekend
barbecues are a popular feature, especially
in summer. Inside, food is served in a pine-
furnished dining area next to the cosy, low-
ceilinged bar. Bill Herbert and his smartly
dressed staff will guide you through the
appetising counter display of cold meats,
fresh seafood and salads, first-rate pies like
flavoursome steak and mushroom, ploughman's and enjoyable sweets from the trolley
– perhaps chocolate fudge cake or Swiss
apple pie made with excellent pastry. A
traditional roast joint is the highlight of
weekday evening meals and weekend
lunches. *Typical prices:* Chicken pie in white
wine £3.75   Turkey & ham pie £3.75 (Last
bar food 10pm) ⊖

ACCOMMODATION 3 bedrooms £C (No dogs)
Check-in: all day

Upstairs, the three simple, cottage bedrooms
with colour TVs and tea-makers share a
public bathroom.

Pett Bottom   (Food)   Duck Inn

Bridge, Near Canterbury · Kent · Map 6 D3
Canterbury (0227) 830354

Free House
Landlords Mr & Mrs L. C. Boothright

Credit Access, Amex
🍺 Marston's Pedigree; Gibbs Salisbury; Fuller's
London Pride; Wem Bitter; cider. ♀

Chef Gary's bar snacks have plenty of zip at
this friendly old country pub. Try a bowl of
his fiery chilli, or some garlicky cheese-
topped mushrooms, served with piping hot
rye bread – or opt for a milder dish, perhaps
cottage pie, or a salad. Memorable sweets
from the restaurant menu include rich cream-
filled brandy snaps. Closed Mon (except
Bank Hols). Garden. *Typical prices:* Garlic
mushrooms £2.35   Stuffed potatoes £1.95
(Last bar food 9.45 pm) ⊖

Petworth *(B & B)*   *Angel*

Angel Street · *West Sussex* · Map 6 B4
Petworth (0798) 42153
Free House
Landlords Derrick & Susan Pope
Children welcome
Credit Access, Amex, Diners, Visa
🍺 Flowers Bitter; Whitbread Best Bitter, Mild;
Courage Best Bitter; Guinness; Stella Artois;
Heineken; cider. 🍷
ACCOMMODATION   4 bedrooms   £C
Check-in: all day

Black beams contrast with white plasterwork
walls in the characterful bedrooms of this
fine old inn near the town centre. Pretty soft
furnishings contribute colour, and the four
rooms share two carpeted public bathrooms
with pristine modern suites. Downstairs,
there are more beams in the spacious bar,
where a log fire and a variety of homely knick-
knacks add to its cosy appeal. Garden.

Petworth *(Food)* `New Entry`   *Welldiggers Arms*

Pulborough Road · *West Sussex* · Map 6 B4
Petworth (0798) 42287

Free House
Landlord Mr E. H. Whitcomb

Credit Access, Amex, Diners, Visa
🍺 Young's Bitter, Special Bitter; Guinness;
Carlsberg; Budweiser; cider.

East of Petworth on the A283, this pleasantly
rustic pub specialises in robust home cooking, with an emphasis on seafood and local
game. There's a regular printed menu, plus
blackboard specials like salade niçoise,
grilled halibut, roast partridge and oxtail
casserole. Leave room for a nice sweet,
perhaps ice cream or chocolate gâteau.
Typical prices: Roast partridge £6.95
French onion soup £1.95 (Last bar food
10pm) 🍴

Pewsham *(Food, B & B)*   *Lysley Arms*

Near Chippenham · *Wiltshire* · Map 7 A2
Chippenham (0249) 652864

Free House
Landlord Peter C. Reeves

Children welcome
Credit Access, Visa
🍺 Bass; Worthington Best Bitter; Guinness;
Carling; Tennent's Extra; cider.

Peter Reeves has spent half a lifetime at this
distinctive white inn, which stands on the A4
just outside Chippenham (Calne direction).
He's a most courteous host, and his affability
rubs off on his charming young staff. The
bars are cheerful and traditional, and there's
a summery conservatory that overlooks the
garden. Enjoyable bar fare ranges from filled
rolls and ploughman's platters to omelettes,
baked crab and steak and kidney pie. Moules
marinière is a special much in demand, and
sweets include a good sherry trifle. *Typical
prices:* Steak & kidney pie £2.50 Moules
marinière £2.50 (Last bar food 10pm) 🍴

ACCOMMODATION   4 bedrooms   £C
Check-in: all day

Bedrooms have a deal of cottage charm, with
homely furnishings and restful colour
schemes. They're comfortable, too, thanks
to central heating, full carpeting and softly
sprung beds. Colour TVs and tea-makers are
standard, and each room has its own neat
bath or shower room with generous towels.

Philleigh   *(Food)*   *Roseland Inn*

Near Truro · *Cornwall* · Map 9 A4
Portscatho (087 258) 254

Brewery Cornish Brewery Company
Landlord Desmond Sinnott

Children welcome
🍺 John Devenish Bitter, Cornish Original, Great
British Heavy; Guinness; Heineken; cider.

Off the beaten track, this 17th-century inn
has abundant rustic charm. Most of the
snacks served in the beamed bar are home
made, with local crab and seafood mornay
two popular items. Other choices include
sandwiches, pâté, good cheeses and a nice
chocolate biscuit cake served with clotted
cream. *Typical prices:* Seafood mornay £2.50
Treacle tart & cream £1 (Last bar food 9pm.
No bar food winter eves) ☕

Pickhill   *(B & B)*   *Nag's Head*

Near Thirsk · *North Yorkshire* · Map 4 C2
Thirsk (0845) 567391
Free House
Landlords R. J. & J. E. Boynton
Children welcome
Credit Access, Visa
🍺 Theakston's Best Bitter, Old Peculier, XB;
Tetley's Bitter; Carlsberg Hof; Slalom Pilsner;
cider. ♀
ACCOMMODATION   10 bedrooms   £C
Check-in: all day

A popular inn situated in an unspoilt village
not far from the A1. Behind a fairly stark
exterior are two pleasant bars (one featuring
a collection of neckties) and an attractively
flagstoned reception area. Eight of the bedrooms are in the main building, the other two
in a separate cottage. All are equipped with
duvets, decent pine furniture, colour TVs,
digital radio-alarms and good modern
shower/bathrooms.

Pin Mill   *Butt & Oyster*

Standing right on the banks of the river Orwell, this splendid old inn is a
great favourite of the seafaring locals. Take the sea air from the sunny
terrace, or enjoy a pint drawn from the wood in the characterful main bar
with its yellowing walls, sturdy furniture and nautical bric-à-brac.

Near Chelmondiston, Ipswich · *Suffolk* · Map 5 D2
Woolverstone (0473) 84764   *Brewery* Tollemache & Cobbold
Landlords Mr & Mrs Mainwaring   **Children welcome**
🍺 Tolly Cobbold Bitter, Mild, Original, 4X; Hansa Lager; cider.

Pinner   *Queen's Head*

This attractive, half-timbered pub has a sign dated 1705. Its foundations
are even older, and some of the original character survives in the blackened
beams and abundant dark oak panelling. Coal fires warm the bars, where
nicely upholstered benches provide ample seating.

31 High Street · *Middlesex* · Map 7 C2
01-868 4607   *Brewery* Benskins   *Landlords* Mr & Mrs Derek & Susie
Passey
🍺 Ind Coope Burton Ale; Benskins Ale; John Bull Bitter; Castlemaine;
Löwenbräu; Skol; cider.

Our inspectors never book in the name of Egon Ronay's Guides; they disclose their identity only after paying their bills.

Pitton *(Food)* **New Entry** — Silver Plough

Salisbury · *Wiltshire* · Map 6 A3
Farley (0722 72) 266 *Free House* *Landlord* Mr Michael Beckett
Children welcome *Credit* Access, Amex, Diners, Visa
🍺 Wadworth's 6X; Hook Norton; Ushers Best Bitter; Webster's
Yorkshire Bitter; Guinness; Carlsberg Hof; cider.

★ Chef Rupert Wilcox prepares a harvest of fine fare at this attractively converted farmhouse. Seafood plays a leading role, with dishes like pasta marinara, bouillabaisse and monkfish in a superb sauce armoricaine among many mouthwatering choices. Game also appears in seasonal specials, and the regular menu runs from soup and pâté to steak and kidney pie, spare ribs and tarragon chicken. Vegetables and salads are excellent, too, and if you're not tempted by a splendid sweet like chocolate fudge cake or blueberry ice cream, you could sample the delights of a first-rate cheeseboard. The two bars and restaurant feature beams, paintings and handsome antique tables. Note also a collection of engraved Bristol glass rolling pins. *Typical prices:* Mussels in cream & white wine £2.95 Gâteau St Honoré £1.40 (Last bar food 10pm) ★

Plumley *(Food)* — Smoker Inn

Near Knutsford · *Cheshire* · Map 3 B3
Lower Peover (056 581) 2338

Brewery Robinson
Landlord Mr Jorge Masso

Children welcome (lunchtime only)
🍺 Robinson's Best Bitter, Best Mild, Lager;
Guinness. ♀

Decent home cooking in a mellow thatched pub by the A556. The menu spans sandwiches, salads and hot dishes like liver and onions, fresh plaice and moussaka, plus sweets such as sherry trifle or crème brûlée. Sandwiches are the only choice Saturday evening and all day Sunday, though a traditional Sunday lunch is served in the restaurant. *Typical prices:* Kofta curry £1.95 (£2.70 at night) Crème brûlée £1 (Last bar food 9.45pm). Garden.

Plymouth *(Food)* — Unity

Eastlake Street · *Devon* · Map 9 B4
Plymouth (0752) 262622

Brewery Halls
Landlord Mrs S. Bibby

🍺 Halls Plympton Pride; John Bull Bitter;
Tetley's Bitter; Skol; Löwenbräu; Castlemaine
4X; cider. ♀

The honest, enjoyable bar food continues to draw lunchtime support for this bustling modern pub in the city centre. Cold cuts and prawns are the basis of fresh salads and granary bread sandwiches, and there are a couple of hot daily specials like lasagne or shepherd's pie. Good Stilton. Evening snacks may be introduced. *Typical prices:* Chilli with baked potato £2 Lasagne £2 (No bar food eves). Pub closed Sunday.

Pocklington   (B & B)   *Feathers Hotel*

56 Market Place · *Humberside* · Map 4 D3
Pocklington (0759) 303155

Brewery Younger
Landlord K. F. Suttle
Children welcome
Credit Access, Amex, Diners, Visa
🍺 Younger's Scotch Bitter, No. 3 Bitter, IPA;
Guinness; Kestrel; McEwan's Lager; cider. ♀
ACCOMMODATION 12 bedrooms £B (No dogs)
Check-in: all day

Overnight accommodation is both attractive and comfortable at this smart, pebbledash hotel in the market place. Six rooms in the main building have a fairly traditional look, while the other six, which are in a chalet-style block across the car park, are in tasteful modern style. All rooms offer TVs, telephones, trouser presses and private facilities. There's a warm, roomy lounge bar. Staff could be more on the ball.

Poole   (B & B)   *Inn in the Park*

Pinewood Road, Branksome Park · *Dorset*
Map 6 A4
Bournemouth (0202) 761318
Free House
Landlords Alan & Paula Potter
Children welcome (lunchtime)
🍺 Younger's Tartan Bitter; Ringwood Potters
Bitter; Wadworth's 6X, IPA; Guinness; Stella
Artois; cider. ♀
ACCOMMODATION   5 bedrooms   £C
Check-in: all day

Just a short walk from Branksome Dean Chine and the sea, this converted Victorian house has been much modernised. The Potters work hard to keep standards high, and the bedrooms are bright and practical, with TVs and tea-makers; three have private facilities. The large open-plan bar features a fine collection of stamps, and there's a patio for fine-weather drinking.

Pooley Bridge   (B & B)   *Crown Hotel*

Near Penrith · *Cumbria* · Map 3 B1
Pooley Bridge (085 36) 217

Brewery Whitbread
Landlords Mr & Mrs Simcox

🍺 Whitbread Trophy, Mild; Guinness; Stella
Artois; Heineken; cider.
ACCOMMODATION 5 bedrooms £D (No dogs)
Check-in: all day

Spacious bars and a central location with a pleasant garden running down to the banks of the river Earmont help to make this village pub a popular meeting place. Bright, good-size bedrooms have a nice old-fashioned character and share a single public bathroom; all are equipped with tea-makers. Residents can enjoy TV in the cosy first-floor lounge.

Porlock Weir   (B & B)   *Anchor Hotel & Ship Inn*

Near Minehead · *Somerset* · Map 9 C3
Porlock (0643) 862636

Free House
Landlords Pandy Sechiari & Donald Wade
Children welcome
Credit Access, Amex, Visa
🍺 Ushers Best Bitter, Exmoor Ale, Triple
Crown; Guinness; Foster's; Holsten; cider.
ACCOMMODATION   30 bedrooms   £A
Check-in: all day

The thatched 16th-century Ship Inn, the 19th-century Anchor Hotel and a recently converted annexe enjoy a delightful setting overlooking the pretty harbour, with views across the Bristol Channel to the Welsh coast. All the bedrooms have TVs and tea-makers; 20 have private facilities and many enjoy sea vistas. There are a number of lounge areas and several bars. Accommodation closed two weeks January. Patio.

Port Gaverne *(B & B)*

Port Gaverne Hotel

Near Port Isaac · *Cornwall* · Map 9 B4
Bodmin (0208) 880244

Free House
Landlords Mr & Mrs F. P. Ross
Credit Access, Amex, Diners, Visa
McEwan's Export; Flowers Best, IPA;
Whitbread Best; St Austell Hicks Special; Stella
Artois; Guinness; cider. ♀
ACCOMMODATION 19 bedrooms £A
Check-in: all day

Charm is in plentiful supply at this early 17th-century inn set in a rugged cove half a mile from Port Isaac. The three cosy bars – decorated with old photographs and water-colours – are full of character, and the pleasant little lounge has a seaview balcony. Pretty, spotless bedrooms – all with modern bathrooms – have thoughtful extras like books and magazines and quality soap. Closed mid January to end February. Garden.

Powerstock *(Food, B & B)*

Three Horseshoes

Bridport · *Dorset* · Map 9 D3
Powerstock (030 885) 328

Brewery Palmer
Landlords Pat & Diana Ferguson

Children welcome
Credit Access, Visa
Palmer's Bridport Bitter, IPA; Guinness;
Faust; Shilthorn; cider. ♀

Customers are attracted both by the do-it-yourself garden barbecues which are a feature of this Victorian pub and by the adventurous fare served in the handsome pine-panelled bars. Fresh crab, plaice, mullet and sea bass dominate the menu, with perhaps mussels and lobsters as well. There are also lamb cutlets and roast beef, with soup, sandwiches, omelettes, ploughman's and wholewheat pancakes for those who want only a snack. Simple home-made puds such as apple pie, and there are always three or four excellent farmhouse cheeses. *Typical prices:* Moules marinère £2.75   Grilled fresh plaice £3.95 (Last bar food 10pm. No bar food Mon) ⊖

ACCOMMODATION 3 bedrooms £D
Check-in: restricted

The three cottage bedrooms – which share a well-kept bathroom – provide comfortable overnight accommodation. All have tea/coffee-making facilities.

Priors Hardwick

Butchers Arms

The Portuguese family owners provide a warm welcome at their solid stone-built village inn which dates back to 1375. Flagstoned floors, splendid fireplaces and handsome antique furniture characterise the oak-beamed bars, and drinks can also be enjoyed in the peace of the conservatory or in the well-kept grounds.

Near Southam · *Warwickshire* · Map 7 B1
Byfield (0327) 60504   *Free House   Landlords* Pires family
Children welcome
Bass; Mitchell & Butlers Springfield Bitter, Brew XI; Carling Black
Label; Carlsberg Hof; Tennent's Lager. *No real ale.* ♀

Pulborough   *(Food)*   *Waters Edge*

Station Road · *West Sussex* · Map 6 B4
Pulborough (07982) 2451

Brewery Friary Meux
Landlords John & Margaret Salmon

Children welcome
Credit Access, Amex, Diners, Visa
🍺 Friary Meux Best Bitter, Mild; Ind Coope
Burton Ale; John Bull; Löwenbräu, cider. ♀

An excellent carvery of roast meats and
fresh, crisp vegetables is a big attraction at
this comfortable pub by an inlet on the river
Arun. There's also a cold table, but neither is
available on Sunday evening or all day
Monday, when various other things, from
sandwiches to steaks, are served. Good
home-made sweets and puddings. *Typical
prices:* Steak & kidney pie with Guinness
£3.60   Lemon meringue pie £1.10 (Last bar
food 9.30pm) ⊖

Pulverbatch   *(Food)*   *White Horse*

Near Shrewsbury · *Shropshire* · Map 8 D1
Dorrington (074 373) 247

Brewery Whitbread
Landlords Margaret & Hamish MacGregor

Children welcome
🍺 Wadworth's 6X; Flowers Original; Whitbread
Best Bitter; Guinness, Stella Artois; cider. ♀

Follow the country lanes from the A49 at
Dorrington to find the MacGregors' busy inn.
Scottish flavour abounds, from the tartan
decor to the popular Rob Roy sandwich – hot
French bread with roast beef and melted
cheese. The menu offers a vast choice,
including warming soups, home-made burgers, omelettes, grills and salads, plus fruit
pies, cheese cake and ice creams. *Typical
prices:* Anytime breakfast £3.10   Superbur-
ger £1.75 (Last bar food 10pm) ⊖

Pyrton   *(Food)*   *Plough Inn*

Near Watlington · *Oxfordshire* · Map 7 B2
Watlington (049 161) 2003

Free House
Landlords Jackie & Jeremy Hunt

Children welcome
Credit Access, Visa
🍺 Adnams Bitter; Brakspear's Bitter;
Barleycorn Pale Ale; Badger Bitter; Theakston's
XB; Guinness, cider. ♀

Sandwiches, ploughman's and jacket potatoes top up the lunchtime menu at this
archetypal English country pub. Its considerable charms include a thatched roof, grand
old fireplace and friendly owners, who enjoy
dispensing real ale and tasty food. Soup,
pâté, steaks, chilli and scampi are always
available, plus scrumptious home-made
puds. *Typical prices:* Vegetarian stuffed vine
leaves £4.95   Jacket potatoes with garlic
prawns £1.75 (Last bar food 10pm) ⊖

Ramsbury   *(Food)*   *Bell at Ramsbury*

The Square · *Wiltshire* · Map 7 A2
Marlborough (0672) 20230

Free House
Landlord Mr Michael Benjamin

Children welcome
🍺 Wadworth's IPA; 6X; Guinness; Carlsberg
Hof; cider. ♀

In winter a log fire warms the comfortable
bar of this smartened-up pub by the village
square. Unusual pies like Bernese Oberlan-
der (bacon, sausage and cabbage) and
Gobble and Grunt (turkey and pork) are a
feature of the menu, which also offers a
hearty vegetable soup, pâté, ploughman's
and kedgeree. Delicious sweets, too. Garden. *Typical prices:* Gobble & grunt pie
£2.45   Taramasalata £1.80 (Last bar food
10pm. No bar food Sat eve) ⊖

Ringmore   *(Food, B & B)*   *Journey's End Inn*

Kingsbridge · Devon · Map 8 B4
Bigbury-on-Sea (0548) 810205

Free House
Landlords Ray & Hazel Hollins
Children welcome
Credit Access, Visa
🍺 Wadworth's 6X; Hall & Woodhouse Badger
Best Bitter; Hall's Plympton Bitter; Guinness;
Carlsberg; cider. ⚫

A narrow lane leads to this delightfully rambling pink-washed pub which rejoices in low ceilings, paved floors and lots of cosy corners. The panelled lounge bar is particularly inviting and here you can enjoy tasty bar snacks to suit all appetites – from soup and toasted double-decker sandwiches, salads and ploughman's to hearty offerings like sausage and mash with onion sauce, fried plaice, chicken curry and pizzas. There are vegetarian specials, too, and home-made fruit pies topped with lovely clotted cream to round things off nicely. *Typical prices:* Giant beefburger £1.95   Shepherd's pie £2.50 (Last bar food 10pm) ⊖

ACCOMMODATION 4 bedrooms £C (No dogs)
Check-in: all day

A fresh rose each day in the cheerful, cottagy bedrooms is a typically thoughtful touch. Colour TVs and tea-makers are standard throughout. Two rooms have private facilities, and the other two share a spotless public bathroom. No under-tens overnight.

Children welcome *indicates a pub with an area where children are allowed whether eating or not.*

Ringwood   *(Food, B & B)*   *Original White Hart*

Market Place · *Hampshire* · Map 6 A4
Ringwood (042 54) 2702

Brewery Eldridge Pope
Landlords Terry & Mary Eales

Children welcome
Credit Access, Amex, Visa
🍺 Eldridge Pope Dorchester Bitter, Dorset IPA,
Royal Oak, 1880; Guinness; Faust; cider. ⚫

Old beams and mellow panelling in a series of cosy interconnecting rooms at this fine old tavern in the town centre create an attractive setting in which to enjoy Mary Eales' simple home cooking. Her home-made soup can be followed by steak and kidney pie or a tasty steak sandwich, rounded off with a nice apple pie. There is also an appetising display of salads at lunchtime which includes flavoursome honey roast ham. *Typical prices:* Steak & kidney pie £1.50   Filled jacket potato 95p (Last bar food 10pm) ⊖

ACCOMMODATION 8 bedrooms £C
Check-in: all day

Modest, traditionally furnished bedrooms provide basic comforts. They are equipped with TVs, radios and tea/coffee-making facilities. Improvements are planned.

Ripley *(Food)*   *Anchor*

High Street · *Surrey* · Map 7 C2
Guildford (0483) 224120

Brewery Friary Meux
Landlord Mrs Christine Beale

🍺 Friary Meux Bitter; Ind Coope Burton Ale;
Guinness; Skol; Löwenbräu; cider.

This mellow village pub is over 700 years old,
and its cosy, low-beamed bars are filled with
burnished brass and pretty porcelain. Christine Beale's tasty, home-baked savoury pies
are the favourite choice at lunchtime, with
soup, sandwiches and ploughman's providing lighter bites. Beef curry is a typical daily
special and there's a traditional roast on
Sunday. *Typical prices:* Steak & kidney pie
with vegetables £2.25   Ham salad £2.50 (No
bar food eves) ℮

Ripley *(Food)*   **New Entry**   *Seven Stars*

Newark Lane · *Surrey* · Map 7 C2
Guildford (0483) 225128

Brewery Friary Meux
Landlord Rodney Dean

🍺 Friary Meux Best Bitter, Mild; Ind Coope
Bitter; Benskins; Guinness; Löwenbräu; cider.

Prize-winning pizzas are among the tasty
home-prepared snacks served in this cheerful pub, which stands by the B367 just north
of Ripley. Other dishes marked up on the
blackboard could include lasagne (with a
good meaty sauce), jumbo sausage or seafood platter, with apricot crumble or a splendid trifle to finish. Also sandwiches, winter
soup and a lunchtime cold buffet. *Typical
prices:* Goulash with salad £1.30   Special
pizza £2.10 (Last bar food 9pm) ℮

Ripon *(B & B)*   *Unicorn Hotel*

Market Place · *North Yorkshire* · Map 4 C2
Ripon (0765) 2202
Free House
Landlords Mr & Mrs D. T. Small
Children welcome
Credit Access, Amex, Diners, Visa
🍺 Theakston's Best Bitter, XB; John Smith's
Bitter; Younger's Scotch Bitter; Guinness;
Carlsberg Export; cider.
ACCOMMODATION   27 bedrooms   £C
Check-in: all day

An old posting house standing in the market
place of a historic city that was granted its
first charter 1100 years ago. The public bar
is a favourite meeting place for the locals,
and there's a comfortable lounge bar along
with a residents' lounge. Bedrooms are light,
spacious and quite well equipped (TVs, tea-
makers, direct-dial telephones). Private bath
or shower in every room.

Ripponden *(Food)*   *Old Bridge Inn*

Priest Lane · *West Yorkshire* · Map 4 C3
Halifax (0422) 822595

Free House
Landlord Mr Ian Hargreaves Beaumont

Children welcome (lunchtime)
Credit Amex, Visa
🍺 Younger's Scotch Bitter; Timothy Taylor's
Best Bitter; Tetley's Falstaff Mild; Guinness;
Tuborg; cider.

Cottagy beamed bars and a riverside setting
add to the charm of this whitewashed inn,
said to be the oldest in Yorkshire. At lunchtime, the help-yourself cold buffet featuring
cooked meats, salads and quiches is a
popular attraction, while evenings bring
soup, sandwiches and tasty hot dishes like
fisherman's pie. There's also a restaurant
open for dinner. *Typical bar prices:* Kyrenian
beef £2.50   Smoked trout £2.25 (Last bar
food 10pm. No bar food Sat eve & Sun lunch)

Risplith   (B & B)

Black-a-Moor Inn

Near Ripon · North Yorkshire · Map 4 C2
Sawley (076 586) 214

Free House
Landlords Mr & Mrs David Beckett
Children welcome
Credit Access, Visa
🍺 Younger's Scotch Bitter, IPA, No. 3;
McEwan's Lager; Hofmeister; cider.
ACCOMMODATION 3 bedrooms £D (No dogs)
Check-in: all day

A pretty stone-built pub located on the B6265 about five miles west of Ripon. It's a good spot for an overnight stop, and the three bedrooms are all of quite a decent size; they share a neat, functional bathroom. The single spacious bar is divided into public (games and jukebox) and plusher lounge areas. Pub closed Monday lunchtime except for Bank Holidays. Garden.

Any person using our name to obtain free hospitality is a fraud. Proprietors, please inform the police and us.

Rochester   (B & B)

Redesdale Arms

Near Otterburn · Northumberland · Map 2 D4
Otterburn (0830) 20668

Free House
Landlords Hilda & Johnny Wright

Credit Access, Visa
🍺 Drybrough Heavy; McEwan's Best Scotch, Export; Carlsberg; cider. *No real ale.* ♀
ACCOMMODATION 11 bedrooms £D (No dogs)
Check-in: all day

This mellow stone inn stands in beautiful countryside by the A68, just 12 miles from the Scottish border. Horse brasses hang on rough plaster walls in the beamed lounge bar, and there are some inviting easy chairs in the residents' sitting room; there's also a simply appointed public bar. Bedrooms are traditional in style and furnishings; all have TVs and three offer private facilities. Garden.

Rockcliffe   (Food)

Crown & Thistle

Near Carlisle · Cumbria · Map 3 B1
Rockcliffe (022 874) 378

Brewery Scottish & Newcastle
Landlords Kevin & Joanne Dempsey

Children welcome
🍺 McEwan's 70/-; Younger's Traditional IPA; Harp; Guinness; cider.

If the choice on the bar menu of this pleasant old pub on the outskirts of the village looks ordinary, the preparation certainly isn't. Succulent home-cooked ham heads the list of tasty fare, and the steaks are good, too. Other offerings include soup and sandwiches (these two are all that's available on Mondays) and the popular hot pot. The favourite sweet is a creamy apple gâteau. *Typical prices:* Hot pot £1.75   Ham platter £2.40 (Last bar food 9 pm. No bar food Sun eve) ⊖

Romaldkirk   *(Food, B & B)*   *Rose & Crown Hotel*

Teesdale · *Co. Durham* · Map 4 C2
Teesdale (0833) 50213

Free House
Landlords David & Jill Jackson

Credit Access, Amex, Diners, Visa
🍺 Tawny Bitter; Theakston's Bitter; Matthew
Brown's Bitter; Slalom, Slalom D Lager; cider.

ACCOMMODATION   11 bedrooms   £B
Check-in: all day

Once a major coaching house, this 18th-
century inn stands next to the ancient church
overlooking the green. Hospitality's still the
name of the game, and both the food and the
accommodation are excellent. The lunchtime
bill of fare includes a popular cold buffet
(summer only), along with pâté, soup, sandwiches and hot dishes like fish and chips or
chilli con carne. No sandwiches in the evening, when a wider choice of main courses
could include gammon, sirloin steak, pan-
fried trout and barbecue-sauced breast of
chicken. *Typical prices:* Soup 95p   Fillets of
lemon sole £4.95 (Last bar food 10pm) 🍴

Seven very comfortable bedrooms in the
main building are traditionally furnished and
have either a settee or a couple of armchairs
each and a choice of duvets or sheets and
blankets. Smart modern chalet-style rooms
in the courtyard block include a honeymoon
room complete with four-poster. Private
bathrooms and lots of little extras throughout.

Rosedale Abbey   *(B & B)*   *Blacksmiths Arms Hotel*

Hartoft End, Near Pickering · *North Yorkshire*
Map 4 D2
Lastingham (075 15) 331
Free House
Landlords M. P. & J. K. Barrie
Credit Access, Visa
🍺 Younger's Scotch Bitter; John Smith's Best;
Newcastle Exhibition; Guinness; Carlsberg;
cider. 🍷
ACCOMMODATION   12 bedrooms   £B
Check-in: all day

At the foot of Rosedale in the North Yorkshire
Moors National Park, this 16th-century farmhouse – built with stone from the nearby
Abbey – makes a comfortable and welcoming
place to stay. Attractively decorated bedrooms, most with private facilities, have
simple modern furniture and tea-making
facilities. The two cottage bars are full of
charm and character, with their homely bric-
à-brac, and there's a splendid garden.

Rosedale Abbey   *(B & B)*   *White Horse Farm Hotel*

Near Pickering · *North Yorkshire* · Map 4 D2
Lastingham (075 15) 239

Free House
Landlords Mr & Mrs D. C. Wilcock

Credit Amex, Diners
🍺 Tetley's Best Bitter, Mild; Cameron's Lion
Bitter, Strongarm; Hansa; Skol; cider. 🍷
ACCOMMODATION   15 bedrooms   £B
Check-in: all day

Stunning moorland views are a bonus of this
sturdy stone pub, well placed as a base for a
touring holiday. The stone-walled bar with its
wealth of old beams and church pew seating
is splendidly rustic, and spacious bedrooms
with pleasing colour schemes and attractive
fitted units are very comfortable. All have tea-
makers, colour TVs, and compact bath or
shower rooms. Patio and garden.

Rotherwick   *(Food)*   *Coach & Horses*

The Street, Near Hook · *Hampshire* · Map 7 B2
Hook (025 672) 2542

Free House
Landlord Mrs Terry Williams

Children welcome
🍺 Hall & Woodhouse Badger Pedigree,
Tanglefoot; Royal Oak; Kingsdown; Ringwood
Old Thumper; Guest Beer; cider.

The owner's son Liam prepares the tasty bar
fare in this agreeable pub that features an
excellent selection of real ales. His pizzas
and meaty burgers are particularly popular,
and there are sandwiches, quiches and
heartier dishes like roast duck or mixed grill.
A cold buffet in summer and carvery in winter,
which run from Thursday to Sunday, provide
appetising fare. *Typical prices:* Hamburger
£1.75   Carvery or cold table £5.75 (Last bar
food 10.30pm) 🍽

Rowhook   *(Food)*   *Chequers Inn*

Near Horsham · *West Sussex* · Map 6 B3
Slinfold (0403) 790480

Brewery Whitbread
Landlord Mr P. A. Barrs

Credit Visa
🍺 Flowers Original; Whitbread Strong Country
Bitter; Samuel Whitbread; Stella Artois;
Heineken; cider.

An unpretentious 15th-century inn whose
snack menu changes daily, with home-made
pies and casseroles among the regular
favourites. There are also sandwiches and
ploughman's, home-cooked ham, grilled sole
and a particularly good toad in the hole.
Evening extras could include rainbow trout
and chicken Kiev. Standard puds. *Typical
prices:* Home-cooked ham £2.95   Stilton
ploughman's £1.90 (Last bar food 10.30pm.
No bar food Sun eve) 🍽

Running Waters   *(B & B)*   *Three Horse Shoes*

Sherburn House, Near Durham · *Co. Durham*
Map 4 C1
Durham (0385) 720286
Free House
Landlords Derek & Lesley Crehan
Children welcome (lunchtime)
Credit Access, Visa
🍺 Vaux Samson, Lorimer's Scotch, Sunderland
Bitter; Tuborg; Stella Artois, cider. *No real
ale.* 𝅘
ACCOMMODATION   4 bedrooms   £C
Check-in: all day

Derek and Lesley Crehan take great pride in
their neat, cream-painted pub, which stands
high up on the A181 between Durham and
Hartlepool. You can be sure of a friendly
welcome, whether pausing for a drink in the
two simple bars hung with prints and water-
colours of the Yorkshire Dales or staying
overnight in one of the pleasant, well-kept
bedrooms. Three rooms have shower cabinets and washbasins, and there's a very
pretty bathroom. Good breakfasts. Garden.

Rusthall   *(Food)*   *Red Lion*

Near Tunbridge Wells · *Kent* · Map 6 C4
Tunbridge Wells (0892) 20086

Brewery Whitbread
Landlords Mr & Mrs B. Cooter

🍺 Whitbread Best, Mild; Fremlins Bitter; Stella
Artois; Guinness; Heineken; cider. 𝅘

Two bars – one plushly comfortable, the
other beamed and full of character – provide
a choice of venue for enjoying the Cooters'
appetising snacks. Stick to old favourites
such as soup, salads, sausages and steaks,
or opt for something more unusual like our
savoury meatballs in a vegetable-packed
curry sauce. Less choice in the evening.
Garden. *Typical prices:* Smoked salmon pâté
£1.50   Fried scallops & chips £2.40 (Last bar
food 10pm) 🍽

St Dominick   *Who'd Have Thought It Inn*

The Potter family have achieved an impressive standard of comfort and hospitality over the 30-odd years that they've been welcoming visitors to this sturdy, 19th-century inn. Handsome old furnishings, china and objets d'art create a homely air in the three bars, which include a delightful beamed lounge bar overlooking the Tamar Valley.

Saltash · *Cornwall* · Map 9 B4
Liskeard (0579) 50214   *Free House*   *Landlords* Potter family
Children welcome (lunchtime Mon-Sat)
🍺 Courage Directors Bitter; Bass; Worthington Best Bitter; Guinness; Hofmeister; Carling Black Label; cider. ♀

St Margaret's at Cliffe   *(B & B)*   *Cliffe Tavern*

High Street, near Dover · *Kent* · Map 6 D3
Dover (0304) 852749
Free House
Landlords Westby family
Children welcome
Credit Access, Amex, Diners, Visa
🍺 Shepherd Neame Masterbrew; Fremlins Bitter; Webster's Yorkshire Bitter; Guinness; Carlsberg; Hurlimann; cider. ♀
ACCOMMODATION   12 bedrooms   £C
Check-in: restricted

This white-painted clapboard pub in a pretty village just outside Dover offers handy overnight accommodation for ferry passengers. Whether in the main building or two adjacent cottages, all rooms have pretty furnishings, practical units (including a desk), TVs, tea-makers and neat modern bathrooms. The spacious mock-beamed bar has a cheerful atmosphere, and the walled garden is a pleasant spot for a summer drink.

St Mawgan   *(B & B)*   *Falcon Inn*

Near Newquay · *Cornwall* · Map 9 A4
St Mawgan (0637) 860225

Free House
Landlords Mr & Mrs P. Joyce

Children welcome
🍺 St Austell Best Bitter, Pinner's Ale; McEwan's Bitter; Worthington Bitter; Bass; Guinness; Carlsberg; cider.
ACCOMMODATION   4 bedrooms   £D
Check-in: all day

The Joyces are hospitable hosts at their handsome old pub in the wooded valley of Lanherne. The huge garden with its wishing well makes an inviting spot for summer drinks, while the popular bar is roomy and convivial. Upstairs, the cosy residents' TV lounge and four bedrooms (sharing a spotless bathroom) are delightfully homely and comfortable. No children overnight July and August. Accommodation is closed a week at Christmas.

St Neots   *(Food)*   *Chequers Inn*

St Mary's Street, Eynesbury · *Cambridgeshire*
Map 5 B2
Huntingdon (0480) 72116

Free House
Landlord David James Taylor

Children welcome
Credit Access, Amex, Diners, Visa
🍺 Paine's 3X, Stones Bitter; Younger's Tartan; Carlsberg; Carling Black Label. ♀

Lunchtime is the busy period at this attractive 16th-century pub, whose cosy, low-beamed bar has great atmosphere. Fresh plaice is one of the house specialities (two fish choices are always available) and other favourites include garlic mushrooms, steak and kidney pie and peppered pork chop. Home-made puddings are tempting, and there's a selection of cheeses. *Typical prices:* Pâté £1.95 Grilled gammon & pineapple £3.85 (Last bar food 10pm) 🍽

St Neots *(B & B)* — *Rocket*

Grosshall Road, Eaton Ford · *Cambridgeshire*
Map 5 B2
Huntingdon (0480) 72773

Free House
Landlord Mrs V. Stephenson
Credit Access, Amex, Diners, Visa
🍺 Adnams Bitter; Greene King IPA; Paine's 3X;
Wells Gold Eagle; Guinness; Kellerbräu.
ACCOMMODATION 9 bedrooms £B (No dogs)
Check-in: all day

The Stephenson family are relations of George – hence the name of this former farmhouse at the junction of the A1 and A45. The pleasant panelled bar is in the original building, while the roomy overnight accommodation is in an adjoining modern block. All bedrooms have central heating, plus TVs, direct-dial phones, and tea-making facilities. Well-fitted private facilities throughout. Patio.

We welcome complaints and bona fide recommendations on the tear-out pages for readers' comments. They are followed up by our professional team. Please also complain to the management instantly.

Saffron Walden *(Food, B & B)* — *Eight Bells*

Bridge Street · *Essex* · Map 7 D1
Saffron Walden (0799) 22790

Brewery Benskins
Landlord Mr R. Moore

Children welcome
Credit Access, Amex, Diners, Visa
🍺 John Bull Bitter; Benskins Best Bitter; Burton Ale; Guinness; Skol; Oranjeboom; cider. ♀

Polished oak furniture, beamed walls hung with old prints and candlelight at night make this 500-year-old inn a particularly appealing place for a thoroughly enjoyable snack. The imaginative selection of dishes suits all tastes, from guacamole and farmhouse cheese ploughman's to surf 'n' turf (rump steak and giant prawns), fried plaice and Stilton-topped mushrooms baked in cider and thyme. Daily specials such as fresh crab and chicken in champagne sauce expand the choice, and delicious sweets include home-made blackberry and apple crumble. There's a cold buffet in summer, and a thoughtful children's menu, too. *Typical prices:* Saffron gilded chicken £4.55 Steak & kidney pie £3.95 (Last bar food 9.30pm) ☻

ACCOMMODATION 2 bedrooms £C (No dogs)
Check-in: all day

Upstairs the two beamed, good sized bedrooms have a comfortable, homely appeal. Both offer tea-makers and share a carpeted bathroom. Garden.

Saffron Walden   (Food, B & B)   Saffron Hotel

High Street · *Essex* · Map 7 D1
Saffron Walden (0799) 22676

Free House
Landlords Craddock family

Children welcome
Credit Access, Visa
🍺 Greene King IPA; Younger's Tartan; John
Smith's Yorkshire Bitter; Guinness;
Kronenbourg 1664; Carlsberg; cider. 🍷

Lanzarote-born Domingo Berriel is in charge
of culinary affairs at this 16th-century high-
street hotel. The restaurant is his main outlet,
but his bar snacks are also excellent. There's
quite a large seafood section on the menu
(though our super grilled herring was one of
the blackboard specials), and other choices
run from delicious creamy vegetable soup to
spaghetti bolognese, Spanish omelette,
gammon steak and the very popular tandoori
chicken with curried vegetables. Just a few
sweets, including bread and butter pudding
and apple pie. *Typical prices:* Chicken liver &
brandy pâté £1.95   Grilled trout £3.75 (Last
bar food 9.30pm. No bar food Sat eve or
Sun) ☺

ACCOMMODATION   18 bedrooms   £B
Check-in: all day

Bedrooms vary in size, the smallest (but at
the same time the most characterful) being
those under the eaves. Six rooms offer
private facilities and six others have shower
cubicles. The bar is smart and comfortable
and there's a traditional lounge. The hotel is
closed for five days at Christmas.

Salisbury   Haunch of Venison

Overlooking the ancient Poultry Cross in the city centre, this fine half-
timbered inn has a history spanning seven centuries. A choice of cosy
drinking spots is provided by the intimate bar with its solid metal counter
and three other little rooms — including the House of Lords, reputedly
once a discreet tippling place for local church dignitaries.

1 Minster Street · *Wiltshire* · Map 6 A4
Salisbury (0722) 22024   *Brewery* Courage   *Landlords* Mr & Mrs Leroy
Children welcome   *Credit* Access, Amex, Diners, Visa
🍺 Courage Directors Bitter, Best Bitter; Guinness; Hofmeister.

Salisbury   (B & B)   King's Arms

9 St John Street · *Wiltshire* · Map 6 A4
Salisbury (0722) 27629
Owners Westward Hosts
Landlord Mr Anthony Wilkinson
Children welcome
Credit Access, Amex, Diners, Visa
🍺 Usher's Best Bitter, Founder's Ale, Triple
Crown; Webster's Yorkshire Bitter; Holsten;
Carlsberg; cider. *No real ale*
ACCOMMODATION   15 bedrooms   £C
Check-in: all day

Close to the cathedral, this splendid old half-
timbered inn simply oozes period charm. The
oak-panelled residents' lounge with its original Tudor fireplace and tapestries is particularly fine, and the two cosy beamed bars are
full of character. Appealingly old-fashioned
bedrooms (one boasts a handsome William
and Mary four-poster) offer homely comforts;
they have TVs and tea-makers, and private
facilities are well equipped.

Sandon Bank (Food)

Seven Stars Inn

Near Stafford · Staffordshire · Map 4 C4
Sandon (088 97) 316

Brewery Burtonwood
Landlords Jill & Ron Roestenburg

Children welcome
Credit Access, Visa
🍺 Burtonwood Bitter, Dark Mild, Top Hat Strong Ale; Guinness; Tuborg Gold, Pilsner; cider.

A popular family pub with five cosy bar-food areas, a cocktail bar, a 40-seat restaurant and a large garden. Ploughman's lunches, steak and kidney pie, steaks and curries are served in bumper portions, along with specials like seafood mornay or beef mexicana. There's a roast for Sunday lunch and a weekday cold buffet in summer. *Typical prices:* Chicken à la king £3.50 Ploughman's lunch £1.80 (Last bar food 9.45pm) ℮

Sandside (B & B)

Ship Inn

Near Milnthorpe · Cumbria · Map 3 B2
Milnthorpe (044 82) 3113

Brewery William Younger's Inns
Landlord Mr John Nancarrow
Children welcome
Credit Access, Visa
🍺 William Younger's No. 3 Scotch Ale; McEwan's 70/-, Lager; Beck's Bier; cider.
ACCOMMODATION 6 bedrooms £C
Check-in: all day

Morecambe Bay and the Lakeland hills make a most attractive backdrop for this cheerful inn, which is less than ten minutes' drive from the M6 (junction 36). The bedrooms, all with TVs and tea-makers, have attractive pine wardrobes and chests of drawers; one double has an en suite bathroom, and the rest share a public one. Children are not accommodated overnight, but they are admitted to the pub, and there's a play area. Friendly, obliging staff.

Sandwich (B & B)

Fleur-de-Lis

Delf Street · Kent · Map 6 D3
Sandwich (0304) 611131

Brewery Whitbread
Landlord Mr R. J. Tillings
Children welcome
Credit Access, Amex, Diners, Visa
🍺 Fremlins Bitter; Flowers Original; Guest Beer; Guinness; Stella Artois; Heineken; cider. ♀
ACCOMMODATION 8 bedrooms £C
Check-in: restricted

Oil lamps light one of the three pleasant bars at this mellow old red-brick pub, making it a particularly inviting spot at night. There's also a well-equipped games room featuring two pool tables. Comfortable bedrooms are furnished in traditional style and all provide TVs and tea-makers. Those in the main building share a modern bathroom, while each of the annexe rooms has a shower cubicle.

Sandygate (Food)

Blue Ball

Old Rydon Lane, Exeter · Devon · Map 9 C3
Topsham (039 287) 3401

Brewery Whitbread
Landlords Mike & Linda Ward

🍺 Flowers Original, IPA, Best Bitter; Whitbread Best Bitter; Guinness; Stella Artois; Heineken; cider. ♀

This peaceful thatched pub is to be found down a lane near junction 30 of the M5 (follow signs for Topsham). Traditional snacks can be enjoyed – lunchtime and evenings – in the friendly beamed lounge bar. Choice ranges from hearty soup, pâté and smoked mackerel to a farmhouse grill, lasagne, or ham and eggs. Sandwiches and salads too. Garden. *Typical prices:* Steak & kidney pie £2.85 Chicken curry Madras £2.60 (Last bar food 10pm) ℮

Saunderton *(B & B)*   *Rose & Crown Inn*

Wycombe Road, Near Princes
Risborough · *Buckinghamshire* · Map 7 B2
Princes Risborough (084 44) 5299
Free House
Landlords Robert & John Watson
Credit Access, Amex, Diners, Visa
🍺 Morlands Bitter; Wethereds Bitter; Morrell's
Varsity Bitter; Stella Artois; Heineken. ♀
ACCOMMODATION 15 bedrooms £A (No dogs)
Check-in: all day

Both modern and period styles grace the
pretty bedrooms of this large white-painted
inn on the A4010. All are spacious and
attractively furnished, with colour TVs and
tea-makers, and most have neat private
bathrooms. Housekeeping is excellent.
Guests can relax in the cosy bow-windowed
bar, or take their ease in the large beer
garden at the rear. No children under eight
overnight; accommodation closed one week
Christmas.

Scole *(B & B)*   *Crossways Inn*

Near Diss · *Norfolk* · Map 5 D2
Diss (0379) 740638

Free House
Landlord Peter Black
Children welcome
Credit Access, Visa
🍺 Adnams Bitter; Tolly Cobbold Bitter; Hansa;
Dortmunder; cider. ♀
ACCOMMODATION   5 bedrooms   £B
Check-in: restricted

Dating back to 1560, though now largely
modernised, this busy pub stands alongside
the A140. The spacious main bar sports
beams and solid darkwood furnishings, and
there's a lounge area by reception. Good-
size, attractively decorated bedrooms all
have TVs, telephones, washbasins and WCs,
and three have baths en suite. At the back of
the pub is a well-tended garden covering
three acres.

Scole *(B & B)*   *Scole Inn*

Near Diss · *Norfolk* · Map 5 D2
Diss (0379) 740481
Free House
Landlord Mr Bob Nylk
Children welcome
Credit Access, Amex, Diners, Visa
🍺 Adnams Bitter; Greene King Abbot;
McEwan's Export Bitter; Guinness; Carling
Black Label; Tennent's Lager; cider. ♀
ACCOMMODATION   23 bedrooms   £B
Check-in: all day

Once an important coaching stop and
adopted headquarters of a highwayman, this
impressive roadside inn dating from 1655 is
full of character and atmosphere. The bar
has heavy oak furniture and a huge inglenook
fireplace, and spacious main-house bedrooms (some are in a converted stable block)
are approached by a magnificent carved oak
staircase. All rooms offer private facilities
and are equipped with TVs, tea-makers and
trouser presses.

Seahouses *(B & B)*   *Olde Ship Hotel*

Northumberland · Map 2 D4
Seahouses (0665) 720 200

Free House
Landlords Alan & Jean Glen

🍺 Scottish & Newcastle Exhibition, Newcastle
Bitter; McEwan's Best Scotch 80/-; Guinness;
McEwan's Lager; cider. *No real ale.* ♀
ACCOMMODATION   10 bedrooms   £C
Check-in: all day

The Glens take great pride in their homely
little harbourside inn. Everything is spotlessly
kept, from the two peaceful residents'
lounges to the saloon and cabin bars
crammed with nautical bric-à-brac and popular with local fishermen. There's a charming
garden with a summerhouse and a terrace,
too. Snug, simply furnished bedrooms with
bath or shower rooms have TVs and tea-
makers. Accommodation is closed from November to March.

Sedgefield (B & B)

Dun Cow Inn

43 Front Street · *Co. Durham* · Map 4 C1
Sedgefield (0740) 20894
Owner Ramside Estates
Landlord Mr Geoff Rayner
Children welcome
Credit Access, Amex, Diners, Visa
🍺 Younger's No. 3, Tartan; McEwan's 80/-,
Best Scotch; Newcastle Exhibition; Guinness;
Harp; cider.
ACCOMMODATION 6 bedrooms £C
Check-in: all day

Window boxes and hanging flower baskets
add a touch of colour to this trim, white-
painted pub. The main bar is a smart affair,
with plush banquettes and photographs of
old Sedgefield. Mock beams give a rustic
character to the pleasant bedrooms, which
have modern furniture, brass light fittings
and plenty of thoughtful extras, from fresh
fruit and sweets to tea-makers and TVs.

Sedgefield (Food)

Nag's Head Inn

8 West End · *Co. Durham* · Map 4 C1
Sedgefield (0740) 20234

Brewery Charrington
Landlords Mr & Mrs I. Campbell

Children welcome
Credit Access, Amex, Diners, Visa
🍺 Stones Bitter, Best Scotch Bitter; Carling
Black Label; cider.

The friendly Campbell family keep their 300-
year-old pub in tip-top condition and the main
bar, with its horsy pictures and plush velvet
seating, is a most inviting place. The menu,
available in both bar and restaurant, includes
several Mexican specialities like tacos and
chilli as well as more familiar items such as
soup, pâté, burgers and steak. Super sweets,
too. Garden. *Typical prices*: Sirloin steak
£4.95   Trout £2.50 (Last bar food 10 pm) ⊝

*We publish annually
so make sure you use
the current edition.*

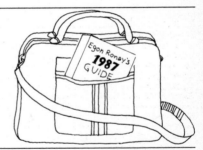

Sellack (Food)

Lough Pool Inn

Ross-on-Wye · *Herefordshire* · Map 8 D2
Harewood End (098 987) 236

Free House
Landlords Paul & Karen Whitford

🍺 Bass; Mitchells & Butlers Springfield Bitter,
Hereford Bitter; Guinness; Tennent's; Carling
Black Label; cider. 🍷

Situated in a dip on the Hoarwithy–Bridstow
road, this 16th-century former cider house
oozes old-world charm. Under the beams in
the bar you can enjoy traditional and more
elaborate snacks, from deep-fried Brie or
Stilton and port pâté to seafood lasagne and
trout stuffed with crab, spinach and almonds.
Sweets include home-made ice-creams, sorbets and fruit pies. *Typical prices:* Garlic
chicken £4.20   Chocolate rum pot £1.25
(Last bar food 9.45pm) ⊝

Semley   *(Food, B & B)*   *Benett Arms*

Near Shaftesbury · *Wiltshire* · Map 9 D3
East Knowle (074 783) 221

Brewery Gibbs Mew
Landlord Joseph Duthie

Children welcome
Credit Access, Amex, Diners, Visa
🍺 Gibbs Mew Salisbury Best Bitter; Adnams
Bitter; Marston's Pedigree; Wiltshire Regency;
Guinness; Carlsberg Hof; cider. ♀

A pleasant, lively pub opposite the village green, run by a friendly landlord. The bar is both cosy and comfortable and makes an ideal spot for lunch or an evening snack. There are enjoyable soups, pâté, freshly made salads and ploughman's. For hungrier visitors the choice expands to ample portions of home-made pies, scampi or local trout, grilled gammon, steak or chilli con carne, all served with peas and chipped potatoes. There's a tempting selection of desserts (from the restaurant menu), including a creditable sherry trifle. *Typical prices:* Wiltshire ham £3   Steak & kidney pie £2.80 (Last bar food 10pm) ⊖

ACCOMMODATION   6 bedrooms   £C
Check-in: all day

The six bedrooms are most comfortable: two in the main house are pleasingly traditional and those in the annexe more modern with their own bath/shower rooms. All rooms have colour TVs and tea-makers. The good cooked breakfasts are accompanied by fresh strong tea.

Sennen Cove   *(B & B)*   *Old Success Inn*

Land's End · *Cornwall* · Map 9 A4
Sennen (073 687) 232
Free House
Landlord Mr F. Carroll
Children welcome
Credit Visa
🍺 John Smith's Yorkshire Bitter; St Austell
Cornish Best Bitter, Tinners Ale (summer only);
Guinness; Carlsberg; cider (summer only).
ACCOMMODATION 14 bedrooms £C (No dogs)
Check-in: all day

Down on the sea front, with a fine view of the broad, sandy sweep of Sennen Cove, this pebbledash pub is just the place for those who enjoy surfing, walking and cliff climbing. The pleasant bars and spacious residents' lounge offer scope for relaxing, and the simply furnished bedrooms, eight with their own bathrooms, look fresh and cheerful. It's essential to book in advance for winter accommodation. Terrace.

Shalfleet   *(Food)*   *New Inn*

Yarmouth Road · *Isle of Wight* · Map 6 A4
Isle of Wight (0983) 78314

Brewery Whitbread
Landlords Nigel & Brenda Simpson

Children welcome
🍺 Whitbread's Pompey Royal, Strong Country,
Flowers Original, Fremlins; Stella Artois;
Guinness; cider.

Marine delights like garlic mussels, a shellfish cocktail or a pint of prawns in the shell get you off to a good start at this characterful country pub. All sorts of local fish including conger eels turn up on ex-fisherman Nigel Simpson's menu, but there are also meat pies and pasties, ploughman's, giant country sausages and sandwiches. Expect to share a table with fellow fish-lovers. *Typical prices:* Fresh mussels from £2   Poacher's pie £3.95 (Last bar food 10pm) ⊖

Shamley Green   *(Food)*

Red Lion

Near Guildford · *Surrey* · Map 6 B3
Guildford (0483) 892202

Brewery Friary Meux
Landlords Ben & Brenda Heath

Credit Access, Amex, Diners, Visa
■ Friary Meux Bitter, Mild; Red Lion Bitter; Ind
Coope Burton Ale; Guinness; Castlemaine;
cider.

Cheerful fires, shelves of books and fresh
flowers create a welcoming atmosphere at
this pub on the village green. Wholesome
home-cooked dishes are generously served
and range from soup, cheese-topped burgers and game pie to pan-fried squid and liver
with sage and onions. Finish with rich, moist
chocolate and truffle cheesecake. Garden.
Typical prices: Seafood salad £5.95   Steak,
kidney & Guinness pie £4.25 (Last bar food
10.30pm) ☺

Shave Cross   *(Food)*

Shave Cross Inn

Marshwood Vale, near Bridport · *Dorset*
Map 9 D3
Broadwindsor (0308) 68358

Free House
Landlords Mr & Mrs Slade

Children welcome
■ Badger Best Bitter; Bass; Royal Oak;
Guinness; Carlsberg Hof; Black Label; cider. ♀

Set at a small crossroads in the beautiful
Marshwood Vale, this 14th-century thatched
inn and its garden have a traditional country
charm. In the beamed bar a simple range of
snacks is available – ploughman's, salads
and a few sweets like Dorset apple cake. The
colder months bring basket meals, including
excellent local sausages. *Typical prices:*
Sausages & chips £1.65   Dorset apple cake
70p (Last bar food 9.30pm. No bar food Mon
except Bank Hols) ☺

Shelley   *(Food, B & B)*

Three Acres Inn

Near Huddersfield · *West Yorkshire* · Map 4 C3
Huddersfield (0484) 602606

Free House
Landlords D. & N. F. Truelove & B. A. Orme

Children welcome
Credit Access, Amex, Diners, Visa
■ Tetley's Bitter, Mild; Younger's No. 3, IPA;
McEwan's 80/-; Guinness; Beck's Bier;
cider. ♀

Situated in the Pennine foothills within striking distance of the Peak District and the
Holmfirth area known as 'the land of summer
wine', this stone-built pub converted from a
row of cottages provides good accommodation and excellent bar snacks. The menu,
which changes each week, includes sardine
pâté, soup, Gruyère and brandy vol-au-vent,
potted ham and more substantial fare like
beef and herb pancake, goulash, poached
salmon or cold meat salads. There are always
some vegetarian dishes on the menu, and a
tempting selection of sweets including a trifle
made with seasonal fruits. *Typical prices:*
Sardine pâté £1.75   Haddock and prawn
bake pie £3.25 (Last bar food 10pm) ☺

ACCOMMODATION 10 bedrooms £B (No dogs)
Check-in: all day

The bedrooms, prettily decorated with pine
furniture, have shower rooms en suite, colour
TVs, radio alarms and tea-making facilities,
as well as direct-dial telephones.

Shenington *(Food, B & B)* *Bell*

Near Banbury · *Oxfordshire* · Map 7 B1
Edge Hill (029 587) 274   *Free House*   *Landlords* Mr & Mrs Keith Brewer
Children welcome
🍺 Wadworth's 6X; Northgate Bitter; Hook Norton Best Bitter;
Löwenbräu; cider. ⌢

★

This attractive stone-built pub dating from the early 18th century enjoys
an attractive setting near the green in a lovely quiet village. The little bars
are full of character, and you couldn't ask for friendlier hosts than the
Brewers. Vanessa's menus are varied and imaginative, her cooking
consistently excellent: creamy onion soup or mixed seafood pâté could
be your starter, followed by a main course such as shrimps Phoebe
(tomatoes, peppers, garlic and herbs), kidneys à la crème or crispy-topped
lamb. Vegetables and rice are spot-on and there are some tempting
sweets like fruit Pavlova or a beautifully light peach and almond tart.
Typical prices: Carrot & orange soup £1   Lamb & almond casserole £4.50
(Last bar food 10.30pm. No bar food Sun eves)

★

ACCOMMODATION   4 bedrooms   £C
Check-in: all day

Four bedrooms have recently been opened, one of them with its own
shower, the others sharing a simply appointed bathroom. Furnishings are
country style, and sloping ceilings add to the cosy, homely feel.

Shepperton *(B & B)* *Anchor Hotel*

Church Square · *Middlesex* · Map 7 C2
Walton-on-Thames (0932) 221618

Free House
Landlord Mr Goddard
Children welcome
Credit Access, Amex, Diners, Visa
🍺 Flowers Original Bitter; Eldridge Pope Dorset
IPA, Royal Oak; Heineken; Faust Export, Lager;
cider. ⌢
ACCOMMODATION   24 bedrooms   £B
Check-in: all day

This 400-year-old inn just a few yards from
the Thames is named after the symbol of the
adjoining church. It's a friendly, well-run
place, and the bar, with its original beams
and lovely carved oak panelling, is a very
pleasant spot for a drink. Double-glazed
bedrooms with simple colours and mainly
modern furnishings have TVs, direct-dial
phones and compact shower rooms.

Shepperton *King's Head*

Nell Gwyn is reputed to have put up at this 300-year-old inn close to the
Thames and overlooking a quaint little square. Although the cosy main bar
with its inglenook fireplace gets crowded, several tiny rooms lead from it,
and there are lots of nooks and crannies for a quiet chat. Garden.

Church Square · *Middlesex* · Map 7 C2
Walton-on-Thames (0932) 221910   *Brewery* Courage   *Landlord* Mr D.
K. Longhurst
🍺 Courage Directors Bitter, Best Bitter, JC, Strong Bitter; Guinness;
Kronenbourg; Hofmeister; cider.

Shepperton   *(Food)*

Thames Court

Towpath · *Middlesex* · Map 7 C2
Walton-on-Thames (0932) 221957

Free House
Landlord Mr Matthew Negus

Children welcome
🍺 Bass Bitter; Charrington's IPA; Stones Bitter;
Guinness; Tennent's Extra; Carling Black Label;
cider. ♉

This handsome brick-built pub enjoys a
garden setting by the Thames. In the food
area, a tempting cold buffet is laid out at
lunchtime (also summer evenings). There are
always a couple of hot dishes – perhaps beef
curry and delicious roast pork – plus jacket
potatoes, sandwiches and several sweets.
Restaurant meals, too. *Typical bar prices:*
Wholemeal courgette & prawn quiche £1.10
Roast beef & Yorkshire pudding £3 (Last bar
food 9.30pm) ⊗

Shepperton   *(B & B)*   **New Entry**

Warren Lodge

Church Square · *Middlesex* · Map 7 C2
Walton-on-Thames (0932) 42972

Free House
Landlord Mr Douglas Gordon

Children welcome
Credit Access, Amex, Diners, Visa
🍺 Whitbread Tankard; Heineken. *No real ale.*
ACCOMMODATION 45 bedrooms £A (No dogs)
Check-in: all day

Walnut and mulberry trees grow in the garden
of this white-painted 18th-century house by
the Thames. The riverside terrace is a popular
place in fine weather, and when the wind
blows the bar is a cosy refuge. Bedrooms in
two modern wings are generally of a good
size, and pleasantly light and airy. Direct-dial
phones, TVs, drinks fridges, hairdryers, private bath or shower (three not en suite).

Shepton Mallet   *(B & B)*

Kings Arms

Leg Square · *Somerset* · Map 9 D3
Shepton Mallet (0749) 3781

Brewery Hall
Landlords Mr & Mrs P. W. Swan
Children welcome
🍺 Hall's Harvest Bitter; Wadworth's 6X; Ind
Coope Burton Ale; Ruddle's County Ale;
Guinness; Skol; Löwenbräu; cider. ♉
ACCOMMODATION 3 bedrooms £D
Check-in: all day

Built in the 17th century from local stone, this
handsome pub became a favourite of nearby
quarry workers and is still affectionately
known to many as the 'Dusthole'. Today's
vistors can be sure of spotlessly clean
accommodation in three comfortable, traditionally furnished bedrooms which share a
modern carpeted bathroom. There is a relaxing residents' lounge with TV, too, and the
three beamed bars are full of character. Good
breakfasts.

*We welcome complaints
and bona fide
recommendations on the
tear-out pages for readers'
comments. They are
followed up by our
professional team. Please
also complain to the
management instantly.*

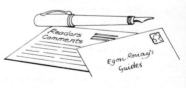

241

Shiplake   *(Food, B & B)*   ## *Baskerville Arms*

Near Henley-on-Thames · *Oxfordshire*
Map 7 B2
Wargrave (073 522) 3332

Brewery Wethered
Landlords Derek & Janice Tomlin

Children welcome
Wethered's Bitter, SPA, Winter Royal (winter only); Flowers Original; Guinness; Stella Artois; cider.

The Tomlins have recently taken over at this solid 1930s pub, with Derek pulling a sociable pint in the roomy bar and Janice preparing homely snacks in the kitchen. The basic menu offers sandwiches, salads and variations on the ploughman's theme, plus hot dishes like steak, scampi or ham, egg and chips. Additionally there's a daily-changing selection posted on the blackboard: turkey and ham pie, lasagne, quiche and curry (a Janice special!) show the range. A few sweets, too, like apple pie or ice cream. There's a garden. *Typical prices:* Beef curry £2.60   Apple pie 90p (Last bar food 9.30pm. No bar food Sun or Mon eves)

ACCOMMODATION   3 bedrooms   £C
Check-in: all day

Upstairs are three freshly decorated bedrooms of decent size, with traditional freestanding furniture and TV sets. The bathroom they share has both tub and shower cubicle, and there's a separate toilet.

Shipston-on-Stour   *(B & B)*   ## *Bell Inn*

Sheep Street · *Warwickshire* · Map 7 A1
Shipston-on-Stour (0608) 61443

Brewery Whitbread
Landlords Mr & Mrs Edward Fila
Children welcome
Credit Access, Amex, Diners, Visa
Flowers IPA, Original, Best; Guinness; Stella Artois; Heineken; cider.
ACCOMMODATION   6 bedrooms   £C
Check-in: all day

Comfortable overnight accommodation is provided at this town-centre inn, which dates from 1730. Large floral print fabrics are pleasing in the bedrooms, which are centrally heated and have tea-makers, trouser presses and TVs with free in-house movies; three have their own spacious bathrooms. There are two bars, the public one in simple, traditional style, the lounge with exposed stonework and a log fire in winter. Patio.

Shipston-on-Stour   *(Food, B & B)*   ## *White Bear*

High Street · *Warwickshire* · Map 7 A1
Shipston-on-Stour (0608) 61558   *Brewery* Bass   *Landlords* Suzanne & Hugh Roberts
Children welcome   *Credit* Access, Amex, Diners, Visa
Bass; Mitchells & Butlers Mild, Brew XI, Springfield Bitter; Guinness; Carling Black Label; cider.

Suzanne and Hugh Roberts' sensational bar food has won them many friends at this welcoming little hotel. Large blackboards proclaim the day's offering in the cosy beamed bars, with carrot and coriander soup, poached chicken breast with watercress sauce, Guinness-enriched beef pie and vegetarian mushroom, spinach and cream cheese lasagne among typically tasty items. In addition, the standard menu has ploughman's and salads with home-baked ham, jacket potatoes and baguette sandwiches (the only choice Sun lunchtime). Splendid, too, are old fashioned sweets like traditional steamed fruit pudding and lovely treacle tart. *Typical prices:* Fish terrine £1.75   Lamb curry £3.50 (Last bar food 9.30pm. No bar food Sun eve) ☺

ACCOMMODATION   9 bedrooms   £C
Check-in: all day

Prettily decorated bedrooms all have private bath/shower rooms and are equipped with tea-makers and televisions. Accommodation closed 4–5 days Christmas.

Shipton-under-Wychwood   *(Food, B & B)*   *Lamb Inn*

High Street · *Oxfordshire* · Map 7 A1
Shipton-under-Wychwood (0993) 830465

Free House
Landlords Hugh & Lynne Wainwright

Credit Access, Amex, Diners, Visa
🍺 Hook Norton Best Bitter, Old Hookey (winter only); Wadworth's 6X; Guinness; Löwenbräu; cider. ♈

The welcome is wonderfully warm and the eating excellent at the Wainwrights' pleasant old inn built of Cotswold stone. Consult the blackboard in the mellow beamed bar for the day's delights – perhaps duck and orange pâté or hot buttered shrimps to start, garlicky roast lamb, pan-fried sole or juicy rump steak as your main course. Simple but enjoyable sweets like bread and butter pudding or trifle round off a thoroughly satisfying meal. A cold table operates during summer lunchtimes, with less choice on Sundays, and full meals are available in the restaurant. *Typical bar prices:* Avocado mousse with prawns £1.50 Roast lamb £3.50 (Last orders 10pm) ☺

ACCOMMODATION 5 bedrooms £B (No dogs)
Check-in: all day

Up a steep staircase are five spacious, impeccably kept rooms with pretty soft furnishings and a few handsome period pieces. All have good private bathrooms and tea-makers; mineral water is a thoughtful extra touch. Huge and hearty breakfasts feature black pudding and fine lean bacon. No children under 14 overnight. Patio.

Shipton-under-Wychwood   *(B & B)*   *Shaven Crown Hotel*

High Street · *Oxfordshire* · Map 7 A1
Shipton-under-Wychwood (0993) 830330

Free House
Landlords Brookes family

Credit Access, Visa
🍺 Hook Norton Best Bitter; Flowers Original, Best Bitter; Heineken; Tuborg Gold; cider.
ACCOMMODATION 8 bedrooms £C (No dogs)
Check-in: all day

As its name suggests, monks were the original hosts of this 14th-century inn, which boasts an impressive medieval hall, now used as a reception and lounge. There are two beamed bars, and a delightfully monkish courtyard garden with a pond. Bedrooms of varying sizes and furnishings – half with private facilities – have TVs and tea-makers. The staff are friendly and there's a good breakfast in the morning.

Shirley (B & B) New Entry — Saracens Head Hotel

Stratford Road · *West Midlands* · Map 5 A2
021–744 1016

Brewery Ansells
Landlord Mr Michael Stevens

Credit Access, Amex, Diners, Visa
🍺 Ansells Traditional Bitter, Mild; Tetleys Bitter;
Guinness; Castlemaine 4X; Skol; cider.
ACCOMMODATION 34 bedrooms £B (No dogs)
Check-in: all day

On the A34 Birmingham–Stratford Road, this substantial hostelry has comfortable, well-equipped modern bedrooms. Attractive pastel colour schemes, brass lamps, nice prints and lightwood units are common to all rooms, along with double-glazing, direct-dial phones, colour TVs and good private facilities. There are two pleasant bars – a cocktail bar with rattan-backed chairs and another in Victorian style. First-class housekeeping. No children under eight overnight. Patio.

Shoreham-by-Sea (Food) — Red Lion

Old Shoreham · *West Sussex* · Map 6 B4
Shoreham (0273) 453171

Brewery Phoenix
Landlord Norman Stevens

🍺 Gale's HSB; Usher's Best Bitter; Webster's
Yorkshire Bitter; Carlsberg Pilsner; Holsten;
cider. ♀

There are fine views over the South Downs from this white-painted pub that was originally a Saxon chapel. In the comfortable bars (one for non-smokers) or walled garden you can enjoy very good snacks, from sandwiches and salads to smoked haddock pasta and chilli con carne. *Typical prices:* Garlic prawns £2.75   Spiced apple cake 90p (Last bar food 9pm. No bar food Mon eve or all Sun) ⊖

Silk Willoughby (Food) — Horseshoes

Near Sleaford · *Lincolnshire* · Map 5 B1
Sleaford (0529) 303153

Brewery John Smith
Landlord Francisco Cuñago

Children welcome
Credit Access, Visa
🍺 John Smith's Bitter; Guinness; Kronenbourg;
Hofmeister; cider.

A plush and attractively decorated pub alongside the A15, with subdued lighting and comfortable banquette seating in its roomy bar. The menu changes daily, offering a good variety of well-prepared and satisfying dishes, from cream of cauliflower soup to steak and oyster pie, roast turkey with stuffing and poached haddock with prawn sauce. Garden. *Typical prices:* Game pie £3.80   Lasagne romana £2.50 (Last bar food 10pm) ⊖

Sindlesham (Food) — Walter Arms

Bearwood Road, Near Wokingham · *Berkshire*
Map 7 B2
Wokingham (0734) 780 260

Brewery Courage
Landlord Mr W. Mansfield-Cox

🍺 Courage Best Bitter, Directors Bitter, John
Courage; Guinness; Kronenbourg;
Hofmeister. ♀

Hearty fare brings the customers to the three cheerful bars of this sturdy roadside pub. Soup, ploughman's, quiche and salads cater for more modest appetites, while the starving can tuck into such favourites as chilli, moussaka, lasagne, and burgundy beef. Sinful sweets include chocolate fudge cake, vicar's delight, and a gorgeously sticky treacle tart. Terrace. *Typical prices:* Country pie & vegetables £2.60   Beef in burgundy £3.15 (Last bar food 10pm) ⊖

Skidby   (Food)   Half Moon Inn

16 Main Street · *Humberside* · Map 4 D3
Hull (0482) 843403

Brewery John Smith
Landlord Mr Peter Madeley

Children welcome
🍺 John Smith's Bitter, Chestnut Mild; Guinness;
Hofmeister; Kronenbourg; cider.

They're ready for healthy appetites at this smart, white-painted pub, where the bar snacks are tasty and satisfying. Man-sized Yorkshire puddings are the speciality, served in various ways – with onion gravy, chilli, curry or traditional roast beef. Toad and lamb in the hole are other variants, and there are burgers, ploughman's and steak and kidney pie. *Typical prices:* Yorkshire pudding with curry £2.95   Cheeseburger £1.55 (Last bar food 10pm) 🍴

Slaidburn   (B & B)   Hark to Bounty Inn

Near Clitheroe · *Lancashire* · Map 3 B2
Slaidburn (020 06) 246
Free House
Landlord Mrs Pat Holt
Children welcome
Credit Access, Amex, Diners, Visa
🍺 John Smith's Bitter, Tawny Mild, Chestnut
Mild; Moorhouse's Bitter; Guinness; Hofmeister;
cider.
ACCOMMODATION   7 bedrooms   £C
Check-in: all day

The name dates from Victorian times and commemorates a loud-barking member of a local pack of hounds. It is still very much a village pub, with a friendly atmosphere in the large, unpretentious bar. Exposed beams give a touch of character to the simple bedrooms, which all have tea-makers and private facilities. Residents can watch TV in a neat, comfortable lounge. Garden.

Slaithwaite   (Food)   White House

Holthead, Huddersfield · *West Yorkshire*
Map 4 C3
Huddersfield (0484) 842245

Free House
Landlords Gillian & Alan Swift

Children welcome (till 8.30pm)
Credit Access, Amex, Diners, Visa
🍺 Tetley's Bitter, Mild; Younger's Bitter, Mild;
Guinness; McEwan's Lager. ♀

A whitewashed inn set high above the village, where the Swifts serve hearty fare like Yorkshire pudding with gravy for starters and then steak pie or beef with dumplings. Dishes such as chilli in pitta bread and Peruvian stew offer further choice, and simple snacks include sandwiches, salads, real chips plus interesting sweets like chocolate roulade. *Typical prices:* Steak & kidney pie with vegetables £2.50   Fried mussels with garlic mayonnaise £2.25 (Last bar food 10.30pm) 🍴

Sleights   (B & B)   Salmon Leap

Near Whitby · *North Yorkshire* · Map 4 D2
Whitby (0947) 810233

Brewery Cameron
Landlords Mr & Mrs B. Gibson

Children welcome
🍺 Cameron's Best Bitter, Strongarm, Lion;
Guinness; Hansa; cider.
ACCOMMODATION   11 bedrooms   £B
Check-in: all day

Standing high above the Esk valley some four miles from Whitby, this solidly built stone inn adorned with colourful flower boxes offers a cheerful welcome and neat, simple overnight accommodation. Some of the bedrooms have darkwood fitted units, others are furnished with older freestanding pieces; they share three public bathrooms. The spacious lounge bar in a modern extension has regular sessions of live music, and there are two smaller public bars. Garden.

Smarden   *(Food, B & B)*   *Bell*

Bell Lane, Near Ashford · *Kent* · Map 6 C3
Smarden (023 377) 283

Free House
Landlord Mr I. J. Turner

Children welcome
Credit Access, Visa
Fremlins Bitter; Theakston's Best Bitter, Old
Peculier; Shepherd Neame Masterbrew;
Murphy's Stout; Fuller's London Pride; Young's
Special; cider.

ACCOMMODATION   4 bedrooms   £D
Check-in: restricted

Three traditional bars, their beams garlanded
with hops and log fires burning in the
inglenooks, provide a friendly setting for the
patrons of this popular weatherboarded pub
in one of the prettiest corners of Kent. It's
worth the wait for the popular snacks, which
include soup, pâté, ploughman's, pizzas,
salads and sandwiches, as well as excellent
steaks and a flavoursome Greek shepherd's
pie. And save room for the crisp apple
crumble. Less choice at Sunday lunchtime.
Typical prices: Greek shepherd's pie
£1.95   Rump steak £5.60 (Last bar food
10pm)

An outside staircase spirals to the comfortable bedrooms, which have pleasing decor
and attractive furniture. All have TVs and tea-
makers, and continental breakfast is served
in the rooms. Garden.

Smarden   *(Food)*   *Chequers Inn*

Near Ashford · *Kent* · Map 6 C3
Smarden (023 377) 217

Brewery Courage
Landlord Mr Frank Stevens

Credit Access
Courage Best Bitter, Directors Bitter;
Guinness; Hofmeister; Kronenbourg; cider.

Frank Stevens is a talented and thoughtful
chef, and you will certainly eat well in this
attractive weatherboarded pub with garden.
There's always a splendid soup, and main
courses run from halibut to ham and eggs,
from beef carbonnade to a lovely dish of
gratinated asparagus, carrots and courgettes. Puds include raspberry Pavlova and
Mississippi mud pie. *Typical prices:* Vegetarian risotto £2.45   Beef carbonnade £3.75
(Last bar food 10.30pm).

Snainton   *(B & B)*   *Coachman Inn*

Near Scarborough · *North Yorkshire* · Map 4 D2
Scarborough (0723) 85231

Brewery Camerons
Landlord Mr G. Senior
Children welcome
Credit Access, Amex, Diners, Visa
Cameron's Best Bitter, Strongarm; Hansa;
cider. *No real ale.*
ACCOMMODATION   12 bedrooms   £B
Check-in: all day

A jolly landlord and comfortable, well-kept
accommodation keep up the tradition of
hospitality at this 200-year-old coaching inn
in pleasant gardens and paddocks set back
from the A170. Neat, good-sized bedrooms
– most with their own bath/shower rooms –
have modern units and floral fabrics. There
are two bars, and a cosy TV lounge well
stocked with flowers and magazines.

Snettisham — *Rose & Crown Inn*

Colourful hanging baskets decorate this delightfully secluded village pub, an extended 14th-century building with a covered barbecue area which opens on to a neat garden. Inside, there are three cosy bars, including the beamed public featuring a settle with a hole in its seat where visitors can pitch pennies.

Old Church Road, Near King's Lynn · *Norfolk* · Map 5 C1
Dersingham (0485) 41382   *Free House*   Landlords Margaret & John Trafford
Children welcome
🍺 Adnams Bitter; Greene King IPA, Abbot Ale; Wadfords Norfolk Pride; Webster's Yorkshire Bitter; Guinness; cider.

Sonning-on-Thames   *(Food, B & B)* — *Bull Inn*

High Street · *Berkshire* · Map 7 B2
Reading (0734) 693901

Brewery Wethered
Landlord Mr D. T. Catton

🍺 Wethered's Bitter, SPA, Winter Royal; Flowers Original; Heineken; cider.

Standing next to the village church, this 600-year-old pub makes a charming picture, its smartly painted black and white exterior festooned with climbing wistaria. The interior is just as delightful, with heavy beams, an inglenook fireplace, even an old penny farthing bicycle propped against one of the bar walls. A cold buffet display at lunchtime offers cooked meats, pies, cheese and crisp, fresh salads, and in winter soup and a daily hot special warm things up. Sandwiches only in the evening. *Typical prices:* Mixed meat salad £3.80   Meat pie with salad £3.30 (Last bar food 10pm) ☺

ACCOMMODATION 5 bedrooms £A (No dogs)
Check-in: restricted

Black beams and rough white walls characterise the five simply furnished bedrooms, which all have TVs and share a single public bathroom. No children overnight. Accommodation closed 1 week Christmas. Patio.

South Dalton   *(Food)*   **New Entry** — *Pipe & Glass*

West End · *Humberside* · Map 4 D3
Dalton Holme (069 64) 246

Owner Mr William Jackson
Landlord Mr M. A. Crease

Children welcome
Credit Access, Visa
🍺 Webster's Choice; Clarks HB Bitter; Stones Bitter; Guinness; Foster's; Carlsberg; cider.

Three bars cater for different moods and styles at this friendly pub, and there's also a restaurant and a lovely beer garden. A blackboard lists the day's bar fare, which typically ranges from starters like burgundy mushrooms or Yorkshire pudding with onion gravy to hot smoked mackerel and pork chop in mustard sauce. Also sandwiches, a summer cold table and some sweets. *Typical prices:* Pheasant pie with vegetables £3 Chicken piri-piri £3 (Last bar food 10pm) ☺

South Leigh   *(Food)*   *The Mason Arms*

Near Witney · *Oxfordshire* · Map 7 B1
Witney (0993) 2485

Free House
Landlords Mr & Mrs A. W. Ferguson

Children welcome
Credit Access, Visa
▉ Glenny's Witney Bitter; Younger's Scotch Ale;
Newcastle Bitter; Guinness; Beck's Bier. ♀

Home-cured salt beef is a continuing favourite snack at this lovely old thatched pub in a tiny village. Enjoy it with chips and vegetables, in salads or sandwiches, or opt for a tasty and generously served alternative such as gala pie, seafood pancakes, a ploughman's or jumbo sausages. To finish, there are pleasant sweets like trifle. There's also a restaurant. *Typical bar prices:* Lasagne £3.50 Ploughman's £1.95 (Last bar food 10pm. No bar food Sun eve) Closed Mon. ℮

South Zeal   *(B & B)*   *Oxenham Arms*

Near Okehampton · *Devon* · Map 9 C3
Okehampton (0837) 840244

Free House
Landlords Mr & Mrs J. H. Henry
Children welcome
Credit Access, Amex, Diners, Visa
▉ Flowers Best Bitter; Tinners; Guinness; Stella
Artois; Kronenbourg 1664; cider. ♀
ACCOMMODATION 8 bedrooms £B/C
Check-in: all day

Full of mellow charm, this creeper-clad inn (first licensed in 1477) enjoys a quiet village setting just off the A30. The beamed bar is cosy and welcoming, and there's a delightful lounge with comfortable armchairs and the odd antique. Bedrooms – often also with beams and antiques – combine homeliness with modern amenities like direct-dial phones and colour TVs; six have their own bathrooms. Garden.

Southwold   *(Food, B & B)*   *Crown Hotel*

High Street · *Suffolk* · Map 5 D2
Southwold (0502) 722275

Brewery Adnams
Landlord Mr Stephen Bournes

Children welcome
Credit Access, Amex, Visa
▉ Adnams Bitter, Extra; Guinness; Stella Artois;
Skol. ♀

Sympathetically restored throughout, this fine 18th-century inn in the town centre is a most attractive place to visit, whether for a quiet drink in the snug back bar or in the smartly rustic bar-café. Here you can read the papers over a pot of coffee or, at mealtimes, enjoy a glass of wine from the excellent range on the Cruover machine. The imaginative selection of bar snacks changes daily, with fish soup, a hot salad of pigeon breasts with juniper and pork fillet with tarragon sauce among typically tempting offerings. To finish, be tempted by tangy blackcurrant fool or poached peaches with raspberries. *Typical prices:* Carrot & orange soup £1.20 Cod in pesto sauce £3.65 (Last bar food 10pm) ℮

ACCOMMODATION 12 bedrooms £C
Check-in: all day

Simple, bright bedrooms, all with well-kept bathrooms, have fitted units and candlewick bedspreads and are equipped with televisions and digital clock-radios. Super breakfasts feature freshly squeezed orange juice and quality teas.

Staddle Bridge   *(Food, B & B)*   *McCoy's at the Tontine*

Near Northallerton · *North Yorkshire* · Map 4 C2
East Harsley (060 982) 671   *Free House   Landlords* McCoy brothers
Children welcome   *Credit* Access, Amex, Diners, Visa
🍺 Cameron's Bitter; Guinness; Hansa.

Eugene McCoy presides over a splendid choice of bar food in the
atmospheric cellar bar of the brothers' sturdy stone house. You can snack
off starters like soup, pâté, spare ribs, lasagne or smoked salmon quiche,
★ or feast on steaks, chicken and sole dishes, a superb beef Wellington, ★
prawns in garlic and ginger, all prepared with flavoursome flair. And don't
forget to spoil yourself with a really indulgent sweet such as treacle tart.
Typical prices: Seafood pancake £3.20   Tandoori chicken £6.25 (Last bar
food 10.30pm)

ACCOMMODATION   6 bedrooms   £A
Check-in: all day

Accommodation is at the luxury level for an inn: each room is individually
decorated and features high-grade wallpapers and handsome matching
pine furniture. Air-conditioning, colour TVs and direct-dial phones cater
for modern requirements, and all the bathrooms are en suite. The lounge
has a definite lived-in charm, and thirsts can be quenched in the armchaired
comfort of the bar. Amenities include coarse fishing.

Stafford   *(B & B)*   *Swan Hotel*

46 Greengate Street · *Staffordshire* · Map 4 C4
Stafford (0785) 58142

Owners Berni & Host Group
Landlord Mr J. Fiddler
Children welcome
Credit Access, Amex, Diners, Visa
🍺 Ind Coope Burton Bitter; Ansell's Bitter, Mild;
Guinness; Castlemaine; Skol; cider. ⚲
ACCOMMODATION 32 bedrooms £A (No dogs)
Check-in: all day

Improvements are in hand at this rambling
old hotel in a shopping precinct in the town
centre. Reception and a cocktail lounge flank
the beamed foyer, and other day rooms
include a public bar and residents' lounge.
The car park's at the back, with access from
Mill Street. A maze of corridors links the
bedrooms, which have TVs, telephones, easy
chairs and private bathrooms. Try for one of
the large-windowed front rooms. Garden.

Stamford   *(B & B)*   *Bull & Swan Inn*

St Martin's · *Lincolnshire* · Map 5 B1
Stamford (0780) 63558

Free House
Landlords William & Rosa Morgado
Children welcome
🍺 Sam Smith's Old Brewery Bitter, Mild,
Sovereign; Guinness; Diat Pils; Ayinger Bräu
Lager; cider.
ACCOMMODATION   6 bedrooms   £C
Check-in: all day

The Morgados take pride in keeping the
brass well polished and everywhere spick-
and-span at their delightful old coaching inn
not too far from the town centre. There's
smart velour seating in the handsome
beamed bar, and fresh flowers adorn the
cosy, simply furnished little bedrooms. All
have washbasins and TVs and they share
two public bathrooms. Patio.

Stamford *(B &B)*   *Crown Hotel*

All Saints Place · *Lincolnshire* · Map 5 B1
Stamford (0780) 63136

Free House
Landlords R. D. & E. W. McGahon
Children welcome
Credit Access, Amex, Diners, Visa
Ruddle's County; Burton Ale; Ansells Bitter;
Whitbread Trophy; Guiness; Stella Artois.
ACCOMMODATION 18 bedrooms £B
Check-in: all day

This handsome town-centre inn overlooking All Saints Church dates from 1678, and the McGahons enjoy preserving a traditional, welcoming atmosphere with fresh flowers and polished wood in the friendly, comfortable bar and lounge. Spacious bedrooms – most with private bathrooms – have simple modern furnishings, tea-makers, TVs and telephones. Excellent fishing facilities (including instruction) are an added attraction.

Any person using our name to obtain free hospitality is a fraud. Proprietors, please inform the police and us.

RECEPTION

Stamford *(Food, B & B)*   *George of Stamford*

71 St Martins · *Lincolnshire* · Map 5 B1
Stamford (0780) 55171

Free House
Landlord Mr Jolyon Gough

Children welcome
Credit Access, Amex, Diners, Visa
Samuel Smith's Old Brewery Bitter; Ruddle's
Best Bitter; Beck's Bier; Kestrel. *No real ale*

The airy garden lounge with its exotic plants and summery white furniture is a delightful setting in which to enjoy the first-class snacks served at this renowned 16th-century coaching inn. A fine display of roast meats, poached salmon, salads, good cheeses and delicious sweets makes up the magnificent cold buffet, while hot choices include minestrone, ravioli in a creamy mushroom sauce and seafood pancakes. Alternative eating venues include the elegant lounge with its open log fire and the pretty walled garden. There's also an excellent restaurant. *Typical bar prices:* Gruyère fritters £3.95 Rutland Water trout £5.95 (Last bar food 11pm)

ACCOMMODATION 47 bedrooms £A
Check-in: all day

Stunning bedrooms (including four with four-posters) are individually decorated to a very high standard and feature stylish fabrics, quality furniture and modern accessories such as hairdryers, trouser presses and digital radio-alarms. All have well-equipped private bathrooms.

Standerwick   *(Food)*

Bell Inn

Near Frome · *Somerset* · Map 9 D3
Frome (0373) 830413

Brewery Usher
Landlords Mr & Mrs Paul Kimber

Children welcome (over 4 years)
Credit Access, Visa
🍺 Usher's Best Bitter, Pale Ale, Country Bitter;
Ben Truman; Guinness; Carlsberg Lager. ⛄

This 200-year-old pub has an open plan bar,
and a beamed restaurant where Sunday
lunch is served. A good selection of snacks
is available – ploughman's, salads, toasted
sandwiches, baked potatoes and soups. A
blackboard gives daily specials – seafood
quiches or, in winter, liver and bacon or beef
casserole. *Typical prices:* Smoked trout &
prawn salad £3.50   Lasagne & salad £2.45
(Last bar food orders 10.30pm) ©

Standish   *(Food)*

Foresters Arms

Shevington Moor, near Wigan · *Greater
Manchester* · Map 3 B3
Standish (0257) 421337

Brewery Greenall Whitley
Landlords Ronnie & Jean Baxendale

Children welcome
🍺 Greenall Whitley Bitter, Mild; Guinness;
Grünhalle Lager; cider. ⛄

You'll find hospitality and good food aplenty
at the Baxendales' friendly little pub, which
stands in a row of terraced houses near
junction 27 of the M6. Plain or toasted
sandwiches come with generous fillings like
ham, beef or prawns, and other favourites
include pizza, savoury pies, curries and
steaks, with a delicious apple pie to fill any
remaining gaps. *Typical prices:* Chicken pie
£1.60   Sirloin steak £3.50 (Last bar food
10pm) ©

---

*Prices given are as at the time of our research
and thus may change.*

Stanford Dingley   *(Food)*

Old Boot Inn

Near Bradfield · *Berkshire* · Map 7 B2
Bradfield (0734) 744292   *Free House*   *Landlords* Mr & Mrs J. M. Pratt
Credit Diners
🍺 Arkell's Bitter; Theakston's Best Bitter; Fuller's London Pride;
Ruddle's County; Guinness; Stella Artois. ⛄

★ It's worth a special expedition to find this delightful 18th-century pub in a ★
pretty village. The Pratts will give you a warm welcome, and their beamed
bar with its open fire makes an attractive setting for their small but
interesting and imaginative blackboard menu. Quality ingredients go into
everything from a subtle courgette and tomato soup to tempting main
dishes like freshly baked chicken pie, jambon à la crème and crab New
Orleans, with quiches, a rare roast beef salad, langoustines mayonnaise
or, on the lighter side, a ploughman's with flavourful Cheddar. Delicious
sweets, too. Garden. *Typical prices:* Lamb and apricot pie £3.95   Salade
niçoise £3.75 (Last bar food 9.30pm)

251

Stanton Harcourt   *(Food, B & B)*   *Harcourt Arms*

Near Eynsham · *Oxfordshire* · Map 7 B1
Oxford (0865) 882192   *Brewery* Morrell's   *Landlord* Mr George Dailey
Children welcome   *Credit* Access, Amex, Diners, Visa
🍺 Morrell's Best Bitter, Varsity Bitter; Guinness; Harp; cider.

★ This mellow, creeper-clad pub is renowned for the excellence of its food.
A number of cheerful interconnecting rooms provide an informal setting
for George Dailey's superb seafood. Choices like grilled king prawns with
garlic mayonnaise and a splendid pie filled with white fish, scallops and
prawns are typical – plus meaty delights like honey-baked rack of lamb
and chicken with spicy cream and apricot sauce. Lighter dishes include
Malaysian satay platter and a brandy-enriched pâté, while to finish there's
homely treacle tart or good-looking Stilton. More elaborate meals available
in the restaurant. *Typical prices:* King prawns £2.75   Satay £2.75 (Last
bar food 10pm) 🍽 ★

ACCOMMODATION   16 bedrooms   £B   (No dogs)
Check-in: all day

Ten splendidly equipped bedrooms with excellent modern bathrooms are
in an adjacent building, while two cottages house the remaining rooms –
each with a kitchen and use of a TV lounge. No under-12s overnight.

*We welcome complaints
and bona fide
recommendations on the
tear-out pages for readers'
comments. They are
followed up by our
professional team. Please
also complain to the
management instantly.*

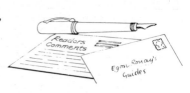

Staple Fitzpaine   *(Food)*   *Greyhound Inn*

Near Taunton · *Somerset* · Map 9 C3
Hatch Beauchamp (0823) 480227

Free House
Landlords David Townsend & Paul Aiston

Children welcome
Credit Access, Visa
🍺 Golden Hill Exmoor Ale; Wadworth's 6X;
Bishop's Best Bitter; Guinness; Carlsberg; Stella
Artois; cider. ♀

The new owners of this creeper-clad country
pub are putting greater emphasis on healthy
eating, with wholemeal bread and pasta,
steamed vegetables and many vegetarian
dishes available. Ingredients are of high
quality (lovely fresh grilled plaice), though
some flavour combinations work better than
others. Some meat dishes; excellent cheeses
and puddings. *Typical prices:* Venison & pork
sausages in red wine £1.95   Kipper & black
olive pâté £1.35 (Last bar food 10pm) 🍽

Stapleton *(Food)* — *Bridge Inn*

Near Darlington · *Co. Durham* · Map 4 C2
Darlington (0325) 50106 *Brewery* Vaux *Landlords* Nicholas &
Catherine Young
Children welcome *Credit* Access, Amex, Diners, Visa
🍺 Vaux Samson; Lorimer Scotch Bitter; Guinness; Stella Artois; cider.

★ Nick Young loves to prepare good food, which goes down very well with
the regulars at this comfortable, unassuming pub three miles out of
Darlington. The regular bar menu offers familiar fare like ploughman's,
salads, excellent home-made burgers and bumper toasted sandwiches,
plus black pudding to remind us we're in the North. Each day brings a new
blackboard list featuring soups and terrines, steaks, offal and zingy fresh
fish (brill, sole and turbot are particular favourites). Vegetables are spot
on, and sweets could include chocolate brandy cake and rich banana and
toffee pudding. Good English cheeses often available. *Typical prices:*
Lamb's kidneys in a creamy mustard sauce £2.70   Chocolate brandy cake
£2 (Last bar food 10pm. No bar food Sun or Mon eves) ★

---

*We neither seek nor accept hospitality
and we pay for all food and drinks in full.*

Starbotton — *Fox & Hounds*

A typical little Yorkshire Dales pub, where you can expect a friendly
welcome from the owners, the Wilkinsons. The exterior is smartly painted
white, and inside there's a tiny bar with a splendid open fireplace, flagstone
floor, rough stone walls and a motley collection of rustic furniture. Garden.

Near Kettlewell, Upper Wharfdale · *North Yorkshire* · Map 4 C2
Kettlewell (075 676) 269 *Free House Landlords* Ann Wilkinson & family
Children welcome *Credit* Access, Visa
🍺 Theakston's Best Bitter, Old Peculier, XB; Younger's Scotch Bitter;
Taylor's Best Bitter; Carlsberg; cider.

Staveley *(Food)* — *Royal Oak*

Near Knaresborough · *North Yorkshire*
Map 4 C2
Copgrove (090 14) 267

Brewery Younger
Landlords Mr & Mrs P. Gallagher

Children welcome
Credit Access, Visa
🍺 Younger's Scotch Bitter; McEwan's Lager;
cider. ⚱

Mrs Gallagher's excellent snacks make this
lovingly run little village pub a popular spot at
lunchtime. Our herby pâté followed by full-
flavoured game pie and crisp vegetables
made a delicious meal; other choices include
soup, salads of beef, ham or smoked trout,
ploughman's and steak and kidney pie. Finish
with delicious chocolate mousse. Garden.
Typical prices: Game pie £3.24   Seafood
platter £3.24 (No bar food eves) 🕗

Staverton (B & B)   *Sea Trout Inn*

Near Totnes · *Devon* · Map 9 C4
Staverton (080 426) 274

Free House
Landlord Mr V. Toffolo
Children welcome
Credit Access, Diners, Visa
🍺 Courage Directors Bitter, Best Bitter; John
Smith's Bitter; Guinness; Hofmeister; cider.
ACCOMMODATION 6 bedrooms £C
Check-in: all day

Huntin', shootin' and fishin' types should feel
welcome at this peaceful old roadside inn.
Displays of mounted fish and fishing flies
decorate the rustic beamed lounge bar,
together with some fine stags' heads and
flint-locks. Those of a gentler disposition will
head for the TV lounge or cosy public bar
with its darts and fruit machines. Cheerful,
cottagy bedrooms with tea-makers share
two up-to-date bathrooms. Patio.

*We publish annually
so make sure you use
the current edition.*

Steep (Food)   *Harrow Inn*

Near Petersfield · *Hampshire* · Map 6 B4
Petersfield (0730) 62685

Brewery Whitbread
Landlord Mr E. C. McCutcheon

🍺 Flowers Original; Whitbread Strong Country
Bitter; Guinness; Heineken; Stella Artois; cider.

Eddie McCutcheon is an innkeeper of the old
school, and time seems to have stood still at
his tile-hung country pub a few miles north of
Petersfield. Bar snacks are wisely limited to
tried and trusted favourites such as huge
bowlfuls of delicious, full-flavoured soup,
superb home-cooked ham for salads, sandwiches and ploughman's, cold roast beef and
simple hot dishes. Garden. *Typical prices:*
Ploughman's £1.70   Ham salad £4 (Last bar
food 9.30pm) 🍽

Stewkley (Food)   *Swan*

Near Leighton Buzzard · *Buckinghamshire*
Map 7 C1
Stewkley (052 524) 285

Brewery Courage
Landlords Colin & Carole Anderson

Children welcome
Credit Access, Amex
🍺 Courage Directors Bitter, Best Bitter, JC;
Guinness; Kronenbourg; Hofmeister; cider. 🍷

The Andersons generate a relaxed and
friendly atmosphere at this mellow brick pub
with a rustic beamed interior. All the tasty bar
food is home cooked; typical lunchtime
choices include ploughman's, pâté, sweet-
cured herrings and steaks, with daily specials
such as lamb korma. The evening range
includes charcoal grills and prawns. *Typical
prices:* Steak & kidney pie with vegetables
£2.70   Lamb korma £2.70 (Last bar food
9.30pm. No bar food Sat eve or all Sun) 🍽

Stockbridge *(Food, B & B)* *Vine*

High Street · *Hampshire* · Map 6 A3
Andover (0264) 810652

Brewery Whitbread
Landlords Michael & Vanessa Harding

Credit Access, Amex, Diners, Visa
🍺 Whitbread Strong Country Bitter, Best Bitter,
Mild; Flowers Original; Guinness; Heineken;
Stella Artois; cider. ♀

Michael and Vanessa Harding are friendly
welcoming hosts at this homely high-street
pub with a trout stream running through its
large rear garden. In the cosily traditional bar
you can enjoy a conventional selection of
appetising bar snacks, from flavoursome
home-made soup served with nice granary
bread to sandwiches and salads, pâtés and
filled jacket potatoes, steaks and tender,
chunky meat pies. Sweets are a particular
strength – note trifle, fresh cream gâteaux
and especially delectable chocolate roulade.
Typical prices: Steak & kidney pie £2.65
Grilled plaice £3.50 (Last orders 10pm) ⊝

ACCOMMODATION 3 bedrooms £D
Check-in: all day

The traditionally furnished bedrooms make
simple but attractive use of natural wood. All
have colour televisions and share a neatly
maintained bathroom. In the morning, a truly
gargantuan breakfast of excellent quality will
set you up for the day.

Stoke-by-Nayland *(Food, B & B)* **New Entry** *Angel Inn*

Suffolk · Map 5 D2
Colchester (0206) 263245

Free House
Landlords Richard E. Wright & Peter G. Smith

Credit Access, Amex, Diners, Visa
🍺 Greene King Abbot, IPA; Ridley's Best Bitter;
Adnams Best; Kronenbourg 1664; cider.

A village inn of style and character, with
beams, exposed brickwork and good-quality
furnishings. The blackboard menu features a
wide variety of carefully prepared dishes,
from simple avocado with prawns and a
superb smooth-as-velvet lentil soup to mushrooms in Madeira, poacher's pie and se-
same-fried chicken pieces with a barbecue
sauce. Fish is a speciality, with four or five
dishes usually being available. Excellent
chips, crisp salads and some interesting
sweets like pear and almond strudel. There's
also a pleasant restaurant. *Typical prices:*
Ham & tomato soup £1 Seafood platter
£5.25 (Last bar food 9.30pm).

ACCOMMODATION 3 bedrooms £B (No dogs)
Check-in: all day

Bedrooms run from the handsome gallery
above the restaurant. All three are roomy,
comfortable and nicely furnished, with well-
upholstered armchairs and antiques that
underline the building's traditional character.
Modern facilities include telephones, remote-
control TVs and good private bathrooms.
Staff are delightful.

Stoke Lacy *(Food)* **New Entry** *Plough Inn*

Near Bromyard · *Hereford & Worcester*
Map 8 D1
Munderfield (088 53) 658

Brewery Greenall Whitley
Landlords Norman & Janet Whittall

Children welcome
Credit Access, Visa
🍺 Greenall Local Bitter, Festival; Wem Special
Bitter; Guinness; Grünhalle Gold; cider.

A smart, white-painted pub on the A465 in
cider country. Apple pie order is kept in the
bay-windowed bar, where Normal Whittall
dispenses good beer and bonhomie. Janet
turns her hand to tasty dishes like rabbit pie,
cidery chicken or the popular salmon tart.
Also sandwiches and grills, with lovely home-
made ice creams and traditional puds. *Typical
prices:* Salmon tart £2 Ice cream selection
90p (Last bar food 10pm) ℮

Stoke St Gregory *(Food, B & B)* *Rose & Crown*

Woodhill · *Somerset* · Map 9 D3
North Curry (0823) 490296

Free House
Landlords Ron & Irene Browning

Children welcome
Credit Access, Visa
🍺 Golden Hill Exmoor Ale; Eldridge Pope Royal
Oak Bitter, Rebellion Bitter, 1880; Bass Toby
Bitter; Guinness; Faust; cider. ♀

Winding country lanes leading off the A361
bring you to this highly appealing old slate-
roofed inn. An illuminated well that's 60 feet
deep is an unusual feature of the cosy
beamed bar, where an appetising range of
food is served. Somerset scrumpy chicken
remains a firm favourite, while lighter bites
include soup served with lovely home-baked
granary bread, sandwiches, omelettes and
cold meat salads. Work off the calories (or
raise a thirst!) with an energetic game in the
skittle alley afterwards. *Typical prices:*
Scrumpy chicken £3.25 Steak & kidney pie
with Guinness £3.25 (Last bar food 10pm) ℮

ACCOMMODATION 3 bedrooms £D (No dogs)
Check-in: all day

Three neat bedrooms with modern built-in
wardrobes, televisions and pretty co-ordi-
nated fabrics share a smart carpeted bathroom. Good cooked breakfasts. Patio.

Stony Stratford *(B & B)* *Bull Hotel*

64 High Street · *Buckinghamshire* · Map 7 B1
Milton Keynes (0908) 567104
Brewery Aylesbury Brewery
Landlords Mr Everett Johnson & Mr Paul Waring
Children welcome
Credit Access, Visa
🍺 ABC Bitter; Everards Tiger; Bass; Burton
Bitter; Guinness; Castlemaine 4X; cider.
ACCOMMODATION 13 bedrooms £C (No dogs)
Check-in: all day

Along with its neighbour the Cock, this old
inn used to provide accommodation for
stagecoach travellers whose many tall tales
of doubtful veracity are said to have led to
the phrase 'a cock and bull story'. Today's
visitors will find friendly hospitality in the
several bars – nicest is the flagstoned Vaults
Bar furnished with pine settles – and neat
accommodation in 13 good-sized bedrooms,
all with TVs and tea-makers, four with private
bathrooms. Patio.

Stony Stratford *(B & B)* **New Entry** *The Cock Hotel*

72 High Street · *Buckinghamshire* · Map 7 B1
Milton Keynes (0908) 562109

Free House
Landlord Mrs V. Pharo
Children welcome
Credit Access, Amex, Diners, Visa
🍺 Hook Norton Bitter; Adnams Bitter;
Younger's Tartan Bitter; Beck's Bier; Carlsberg.
ACCOMMODATION 19 bedrooms £B
Check-in: all day

Like its close neighbour the Bull, this hostelry on the High Street is a good place for an overnight stop. The six most desirable bedrooms have smart darkwood furnishings, pretty floral fabrics and private bath/shower rooms. The others have similar furnishings but more ordinary decor and share six public bathrooms. The bar area is comfortable and cosy, with double doors opening on to an attractive walled garden. Good breakfasts.

Stourbridge *(B & B)* *Talbot Hotel*

High Street · *West Midlands* · Map 8 D1
Stourbridge (0384) 394350

Brewery Wolverhampton & Dudley
Landlords Mr & Mrs M. Chatterton

Credit Access, Amex, Visa
🍺 Banks's Bitter, Black Country Bitter, Mild;
Guinness; Stella Artois; Harp Extra; cider.
ACCOMMODATION 23 bedrooms £B
Check-in: all day

Major improvements have taken place at this 500-year-old coaching inn, notably in terms of the spotless accommodation. Standard and de luxe rooms have attractive freestanding pine units, plus TVs, direct-dial phones and hairdryers. Executive rooms are a lot larger, with period or antique furnishings, and all categories have their own attractive modern bathrooms. Restyled public rooms include a spacious, comfortable lounge bar.

Stow Bardolph *(Food)* *Hare Arms*

Kings Lynn · *Norfolk* · Map 5 C1
Downham Market (0366) 382229

Brewery Greene King
Landlords David & Tricia McManus

Children welcome
🍺 Greene King Abbot Ale, IPA, Mild; Guinness;
Kronenbourg; Harp; cider. ♀

The McManuses are rightly proud of their homely inn and the food they produce. Local fish, shellfish and game find their seasonal way on to the blackboard menu, and there's often lobster in summer. Soups, curries and individual pies are other appealing choices, with sandwiches for quicker snacks and a selection of sweets. *Typical prices:* Stilton & bacon soup £1.10 Pheasant & red wine pie £2.95 (No bar food eves or Sun) ☜

Stow-on-the-Wold *(B & B)* *Royalist Hotel*

Digbeth Street · *Gloucestershire* · Map 7 A1
Cotswold (0451) 30670
Free House
Landlords Mr & Mrs L. Bellorini
Children welcome
Credit Access, Amex, Visa
🍺 Worthington Best Bitter; Wadworth's 6X;
Flowers Bitter; Whitbread Best Bitter; Heineken;
cider.
ACCOMMODATION 13 bedrooms £B
Check-in: all day

The facade is 17th-century Cotswold stone, but timbers dating back over a thousand years can still be seen inside this historic hostelry. Many bedrooms are splendidly old-fashioned (notably the four-poster room), while four in the annexe are more modern and spacious. All have central heating, TVs and tea-makers; nine offer private facilities. Day rooms include two bars, one of which opens on to a small patio garden. Closed first week January.

Our inspectors are our full-time employees; they are professionally trained by us.

Stratford-upon-Avon *(Food)* — Slug & Lettuce

38 Guild Street · *Warwickshire* · Map 7 A1
Stratford-upon-Avon (0789) 299700

Free House
Landlord Mark Coles

▮ Wadworth's 6X, IPA; Arkell's Best Bitter;
Hook Norton Best Bitter; Guinness; Stella Artois;
cider.

A smart, lively pub-cum-bistro with an enthusiastic local following for its excellent and imaginative food prepared from market-fresh produce. Daily-changing menus offer a tempting variety, from creamy soups and fresh squid vinaigrette to brill in asparagus sauce, roast pigeon and featherlight chocolate mousse. *Typical prices:* Chicken baked with avocado £5   Pork chop with apples & Calvados £4.50 (Last bar food 10pm). Closed several days Christmas. ℮

Stretton *(Food, B & B)* **New Entry** — Ram Jam Inn

Great North Road, near Oakham
Leicestershire · Map 5 B1
Castle Bytham (078 081) 776

Free House
Landlord Lucy Goldthorp

Children welcome
Credit Access, Amex, Diners, Visa
▮ Ruddle's County, Bitter; Stella Artois;
Carlsberg; cider.

Travellers on the A1 will find this smart, informal motel a very convenient stopping off point. Snacks – available from 7am onwards – range from a breakfast time choice that includes muesli, yoghurt and local sausages to nourishing soup, huge wholemeal baps, prawns, salads, excellent cheeses and hot dishes like steak and mushroom pie. The snack counter menu is also available in the elegant bar, while the restaurant offers additional hot dishes. Try a warm Danish pastry or the deliciously rich treacle and nut tart for afters. *Typical prices:* Bacon, lettuce & Cheddar bap £1.75   Steak & mushroom pie £3.50 (Last bar food 11pm) ℮

ACCOMMODATION   8 bedrooms   £B
Check-in: all day

Spacious bedrooms, facing away from the road, are attractively furnished with rustic-style pine and pleasing colour schemes. Wicker chairs, remote control TVs, clock radios and tea-makers create a relaxing atmosphere, as do superior, well-equipped bathrooms.

Stuckton *(Food)*   *Three Lions Inn*

Stuckton Road, near Fordingbridge · *Hampshire* · Map 6 A4
Fordingbridge (0425) 52489   *Free House*   Landlords June & Karl
Wadsack
Credit Access, Visa
🍺 Wadworth's 6X; Ind Coope Burton Ale, Harvest Bitter; Guinness;
Löwenbräu; Castlemaine 4X. ♀

★ Though nominally an inn, this welcoming place is run more on the lines of
a restaurant with bar. Karl Wadsack is a highly skilled chef who goes to
great lengths to secure the very best raw materials (even importing fish
from the Seychelles every week!). The menu thus changes constantly,
tempting with delights that run from game soup and home-made bratwurst
to roulade of plaice stuffed with the lightest and moistest of salmon
mousses and served with a sublime white wine sauce. Desserts include
fresh fruit sorbets, chocolate marquise and crème brûlée. Also a good
selection of English and Continental cheeses. *Typical prices:* Hot spinach
& cheese strudel £2.30   Sauté of beef in Guinness with oysters £5.50
(Last bar food 9.30pm. No bar food Sun eve or all Mon) ★

Surbiton *(Food)*   *Oak*

Maple Road · *Surrey* · Map 7 C2
01–399 1662

Brewery Charrington
Landlord Robert Mahon

🍺 Charrington's IPA; Bass; Guinness;
Tennent's Extra, Pilsner; Carling Black Label;
cider. ♀

On a corner site in a tree-lined road, this is a
pleasant, roomy place for enjoying a lunchtime snack. There's an appetising display of
ham, beef and pâté, coronation turkey and
egg mayonnaise, plus a choice of hot dishes
– perhaps stuffed peppers, freshly baked
quiche and Lancashire lamb pie. To round
things off, cheese or the day's pud such as
apple and orange flan. *Typical prices:* Lancashire lamb pie £2.20   Egg mayonnaise
£1.50 (No bar food eves or Sun)

Children welcome *indicates a pub with an area
where children are allowed whether eating or not.*

Sutton *(Food)*   *Anne Arms*

Suttonfield Road, Near Doncaster · *South
Yorkshire* · Map 4 C3
Doncaster (0302) 700500

Brewery John Smith
Landlords Mr & Mrs J. R. Simm

🍺 John Smith's Bitter, Lager; Guinness;
Hofmeister; cider. *No real ale.*

Mrs Simm's excellent cooking is just one of
the attractions of this delightful, ivy-clad pub
with a wealth of beams, brass and homely
bric-à-brac filling every nook and cranny. Her
pies – sweet or savoury – boast superb
pastry, and there's a daily roast plus favourites like ham salad and liver with onions.
There's a garden. *Typical prices:* Rabbit pie
£2   Lasagne £2 (Last bar food 9.30pm. No
bar food Sun)

Sutton   (Food, B & B)   `New Entry`   Sutton Hall

Bullocks Lane, near Macclesfield · *Cheshire*
Map 4 C4
Sutton (02605) 3211

Free House
Landlords Robert & Phyllida Bradshaw

Children welcome
Credit Access, Amex, Visa
🍺 Bass; Stones Bitter; Marston's Bitter; Bass
4X Mild; Guinness; Tennent's Lager; cider.

ACCOMMODATION   10 bedrooms   £A
Check-in: all day

Originally a private residence and sometime
a nunnery, Sutton Hall is now a very splendid
inn offering good cheer and a comfortable
stay. In the beamed bar, where a suit of
armour and a grandfather clock enhance the
old-world feel, enjoyable snacks may be had:
French onion soup, chicken liver pâté, pot-
roast pigeon and seafood pancakes typify
the choice, and fresh-cut baps filled with cold
meat or hot steak are favourite light meals.
Daily specials could include dressed crab
and grilled lamb chops. More formal meals
are served in the dining room. *Typical bar
prices:* Crab & asparagus quiche £2.50
Roast beef bap 90p (Last bar food 10pm) 🍽

A handsome oak staircase climbs to the
bedrooms, which are particularly spacious
and characterful: all have four-poster beds,
and two feature some fine panelling. Good-
quality carpeting extends to the modern
bathrooms. TVs, direct-dial phones and tea-
making facilities.

Sutton Howgrave   (Food)   White Dog Inn

Near Ripon · *North Yorkshire* · Map 4 C2
Melmerby (076 584) 404

Free House
Landlords Mr & Mrs Bagnall

Children welcome
🍺 Webster's Pennine Bitter; Carlsberg Hof.
No real ale. ♀

Lunchtime snacks are full of variety at this
pleasant village pub named in memory of a
beloved bull terrier. Cooking is robust and
dependable, with things like venison pie,
mariner's hot pot and chicken casserole
among the stalwarts. Also sandwiches and
salads, omelettes, steaks and sweets. Restaurant meals in the evening. There's a
garden. *Typical prices:* Mariner's hot pot
£2.50   Iced rum truffle £1.25 (No bar food
eves). Closed Mon. 🍽

Sutton-upon-Derwent   (Food)   St Vincent Arms

York · *Humberside* · Map 4 C3
Elvington (090 485) 349

Free House
Landlords Max Royd & Kate Smith

Children welcome
🍺 Theakston's Best Bitter, Old Peculier;
Tetley's Bitter; Younger's Scotch; Guinness;
Carlsberg; cider. ♀

New owners keep the cosy, welcoming feel
at this agreeable timbered pub, and the bar
menu has also remained much the same. An
extensive choice of freshly made sandwiches
is available for quick snacks, and other
options range from thick mulligatawny soup
to grilled sardines, gammon, roast chicken
and a tasty, well-put-together beefsteak and
Guinness pie. *Typical prices:* Hot smoked
mackerel £1.10   Steak pie £3.30 (Last bar
food 10pm) 🍽

Symonds Yat West   (B & B)   New Entry   Old Court Hotel

Near Ross-on-Wye · *Hereford &*
Worcester · Map 8 D2
Monmouth (0600) 890367
Free House
Landlords Mr & Mrs John Slade
Children welcome
Credit Access, Amex, Diners, Visa
🍺 Wadworth's 6X; Flowers Original, Best Bitter;
Heineken; Stella Artois; cider.
ACCOMMODATION   17 bedrooms   £B
Check-in: all day

An impressive mansion near the river Wye.
The main building dates from about 1570,
and it's here that you'll find the lofty dining
room, the oak-panelled bar and the lounge
that leads to the garden (note swimming pool
and children's play area). Here, too, is the
roomiest accommodation – six pleasant,
chintzy rooms, two with ingeniously fitted
bathrooms. The other rooms are in a modern
wing, compact and simply furnished. All are
equipped with TVs, radios, tea-makers.

Talkin Village   (Food, B & B)   Hare & Hounds Inn

Near Brampton · *Cumbria* · Map 3 B1
Brampton (069 77) 3456

Free House
Landlords Joan & Les Stewart

Children welcome
🍺 Theakston's Best Bitter, Old Peculier, XB;
Hartley's Bitter; Younger's Tartan; Carlsberg
Pilsner; cider. ♀

Owners Joan and Les Stewart keep the
welcome mat rolled out at this 200-year-old
village inn, where decently prepared snacks
are served in the simple, traditional bars.
Filled jacket potatoes (Talkin tatties) are one
of the regular favourites, along with sandwiches, pizzas, rainbow trout and steaks.
Daily specials like spaghetti bolognese or
chilli con carne broaden the choice, and
kiddies have their own menu of jokily named
dishes. Sweets are mainly of the ice cream
variety. The bars are closed lunchtime Mon–
Fri except during school holidays. *Typical
prices:* Barbecued bangers £1.75   Rainbow
trout £2.95 (Last bar food 9pm) ⊘

ACCOMMODATION   4 bedrooms   £D
Check-in: All day

Two of the bedrooms boast fine old wardrobes, splendid beds and private bathrooms,
while the other two are more modern and
functional in style. There's a plainly appointed
upstairs residents' lounge for those wishing
a break from the bonhomie of the bars. Beer
garden.

Tarporley   (B & B)   Swan Hotel

50 High Street · *Cheshire* · Map 3 B4
Tarporley (082 93) 2411
Brewery Greenall Whitley
Landlords Alain Rutter
Children welcome
Credit Access, Amex, Diners, Visa
🍺 Greenall Whitley Bitter, Mild; Guinness;
Grünhalle; cider. ♀
ACCOMMODATION 9 bedrooms £C (No dogs)
Check-in: all day

This welcoming high-street inn has an imposing Georgian facade. The Old Kitchen Bar,
with its flagstoned floor, open fire and
gleaming copperware, is a particularly popular spot, and there's also the cosy Den Bar
and a comfortable residents' lounge. Traditionally furnished bedrooms with cheerful
fabrics, central heating and fitted carpets all
have TVs and tea-makers.

Tarrant Monkton   *(Food, B & B)*   **New Entry**   *Langton Arms*

Blandford Forum · *Dorset* · Map 9 D3
Tarrant Monkton (025 889) 225

Free House
Landlords Diane & Chris Goodinge

Children welcome
Credit Access, Amex, Diners, Visa
🍺 Bass; Wadworth's 6X; Stones Best Bitter;
Worthington Best Bitter; Guinness; Carling Black
Label; cider.

ACCOMMODATION   6 bedrooms   £C
Check-in: all day

The beamed bar of this 17th-century thatched
pub in an unspoilt village in Hardy country
makes a cosy setting in which to enjoy tasty
snacks. The menu ranges from soups and
ploughman's to shepherd's pie, chilli con
carne and blackboard specials such as
seafood lasagne and casseroles. Evenings
bring grills and regular weekly pizza (Tues &
Fri), curry (Wed) and Chinese (Thurs) nights.
Large skittle alley and garden, also a popular
restaurant that's open evenings and Sunday
lunch. *Typical bar prices:* Moussaka £2
Chocolate & walnut fudge gâteau 90p (Last
bar food 10.30pm) ☺

The six spacious bedrooms, in a brand new
block, have pine furniture and pretty duvets
and curtains. All have en suite bathrooms,
tea-makers and colour TVs. Charming owners and staff provide excellent breakfasts.

Teddington   *(B & B)*   *Clarence Hotel*

19 Park Road · *Middlesex* · Map 7 C2
01–977 8025

Free House
Landlords Ron & Rose Currall

Children welcome
Credit Access, Amex, Diners, Visa
🍺 Webster's Yorkshire Bitter; Marston's
Pedigree; Wadworth's 6X; Young's Special
Bitter; Guinness; Holsten; cider.
ACCOMMODATION   15 bedrooms   £C
Check-in: all day

Private bathrooms are planned for all the
bedrooms in this friendly Victorian hotel,
which stands about six miles from Heathrow.
The rooms have plain colour schemes, a
mixture of furnishing styles and no shortage
of space. All are equipped with tea-makers,
and TVs are available on request. The bar is
lively and cheerful, with lots of plants, a video
jukebox and plenty of elbow room.

Teffont Magna   *(Food)*   *Black Horse Inn*

Near Salisbury · *Wiltshire* · Map 6 A3
Teffont (072 276) 251

Brewery Usher
Landlords Colin & Jacqui Carter

Credit Access, Visa
🍺 Usher's Best, Founders; Bass; Webster's
Yorkshire; Guinness; Foster's; cider. ♀

One of the sleepiest of villages is home to
this creeper-clad stone pub with a large
pleasant bar. You can snack on freshly made
sandwiches, salads and ploughman's, or
tuck into something more substantial like
pan-fried trout, pork Marengo, or home-
cooked Wiltshire ham with a fried egg and
golden chips. Home-made ice cream and
fruit pie for afters. Garden. *Typical prices:*
Lasagne £3.60   Meringues £1.50 (Last bar
food 9.30pm. No bar food Mon eve) ☺

Temple Grafton *(Food)* **New Entry**   *Blue Boar*

Near Alcester · *Warwickshire* · Map 5 A2
Stratford-upon-Avon (0789) 750010

Free House
Landlord Mr G. Ponzi

Children welcome
Credit Access, Visa
🍺 Whitbread Mild; Flowers IPA, Original, Best;
Heineken; Stella Artois; cider.

A very popular pub in a village just off the
A422 Stratford–Alcester road. The central
bar is surrounded by cosy seating areas
where hungry folk can enjoy anything from a
ham sandwich or ploughman's platter to
deep-fried mushrooms, fish soup or poached
salmon. Plentiful vegetables accompany
main courses and there are some home-
made sweets. Patio. *Typical prices:* Steak &
kidney pie with vegetables £3.10   Gammon
£3.30 (Last bar food 10pm) 🏠

Terrington *(B & B)*   *Bay Horse Inn*

Near York · *North Yorkshire* · Map 4 C2
Coneysthorpe (065 384) 255

Free House
Landlord Grace Hoggard
Children welcome (till 8pm)
🍺 John Smith's Bitter; Younger's Scotch Bitter;
Tetley's Bitter; Guinness; Hofmeister; Carlsberg
Hof; cider. *No real ale.* ♀
ACCOMMODATION   4 bedrooms   £C
Check-in: restricted

Kept in pristine condition throughout, this
smart black and white village inn hung with
pretty window boxes has a genuinely hospitable air. Roaring fires warm the two cosy
bars, while central heating and hot-water
bottles keep overnight guests snug in the
cheerful little bedrooms. All have pretty soft
furnishings, washbasins and tea-makers and
they share two public bathrooms. Pub closed
Monday lunchtime except Bank Holidays.

Testcombe *(Food)*   *Mayfly*

Near Stockbridge · *Hampshire* · Map 6 A3
Chilbolton (026 474) 283

Brewery Whitbread
Landlords Barry & Julie Lane

Children welcome
🍺 Flowers Original, Strong Country Bitter;
Whitbread Best Bitter; Guinness; Stella Artois;
cider.

Eating in the garden is particularly agreeable
at this attractive red-brick pub alongside the
river Test. Cold meats with imaginative
salads are just the thing in summer, while for
colder days there are delicious soups and
maybe braised venison, lasagne or hare pie.
Nice puds and lots of cheeses. *Typical prices:*
Chicken tandoori £2.90   Quiche £1.95 (Last
bar food 10pm. No bar food Sun eve) Closed
Mon, Tues and Wed eves in winter. 🏠

Thames Ditton *(Food)*   *Albany*

Queens Road · *Surrey* · Map 7 C2
01-398 7031

Brewery Charrington
Landlord A. R. Christie

🍺 Bass; Charrington's IPA; Fuller's ESB;
Guinness; Tennent's Extra; Grolsch;
cider. ♀

Someone really cares for this Victorian pub
in a marvellous position on the Thames.
There are bowls of fresh flowers, open fires
and super food. At lunchtime the cold table
groans with platters of rare roast beef, ham,
turkey, pies, pâtés and salads. Bar snacks
are made up from this buffet or from daily hot
dishes that include a pie. No puds but a good
cheeseboard. *Typical prices:* Coronation turkey salad £2.95. Beef bourguignon pie £2.40
(No bar food eves or Sun) 🏠

Thetford   (B & B)   *Historical Thomas Paine Hotel*

White Hart Street · *Norfolk* · Map 5 C2
Thetford (0842) 5631
Free House
Landlord Mr T. Muir
Children welcome
Credit Access, Amex, Diners, Visa
🍺 Adnams Southwold Bitter; Stones Bitter;
Bass Best Bitter; Guinness; Carlsberg Hof;
McEwan's Lager; cider.
ACCOMMODATION   14 bedrooms   £B
Check-in: all day

Named after a political pamphleteer who was
reputedly born here in 1737, this attractive
white-painted hotel is a good place for an
overnight stop. The bedrooms – double-
glazed when appropriate – have individual
colour schemes and well-chosen modern
furnishings, plus TVs, telephones and tea-
makers. Day rooms include a comfortable
bar, a relaxing residents' lounge and a
strikingly decorated breakfast room. Garden.

Thurnham   (Food)   *Black Horse*

Pilgrims Way · *Kent* · Map 6 C3
Maidstone (0622) 37185

Brewery Whitbread
Landlords Les & Clare Broughton

Credit Access, Visa
🍺 Whitbread Best Bitter; Flowers Original;
Fremlins Bitter; Wethered's SPA; Stella
Artois. ♀

A warmly welcoming atmosphere immediately envelops visitors here. In the pretty
beamed bar hung with pewter mugs and
teapots you can snack on a tastily topped
open sandwich or opt for something more
substantial like cottage pie or chicken curry.
Filled baps only on weekends. There's also
a restaurant open evenings. *Typical bar
prices:* Chicken, gammon & mushroom pie
£3.25   Bacon & mushroom bap 75p (Last
bar food 10pm. No bar food Sat eve) ☺

Tichborne   (Food)   *Tichborne Arms*

Near Alresford · *Hampshire* · Map 6 B4
Alresford (096 273) 3760

Free House
Landlord Mrs Lynn O'Callaghan

🍺 Wadworth's 6X; Marstons Pedigree; Courage
Best; Eldridge Pope Royal Oak; Guinness;
Heineken; cider.

Simple home cooking (by local ladies) can be
enjoyed in the pleasant bar of this redbrick
thatched pub or in its delightfully peaceful
garden. Choice ranges from soup, sandwiches, salads and jacket potatoes to daily
specials like a mild chicken curry, paella or
mixed grill. Save room for a delicious – and
filling – syrup sponge, bread pudding, or a
crunchy fruit crumble. *Typical prices:* Barbecued spare ribs £2.95   Syrup sponge &
custard £1 (Last bar food 9.45pm) ☺

Timberscombe   (B & B)   *Lion Inn*

Near Minehead · *Somerset* · Map 9 C3
Timberscombe (064 384) 243

Free House
Landlord Andy Richardson
Children welcome
🍺 Usher's Best Bitter, Triple Crown; Webster's
Yorkshire Bitter; McEwan's Export; Carlsberg
Pilsner; cider.
ACCOMMODATION   4 bedrooms   £D
Check-in: restricted

A whitewashed village pub of unpretentious
charms, standing in lovely country on the
edge of Exmoor National Park. The new
landlord is energetic and efficient, and evenings in the bar are full of good fellowship.
Opposite the bar is a games room where
children may sit. Bedrooms are spacious,
well kept and warm, with comfortable beds
and practical modern furniture. One room
has its own bathroom, the others share.

Timperley *(Food)*   *Hare & Hounds*

1 Wood Lane, Near Altrincham · *Cheshire*
Map 3 B3
061–980 5299

Brewery Marston, Thompson & Evershed
Landlords Jim & Fran Cunningham

Children welcome
Credit Access, Amex, Diners, Visa
🍺 Marston's Pedigree, Mild; Burton Bitter;
Guinness; Stella Artois; Marston's Pilsner. 🍷

A beautifully presented cold table is the main lunchtime attraction at this popular creeper-clad pub. Super cooked meats and fish, savoury flans, imaginative salads and excellent cheeseboard make up the appetising picture. Tasty hot dishes, too – perhaps pork Neapolitan-style and curry – and delicious sweets like peach tart. (Limited choice Sunday lunchtime.) *Typical prices:* Pork napolitaine £2.50 Cod fillet with mushrooms & cream £2.50 (No bar food eves) ☕

Toot Hill *(Food)*   *Green Man*

Near Ongar · *Essex* · Map 7 D2
North Weald (037 882) 2255

Brewery Watneys
Landlord Mr John Rhodes

Children welcome
Credit Access, Diners, Visa
🍺 Webster's Yorkshire Bitter; Combes Bitter;
Ben Truman; Watneys Dark Mild; Guinness;
Carlsberg; cider. 🍷

The flower-filled front patio of this pleasant, creeper-clad pub is just the place on a fine summer's day to sample John Rhodes' excellent champagnes. His bar snacks are a treat at any time of year, and in the comfortable bar you can tuck into veal Kiev, grilled sardines and Mexican chicken, as well as standard soups, salads and sandwiches. Garden. *Typical prices:* Veal Kiev with vegetables £4.75 Liver & bacon with vegetables £3.50 (Last bar food 10pm) ☕

Tormarton *(B & B)*   *Compass Inn*

Near Badminton · *Avon* · Map 8 D2
Badminton (045 421) 242
Free House
Landlord Mr P. Monyard
Children welcome (lunchtime)
Credit Access, Amex, Diners, Visa
🍺 Archer's Village Bitter; Wadworth's 6X, Old
Timer (winter only); Bass; Carlsberg Hof;
Kronenbourg. 🍷
ACCOMMODATION 19 bedrooms £A
Check-in: all day

Motorists leaving the M4 at junction 18 can be sure of comfortable overnight accommodation at this creeper-clad coaching inn. Two extensions house the majority of bedrooms, which have modern built-in units, TVs, teamakers and good bathrooms. Four characterful bedrooms in the original building are without private facilities. There are four rustically cosy bars, plus a plant-filled orangery. Patio and garden.

Towersey *(Food)*   *Three Horseshoes*

Chinnor Road, Near Thame · *Oxfordshire*
Map 7 B2
Thame (084 421) 2322

Brewery Aylesbury
Landlords Mr & Mrs Worsdell

🍺 ABC Bitter; Beechwood; Everards Tiger;
Guinness; Skol; Castlemaine; cider. 🍷

A large beer garden fronts this mellow brick pub, where you can enjoy the Worsdells' appetising home-cooked fare on sunny days. Crisp salads go well with a good variety of cold meats and fish, or you can select something from the restaurant to eat in the flagstoned bar: perhaps a tasty home-made soup or a vegetarian special like herby Brazil nut croquettes. *Typical prices:* Lasagne £2.55 Steak & kidney pie £2.95 (Last bar food 10pm) ☕

Trebarwith   *(B & B)*   *Mill House Inn*

Near Tintagel · *Cornwall* · Map 9 B4
Camelford (0840) 770200

Free House
Landlords Jennifer & David Liddiard-Jenkin
Children welcome
Credit Access, Visa
🍺 Flowers Original, IPA; Whitbread Best Bitter, Mild; Guinness; Stella Artois; cider.
ACCOMMODATION   9 bedrooms   £B
Check-in: restricted

This slate-built former corn mill provides a pleasant retreat that's far from the urban grind and just a few minutes' walk from the sea. The bar is very rustic in character, and there's a homely residents' lounge. Prettily papered bedrooms (all with private bath or shower) feature some nice old pine furnishings, and TVs, tea-makers and hairdryers are standard. New owners are tackling the odd maintenance problem. No children under 14 overnight. Garden.

Troutbeck   *(Food, B & B)*   *Mortal Man*

Near Windermere · *Cumbria* · Map 3 B2
Ambleside (0966) 33193

Free House
Landlord Mr C. J. Poulsom

Children welcome
🍺 Scottish & Newcastle Chieftain Mild, Newcastle Bitter; Guinness; Harp; cider. *No real ale*

As far back as the Lakeland poets, locals and tourists have succumbed to the charm of this old inn in a magical position overlooking Lake Windermere. Residents and visitors may prefer the more comfortable of the two characterful beamed bars – the simpler one echoes with early Westmorland songs of a night. The lunchtime choice of snacks ranges from soup, pâté and sandwiches to salads and a daily special such as mushroom, cheese and leek flan with a jacket potato. Sweets include lemon meringue sponge and a delicious sherry trifle. There are no sandwiches at night, but items from the restaurant menu are available. *Typical prices:* Chicken breast stuffed with cheese & ham £4   Dish of the day £2.50 (Last bar food 9pm) ☺

ACCOMMODATION   13 bedrooms   £A
Check-in: all day

Traditionally furnished bedrooms – eight with their own bathrooms – offer clean, comfortable accommodation, with plenty of books and a good breakfast. No under-fives overnight. Accommodation closed mid November–mid February. Garden.

Turville   *(Food)*   *Bull & Butcher*

Near Henley-on-Thames
Buckinghamshire · Map 7 B2
Turville Heath (049 163) 283

Brewery Brakspear
Landlords Mr & Mrs Jim Cowles

Children welcome
🍺 Brakspear Ordinary Bitter, Special, Old; Heineken. ♀

Landlord Jim Cowles, who used to race saloons, has made his black and white village pub into a haven for motor racing fans. When not admiring the photographs, enthusiasts can tuck into tasty hot dishes like devilled pork or cranberry lamb stew, game pie, salads and sandwiches, while winter brings a variety of jacket potatoes. Simple sweets like plum crumble. Lovely garden. *Typical prices:* Avocado prawns £2.50 Devilled pork chop £3.50 (Last bar food 10pm) ☺

Tutbury   *(Food, B & B)*

High Street · *Staffordshire* · Map 4 C4
Burton-on-Trent (0283) 813030

Free House
Landlord Mr D. J. Martindale

Children welcome
Credit Access, Amex, Diners, Visa
🍺 Marston's Pedigree, John Marston's Bitter,
Pilsner Lager; Stella Artois; Löwenbräu; cider.
No real ale. ♀

ACCOMMODATION   18 bedrooms   £A
Check-in: all day

Ye Olde Dog & Partridge

Prize-winning gardens provide a delightful
setting for this characterful pub, a half-
timbered building dating from the 15th century in the town centre. Arrive early to get the
best of freshly prepared bar snacks, which
are served from a colourful carvery in the
cosy converted stable block and range from
cold meats and steak and kidney pie to
taramasalata and superb roast beef, sliced
to order, with help-yourself vegetables. *Typical prices:* Roast beef £4.30   Poached
salmon £4.50 (Last bar food 10pm) ☕

Steep, rickety stairs lead to quaint bedrooms
with beams, sloping floors and traditional
furnishings, but the best bedrooms are in an
adjacent Georgian house. Garden views here
add to the charm of floral wallpaper and
fabrics, and rooms are most comfortably
equipped with tea-makers, mini-bars, hairdryers, TVs and well-stocked bathrooms.

Twickenham   *(Food)*

30 Hampton Road · *Middlesex* · Map 7 C2
01–894 3963

Brewery Fuller
Landlords Elizabeth & Bruce Lunn

🍺 Fuller's London Pride, ESB Bitter, Chiswick
Bitter; Tennent's Extra; Guinness;
Heineken. ♀

Prince Albert

A really delightful Victorian pub, with affable
staff, excellent food and a real feeling of rus
in urbe. Elizabeth Lunn puts a lot of effort
into her lunchtime menus, which offer delights as diverse as mussels bretonne, liver
and bacon, seafood grill and tasty pork
casserole with wine and mushrooms. Pancakes are a popular pud. Toasted sandwiches are the only evening choice. *Typical
prices:* Seafood grill £6   Pork with herbs
£3.50 (No bar food Sun) ☕

Twickenham   *(Food)*

Riverside · *Middlesex* · Map 7 C2
01-892 2166

Brewery Watney Combe Reid
Landlord Shirley Sutton

Children welcome (lunchtime)
🍺 Watney's Special Bitter; Combes Bitter;
Webster's Yorkshire Bitter; Guinness; Foster's,
Carlsberg; cider. ♀

White Swan

A friendly pub with a garden that takes full
advantage of the riverside setting. Eat here
or in the homely bar where, from about 1
o'clock, Shirley Sutton's freshly prepared
snacks are served: creamy soups, pâtés and
ploughman's, cidery pork chops and vegetarian specials like grilled avocado and Stilton
salad. Rolls and sandwiches only in the
evening. *Typical prices:* Beef hot pot
£2.60   Home-made soup £1.20 (Last bar
food 10.30pm. No bar food Sun) ☕

Umberleigh (B & B)   *Rising Sun*

Devon · Map 9 B3
High Bickington (0769) 60447

Owners Wessex Hosts
Landlord Peter Gardner

Credit Access, Visa
🍺 Usher's Country Bitter, Triple Crown;
Holsten. *No real ale*
ACCOMMODATION 8 bedrooms £B
Check-in: all day

Fishing is a favourite pastime at this nice old inn, which owns extensive rights on the river Taw. Fishy photographs feature in one of the cosy bars, while the other, with a flagstone floor, has murals depicting the four seasons. There's also a very comfortable residents' lounge with TV and the odd antique. The comfortable bedrooms, named after pools in the river, are attractively decorated.

Upper Oddington (B & B)   *Horse & Groom Inn*

Near Stow-on-the-Wold · *Gloucestershire*
Map 7 A1
Cotswold (0451) 30584
Free House
Landlord Mr C. Howarth
Children welcome
🍺 Wadworth's Devizes Bitter, 6X; Worthington
Best Bitter; Younger's Tartan; Guinness;
Heineken; Tuborg; cider.
ACCOMMODATION 7 bedrooms £C (No dogs)
Check-in: all day

A 16th-century building in Cotswold stone, standing in a little village about two miles from Stow-on-the-Wold. There are two traditionally appointed bars (beams, brasses, rustic tackle), and a splendid garden with swings and other things keeps the children happy. Modernised bedrooms are neat and cosy; all have private facilities (mainly showers) and two are equipped with TVs.

Upton Grey (Food) **New Entry**   *Hoddington Arms*

Near Basingstoke · *Hampshire* · Map 6 B3
Basingstoke (0256) 862371

Brewery Courage
Landlords Ian & Irene Fisher

Children welcome
Credit Access, Visa
🍺 Courage Best, Directors; John Smith's
Yorkshire Bitter; Guinness; Kronenbourg;
Hofmeister; cider.

Enjoyable home cooking in an 18th-century village pub. The lunchtime menu offers ploughman's, sandwiches, summer salads and hot dishes like corn chowder, garlicky prawns, lemon chicken and mixed grill. Similar, but slightly more expensive, evening choice of starters and mains (seafood platter a speciality). Clafoutis is an unusual pub pud. *Typical prices:* Seafood platter £7   Steak & oyster pie £3.25 (Last bar food 10pm. No bar food Sun eve) 🍴

Uttoxeter (B & B)   *White Hart Hotel*

Carter Street · *Staffordshire* · Map 5 A1
Uttoxeter (088 93) 2437

Brewery Allied Lyons
Landlord Mrs H. V. Porteous
Children welcome
Credit Access, Amex, Diners, Visa
🍺 Ind Coope Special Bitter, Dark Mild; Burton
Ale; Guinness; Skol; Löwenbräu; cider. ♈
ACCOMMODATION 28 bedrooms £B
Check-in: all day

A wealth of oak beams and some fine linenfold panelling are treasures of this 16th-century former coaching inn in the town centre. Spacious bedrooms range from simply fitted to one with a four-poster and much old-fashioned charm. All are equipped with TVs and tea-makers; and most have private bathrooms. The large split-level bar offers plush comfort, and the former dining room with its superb woodwork is much admired. There's a patio.

Walkern   *(Food)*   *White Lion*

High Street · *Hertfordshire* · Map 7 D1
Walkern (043 886) 251

Brewery Greene King
Landlords Mike & Jenny Windebank

Children welcome
Greene King Abbot Ale, IPA Bitter, Light,
Mild; Guinness; Kronenbourg; Harp; cider.

The Windebanks have been here 17 years,
the building itself more than 400. In the cosy
bar they offer a varied selection of enjoyable
snacks from celery and Stilton soup to three-
bean stew, chicken curry and beef with white
wine and garlic. Fresh fish features on
Tuesday and Thursday. The cold table includes home-made pâté and a reasonable
cheeseboard. *Typical prices:* Pâté £1.95
Steak & kidney pie £3 (Last bar food 10pm.
No bar food Sun & Mon eves)

Wall   *(B & B)*   *Hadrian Hotel*

Near Hexham · *Northumberland* · Map 4 C1
Humshaugh (043 481) 232

Brewery Vaux
Landlords Mr & Mrs Malcolm Mellors

Credit Access
Vaux Samson, Lorimer's Scotch; Guinness;
Tuborg; Stella Artois; cider.
ACCOMMODATION   9 bedrooms   £D
Check-in: all day

Hadrian's wall is only a few minutes' walk
from this sturdy stone inn to the north of
Hexham. The characterful beamed bar looks
most inviting, and there are handsome
leather chairs in the welcoming foyer-lounge.
The three best bedrooms, with pretty views,
are in traditional style and have private
bathrooms; others are more modestly fitted,
and five are equipped with shower cubicles.
No children under 12 overnight. Garden.

Waltham on the Wolds   *(B & B)*   *Royal Horseshoes*

Melton Road, Near Melton
Mowbray · *Leicestershire* · Map 4 D4
Waltham (066 478) 289

Brewery John Smith
Landlords Mr & Mrs Wigglesworth

John Smith's Bitter, Chestnut Mild; Courage
Bitter; Hofmeister; Kronenbourg; cider.
ACCOMMODATION   14 bedrooms   £C
Check-in: restricted

Built around 1500, this thatched pub stands
at a crossroads in the heart of the village.
Much refurbished internally, only the beams
and brass ornaments in the comfortable bar
provide a reminder today of its antiquity. The
four bedrooms are housed in a converted
stable block across the car park. Neatly
decorated in attractive, contemporary style,
all have colour TVs, tea-makers and smart
carpeted bathrooms.

Waltham St Lawrence   *(Food)*   *Bell*

Near Reading · *Berkshire* · Map 7 C2
Twyford (0734) 341788

Free House
Landlords Mr & Mrs L. A. G. Hall

Credit Access, Amex, Diners, Visa
Brakspear's Pale Ale; Adnams Best Bitter;
Wadworth's 6X, Farmer's Glory; Guinness;
Löwenbräu; cider.

This delightful timber-framed inn provides
good eating in a cosily rustic setting. Typical
light bites include prawn and asparagus
pancake, a steak sandwich or ploughman's
while heartier main courses range from
curries and savoury pies to cold meat salads
and evening grills. Delicious home-made
sweets like tangy gooseberry cheesecake to
finish. Garden. *Typical prices:* Steak & kidney
pie £2.40   Seafood platter £2.85 (Last bar
food 10 pm. No bar food Sun)

Waltham St Lawrence *(Food)* *Plough Inn*

West End · *Berkshire* · Map 7 C2
Twyford (0734) 340015

Brewery Morland
Landlord Mrs B. Boulton-Taylor

Credit Visa
🍺 Morland's Best Bitter, Pale Ale; Heineken.

For 35 years Mrs Boulton-Taylor has been delighting visitors to this charming old roadside pub with her fine traditional cooking. Onion and sherry soup, cold veal pie and liver with bacon are typical favourites, while splendidly old-fashioned sweets include treacle tart and lovely plum pie. Book at night. *Typical Prices:* Onion & sherry soup £1.20 Pork pie £1.50 (Last bar food 10pm. No bar food Sun & Mon) ✆

Wansford *(Food, B & B)* *Haycock Hotel*

Near Peterborough · *Cambridgeshire* · Map 5 B1
Stamford (0780) 782223

Free House
Landlord Mr Richard Neale

Children welcome
Credit Access, Amex, Diners, Visa
🍺 Rutland Bitter; Ruddle's County; Bass; Younger's Scotch Bitter; Carling Black Label, Tennent's Extra; cider. ♀

When the future Queen Victoria stayed here in 1835, this busy, well-run hotel was already 200 years old. It stands in a picturesque village in six acres reaching to the river Nene. The River Lounge, overlooking the walled garden, and the comfortable bar are pleasant places for a snack: a cold buffet is spread out in the former, and hot options are quite varied, from garlicky baked mushrooms and grilled sardines to beef curry, deep-fried chicken fillets and wild rice risotto with hazelnuts. Steamed spotted dick is a favourite pud. *Typical prices:* Trio of pâtés £3.95 Game casserole £5.75 (Last bar food 10.30pm) ✆

ACCOMMODATION 26 bedrooms £A
Check-in: all day

Accommodation is exceptionally good, with each bedroom individually decorated to a very high standard. There's good reproduction furniture in all rooms, and the most expensive ones feature four-posters. Remote-control TVs, direct-dial phones, hairdryers and trouser presses are part of a comprehensive list of accessories, and all the bathrooms are en suite.

Wanstrow *(Food)* *King William IV*

Shepton Mallet · *Somerset* · Map 9 D3
Upton Noble (074 985) 247

Brewery Ushers
Landlords Kathy and John Green

Children welcome
🍺 Usher's Best Bitter, Triple Crown; Ben Truman; Watneys SP Mild; Guinness; Carlsberg.

Kathy Green's sound bar snacks warrant a visit to this modest, neatly kept pub, whose lounge features an interesting collection of the tools of various trades. Soup, ploughman's, gammon, rump steak and a couple of salads are supplemented by daily specials like beef and mushroom casserole and a very good, mildly spiced chicken curry. *Typical prices:* Chicken curry £2.95 Meringue nest 85p (Last bar food 9.30pm) ✆

Warborough *(Food)* `New Entry` *Six Bells*

The Green South · *Oxfordshire* · Map 7 B2
Warborough (086 732) 8265

Brewery Brakspear
Landlords Mr & Mrs Bethell

Credit Access, Visa
🍺 Brakspear's Ordinary Bitter, Special, Old Ace (winter); Heineken.

There's a warm welcome at this attractive thatched pub, where beams, low ceilings and exposed stonework impart much old-fashioned charm. The bar food is tasty and satisfying, with things like moussaka and saucy chicken among the robust mains. Simpler snacks are available at lunchtime, and there's a nice home-made apple pie. *Typical prices:* Beef & mushroom pie £2.95 Lasagne £2.95 (Last bar food 9.30pm. No bar food Sun) Garden 🍽

Warenford *(Food)* *Warenford Lodge*

Near Belford · *Northumberland* · Map 2 D4
Belford (066 83) 453

Free House
Landlords Ray & Marion Matthewman

Credit Diners, Visa
🍺 Drybrough Heavy; McEwan's Scotch; Carlsberg; cider. *No real ale.* ♀

In a little village just off the A1, this warm, cosy pub is a splendid place to stop for a sustaining snack. The cooking is both imaginative and accomplished, and dishes range from delicious fresh tomato soup to Normandy-style guinea fowl, leek and tomato flan and fillets of sole in a lovely light mornay sauce. Nice sweets, too. *Typical prices:* Leek & tomato flan £2.20 Grilled mussels £2.20 (Last bar food 9.30pm. No bar food Mon & Tues Nov–Easter) 🍽

Warfield *(Food)* *Cricketers*

Cricketers Lane, Near Bracknell · *Berkshire*
Map 7 C2
Winkfield Row (0344) 882910

Free House
Landlords Mr & Mrs R. Turner

Children welcome
Credit Access, Amex, Diners
🍺 Brakspear's Bitter; Wethered's Bitter; Flowers Original; Guinness; Stella Artois. ♀

Hidden away in Windsor Great Park, this former hunting lodge is full of rustic charm, with its old beams and wooden settles. In the cosy bars you can tuck into a wide variety of fare, from pâtés, pies and quiches to winter soups and substantial main courses such as beef Stroganoff and whole baby salmon. Simple sweets like ices and cheesecakes to finish. Garden. *Typical prices:* Baked plaice in a bag £6.20 Curry £3.75 (Last bar food 10pm. No bar food Sun eve) 🍽

Wark *(B & B)* *Battlesteads Hotel*

Near Hexham · *Northumberland* · Map 4 C1
Bellingham (0660) 30209

Free House
Landlords Robert & Jane Dodd

Children welcome
🍺 Drybrough Heavy, Scotch; Guinness; Carlsberg; cider. *No real ale.*
ACCOMMODATION 7 bedrooms £D
Check-in: all day

The Dodds are engagingly friendly hosts of this village pub which provides a handy stopover for those visiting Hadrian's Wall. It's easy to relax in the cosy beamed bar with its blazing fire or in the delightful upstairs lounge with its sunny views across the cornfields. Simple, cheerful bedrooms share two spotless, old-fashioned bathrooms. Closed Mon lunchtime October–March.

Warmington (Food) **New Entry**   *Wobbly Wheel Inn*

Near Banbury · *Warwickshire* · Map 7 B1
Farnborough (029 589) 214

Free House
Landlord Mike Hayden

Children welcome
Credit Access, Diners, Visa
🍺 Younger's Scotch Bitter; Wilsons Original
Bitter; Webster's Yorkshire Bitter; Guinness;
Carlsberg; Holsten.

This sturdy stone pub stands alongside the busy A41 near the site of the battle of Edge Hill. The staff are very civil, making it a pleasant place to pull in for a snack. Choice varies from pâté and ploughman's to deep-fried Camembert, smoked haddock and exotic nasi goreng. Robust, dependable cooking (there's a restaurant, too). *Typical bar prices:* Steak & kidney pie £3.50 Pork royale £3.25 (Last bar food 10pm) ⊖

Any person using our name to obtain free hospitality is a fraud. Proprietors, please inform the police and us.

RECEPTION

Warminster (Food, B & B)   *Old Bell Hotel*

Market Place · *Wiltshire* · Map 9 D3
Warminster (0985) 216611

Brewery Wadworth
Landlord Mr Howard Astbury

Children welcome
Credit Access, Amex, Diners, Visa
🍺 Wadworth's 6X, Devizes Bitter; Bass;
Guinness; Harp; Heineken; Stella Artois. ♀

A handsome colonnaded facade distinguishes this former coaching inn, now run with pride and efficiency by the Astburys. Snacks can be enjoyed in the delightful courtyard, the beamed Chimes Bar – scene of a vast turkey being freshly carved – or in front of the fire in the cosy lounge. The evening choice is limited to soup, sandwiches and salads, but at lunchtime the menu is enlarged by hot dishes such as shepherd's pie, lasagne and bubble and squeak, as well as old fashioned puds like baked jam roll. *Typical prices:* Steak & kidney pie £1.80 Liver & onions with bacon £1.80 (Last bar food 10.30pm) ⊖

ACCOMMODATION 16 bedrooms £C
Check-in: all day

Neat bedrooms with practical fitted units have tea-makers and TVs. Ten have their own bath or shower rooms. Patio.

Warren Street   (Food, B & B)   *Harrow Inn*

Near Lenham · *Kent* · Map 6 C3
Maidstone (0622) 858727

Free House
Landlord Mr Mark Watson

Credit Access, Visa
🍺 Goacher's Maidstone Ale; Young's Bitter;
Shepherd Neame Masterbrew, Mild; Guinness;
Becks Bier; Hurlimann; cider. ♀

Once the forge and rest house for travellers
to Canterbury along the Pilgrim's Way, this
carefully converted inn is kept in meticulous
order by owner Mark Watson. The comfortable, spacious lounge bar is an inviting setting
for some delicious food from a frequently
changing menu. As well as staples like
sandwiches, salads and ploughman's there
are interesting daily specials such as wild
rabbit and walnut casserole and pork chops
with white wine and mushroom sauce.
Finish with traditional bread and butter pudding or colourful strawberry and gooseberry tart. *Typical prices:* Harvest pie £2.85
Goacher's casserole £3.25 (Last bar food
9.45pm) ◔

ACCOMMODATION 7 bedrooms £C (No dogs)
Check-in: all day

Bedrooms are luxuriously furnished in traditional style and have pretty floral curtains
plus radio-alarms. Three boast excellent
private bathrooms thoughtfully equipped
with extras like bath foam and shampoo.
Good breakfasts. Garden.

Warrington   **New Entry**   *Barley Mow*

Falstaff might feel at home in this splendid Tudor pub on the corner of a
smart shopping precinct. It's handsome without and historic within, with
old prints setting off the carefully preserved panelling and old oak beams.
Book-loving beer drinkers will appreciate the delightful library room that's
lined with books.

Golden Square · *Cheshire* · Map 3 B3
Warrington (0295) 31153   *Brewery* Tetley Walker   *Landlord* Susan
Harkey
🍺 Ind Coope Burton Ale; Tetley Bitter; Guinness; Castlemaine.

Warwick-on-Eden   (B & B)   *Queen's Arms Inn & Motel*

Near Carlisle · *Cumbria* · Map 3 B1
Wetheral (0228) 60699

Free House
Landlords Mr & Mrs Jenkins
Children welcome
Credit Access, Amex, Diners, Visa
🍺 Tetley's Bitter, Mild, Traditional; Guinness;
Skol; Oranjeboom; cider. ♀
ACCOMMODATION 8 bedrooms £C
Check-in: all day

A friendly welcome awaits at this popular
18th-century inn off the A69, just a few
minutes' drive from junction 43 of the M6.
Open fires warm the two convivial beamed
bars, and the brightly decorated bedrooms,
which are of quite a high standard, are equally
inviting. All have TVs, tea-makers and clock
radios, as well as up-to-date private facilities.
Patio and garden.

Wasdale Head   (Food, B & B)   *Wasdale Head Inn*

Near Gosforth · *Cumbria* · Map 3 B2
Wasdale (094 06) 229

Free House
Landlord Mr J. R. M. Carr

Children welcome
Credit Access, Visa
🍺 Jennings Traditional Bitter; Theakston's Best
Bitter, Old Peculier; Guinness; Carlsberg;
cider. ⚲

Walking and climbing are favourite pastimes
around this splendid inn, which stands in a
secluded position at the head of one of
Lakeland's unspoilt valleys. The panelled
bars have a very straightforward choice of
appetising fare (there's also a restaurant).
Chicken liver pâté is fresh and well flavoured,
and main courses include cheese and onion
flan, chicken casserole and tasty pies. The
platter of local smoked meats is a popular
choice, and a daily-changing choice of
sweets nearly always includes a fruit pie.
Typical prices: Smoked meat platter
£3.20 Shepherd's pie £2 (Last bar food
10pm) 🖰

ACCOMMODATION   10 bedrooms   £B
Check-in: all day

Overnight accommodation (half-board only)
comprises ten comfortable, cosy bedrooms,
all with practical tiled bath/shower rooms and
most with lovely views. Day rooms include a
delightful residents' lounge featuring a restored Victorian fireplace. Good management and staff. Pub closed January 19–
March 27 & November 16–December 28.

Washbrook   (Food)   **New Entry**   *Brook Inn*

Back Lane, near Ipswich · *Suffolk* · Map 5 D2
Copdock (047 386) 455

Brewery Tollemache & Cobbold
Landlords William & Nicky Freeth

Credit Access, Visa
🍺 Tolly Cobbold Original, 4X, Mild; Guinness;
Dortmunder Lager; cider.

Homely lunchtime snacks are served in this
comfortable village pub, which William and
Nicky Freeth run with care and enthusiasm.
The menu is shortish and quite simple, and
the day's savoury pie is always one of the
most popular dishes. Other choices might be
warming leek soup, smoked trout and grilled
duck breast. Good selection of cheeses.
Typical prices: Curried parsnip soup 95p
Steak & kidney pie £2.75 (No bar food eves,
Sun or Bank Holidays) 🖰

Washington   (Food)   *Frankland Arms*

Near Storrington · *West Sussex* · Map 6 B4
Ashington (0903) 892220

Brewery Whitbread
Landlords Bob & Jane Carey

Credit Access, Visa
🍺 Whitbread Best Bitter; Flowers Original, IPA,
Strong Country Bitter; Guinness; Stella Artois;
cider. ⚲

The blackboard specials provide the pick of
the eating in this whitewashed pub just off
the A24. Puff pastry pies (lamb and apricot,
steak and kidney, chicken with leeks and
sweetcorn) are the house speciality, and
other favourites include lasagne, game casserole and a roast every Sunday and
Wednesday. Ploughman's and open granary
sandwiches for quick bites. *Typical prices:*
Chicken, leek & sweetcorn pie £2.65 Stilton
ploughman's £1.50 (Last bar food 9.45pm) 🖰

Waterley Bottom *(B & B)*   *New Inn*

Near North Nibley, Dursley · *Gloucestershire*
Map 8 D2
Dursley (0453) 3659
Free House
Landlord Mrs R. D. Sainty
🍺 Smiles Best Bitter; Cotleigh Tawny Bitter;
New Inn WB; Greene King Abbot Ale; Guinness;
Hofmeister; Stella Artois; cider. ♀
ACCOMMODATION 2 bedrooms £D (No
dogs)
Check-in: restricted

Ask directions to this pleasant country pub
peacefully situated in a lovely valley. It may
not be very ancient but its bars have plenty
of traditional character. Locals enjoy a game
of darts or dominoes in the cheerful public
bar, while the lounge bar – overlooking the
attractive garden – is just the place for mulling
over a pint of excellent real ale. Two modern
bedrooms with TVs and tea-makers share a
good bathroom.

Wath-in-Nidderdale *(Food, B & B)*   *Sportsman's Arms*

Pateley Bridge, Near Harrogate · *North
Yorkshire* · Map 4 C2
Harrogate (0423) 711306

Free House
Landlords Ray & Jane Carter

Children welcome
Credit Access, Amex, Diners, Visa
🍺 Theakston's Bitter; Younger's Scotch Bitter;
McEwan's Export; Guinness; Carlsberg Hof;
Harp; cider. *No real ale*

The river Nidd runs not a hundred yards from
this handsome sandstone hotel, which
stands in an area of great natural beauty just
a quarter of a mile from Gouthwaite Reser-
voir, famous for its birdlife. Enjoyable snacks
may be ordered in the bar between noon and
2; there's also a restaurant with à la carte
and prix fixe menus. Soup, pâté and ploughman's, garlic prawns, rarebit and pasta are
typical snacks, or you can push the boat out
with the day's fish special, perhaps monkfish
with Chablis sauce, or a sirloin steak. Sweets
provide less interest. *Typical prices:* Nidder-
dale trout meunière £3.25   Creamed garlic
mushrooms with bacon & crusty bread £2.50
(No bar food eves) ⊖

ACCOMMODATION 6 bedrooms £C
Check-in: all day

Bedrooms, all of a decent size, are kept very
neat and tidy. Attractive pine furnishings and
pretty floral fabrics take the eye, and two
rooms have their own bathrooms. Besides
the simply appointed bar there's a comfortable lounge and a homely TV room, and the
garden is set for summer sipping.

Watton-at-Stone *(Food)*   *George & Dragon*

Hertfordshire · Map 7 D1
Ware (0920) 830285

Brewery Greene King
Landlord Kevin Dinnin

Credit Access, Amex, Diners, Visa
🍺 Greene King IPA, Abbot Ale, Light Mild,
Yeoman; Harp; Kronenbourg. ♀

Kevin Dinnin cares for his customers at this
smashing village pub: fresh flowers in the
cottagy bars, a daily paper is provided, and
his bar snacks are inventive and delicious.
Skewered prawns with garlic butter and
devilled chicken liver vol-au-vent are typical
of his enterprising range, and there are
sandwiches, salads, ploughman's and super
sweets. Garden. *Typical prices:* Grilled king
prawns £5.75   Smoked trout sandwich £2
(Last bar food 10 pm. No bar food Sun) ⊖

Welford-on-Avon *(Food)* `New Entry` — Shakespeare Inn

Chapel Street · *Warwickshire* · Map 7 A1
Stratford-upon-Avon (0789) 750443

Brewery Whitbread
Landlords Mr & Mrs J. M. Shaw

Children welcome
Credit Access
🍺 Flowers Original Bitter, IPA Bitter; Guinness;
Stella Artois; Heineken; cider.

Paperbacks give a literary feel to the homely bar of this charming village pub which pulls in the customers with superb home-made hot pies. Also on the menu are ploughman's, salads, sandwiches, jacket potatoes and omelettes (lunchtime only) and in the evening the choice widens to include trout, steaks and a mixed grill. Garden. *Typical prices:* Steak & kidney pie £2.85 Ham & cheese jacket potato £1.35 (Last bar food 9.30pm. No bar food Sun eve mid Oct–Easter) ⊖

Well `New Entry` — Chequers

A flourishing vine covers the patio of this quaint 17th-century pub, which has remained delightfully unspoilt. Lovers of the simple life will appreciate old-world details like the low ceiling, panelled walls, carvings and bric-à-brac that make the bar a restful place for a quiet drink. French staff lend a convivial Gallic air.

Near Odiham · *Hampshire* · Map 6 B3
Basingstoke (0256) 862605 *Free House* *Landlord* Maurice Bernard
Credit Access, Diners, Visa
🍺 Hall & Woodhouse Badger, Tanglefoot; Guinness; Stella Artois; cider.

Wendron *(B & B)* — New Inn

Near Helston · *Cornwall* · Map 9 A4
Helston (032 65) 2683

Brewery Cornish Brewery Company
Landlords Bill & Gloria Standcumbe

🍺 Devenish Bitter, Cornish, Falmouth;
Guinness; Grünhalle; Heineken; cider. ♀
ACCOMMODATION 2 bedrooms £D (No dogs)
Check-in: restricted

Opposite the churchyard, this pleasant little stone pub is cheerfully decked with flowers. Horse brasses, post horns and bridles are among the ornaments that hang in the bar, where everything gleams like a new pin. Upstairs are two modest but comfortable bedrooms with traditional furnishings and colour TVs; they share a neat modern bathroom. No children under 14 overnight. Accommodation closed one week Christmas. There's a patio.

Wentworth *(Food)* — George & Dragon

Main Street · *South Yorkshire* · Map 4 C3
Barnsley (0226) 742440

Free House
Landlord Margaret Dickinson

Children welcome (lunchtime only)
🍺 Theakston's Old Peculier, XB; Old Mill
Bullion; Taylor's Bitter; Löwenbräu.

Once a courthouse, now an atmospheric pub with an air of old-fashioned, lived-in comfort. Margaret Dickinson keeps the customers smiling with her good beers and wholesome snacks (sometimes the two combine – real ale gives a kick to the wholemeal bread and the excellent fruitcake). Good sandwiches and ploughman's platters, salads and a few, mainly lunchtime hot dishes like fidget pie. *Typical prices:* Fidget pie £2.65 Fruitcake with cheese 95p (Last bar food 9pm) ⊖

Weobley   (Food, B & B)   Red Lion Hotel

Hereford & Worcester · Map 8 D1
Weobley (0544) 318220

Free House
Landlord E. J. Townley-Berry

Children welcome
Credit Access, Amex, Diners, Visa
🍺 Ushers Founders Ale; Webster's Yorkshire
Bitter; Guinness; Carlsberg Hof; cider. ⚲

Mr Townley-Berry is the urbane host at this
delightful 14th-century inn, one of many half-
timbered buildings in the village. Sandwiches,
toasties and coffee are available at most times
in the bar, but if you're hungrier head for the
comfortable dining room to enjoy the excellent
lunchtime buffet, which offers a wide range of
cooked meats and salads, well-kept English
cheeses and a couple of hot specials. There's
also an evening à la carte menu. Sunday lunch
is table d'hôte at £7.50; sandwiches only
Sunday evening. *Typical prices:* Cold buffet
£3.75   Stilton ploughman's £1.80 (Last bar
food 9.30pm) ♥

ACCOMMODATION   7 bedrooms   £B
Check-in: all day

The seven bedrooms are bright and cheerful,
with simple modern furnishings and plenty of
space for storage and writing. All rooms have
TVs and telephones, plus neat bath or shower
rooms en suite. Amenities include a garden
and a bowling green.

West Adderbury   (Food)   White Hart

Tanners Lane, near Banbury · *Oxfordshire*
Map 7 B1
Banbury (0295) 810406

Free House
Landlords Andrina & Frank Coroon

🍺 Hook Norton Best Bitter; Marston's Bitter;
Webster's Yorkshire Bitter; Foster's;
Kronenbourg.

A very pleasant village inn with a warm,
homely feel. The new landlords keep the
emphasis on quality for the bar snacks, which
include a nicely laid out cold table. Hot
choices might be prawn curry, braised lamb
cutlets and spicy-sauced hamburgers. Tasty
sweets, too, like a nice rummy chocolate rum
pot. Traditional Sunday lunch. *Typical prices:*
Lasagne £2.50   Hamburger pizzaiola £2.50
(Last bar food 10pm. No bar food Sun & Mon
eves) ♥

West Ilsley   (Food)   **New Entry**   Harrow

Near Newbury · *Berkshire* · Map 7 B2
East Ilsley (063 528) 260

Brewery Morland
Landlord Heather Humphreys

Children welcome
Credit Access, Visa
🍺 Morland's Mild, Bitter, Best Bitter; Guinness;
Heineken; cider. ⚲

This attractive pub opposite the village pond
has an interesting and varied bar menu –
spinach and mushroom roulade, baked trout
stuffed with cucumber, casseroled chicken
with lemon and chives are typical delights.
There's traditional fare, too, like steak and
kidney pie and brown bread sandwiches.
Home-made sweets include a very nice
terrine of cheesecake and summer fruits.
Typical prices: Rabbit pie £2   Old English
syllabub £1.50 (Last bar food 9.30pm) ♥

West Lavington   (B & B)   *Wheatsheaf*

Near Devizes · *Wiltshire* · Map 6 A3
West Lavington (0380 81) 3392

Free House
Landlord Mr T. J. Emery

Children welcome
🍺 Wadworth's 6X; Cooper Bitter; Guinness;
Skol; Löwenbräu; cider.
ACCOMMODATION   3 bedrooms   £D

Six bright, cheerful bedrooms with private
facilities and bedside controls head the
accommodation at this pleasant black and
white village pub. Older rooms, though more
modest, are well maintained and share three
good bathrooms. There's a pool table in one
of the simple bars, while farming implements
adorn the other. The large garden has a
children's play area.

West Lulworth   (B & B)   `New Entry`   *Castle Inn*

Dorset · Map 9 D4
West Lulworth (092 941) 311

Brewery Devenish
Landlords Pat & Graham Halliday

Credit Access, Amex, Diners, Visa
🍺 Devenish Bitter, Wessex Bitter; Truman Mild;
Webster's Yorkshire Bitter; Guinness; Foster's.
ACCOMMODATION   13 bedrooms   £C
Check-in: all day

Long, low and picture-postcard-pretty, this
16th-century thatched pub has an attractive
garden with a water terrace and other rustic
features. The bars are in cosy country style,
and the centrally-heated bedrooms, including
five in a newish rear extension, provide
delightfully homely touches like ornaments,
books, biscuits and sweets. TVs and radios
in all rooms, private facilities in all but two.

West Witton   (B & B)   *Wensleydale Heifer*

Near Leyburn · *North Yorkshire* · Map 4 C2
Wensleydale (0969) 22322

Free House
Landlords Major & Mrs Sharp
Children welcome
Credit Access, Amex, Visa
🍺 Younger's IPA; McEwan's Export, Lager;
Stella Artois; cider. ♀
ACCOMMODATION   20 bedrooms   £B
Check-in: all day

Set among splendid Wensleydale scenery on
the A684 Leyburn–Hawes Road, this 17th-
century inn is a comfortable base for tourists
and walkers. Half the bedrooms are in the
main building, the rest in adjacent premises;
decor is quietly appealing, and furnishings
range from modern fitted to attractive period.
TVs and tea-makers are standard, and all
rooms have en suite shower or bathroom.
Charming bar, inviting lounge.

Westbury   (Food)   *Reindeer Inn*

Near Brackley · *Buckinghamshire* · Map 7 B1
Brackley (0280) 704934

Brewery Manns
Landlord J. Hicks

🍺 Usher's Fawder's Bitter; Wilson's Original;
Webster's Yorkshire Bitter; Guinness; Holsten;
Carlsberg; cider.

The beer garden is a fair-weather attraction
at this sturdy, stone-built pub, which serves
a decent selection of straightforward bar
food. Steak and kidney pie, chilli con carne,
burgers and open sandwiches are typical
choices, along with steaks and salads.
There's pâté to start, and sweets include the
very popular and very gooey hot chocolate
fudge cake. *Typical prices:* Chilli con carne
£1.90   Hot chocolate fudge cake 90p (Last
order 9.30pm. No bar food Sun eve). ☺

Weston   *(Food)*   *White Lion*

Near Crewe · *Cheshire* · Map 3 B4
Crewe (0270) 587011

Free House
Landlords Alison & Gordon Davies

Children welcome
Credit Access, Amex, Diners, Visa
🍺 Tetley's Traditional Bitter; Ind Coope Burton
Ale, Bitter, Mild; Guinness; Skol; cider. ♀

Dating from 1652, this village pub has been
extended and improved by the Davieses and
now boasts space, atmosphere, open fires
in its timbered bar and a garden with bowling
green. A huge variety of snacks like soup,
pâtés, toasted sandwiches, cold meats,
steak and weekday roast are home-made,
together with sweets such as trifle or chocolate roulade. *Typical prices:* Toasted steak
sandwich £3.25   Roast £2.50 (Last bar food
9.45pm) ℗

Westwood   *(Food)*   *New Inn*

Near Bradford-on-Avon · *Wiltshire* · Map 9 D3
Bradford-on-Avon (02216) 3123

Brewery Usher
Landlords Mr & Mrs F. McFadden

🍺 Usher's Best Bitter, Founders, PA; Webster's
Yorkshire Bitter; Ben Truman; Carlsberg;
cider. ♀

There's an impressive choice of bar food at
this cosy village inn, where local ladies
produce anything from a quick bite to a slap-
up meal. Fish chowder, lasagne and shepherd's pie are popular one-course orders,
and other goodies range from garlic mushrooms to scampi, gammon and roast duckling
with orange sauce. Puds include a really
super treacle tart. *Typical prices:* Sirloin steak
£4.50   Treacle tart £1.20 (Last bar food
10pm) ℗

Wetherby   *(Food)*   *Alpine Inn*

North Yorkshire · Map 4 C3
Wetherby (0937) 62501

Brewery Samuel Smith
Landlord Mr Paul Emsley

Children welcome
Credit Access, Visa
🍺 Samuel Smith's Old Brewery Bitter, Ayinger
Bräu Lager; cider. ♀

On the southbound carriageway of the A1,
this Alpine-style inn with a large car park is a
handy stopping place for the hungry motorist.
Everything in the food line is home-made, the
house speciality being a fillet steak sandwich
served on a sizzling platter. Burgers, ploughman's, fish pie and jacket potatoes are other
options, with apple pie and gâteau among
the sweets. *Typical prices:* Steak sandwich
£3.95   Corn on the cob 95p (Last bar food
9.30pm) ℗

Whatcote   **New Entry**   *Royal Oak*

Built in 1168 as an ale house for the workers building churches in the area,
this delightful pub features a large chimney with iron rungs leading up to a
hideaway used by Cromwell during the Battle of Edge Hill. Today, the low
beamed bars provide an atmospheric setting for a convivial drink. Garden.

Near Shipston-on-Stour · *Warwickshire* · Map 7 A1
Tysoe (029 588) 319   *Free House*   *Landlords* Matthews family
Children welcome
🍺 Hook Norton Bitter; Flowers Best Bitter; Guinness; Heineken; Stella
Artois; cider. ♀

Whitefield *(Food)*   *Mason's Arms*

Bury New Road · *Greater Manchester*
Map 3 B3
061–766 2713

Brewery Whitbread
Landlords Phil & Carol Spires

Whitbread Castle Eden Ale, Trophy Bitter;
Chester's Best Mild, Bitter; Guinness; Heineken.

A handsome red-brick pub, whose single large bar is a popular spot with those in search of tasty lunchtime snacks. Sandwiches and ploughman's platters are favourite light bites, while for something more substantial there's a very good and very chunky steak pie. Fish, too – perhaps deep-fried fillet of plaice – and some nice puddings like lemon meringue pie. *Typical prices:* Steak pie £1.85 Breaded fillet of plaice £1.70 (No bar food eves) ☕

Whitewell *(B & B)*   *Inn at Whitewell*

Near Clitheroe · *Lancashire* · Map 3 B3
Dunsop Bridge (020 08) 222
Free House
Landlord Mr Richard Bowman
Children welcome
Credit Access, Amex, Diners, Visa
Whitbread Trophy, Best Mild; Moorhouse's Burnley Bitter; Guinness; Stella Artois; Heineken. ♀
ACCOMMODATION 11 bedrooms £B
Check-in: all day

The river Hodder runs by this substantial stone inn, and fishing rights are one of the amenities available to guests. Log fires, old prints and period furnishings lend charm to the foyer and bar, and residents have a jolly little lounge with TV. Bedrooms are being upgraded and half now have their own bathrooms. The setting is both peaceful and beautiful, and the whole place has a splendidly welcoming air.

Whitney-on-Wye *(Food, B & B)* **New Entry** *Rhydspence Inn*

Hereford & Worcester · Map 8 C1
Clifford (04973) 262

Free House
Landlords Peter & Pam Glover

Children welcome
Credit Access, Amex, Visa
Hook Norton Bitter; Robinsons Best Bitter; Bass Export Bitter; Guinness; Carling; cider.

On the A438 near the border of England and Wales, this black and white half-timbered old inn enjoys a lovely setting looking down the Wye Valley. The heavily beamed interior is equally delightful, with its creaky floor, roaring log fire in the bar – even bats in the roof space. Appetising snacks like hot smoked mackerel fillets served with a spicy cream sauce, cheese and onion toasties, grilled sardines basted with olive oil, herbs and garlic, and farm sausages (try Cumberland, venison and bacon or smoked pork with garlic) go down a treat. To finish there are such tempting sweets as chocolate brandy cake and treacle tart. *Typical prices:* Rhydspence pasty £3.50 Seafood Thermidor £7 (Last bar food 9.30pm) ☕

ACCOMMODATION 3 bedrooms £B
Check-in: all day

Spotless, attractively decorated bedrooms offer thoughtful extras like flowers and tissues as well as TVs and tea-makers. Bathrooms are compact. Terrace and garden.

Whittlesey *(B & B)* — *Falcon Hotel*

Paradise Lane · *Cambridgeshire* · Map 5 C1
Peterborough (0733) 203247

Brewery Tollemache & Cobbold
Landlord Mr Brian Ramsden

Credit Access, Amex, Diners, Visa
🍺 Tolly's Original, Bitter; Younger's Scotch
Bitter; Hansa; cider. ♀
ACCOMMODATION 8 bedrooms £C
Check-in: all day

This former coaching inn is an attractive brick building tucked away behind the town square. The redecorated ground floor consists mainly of two warm, comfortable bars, one with a thatched serving area, the other with a handsome carved wooden counter. Welcome revamping is planned for the bedrooms, which are mostly of a good size; furnishings are modern, and all rooms have TVs and central heating. Patio.

We welcome complaints and bona fide recommendations on the tear-out pages for readers' comments. They are followed up by our professional team. Please also complain to the management instantly.

Wickham *(B & B)* — *Five Bells*

Berkshire · Map 7 B2
Boxford (048 838) 242

Brewery Usher
Landlord Mrs D. A. Channing-Williams

Children welcome
🍺 Usher's Country Bitter, PA Bitter, Best Bitter; Guinness; Fosters; Carlsberg; cider.
ACCOMMODATION 4 bedrooms £C
Check-in: all day

This attractive thatched country inn – run in a friendly fashion by Dottie Channing-Williams and her all-female staff – is brimming over with atmosphere and charm. A log fire warms the low-beamed bar, which opens on to a pleasant garden with a swimming pool. The four neat bedrooms – in the adjoining stable block – are simple and spotless and share a spacious bathroom. All have colour TVs and tea-makers. Enjoyable breakfasts.

Wilmcote *(B & B)* — *Swan House Hotel*

Near Stratford-upon-Avon · *Warwickshire*
Map 5 A2
Stratford (0789) 67030
Free House
Landlords Mr & Mrs I. Sykes
Children welcome
Credit Access, Amex, Visa
🍺 Hook Norton Bitter; Wadworth's 6X; Younger's IPA; Carlsberg Hof; 'guest ale' (different each week); cider.
ACCOMMODATION 11 bedrooms £C (No dogs)
Check-in: all day

This sturdy black and white building stands in the middle of a village just three miles from Stratford. The owners are cheerful and friendly, and there's a cosy, welcoming bar with attractive stone walls and an old well. Accommodation (closed 4 days Christmas) comprises 11 well-kept bedrooms with TVs, radio alarms and tea-makers; three have private facilities. Patio and garden.

Wimborne St Giles *(Food, B & B)* *Bull Inn*

Dorset · Map 6 A4
Cranborne (072 54) 284

Brewery Hall & Woodhouse
Landlord Mr A. D. Sharp

🍺 Hall & Woodhouse Badger Best Bitter, Export
Bitter; Guinness; Brock; Carlsberg Hof; Stella
Artois; cider. ☿

Standing peacefully in the middle of the
Shaftesbury Estate, this charming little place
is worth seeking out whether for an overnight
stop or just a bar snack. Charcoal-grilled
steaks are the house speciality, and other
main courses include basket meals, steak
and kidney pie, vegetarian bake and, when
the season's right, crab and lobster from
Poole. Daily specials like stuffed vine leaves
add to the interest, and for lighter bites there
are salads and ploughman's platters (cheese
or meat). Kiddies' dishes, too, and a nice
Bakewell tart among the sweets. *Typical
prices:* Grilled sirloin steak £5.45   Chocolate
fudge cake £1.20 (Last bar food 10pm) ℮

ACCOMMODATION   3 bedrooms   £D
Check-in: restricted

Three simply furnished bedrooms with pretty
fabrics and pleasing views are kept in tip-top
condition and share an equally spotless
modern bathroom. Washbasins and tea-
makers in each room. There's a pleasant
garden and terrace.

Wincham *(Food)* **New Entry** *Black Greyhound Hotel*

Hall Lane, near Northwich · *Cheshire* · Map 3 B3
Northwich (0606) 3053

Brewery Greenall Whitley
Landlords David & Janet Buckley

Children welcome
Credit Visa
🍺 Greenall Whitley Local Bitter, Mild; Export
Gold; Guinness; Grünhalle Lager; cider.

The greeting is genuinely friendly at this
sturdy roadside pub, where the food side of
the business is very important. Rolls and
ploughman's are popular light bites, while
more substantial items could include meatballs with rice, steak and kidney pie and a
traditional jam roll. Also cold meats and
salads, fish dishes and choices for vegetarians and vegans. *Typical prices:* Stuffed plaice
with prawns £2.75   Bread & butter pudding
90p (Last bar food 10pm) ℮

Winchcombe *(B & B)* *George Inn*

High Street · *Gloucester* · Map 7 A1
Winchcombe (0242) 602331

Brewery Whitbread
Landlord Mr Carter
Children welcome
Credit Access, Amex, Diners, Visa
🍺 Flowers Best, Original; Heineken; Stella
Artois.
ACCOMMODATION 8 bedrooms £C (No dogs)
Check-in: all day

Once a hostelry for Benedictine monks, this
ancient, half-timbered inn remains a comfortable, welcoming place to stay. Open fires,
flagstoned floors and beams characterise
the convivial bars, and the handsome residents' lounge features leather seating, a
splendid inglenook and oak dressers displaying fine china. Smart, pine-furnished bedrooms (all but one with private facilities) offer
colour TVs, trouser presses and telephones.

Winchelsea *(B & B)*

Winchelsea Lodge Hotel

Sandrock, Hastings Road · *East Sussex*
Map 6 C4
Rye (0797) 226211
Free House
Landlord George Cunliffe
Children welcome
Credit Access, Amex, Diners, Visa
🍺 Webster's Yorkshire Bitter; Harvey's; King &
Barnes Festive; Carlsberg; Foster's; cider.
ACCOMMODATION   24 bedrooms   £C
Check-in: all day

A 20th-century adaptation of a classic Sussex
barn, this modern complex west of Winchelsea on the A259 offers excellent accommodation in motel-style bedrooms. All the neatly
fitted rooms have built-in wardrobes, colour
TVs and tea-makers, plus their own fully tiled
shower rooms. Exposed brickwork and a
high raftered ceiling give the large split-level
bar considerable traditional appeal. The large
garden has plenty of facilities for children.

Winchester *(Food, B & B)*

Wykeham Arms

75 Kingsgate Street · *Hampshire* · Map 6 A4
Winchester (0962) 53834

Brewery Eldridge Pope
Landlord Graeme Jameson

Children welcome
🍺 Eldridge Pope Royal Oak, IPA, Dorchester
Bitter; Guinness; Faust; cider. �

Cheerful log fires warm the two bars of this
early-Georgian pub named after the founder
of the nearby college, and an awning shades
the attractive outdoor eating area. The bar
food is justly popular: feta cheese salad, tuna
and bean antipasto and vegetarian lasagne
among the lighter bites, with steaks, cutlets
and casseroles providing something more
substantial. Imaginative starters include guacamole and smoked mackerel and celery
pâté, with honey and walnut tart among the
sweet treats. *Typical prices:* Venison steak
au poivre £5.75 Boeuf bourguignonne £4.75
(Last bar food 8.45pm. No bar food Mon eve
or all Sun) ☺

ACCOMMODATION   7 bedrooms   £C
Check-in: restricted

Characterful bedrooms have been thoughtfully improved and are now equipped with
central heating, TVs, tea-makers and mini-
bars. Five have private facilities with showers. Residents can get steamed up in the
sauna or take their ease in a delightful
panelled drawing room. No children overnight.

Winforton *(Food)*   **New Entry**

Sun Inn

Hereford & Worcester · Map 8 C1
Eardisley (054 46) 677

Free House
Landlords Brian & Wendy Hibbard

🍺 Felinfoel Double Dragon; Flowers IPA;
Whitbread Poacher Bitter; Guinness; Stella
Artois; Heineken; cider.

Brian and Wendy Hibbard have built up a
solid trade at this refurbished pub on the
A438. A leafy porch leads into the charming
bar, where large blackboards proclaim an
ever-changing variety of tasty home-cooked
snacks. Favourites include pizzas, hearty
stockpot soup, cheesy seafood crumble and
'piggy pie'. For sweets, perhaps tipsy pear in
pastry. *Typical prices:* Piggy pie £2.75 Haddock florentine £4.25 (Last bar food 9.45pm).
Closed Tues in winter. ☺

Winfrith Newburgh (B & B)   *Red Lion*

Dorchester · *Dorset* · Map 9 D4
Warmwell (0305) 852814
Brewery Hall & Woodhouse
Landlords Michael & Elizabeth Smeaton

Children welcome
🍺 Hall & Woodhouse, Badger Best Bitter,
Tangleroot, Malthouse Bitter, Export; Guinness;
Carlsberg; Brock; cider. ♀
ACCOMMODATION 4 bedrooms £D
Check-in: all day

Earlier incarnations as a farmhouse and
coaching inn lie behind this rebuilt roadside
inn, which has been in the same family for 40
years. The panelled lounge bar is warm and
characterful, and a smaller bar more rustic.
Upstairs is a simple residents' lounge and
four delightful bedrooms with cheerful decor,
practical units, tea-makers and TVs. The
shared bathroom is spotless. Garden.

Winkfield (Food)   *Olde Hatchet*

Hatchet Lane, Near Windsor · *Berkshire*
Map 7 C2
Bracknell (0344) 882303

Brewery Bass Charrington
Landlord Mr M. P. Cass

Children welcome (weekend lunchtimes)
Credit Access, Amex, Visa
🍺 Charrington IPA Bitter; Bass Bitter; Guinness;
Carling Black Label; Tennent's; cider.

There's a fine country feel to this attractive
black and white inn with 16th-century origins.
Bar snacks are tasty and enjoyable: ploughman's and rolls for quick bites; home-made
pâtés; salads; hot dishes like lasagne, chilli
or beef Marengo. Simple sweets include
cheesecake and apple bake. Garden. *Typical
prices: Beef Marengo £3   Grilled swordfish
£4.25 (Last bar food 9.30pm. No bar food
Sun eve).* ⊖

Winkfield (Food)   *White Hart Inn*

Church Road · *Berkshire* · Map 7 C2
Winkfield Row (0344) 882415

Brewery Courage
Landlords Mr & Mrs Haywood

🍺 Courage Directors Bitter, Best Bitter, JC;
Guinness; Hofmeister; Kronenbourg. ♀

Opposite the church, this 16th-century pub
has a pretty garden for summer snacking,
while in winter an open fire makes the bar a
convivial spot. Mrs Haywood provides simple, wholesome fare: soup and salads or hot
dishes like turkey curry and a rich, flavoursome steak and kidney pie. Finish with home-
made blackberry and apple pie. Sandwiches
only Sun eve. *Typical prices: Steak & kidney
pie £3.40   Seafood pancake £2.85 (Last bar
food 9.30pm)* ⊖

Winkleigh (Food)   *King's Arms*

Devon · Map 9 B2
Winkleigh (083 783) 384

Free House
Landlord Mr Wrickard

Credit Access, Amex, Diners, Visa
🍺 Usher's Best Bitter, Triple Crown; Webster's
Bitter, Yorkshire Bitter; Carlsberg; cider.

Highly enjoyable bar food adds to the charm
of this delightful village pub. Home-made
pies, pâtés, cooked meats and salads make
up the excellent cold buffet, while the hot
choice includes hearty vegetable soup and
daily-changing specials such as chicken with
tarragon or local sausages. Traditional roast
on Sun. Restaurant. Closed Mon (except
Bank Hols), 2 weeks Feb & 3 weeks Nov.
*Typical prices: Vegetable soup £1   Beef
Burgundy £2.95 (Last bar food 10pm)*

Winkton (B & B)

Fisherman's Haunt Hotel

Salisbury Road, Christchurch · *Dorset*
Map 6 A4
Christchurch (0202) 484071
Free House
Landlords Mr & Mrs James Bochan
Children welcome
Credit Access, Amex, Diners, Visa
🍺 Ringwood Best Bitter; Bass; Worthington
Best Bitter; Guinness; Hofmeister; cider. ♀
ACCOMMODATION 19 bedrooms £B
Check-in: all day

An ideal centre for walkers and, of course, fisherman, this hospitable 17th-century inn overlooking the river Avon offers thoughtfully equipped accommodation. Bedrooms in the stable and cottage blocks, though compact, are most attractive. Main building rooms are bigger and more traditional; one has a four-poster and another a half-tester. All have TVs and tea-makers. There are two beamed bars – one with a well – and a residents' lounge, along with a garden.

Winsford (B & B)

Royal Oak Inn

Near Minehead · *Somerset* · Map 9 C3
Winsford (064 385) 232

Free House
Landlord Mr Charles Stevens
Children welcome
Credit Access, Amex, Diners, Visa
🍺 Flowers IPA, Best Bitter; Whitbread Best
Bitter; Heineken; Stella Artois; cider.
ACCOMMODATION 14 bedrooms £B
Check-in: all day

Accommodation is of a high standard at this smartly thatched pub, whether you choose a traditional room in the main house or an equally attractive modern one in the outbuilding. All are prettily decorated and offer TVs, tea-makers and excellent private bathrooms; in addition, there's a most luxurious suite. Downstairs, the cosy lounges are warmed by open fires, and there are two rustic bars.

Winslow (B & B)

Bell Hotel

1 Sheep Street, Market Square
Buckinghamshire · Map 7 B1
Winslow (029 671) 2741
Free House
Landlords Mr & Mrs William Alston
Children welcome
Credit Access, Visa
🍺 Hook Norton Bitter; Adnams Bitter; Marston's
Bitter; Sam Smith's Bitter; Carlsberg;
Foster's. ♀
ACCOMMODATION 14 bedrooms £A
Check-in: all day

The charming and jovial Alstons lead a friendly team at this former coaching house in the centre of town. There are various convivial bar areas for the peaceful enjoyment of a pint, including the cosy Neal Snug and a courtyard. Well-kept bedrooms are all of a decent size, with TVs and tea-makers. Most rooms have smart bath/shower rooms en suite. Good breakfasts.

Winster (B & B)

Brown Horse Inn

Near Windermere · *Cumbria* · Map 3 B2
Windermere (096 62) 3443

Free House
Landlords John & Joanne Cummins

🍺 Websters Wilsons, Mild; Guinness;
Hofmeister; Holsten; Carlsberg; cider.
ACCOMMODATION 4 bedrooms £D (No dogs)
Check-in: all day

Set in the pretty Lyth Valley, this unpretentious village hostelry has been a public house since 1848. There are two inviting bars, offering a choice of style and mood for the thirsty. Bedrooms are fairly plain and simple, but well maintained and comfortable, with full central heating. Furnishings are modern functional, and the four rooms share a single bathroom. Children under 14 not accommodated overnight. Patio.

Winterton-on-Sea   (B & B)   *Fisherman's Return*

The Lane · *Norfolk* · Map 5 D1
(049 376) 305

Brewery Norwich
Landlords John & Kate Findlay
Children welcome
🍺 Norwich S&P Bitter, Bitter; Webster's
Yorkshire Bitter; Ruddle's County; Guinness;
Foster's; cider. ♀
ACCOMMODATION 3 bedrooms £C
Check-in: restricted

A traditional Norfolk building of brick and
flint, this village pub stands just a short walk
from the dunes and the sea. The panelled
bars have a cosy, friendly character, and the
first-floor hallway serves as a little lounge
area with TV. Two of the neat bedrooms have
oid furniture, the third modern fitted units; all
have sloping ceilings and one has its own
charming sitting room. No children accommodated overnight. Garden.

Wisbech   (B & B)   *Rose & Crown Hotel*

Market Place · *Cambridgeshire* · Map 5 C1
Wisbech (0945) 583187

Brewery Greene King
Landlords John Martin & David Owen
Children welcome
Credit Access, Amex, Diners, Visa
🍺 Greene King Abbot Ale, IPA; Bass; Guinness;
Harp; Kronenbourg; cider.
ACCOMMODATION 24 bedrooms £C
Check-in: all day

The new owners have initiated an impressive
renovation programme at this charming hotel, where the oldest part dates from 1601.
The day rooms have been the first to benefit,
the residents' lounge being particularly elegant and tasteful. Attention will then turn to
the bedrooms (already comfortable and well
furnished), which offer TVs, direct-dial
phones, fresh flowers and various little
extras. Home-made preserves are a breakfast feature.

Withington   (B & B)   *Mill Inn*

Near Cheltenham · *Gloucestershire* · Map 7 A1
Withington (024 289) 204

Free House
Landlord Mr M. G. P. Stourton

Children welcome
Credit Access, Visa
🍺 Webster's Yorkshire Bitter; Bass; HB Bitter;
Flowers IPA, Best Bitter; Carlsberg Pils; cider.
ACCOMMODATION 3 bedrooms £C
Check-in: restricted

Originally built to accommodate workers at
the nearby mill, this marvellously traditional
inn has a history going back 500 years. The
flagstones, the beams, the yellowed walls
and the rustic furnishings ooze charm, and
the garden is a model of rural tranquillity.
Upstairs to three equally delightful bedrooms, with pretty fabrics and sturdy oak
pieces, that offer simple but comfortable
overnight accommodation.

Withybrook   (Food)   **New Entry**   *Pheasant*

Main Street, Near Coventry · *Warwickshire*
Map 5 A2
Hinckley (0455) 220 480

Free House
Landlords Mr & Mrs D. Guy & Mr & Mrs A. H.
Bean
Credit Access, Via
🍺 Courage Dark Mild, Directors Bitter; Everards
Old Original Bitter; John Smith's Bitter;
Hofmeister; Carlsberg; cider. ♀

A busy brookside pub with a bar adorned
with rural artefacts and stuffed pheasants.
The bar menu is long and varied, with soup
and assorted pâtés preceding anything from
liver and bacon to lasagne, stuffed plaice to
moules marinière to a mixed
grill. Also sandwiches, omelettes, simple
sweets. Sunday lunch at £5.25 is served in
both bar and restaurant. *Typical prices:*
Moussaka £2.95   Apple pie 75p (Last bar
food 10pm) ⊝

Withypool   *(Food, B & B)*   ## *Royal Oak Inn*

Near Minehead · *Somerset* · Map 9 C3
Exford (064 383) 236

Free House
Landlords Mr & Mrs Bradley & Mr & Mrs Lucas

Credit Access, Amex, Diners, Visa
🍺 Usher's Best Bitter, Country Bitter, Founder's Ale; Webster's Yorkshire Bitter; Guinness; Carlsberg; cider. 🍷

Lovers of the great outdoors find both the surroundings and the friendly welcome at this 300-year-old inn very much to their liking. When all that fresh air has roused an appetite, rest assured that some suitably hearty snacks await in the rustic bars warmed by open fires. Choose from giant filled rolls, ploughman's and pâté, spicy tomato or garlicky pork sausages, locally baked pasties, salads and steaks. In addition, weekends and winter months see a warming special such as a substantial beef stew with herb dumplings, and there are pleasant sweets to finish. There's also a restaurant. *Typical prices:* Home-cooked gammon & eggs £3.20   Chocolate brandy cake £1.20 (Last bar food 9.30pm) 🍽

ACCOMMODATION   8 bedrooms   £B
Check-in: all day

A glass of sherry is a typically thoughtful touch in the charming beamed bedrooms, many of which enjoy lovely views. Four have en suite bathrooms, six are equipped with TVs and both tea-makers and radio-alarms are standard throughout. No under-tens overnight. Terrace.

Witney   *(Food, B & B)*   ## *Red Lion Hotel*

Corn Street · *Oxfordshire* · Map 7 A1
Witney (0993) 3149

Brewery Morrell
Landlords Mr & Mrs R. Tams

Children welcome
🍺 Morrell's Bitter, Friar Bitter; Guinness; Harp, Harp Premium; cider. 🍷

A friendly pub standing at one end of the main road through town. The bars derive much of their character from the sociable crowd that gathers to enjoy a drink and a bite. The menu sticks mainly to familiar fare, with main courses such as roast chicken, steak and kidney pie, chilli con carne and cauliflower cheese. Ploughman's, pasties and rarebits make tasty lighter snacks, and there are sandwiches both hot and cold, jacket potatoes and a selection of sweets including a very good treacle tart (don't bother with the custard). *Typical prices:* Lasagne £1.85   Steak & kidney pie £2.65 (Last bar food 10.30pm) 🍽

ACCOMMODATION   2 bedrooms   £B
Check-in: restricted

Accommodation is a new thing here, and is in the process of being increased. The first two rooms have a homely feel helped along by central heating, pretty fabrics and agreeable furnishings. TVs and tea-makers are provided, and each room has its own modern bathroom (not en suite). No smoking in bedrooms. Courtyard.

Wixford

Wixford   *(Food)*   **New Entry**   *Three Horseshoes*

Near Alcester · *Warwickshire* · Map 7 A1
Stratford (0789) 773443

Brewery Flowers
Landlords Mr & Mrs Crumpton

Children welcome
Credit Access, Visa
🍺 Flowers Original Bitter, IPA, Best Bitter;
Guinness; Stella Artois; Heineken; cider. ♀

This large country inn stands in its own
grounds by a pretty little stream. Inside,
there's warmth and character a-plenty, plus
tasty bar snacks ranging from soup and pâté
to fried plaice, prawn curry, poussin and
steaks. Sweets like apple and blackcurrant
pie round things off. *Typical prices:* Chicken
provençale £3.70   Lasagne £2.80 (Last bar
food 10pm. No bar food Mondays except
Bank Holidays). ⊖

Woburn   *(Food)*   *Black Horse Inn*

Bedford Street · *Bedfordshire* · Map 7 C1
Woburn (052 525) 210

Free House
Landlord Mr T. Aldous

Children welcome
Credit Access, Visa
🍺 Marston's Burton Bitter, Pedigree; Tetley's
Bitter; Guinness; Oranjeboom; Löwenbräu;
cider. ♀

With Woburn Abbey nearby, this former
coaching inn is a popular spot with tourists,
who join the locals in enjoying some tasty bar
snacks. Jumbo steak sandwiches and chilli-
filled jacket potatoes are popular quick
meals, and there are also salads, soup and
the day's savoury pie. The cold buffet is
popular in summer when the attractive walled
garden comes into its own. *Typical prices:*
Dish of the day £1.90   Fillet steak £5.30 (Last
bar food 10.15pm) ⊖

Wolvey   *(Food)*   **New Entry**   *Axe & Compass*

Near Hinckley · *Warwickshire* · Map 5 A1
Hinckley (0455) 220240

Brewery Mitchells & Butlers
Landlords Jones family

Children welcome
Credit Access, Visa
🍺 Bass; Brew XI; Highgate Mild; Guinness;
Carling Black Label; Tennent's Pilsner, Extra;
cider.

A real family business this, with the landlord's
son cooking and his daughter running the
restaurant. Customers come from miles
around to enjoy the splendid bar snacks – a
constantly changing choice that runs from
sandwiches and omelettes to veal cutlets,
cottage pie, tagliatelle and chicken curry.
Chocolate sponge pudding is one of the nice
sweets. *Typical prices:* Chicken & prawn
indienne £3.50   Steak & kidney pie £2.45
(Last bar food 10pm) ⊖

Wonersh   *(Food)*   *Grantley Arms*

The Street · *Surrey* · Map 6 B3
Guildford (0483) 893351

Brewery Friary Meux
Landlord Michael Weyl

Credit Access, Amex, Diners, Visa
🍺 Friary Meux Bitter; Ind Coope Burton Ale;
John Bull Bitter; Guinness; Löwenbräu; Skol;
cider.

Pilgrims on the Canterbury trail used to stop
at this ancient black and white inn, and
today's travellers greet the tasty snacks on
offer in the heavily beamed bar. A bowl of
creamy mushroom soup with excellent home-baked bread goes down a
treat, and there are also savoury pancakes,
meat pies, grills, curries, salads and sandwiches. *Typical prices:* Steak, mushroom &
Guinness pie £2.75   Ploughman's £1.50 (Last
bar food 10pm. No bar food Sun eve) ⊖

Woodbridge   (B & B)

Bull Hotel

Market Hill · *Suffolk* · Map 5 D2
Woodbridge (039 43) 2089
Free House
Landlords Anne & Neville Allen
Children welcome
Credit Access, Amex, Diners, Visa
🍺 Adnams Bitter; Younger's Tartan; John Bull;
Bass; Tolly Cobbold Original; Tennent's Lager;
Heineken; cider. ♀
ACCOMMODATION   25 bedrooms   £B
Check-in: all day

The fine Tudor shire hall is opposite this former coaching inn which offers pleasant overnight accommodation. Locals throng the public bar, but there's a quieter bar, as well as a family room and a lounge with TV. Rooms in the courtyard annexe are simple and modern; those in the main building have more character. Most have private shower/bathrooms, and ten are equipped with TVs; all have tea-makers.

Woodhall Spa

Abbey Lodge Inn

Two central back-to-back fireplaces dominate the long bar of this cosy pub which stands in open fields outside the town. Rugby and Air Force photographs adorn the burgundy-coloured walls, and highly polished furniture and lovely flower arrangements create a most inviting atmosphere. Patio.

Tattershall Road, Kirkstead · *Lincolnshire* · Map 4 D4
Woodhall Spa (0526) 52538   *Brewery* John Smith   *Landlords* Mr & Mrs Sloan
Children welcome   *Credit* Visa
🍺 John Smith's Bitter; Guinness; Hofmeister; cider. ♀

Woodstock   (Food)

Black Prince

2 Manor Road · *Oxfordshire* · Map 7 B1
Woodstock (0993) 811530

Free House
Landlords Larry & Gabrielle O'Brien

Credit Access, Amex, Diners
🍺 Flowers Original; Adnams Southwold Bitter;
Theakston's XB; Archer Village Bitter; Guinness;
Stella Artois; cider. ♀

Traditional British and Tex-Mex cooking is the unusual combination at this attractively rustic riverside pub. On the home front there's wine-enriched steak and kidney pie, meat and cheese sandwiches, ploughman's and winter soups, while the American owner's influence is seen in a range of thoroughly authentic burritos, enchiladas, tacos and nachos. *Typical prices:* Tostado £2.35   Beef & Guinness pie £3.25 (Last bar food 10pm. No bar food Mon) ☺

Wooler   (B & B)

Tankerville Arms

Cottage Road · *Northumberland* · Map 2 D4
Wooler (0668) 81581

Free House
Landlords Park & Morton families

Children welcome
🍺 McEwan's 80/-; Drybrough Heavy; McEwan's
Best Scotch; Cavalier; Harp; cider. ♀
ACCOMMODATION   17 bedrooms   £D
Check-in: all day

The easy-going friendliness of the Parks and the Mortons makes their sturdy stone pub on the A697 an attractive place for all the family. One bar is lively, the other relaxing, and there's a TV lounge for residents. Spacious bedrooms in traditional style have practical comforts; seven have private bathrooms and the rest share good modern facilities. There's also a cottage in the garden with a double bedroom, bathroom and sitting room.

Woolhope   *(Food, B & B)*   *Butchers Arms*

Near Hereford · *Hereford & Worcester*
Map 8 D2
Fownhope (043 277) 281

Free House
Landlords Mrs M. Bailey & Mr W. Griffiths

🍺 Younger's Tartan Mild, Bitter; Hook Norton
Best Bitter, Old Hookey; Marston's Pedigree;
Carlsberg; cider. 🍷

In a quiet lane surrounded by meadows and
wooded hills, this black and white 14th-
century pub has the friendly, informal atmosphere of a proper country pub. Open log fires
warm both low-beamed bars in winter, while
the patio garden with its flowering shrubs
and little stream makes a delightful spot for a
peaceful summer's drink. Tasty snacks range
from sandwiches, salads and ploughman's
with home-made apple chutney to full meals:
mushroom and walnut soup or prawn pot
with garlic mayonnaise, say, then vegetable
lasagne or rabbit and bacon pie cooked in
local cider. Finish with scrumptious almond
and apple strudel or frozen ginger and coffee
meringue cake. *Typical prices:* Woolhope pie
£3.15   Apple & almond strudel £1.15 (Last
bar food 10pm) 🏠

ACCOMMODATION 3 bedrooms £C (No dogs)
Check-in: all day

Three bright, airy bedrooms with duvets, TVs
and tea-makers share a thoughtfully
equipped bathroom. No children under 14
overnight.

Woolverton   *(Food)*   *Red Lion*

Near Bath · *Somerset* · Map 9 D3
Frome (0373) 830350

Brewery Wadworth
Landlords Mr B. A. Lander

Children welcome
🍺 Wadworth's 6X, IPA; Bass; Guinness; Stella
Artois; Harp; cider.

This well-run pub by the A36 draws a loyal
following with its highly successful bar food
formula. The choice centres on jacket potatoes with a variety of tasty fillings and an
impressive list of salads ranging from
smoked sausage, cheese and garlic croûtons
to pâté-filled cornets of ham and prawns in
curried mayonnaise. *Typical prices:* Jacket
potato from £2   Caribbean chicken £2.80
(Last bar food 10pm) 🏠

Worcester   *(Food)*   **New Entry**   *Slug & Lettuce*

12 The Cornmarket · *Hereford &
Worcester* · Map 8 D1
Worcester (0905) 28362

Owner Slug & Lettuce
Landlord Mr Brian Hulme

Children welcome
🍺 Ind Coope Burton Ale; Gibbs Wiltshire Bitter;
Guinness; Löwenbräu 1047; Castlemaine 4X;
cider.

One of a small chain of pubs, all putting the
emphasis firmly on food. A blackboard in the
roomy bar proclaims the day's selection,
which includes interesting starters (or
snacks) like hot tuna melt or herring roes in
mustard cream. Main dishes aplenty (pasta,
pies, steaks, vegetarian) and tempting
sweets like gooseberry fool. *Typical prices:*
Herring roes in mustard cream £1.85   Beef
goulash £2.50 (Last bar food 9.30pm. No bar
food Sun). Closed Sun lunch. 🏠

Worthing   *(Food)*   **New Entry**   *Far Post*

Wigmore Road · *West Sussex* · Map 6 B4
Worthing (0903) 39561

Brewery Whitbread
Landlords Nicky & Malcolm MacDonald

🍺 Whitbread Best Bitter; Guest Beers;
Guinness; Stella Artois; Heineken; cider.

Malcolm MacDonald, former England foot-
ball star, is winning new fans as the amiable
and hardworking landlord of this smartly
appointed pub. His wife Nicky tackles the
food side of things, pleasing the crowds with
her omelettes, burgers, baguette sandwiches
and tasty chilli con carne. The dish of the day,
usually a savoury pie, is also a winner. *Typical
prices:* Steak & Guinness pie £2.50   Prawn
baguette £1.65 (Last bar food 9.30pm) ⊖

Wroughton   *(Food)*   *White Hart*

High Street, near Swindon · *Wiltshire* · Map 7 A2
Swindon (0793) 812436

Brewery Wadworth
Landlord Mr A. E. Mitchener

🍺 Wadworth's IPA, 6X, Farmer's Glory, Old
Timer (winter only); Guinness; Heineken;
Löwenbräu; cider. ♀

Excellent sandwiches are one good reason
for hunting down this thatched village pub
just outside Swindon. You can also have
ploughman's, salads, and simple hot dishes
such as macaroni cheese, corned beef hash
and chicken curry, with a tangy apple pie for
afters. *Typical prices:* Prawn cocktail sandwich 95p   Chilli con carne £2.60 (Last bar
food 9.30pm. No bar food Mon & Tues eves
& all Sun) ⊖

Wye   *(B & B)*   *New Flying Horse Inn*

Upper Bridge Street · *Kent* · Map 6 D3
Wye (0233) 812297

Brewery Shepherd Neame
Landlords Barry & Anita Law
Children welcome
Credit Access, Amex, Diners, Visa
🍺 Shepherd Neame Best Bitter, Masterbrew,
Hurlimann; Steinbock Lager; Beamish; cider. ♀
ACCOMMODATION   10 bedrooms   £C
Check-in: all day

Once a busy posting house, this solid old inn
on the A28 has an attractive patio and garden
popular for summer drinks. The main bar is
cosily inviting, with its copper-topped tables
and brick fireplace surrounded by gleaming
brassware. Well-kept bedrooms are generally modern in style; six are housed in the
main building, the remaining four (with neat
bathrooms) in the converted coach house.
All have TVs and tea-makers.

Wykeham   *(B & B)*   *Downe Arms*

Near Scarborough · *North Yorkshire* · Map 4 D2
Scarborough (0733) 862471
Free House
Landlord Mr P. Mort
Children welcome
Credit Access, Amex, Diners, Visa
🍺 Cameron's Best Bitter; Younger's Scotch
Bitter, Mild; Guinness; Carlsberg Export; Skol;
cider. ♀
ACCOMMODATION   9 bedrooms   £B (No dogs)
Check-in: restricted

Originally built as a farmhouse, this fine old
creeper-clad inn makes a most comfortable
place to stay. Gleaming brass and bric-a-
brac give the two bars a cheerful, homely air,
and there's a separate room for children.
Attractively decorated bedrooms with good
carpets and smart whitewood furniture all
have TVs, tea-makers and tiled bath/shower
rooms. The splendidly kept garden adds to
the appeal.

Yarde Down   *(Food)*   *Poltimore Arms*

Near South Moulton · *Devon* · Map 9 C3
Brayford (059 88) 381

Free House
Landlords Mike & Mella Wright

Children welcome
🍺 Usher's Best Bitter, Triple Crown, Country;
Guinness; Carlsberg; cider.

The setting, halfway between South Moulton
and Simonsbath, may be remote, but this
300-year-old pub attracts plenty of trade.
Chief reason for this is Mella Wright's tasty
bar food: there's something for everyone,
from sandwiches to steaks, vegetarian specials, children's dishes and pies both sweet
and savoury. Super chunky chips. Wider
evening choice. *Typical prices:* Turkey pie
£1.50   Smoked mackerel pâté 90p (Last bar
food 9.30pm)

Yarmouth   *(B & B)*   *Bugle Hotel*

The Square · *Isle of Wight* · Map 6 A4
Isle of Wight (0983) 760272
Brewery Whitbread
Landlords Karen Merriman & David Fleetwood
Children welcome
Credit Access, Visa
🍺 Whitbread Best Mild; Flowers Original;
Guinness; Stella Artois; Heineken; cider.
ACCOMMODATION 10 bedrooms £C (No dogs)
Check-in: all day

There's no shortage of atmosphere in the
beamed and panelled Wagon Wheel Bar or
in the nautical Galleon Bar of this attractive
300-year-old inn on the town square. The
Galleon has been extended to include a family
room that opens on to a pretty courtyard, and
there's also a cosy TV lounge. Improvements
are planned to the simple bedrooms (four
with showers) which offer basic comforts.

Yattendon   *(Food, B & B)*   *Royal Oak*

The Square, near Newbury · *Berkshire* · Map 7 B2
Hermitage (0635) 201325   *Free House*   Landlords Richard & Kate Smith
Children welcome   *Credit* Access, Amex, Visa
🍺 Wadworth's 6X; Charrington's IPA; Bass; Guinness; Stella Artois;
cider. ⏣

Full of charm and style, Kate and Richard Smith's creeper-clad 16th-
century village pub is an absolute delight. Log fires warm the snug bars,
where some superlative snacks are served. The imaginative menu
changes daily and might offer such treats as smoked duck with
blackcurrant sauce followed by fresh tuna with herb butter sauce, lamb
steak with red pepper mustard or chicken supreme with oyster mushrooms
in a creamy curry sauce. To finish, try homely rice pudding or an elegant
loganberry and passion fruit sorbet. More elaborate meals in the pretty
little restaurant. *Typical bar prices:* Venison pie £4.75   Halibut with prawns
& mussels £7.25 (Last bar food 10pm) 🕭

ACCOMMODATION   5 bedrooms   £A
Check-in: all day

Immaculate bedrooms with fine fabrics and antique furniture are equipped
with thoughtful extras such as pot-pourri, mineral water, books and
magazines. Splendid bathrooms offer huge fluffy towels and dressing
gowns. Excellent breakfasts. Garden.

SCOTLAND

Airdrie (B & B)   *Staging Post*

8 Anderson Street · *Strathclyde* · Map 2 C3
Airdrie (0236) 67525

Brewery Scottish & Newcastle
Landlord Mr D. Barr
Children welcome
Credit Access, Amex, Diners, Visa
🍺 McEwan's Tartan, Lager; Guinness; Beck's
Bier; cider. ♉
ACCOMMODATION   9 bedrooms   £B
Check-in: all day

The name tells you that this long, low hostelry was once a staging post for horse-drawn coaches. Today's travellers still seek it out for its excellent accommodation: there are nine comfortable, well-kept bedrooms with built-in furniture, tea-makers, TVs and good modern bathrooms. The roomy main bar features some handsome horse brasses and harnesses, and there's a quiet cocktail bar and a garden.

Anstruther (Food, B & B)   *Craw's Nest Hotel*

Bankwell Road · *Fife* · Map 2 D3
Anstruther (0333) 310691

Free House
Landlords Mrs Clarke & family

Children welcome
Credit Access, Amex, Diners, Visa
🍺 McEwan's Export; Tartan Special; Guinness;
Carlsberg Pilsner, Hof; cider. *No real ale.*

Locally caught seafood features prominently on the snack menu offered at this cheerful, much-modernised Scottish manse by the Firth of Forth. In the intimate little cocktail bar (stocked with over 40 malt whiskies) or spacious, contemporary lounge bar you can enjoy an appetising selection that includes fried haddock, lemon sole, plus fresh crab and Tay salmon in salads and sandwiches. Sustaining soups like kidney to start, apple strudel for a pleasant finale. *Typical prices:* Haddock & chips £2.75   Scampi £4.75 (Last bar food 10.30pm) ☕

ACCOMMODATION 50 bedrooms £A (No dogs)
Check-in: all day

Accommodation is neat, practical and attractive, all bedrooms (including some in a recent annexe) have good darkwood units, thick carpets and pretty soft furnishings. Direct-dial telephones, colour TVs, radio-alarms and tea-makers are standard throughout and the private bath/shower rooms are spotlessly kept. Garden.

Anstruther   *Smugglers Inn*

A former resident at this fine old inn was the Earl of Strathmore, who made the proclamation for the Pretender at nearby Anster Cross during the rising of 1715. Today's visitors will find plenty of atmosphere, especially in the upstairs cocktail bar with its barrel chairs, nautical bric-à-brac, cheery log fire and views of the old harbour.

High Street · *Fife* · Map 2 D3
Anstruther (0333) 310506   *Free House*   *Landlords* Mr & Mrs McSharry
Credit Access, Diners, Visa
🍺 McEwan's Special, 80/-, Lager; Guinness; cider. ♉

Ardentinny   *(Food, B & B)*

Ardentinny Hotel

Loch Long · *Argyll* · Map 2 B3
Ardentinny (036 981) 209

Free House
Landlords John & Thyrza Horn & Hazel Hall

Children welcome
Credit Access, Amex, Diners, Visa
🍺 Drybrough Special, Export; Guinness;
Foster's; Holsten; cider. *No real ale.*

Exceptionally friendly owners create a warm atmosphere at this white-painted inn dating back to the early 1700s. Standing on the very edge of Loch Long, where the hotel has its own moorings, it is particularly popular with fishermen and yachtsmen, who stoke up on enjoyable home-prepared fare served. Mulligatawny soup, freshly made sandwiches and salads make tasty snacks, while the truly hungry can tuck into hot specials like lamb in ginger wine, steak or chicken Normandy. Pleasant sweets and cheeses to finish. *Typical prices:* Musselburgh pie £3.25 Prawn, mushroom & garlic tarts £2.50 (Last orders 9.30pm) ☕

ACCOMMODATION   11 bedrooms   £B
Check-in: all day

Comfortable, good-sized bedrooms with lovely views vary in style from solidly traditional to agreeably modern. All have tea-makers and practical bathrooms or shower rooms. There's a cosy lounge with TV for residents' use. The pub is closed end October–mid March.

Busby   *(Food, B & B)*

Busby Hotel

2 Field Road, Clarkston · *Strathclyde* · Map 2 C3
041–644 2661

Free House
Landlord Mr John Hebditch

Children welcome
Credit Access, Amex, Diners, Visa
🍺 McEwan's 80/-, Tartan Special; Guinness;
McEwan's Lager; Beck's; cider. ♀

In a tree-lined road off the A726, overlooking the river Cart, this purpose-built modern hotel is a popular overnight stop with business visitors (20 minutes to Glasgow city centre). There's a smartly contemporary cocktail bar on the first floor, together with a number of function suites, plus a large and very busy lounge bar where simple, satisfying snacks are served by speedy waitresses. Standard favourites like lasagne, steak and kidney, chilli con carne and chicken curry are supplemented by such tasty daily specials as fisherman's pie and roast lamb. Filled rolls and salad platters also available. *Typical prices:* French onion soup 50p Breakfast £2 (Last bar food 9pm) ☕

ACCOMMODATION   14 bedrooms   £B
Check-in: all day

Comfortable, centrally heated bedrooms with pretty duvets and matching fabrics have good modern furniture and up-to-date accessories like direct-dial telephones, colour TVs and tea-makers. Excellent private bath/shower rooms.

Canonbie   *(Food, B & B)*   *Riverside Inn*

Dumfries & Galloway · Map 2 D4
Canonbie (054 15) 295

Free House
Landlords Robert & Susan Phillips

Credit Access, Visa
🍺 Theakston's Bitter; Tennent's 70/-, Lager;
Guinness; Merlin (summer).

Fishermen are enthusiastic patrons of this
handsome, well-kept black and white inn only
yards from a trout- and salmon-filled stretch
of the river Esk. Local produce contributes to
the carefully prepared snacks served in the
smartly rustic bar, which has an appropriate
fly fishing theme. They range from nourishing
soup, pâté and ploughman's to chicken,
steak and fish dishes, with tempting sweets.
Typical prices: Poached salmon fillets £4.55
Rib eye steak £5.95 (Last bar food 9pm). Pub
closed Sun lunch and last 2 weeks Feb. ⏰

ACCOMMODATION 6 bedrooms £B (No dogs)
Check-in: all day

Charming bedrooms – two in a delightful
cottage annexe overlooking the river – have
spotless traditional furnishings and thoughtful extras such as fresh fruit and home-made
biscuits. All have excellent bathrooms.

---

*Our inspectors never book in the name of Egon Ronay's Guides;
they disclose their identity only after paying their bills.*

Castle Douglas   *(B & B)*   *King's Arms Hotel*

St Andrew Street · *Dumfries & Galloway*
Map 2 C4
Castle Douglas (0556) 2626
Free House
Landlord Mr Iain MacDonald
Children welcome
Credit Access, Amex, Diners, Visa
🍺 Younger's Tartan; McEwan's 80/-; Guinness;
Holsten; cider. *No real ale.*
ACCOMMODATION   15 bedrooms   £C
Check-in: all day

Castle Douglas bustles on market days, and
this one-time coaching house attracts its
share of thirsty visitors. For overnighters
there are 15 comfortable, well-kept bedrooms, all with central heating, and eight with
their own bath/shower rooms. Day rooms
include cosy, tartan-carpeted bars, a residents' lounge and a modest TV room. At the
rear of the hotel is a sheltered patio.

Catterline   *(Food)*   *Creel Inn*

By Stonehaven · *Grampian* · Map 1 D2
Catterline (056 95) 254

Free House
Landlords Moire & Geoff Cook

Children welcome
Credit Access, Amex
🍺 Alloa Export; Skol; cider. *No real ale.*

Overlooking the harbour from its clifftop
position, this modest, white-painted pub
offers a limited selection of bar snacks at
lunchtime. Creamy vegetable soup, deliciously sauced seafood specials, shepherd's
pie and salads with beef or scampi are typical
of the appetising range. *Typical prices:* Mixed
seafood in cream sauce £3.95   Salmon in
tarragon cream sauce £4.50 (No bar food
eves). Pub closed Mon & all January. ⏰

Comrie   *(B & B)*   *Royal Hotel*

Melville Square · *Tayside* · Map 2 C3
Comrie (0764) 70200

Free House
Landlords Mr & Mrs I. Gordon
Children welcome
Credit Access, Amex, Visa
🍺 Younger's Tartan Special; McEwan's 80/-,
Heavy, Pale Ale; Harp; cider. *No real ale.* ♀
ACCOMMODATION   14 bedrooms   £B
Check-in: all day

Queen Victoria, en route to Balmoral, stayed at this 18th-century L-shaped inn in the village square, and one bedroom commemorates her visit. The rest have modern functional units, and all have ultra-modern bathrooms, TVs, and tea-makers. Residents have a comfortable lounge, but may prefer the cocktail bar, which is hung with the landlord's Gordon tartan and stocked with over 50 malt whiskies. Garden.

Dulnain Bridge   *(Food, B & B)*   *Muckrach Lodge Hotel*

Near Grantown-on-Spey · *Highland* · Map 1 C2
Dulnain Bridge (047 985) 257   *Free House   Landlords* Ogilvie & Fone
families
Children welcome
🍺 Ind Coope Alloa's Archibald Arrol's 70/-, Diamond Heavy, Export;
Skol. ♀

★ Two charming families run this friendly former shooting lodge situated in rolling countryside just off the A938. They offer a simply marvellous spread at lunchtime – piping hot soups (try the curried apple made with fruit from the garden), pâtés and mousses, superb sandwiches that simply overflow with everything from home-cooked gammon or garlic sausage to poached salmon, together with such gorgeous sweets as Caribbean chocolate pot or delectable raspberry mousse. Booking is advisable on Sun, and the restaurant is open at night for five-course dinners. *Typical prices:* Gammon, cheese & onion sandwich £1.50   Raspberry hazelnut meringue £1.05 (No bar food eves) ◐ ★

ACCOMMODATION   10 bedrooms   £A   (No dogs)
Check-in: all day

Bedrooms are simply furnished in traditional style and all now boast smart modern bathrooms. Downstairs, the comfortable lounge is a pleasant place to relax, and there's a convivial bar lounge. Excellent breakfasts, too. Garden.

Dysart   *(Food)*   *Old Rectory Inn*

West Quality Street · *Fife* · Map 2 C3
Kirkcaldy (0592) 51211

Free House
Landlords Stuart & Kay Nelson

Children welcome
Credit Access, Amex, Diners, Visa
🍺 Alloa Export; Skol; cider.

North of Kirkcaldy in a pretty coastal village, this agreeable Georgian inn provides a good range of bar food. The cold table, set in a bar overlooking the walled garden, is a popular lunchtime feature, and other dishes could be anything from subtle celery and pineapple soup to beef and onion casserole, seafood vol-au-vents and Dutch apple pie. *Typical prices:* Game pie £2.75   Mushrooms in oatmeal £1.65 (Last bar food 9.30pm). Closed Sunday.

Eddleston   *(Food)*   *Horse Shoe Inn*

Borders · Map 2 C3
Eddleston (072 13) 225

Free House
Landlord C. A. McIntosh-Reid

Children welcome
Credit Access, Amex, Diners, Visa
🍺 McEwan's 80/-; Younger's Tartan Special;
Theakston's BB; Greenmantle; Guinness;
Carlsberg Pils; cider. ♀

Once the village smithy, this white-painted inn offers a particularly wide range of bar snacks (there's a restaurant, too). Sandwiches and salads are popular light bites, while hot dishes run from Stilton soup to chicken curry, steaks and a very tasty prawn and mushroom pie. If you've left room for a sweet, try the deliciously indulgent butterscotch pear concoction. *Typical prices:* Walnut & aubergine lasagne £1.90   Apple & blackcurrant crêpe £1.40 (Last bar food 10pm) ☺

Edinburgh   *(Food)*   *Cramond Inn*

Cramond Glebe Road, Cramond · *Lothian*
Map 2 C3
031–336 2035

Free House
Landlord Mr Gordon Duncan

Credit Access, Amex, Diners, Visa
🍺 Lorimer's 80/-; McEwan's Tartan; Guinness;
Carlsberg Export; cider. ♀

On the edge of the Firth of Forth, with a terrace for use in good weather. At lunchtime this pub serves Scottish dishes as well as traditional pub fare: Scotch broth and haggis, tatties and neeps are backed up by cold meats and a fresh display of salads, pâtés, quiches, cottage and steak and kidney pies. The sweets are cheesecake, fruit salad, ice creams and sorbets. *Typical prices:* Haggis, tatties & neeps £2.25   Apple pie 75p (No bar food eves) ☺

Edinburgh   *(B & B)*   *Rutland Hotel*

3 Rutland Street · *Lothian* · Map 2 C3
031–229 3402

Brewery Scottish & Newcastle
Landlord Mr M. McIlwraith

Credit Access, Amex, Diners, Visa
🍺 Younger's Tartan; McEwan's 80/-; Beck's
Bier; Guinness; McEwan's Lager; cider.
ACCOMMODATION   18 bedrooms   £B
Check-in: all day

Major refurbishing of bars and accommodation has taken place at this friendly, well-run hotel, which stands on a corner at the western end of Princes Street. Carpeted corridors lead to quiet, comfortable bedrooms, all with double glazing, central heating and a full range of up-to-date appliances. Half have bathrooms en suite, and the public facilities are spotless. Decor in the bars is heavy Victorian, but the music is light and lively pop.

Elrick   *(Food)*   *Broadstraik Inn*

Near Aberdeen · *Grampian* · Map 1 D2
Aberdeen (0224) 743217

Free House
Landlord Richard Collins

Children welcome (till 7.30pm)
Credit Access, Amex, Diners, Visa
🍺 Younger's No. 3 Ale, Tartan; Guinness;
Carlsberg Pilsner, Hof Export; cider.

Juicy steaks served sizzling on cast-iron skillets are a popular feature at this cheerful roadside inn. Other attractions include mushrooms with garlic mayonnaise, fried fish, burgers and salads, sandwiches and a children's menu that includes sausages and fish fingers (available until 7.30). There's efficient table service in the spacious lounge bar, or you can eat in the garden. *Typical prices:* Steaks from £5.35   Chicken with barbecue sauce £3.70 (Last bar food 9.45pm) ☺

Fochabers (B & B)

Gordon Arms Hotel

High Street · *Grampian* · Map 1 C2
Fochabers (0343) 820508

Free House
Landlord Mr C. Pern
Children welcome
Credit Access, Amex, Diners, Visa
🍺 Alice Ale; Youngers 80/-; McEwan's Export, Tartan; Harp; Guinness; cider. 🍷
ACCOMMODATION 12 bedrooms £B
Check-in: all day

On the high street of Fochabers, this former coaching inn has a white-painted facade adorned with antlers. Inside, the public rooms include a comfortable cocktail bar with a good collection of malt whiskies. The real strength here is the overnight accommodation – 12 well-laid-out rooms with fitted furniture, direct-dial phones, TVs, hairdryers and good carpeted bathrooms. Garden.

We publish annually so make sure you use the current edition.

Glamis (Food) **New Entry**

Strathmore Arms

The Square · *Tayside* · Map 2 C3
Glamis (030 784) 248

Free House
Landlords Messrs Benton & Henderson

Children welcome
Credit Access, Amex, Diners, Visa
🍺 Skol; Alloa Export; cider. *No real ale.*

A friendly village pub serving a popular range of reasonably priced snacks and meals. Lunchtime in the main dining room brings soup, pâté, a fish dish or two, simple roasts and seasonal game. There's a cold buffet, too, and sweets include a delightful steamed syrup sponge. Evening bar food comprises pâté, grills and steaks. *Typical prices:* Pâté with oatcakes 75p Steak & kidney pie £2.80 (Last bar food 9.45pm. No bar food Sat eve). Closed 1 week from 1 January. 🍽

Glasgow (Food)

Archie's

27 Waterloo Street · *Strathclyde* · Map 2 C3
041-221 3210

Free House
Landlord Mr Tony Orr

Credit Access, Amex, Diners, Visa
🍺 McEwan's Tartan, Special, 80/-; Guinness; Becks Bier; Harp; cider.

Atmospheric, smart, modern – this city-centre bar with its soft lights, mirrors and plants is a favourite with the youth of Glasgow. Tasty snacks served from 12.15 to 10pm include burgers, steaks, lasagne and a daily-changing hot special such as chicken provençale. At lunchtime, help yourself from the cold display of meats, raised pies and salads. *Typical prices:* Chicken curry £2.25 Lamb bourguignon £2.45 (Last bar food 10pm) Closed Sun. 🍽

Glasgow *(Food, B & B)* `New Entry` ### Babbity Bowster

16 Blackfriars Street · *Strathclyde* · Map 2 C3
041–552 5055

Free House
Landlords Fraser Laurie & Tom Laurie

Credit Access, Amex, Visa
🍺 Maclays 70/-, 80/-; Guinness; Tennent's lager; Fürstenberg.

Recently delivered from dereliction, this handsome town house (circa 1790) combines café, bar, restaurant and hotel. Snacks and a lavish breakfast start proceedings at 8am, and the complete bar service is available from 11. This includes both lighter items – scones, wheaten rolls, traditional Scottish cheeses with oatcakes – and more substantial fare such as lasagne, casseroles (meat, fish and vegetarian), smoked sausage and, at lunchtime only, wholewheat pancakes, both savoury and sweet. Service is friendly and laid back; live music is a regular feature. *Typical prices:* Spicy chicken pancake £1.75 Vegetarian stroganoff with rice & salad £3.15 (Last bar food 10pm) 🍃

ACCOMMODATION 6 bedrooms £B (No dogs)
Check-in: all day

Six compact, neatly designed bedrooms have modern pine furnishings of stylish aspect, and each features an original print or lithograph. All have carpeted shower rooms en suite. Besides the restaurant and bar there's a little patio for when the sun shines.

Our inspectors are our full-time employees; they are professionally trained by us.

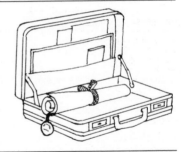

Glencoe *(B & B)* ### King's House Hotel

Highland · Map 1 B2
Kingshouse (085 56) 259

Brewery McEwan's Scottish Brewers
Landlords Mr & Mrs Ian Nicolson
Children welcome
Credit Access, Amex, Visa
🍺 McEwan's Tartan, Special, 80/-, lager; Guinness; cider.
ACCOMMODATION 22 bedrooms £C
Check-in: all day

In a setting of rugged beauty at the head of Glencoe, this modernised old inn is especially popular with tourists and walkers. The granite-pillared cocktail bar sports an admirable array of malt whiskies, and there's a picture-windowed lounge with magnificent mountain views. Bedrooms are neat and simple, and ten have their own bathrooms. Landlords and staff are friendly and relaxed. There's a pleasant beer garden.

Glendevon *(B & B)* — *Tormaukin Hotel*

Near Dollar · *Tayside* · Map 2 C3
Glendevon (025 982) 252
Free House
Landlords Mr & Mrs R. Worthy
Children welcome
Credit Access, Amex, Visa
🍺 Ind Coope Burton Ale, Double Diamond, Diamond Heavy; Alloa's Export; Guinness; Skol; cider. ♀
ACCOMMODATION 6 bedrooms £B (No dogs)
Check-in: all day

Accommodation is a strong point at this pleasantly situated black and white inn with two cosy beamed bars. All the good-sized rooms are neat and bright, with pretty floral wallpaper and smart stripped pine furniture. Five out of six have en suite bath or shower rooms and three rooms offer TV. Back rooms can be noisy at times. Patio.

Glenfinnan *(B & B)* — *Stage House Inn*

Highland · Map 1 B2
Kinlocheil (039 783) 246

Free House
Landlords Helen & Andrew Brooks
Children welcome
Credit Access, Diners, Visa
🍺 Younger's Tartan; Guinness; Tennant's Lager. *No real ale.* ♀
ACCOMMODATION 9 bedrooms £C
Check-in: all day

Fishing rights on nearby Loch Shiel attract many anglers to this smartly painted coaching inn set in breathtakingly lovely scenery on the road to Mallaig. Simple comforts are provided in the modernised bedrooms, which all have private bath or shower rooms. Pine-raftered ceilings are a feature of the two neat bars, and there are two little sun lounges which take full advantage of the spectacular setting. Closed end October–mid March. Terrace.

Inverbeg *(B & B)* — *Inverbeg Inn*

Near Luss, Loch Lomond · *Strathclyde*
Map 2 B3
Luss (043 686) 678
Free House
Landlord Mr J. Bisset
Children welcome
Credit Access, Amex, Diners, Visa
🍺 Strathalbion Bitter; Younger's Tartan; Guinness; McEwan's Lager; Harp; cider. ♀
ACCOMMODATION 14 bedrooms £C
Check-in: all day

Summer tourists flock to this modernised inn on the A82 on the west shore of Loch Lomond. Its attractions include fine views of the loch and facing ben, a pleasant lounge bar hung with paintings of Highland scenes, and bright, cheerful bedrooms. All are comfortably furnished, with TVs and tea-makers, and half have good modern bathrooms.

Invergarry *(B & B)* — *Inn on the Garry*

Highland · Map 1 B2
Invergarry (080 93) 206

Free House
Landlords Iain & Fiona MacLean

Children welcome
🍺 McEwan's 80/-; Younger's No. 3; Guinness; Harp; Tartan Special; cider.
ACCOMMODATION 10 bedrooms £D
Check-in: all day

Standing at the junction of the A82 and A87, this solid Victorian inn has a warm, welcoming air. The rustic bar is a pleasant spot for a drink and a friendly chat, and there are two comfortable lounges. Bright bedrooms (roomiest are on the first floor) are furnished in a variety of styles and all have carpeted modern bathrooms. Accommodation closed October–March, during which period the bar is also closed at lunchtime.

Invermoriston   *(Food, B & B)*   Glenmoriston Arms

Highland · Map 1 B2
Glenmoriston (0320) 51206

Free House
Landlords Mr & Mrs R. Shepherd

Children welcome
Credit Access, Amex, Diners, Visa
🍺 Younger's Tartan; McEwan's 80/-; Guinness; Harp; Carlsberg; cider. 🍷

At the junction of the A82 and the A887, this sturdy, white-painted inn offers simple but delicious bar snacks in its smart bar that's decorated with fishing flies, flintlock guns and Highland pictures. Choose from flavoursome home-made soup and moist pâté with oatcakes, freshly cut sandwiches (look out for salmon in season), juicy local steaks and a variety of meat, fish and cheese platters served with crisp salad and crusty bread. Nice sweets like cherry pie and thick cream to finish. The hotel's restaurant is open for dinner from 6.30pm. *Typical bar prices: Fisherman's lunch £3   Aberdeen Angus steak £6.50 (Last bar food 8.30pm)* 🥘

ACCOMMODATION   8 bedrooms   £C
Check-in: all day

Six of the bright, fresh bedrooms have TVs and tea-makers, as well as their own prettily decorated modern bathrooms. The other two rooms are simpler in style and share a public bathroom. Terrace and garden.

Kelso   *(Food)*   Waggon Inn

10 Coalmarket · Borders · Map 2 D4
Kelso (0573) 24568

Free House
Landlords Scott family

🍺 Drybrough Light, Heavy 80/-; Belhaven 70/-; Guinness; Carlsberg; Foster's; cider. 🍷

Tasty home cooking is the attraction of this sturdy stone pub near the town centre. Mrs Scott's lunchtime menu includes nourishing soup, open sandwiches, salads, sausages and home-made specials, while the evening brings a wider choice of main dishes including half a dozen different steaks. Terrace. *Typical prices: Baked lamb with herb butter £2.50   Crispy fried chicken with onion rice £2.25 (Last bar food 9.45pm)* 🥘

Killin   *(B & B)*   Clachaig Hotel

Falls of Dochart, Gray Street · Central · Map 2 C3
Killin (056 72) 270

Brewery Scottish Brewers
Landlord Mr James Young
Children welcome
Credit Visa
🍺 Younger's Tartan Special; McEwan's 80/-; Guinness; Harp; cider. 🍷
ACCOMMODATION 5 bedrooms £C (No dogs)
Check-in: all day

There are plans to redesign this rambling inn, which enjoys a marvellous setting by the spectacular Falls of Dochart. Bedrooms in the main building are compact but characterful, in the style of ship's cabins and featuring much woodwork from a broken-up liner. Other accommodation is provided in an adjoining cottage. Residents can watch TV in a cosy lounge, or they can join the locals in the bar. Terrace.

Kippen   *(Food, B & B)*   *Cross Keys Inn*

By Stirling · *Central* · Map 2 C3
Kippen (078 687) 293

Free House
Landlords Richard & Penny Miller

Children welcome
🍺 Broughton's Green Mantle Ale; McEwan's
80/-, No. 3, Lager; Guinness; cider. ϙ

Honest, homely bar food matches the unpretentious charms of this friendly pub in the
heart of the village. Old wooden settles line
the atmospheric public bar and a cheery fire
burns in the hearth of the beamed main bar,
whose stone walls are hung with field and
fishing implements. There you can tuck into
tasty offerings like flavoursome leek and
potato soup, delicious salads, traditional
mutton pie and fried haddock. A selection of
home-made ice creams or sorbets makes a
most refreshing finale. *Typical prices:* Baked
trout £3.75   Sirloin steak £7.75 (Last bar
food 9pm. No bar food Mon eve & limited
choice Mon lunch) ☺

ACCOMMODATION   3 bedrooms   £D
Check-in: restricted

Three bright, neatly kept bedrooms share an
equally impeccable bathroom, and two command lovely views. There's an excellent
breakfast in the morning, and your hosts
Richard and Penny Miller are an exceptionally
welcoming couple. Garden.

Lewiston   *(B & B)*   *Lewiston Arms*

Near Drumnadrochit · *Highland* · Map 1 C2
Drumnadrochit (045 62) 225

Free House
Landlords Mr & Mrs N. Quinn

Credit Visa
🍺 Younger's Tartan, No 3; McEwan's Export;
Harp; cider.
ACCOMMODATION   8 bedrooms   £D
Check-in: all day

Simple comforts are on offer at this 250-
year-old pub that's not far from Loch Ness
and that's run by the friendly Quinns. Bright,
pleasant bedrooms (four are in a row of
cottages reached via the pretty garden) have
modest, well-kept furnishings and share two
old-fashioned bathrooms. Public areas include a warm and cosy lounge bar with
classic wheelback chairs, and there are two
comfortable lounges, one with TV.

Linlithgow   *(Food)*   *Champany Inn*

Lothian · Map 2 C3
Philipstoun (050 683) 4532

Free House
Landlords Anne & Clive Davidson

Children welcome
Credit Access, Amex, Diners, Visa
🍺 Belhaven 80/-, 70/-; Skol; cider.

Just-a-biters should make for the cheerful
beamed chophouse at this roadside inn,
where the T-bone steaks, lamb chops and
milk-fed veal are of prime quality. Add a
starter like herrings and sour cream or
garlicky pâté and perhaps hot apple pie for
afters. A splendid cold buffet extends the
range at lunchtime. More formal meals in the
restaurant across the courtyard. *Typical
prices:* Home-made sausage £3   Pickled
fish £1.95 (Last bar food 10pm) ☺

Loch Eck   *(Food)*   *Coylet Inn*

By Dunoon · *Strathclyde* · Map 2 B3
Kilmun (036 984) 426

Free House
Landlord Richard Addis

Children welcome
🍺 McEwan's 80/-; Tartan Special; Younger's
No. 3; Guinness; Tennent's Lager. ♀

This long, low, dormer-windowed pub enjoys
a lovely setting by the loch. The bar has a
cheerful, welcoming feel, and there's a pleasant garden. Bar food is sound and satisfying,
with staples of sandwiches, salads and grills
joined by daily specials like chicken broth or
smoked haddock and egg pie. *Typical prices:*
Grilled rainbow trout with jacket potato
£2.75 Macaroni cheese £1.10 (Last bar
food 10pm) ☺

Lochgair   *(Food, B & B)*   *Lochgair Hotel*

By Lochgilphead · *Strathclyde* · Map 2 B3
Minard (0546) 86333

Free House
Landlords Capt & Mrs G. Paterson

Children welcome
🍺 McEwan's Export, Tartan Special; Guinness;
Harp; McEwan's Lager; cider. *No real ale.*

Just over the A83 from the loch, this white-
painted hotel is a favourite place with both
catchers and eaters of fish. The excellent
local catch featured among the good bar
snacks includes grilled langoustines,
poached trout, haddock and salmon. There's
plenty more choice for healthy eaters (wholemeal bread, vegetable curry, fresh fruit
salad), and among the traditional bar fare are
sandwiches, salads and the perennially popular steak and kidney pie. *Typical prices:*
Steak pie with vegetables £2.75 Grilled
langoustines £4 (Last bar food 9pm) ☺

ACCOMMODATION 18 bedrooms £C (No dogs)
Check-in: all day

The accommodation here is simple, bright
and cheerful, with practical furnishings, duvets and tea-makers in all bedrooms. Ten
rooms offer private facilities, and some have
their own balconies. Besides the two pleasant bars there's a lounge with TV. Amenities
include garden, game & sea fishing, sailing,
hotel boat, mooring and a laundry room.

Lybster   *(Food, B & B)*   *Bayview Hotel*

Russel Street · *Highland* · Map 1 C1
Lybster (059 32) 346

Free House
Landlord Ranald & Norma Hutton

Children welcome
Credit Access, Amex, Diners, Visa

Ranald and Norma Hutton are charming
hosts at this tiny, white-painted inn tucked
away in a side street just a short walk from
the harbour. There are two simple bars (one
warmed by a cheery coal fire), as well as a
cosy, pine-panelled residents' lounge and a
pleasant sun room. Norma is an accomplished cook and her enjoyable bar snacks

🍺 Murphy's Irish Stout; Younger's Tartan; Harp; cider. *No real ale.*

range from soup and fresh, light salmon mousse to juicy roasts, locally caught fish and cold meat salads. Finish with one of her beautifully glazed fresh fruit tarts. *Typical prices:* Roast sirloin of beef £3.50 Salmon steak £3.50 (Last bar food 9pm) ℮

ACCOMMODATION   3 bedrooms   £D
Check-in: all day

The three neat bedrooms with comfortable easy chairs are kept in immaculate order. Two have TVs and all share a modern carpeted bathroom.

Melrose   *(Food, B & B)*   *Burts Hotel*

Market Square · *Borders* · Map 2 D4
Melrose (089 682) 2285

Free House ·
Landlords Graham & Anne Henderson

Children welcome
Credit Access, Amex, Diners, Visa
🍺 Belhaven 80/-, 70/-; Guinness; Skol; Kronenbourg; cider.

Built in 1722, this eye-catching black and white hostelry stands in the centre of town on the market square. Some changes have occurred since last year, including the central resiting of the counter in the main bar. Here you can order from an appetising selection of snacks, including sandwiches, salads, basket meals and roast beef with Yorkshire pudding. They also do a good line in malt whiskies. *Typical prices:* Haddock in bread-crumbs £2.40 Roast beef with Yorkshire pudding £2.60 (Last bar food 9.30pm) ℮

ACCOMMODATION   21 bedrooms   £B
Check-in: all day

Eight of the bedrooms have been very stylishly done out with fine darkwood furni-ture, chic coordinated fabrics and commen-surately smart bathrooms. The other rooms (also with private facilities) are in somewhat starker style; all rooms have direct-dial phones, TVs and tea-makers; the central heating does its job well, and housekeeping leaves little to be desired. Decent breakfast (buffet and cooked).

Melrose   *(B & B)*   *George & Abbotsford Hotel*

High Street · *Borders* · Map 2 D4
Melrose (089 682) 2308
Free House
Landlord Mr John Brown
Children welcome
Credit Access, Amex, Diners, Visa
🍺 Greenmantle Ale; McEwan's Tartan; Younger's Pale Ale; Guinness; Carlsberg Hof, Pilsner; cider.
ACCOMMODATION   35 bedrooms   £B
Check-in: all day

Only a couple of miles from Sir Walter Scott's home, this handsome town-centre hotel right in the town centre makes a handy base for exploring the Border country. The relaxing lounge bar opens on to a pretty rose garden, and there is a simple upstairs lounge with TV. Spacious bedrooms equipped with tea-makers range from smartly modern to mod-estly traditional. Nearly all have private bath-rooms and TVs are available on request.

Moffat   (Food, B & B)   Balmoral Hotel

High Street · *Dumfries & Galloway* · Map 2 C4
Moffat (0683) 20288

Free House
Landlords Robin & Denise Stewart

Children welcome
Credit Access, Amex, Diners, Visa
🍺 Younger's Tartan; McEwan's 80/-, Lager;
Guinness; Carlsberg; cider. *No real ale.*

Summer months bring a throng of visitors to
this smart, white-painted high-street hotel,
where the cheerful beamed bars offer a wide
range of tasty home-made snacks that are
available throughout long opening hours of
11am to 10.30pm. The hearty vegetable soup
makes a warming starter, and to follow there
are popular hot dishes like breaded lamb
chops, chicken curry, chilli con carne and
steak and kidney pie, as well as sandwiches
and ploughman's. Simple sweets include a
homely apple pie. *Typical dishes:* Lasagne
with salad £2.80   Smoked trout salad £2.80
(Last bar food 10pm. No bar food eves
November–March) ⊖

ACCOMMODATION   16 bedrooms   £D
Check-in: all day

Robin and Denise Stewart and their helpful
staff create a pleasant atmosphere. Pretty
bedrooms featuring coordinating floral wallpaper and bedspreads have whitewood furniture and tea-makers. Residents can watch
TV in a quietly formal lounge.

Moffat   (Food)   Black Bull

1 Station Road · *Dumfries & Galloway* · Map 2 C4
Moffat (0683) 20206

Free House
Landlord Mrs H. Poynton

Children welcome
Credit Visa
🍺 McEwan's 70/-; Younger's No. 3 Ale, Tartan;
Greenmantle Ale; Broughton Ale; Guinness;
Carlsberg Hof; cider. ♀

Robert Burns may well have enjoyed a haggis
with his dram at this jolly old characterful inn.
Haggis is still on the simple menu, along with
other tasty hot dishes such as hotpot, fish
pie and chicken and chips, as well as soup,
salads and sandwiches, with a delicious
home-made apple pie for afters. *Typical
prices:* Shepherd's pie £2.35   Quiche lorraine £1.90 (Last bar food 9pm. No bar food
Sun eve or Jan–March) ⊖

Muir of Ord   (B & B)   Ord Arms Hotel

Great North Road · *Highland* · Map 1 C2
Inverness (0463) 870286

Free House
Landlords Mr & Mrs D. Nairn
Children welcome
Credit Access
🍺 McEwan's Export, Extra Pale Ale; Harp;
cider. *No real ale.* ♀
ACCOMMODATION   12 bedrooms   £C
Check-in: all day

General redecoration has given a facelift to
the public areas of this solid red-stone hotel
on the outskirts of the village. Bedrooms,
with boldly patterned decor, are bright and
cheerful. Six have private bath- or shower
rooms and these are particularly spacious.
All have colour TVs and tea-makers, and the
Nairns provide a good breakfast. Garden.

New Abbey *(Food, B & B)*

Criffel Inn

Dumfries · *Dumfries & Galloway* · Map 2 C4
New Abbey (038 785) 305

Free House
Landlords Mr & Mrs McCulloch

Children welcome
🍺 Younger's No. 3 Ale; McEwan's 60/-, 70/-;
Guinness; Tennent's Lager; cider. ♀

Visitors feel instantly at ease at this unspoilt village pub, thanks to the friendly welcome of the warm-hearted McCullochs. Janet's un-pretentious home cooking is another reason why the cosy little bars are popular with the locals. The choice includes home-made soup (lunchtime only), salads and sandwiches, York ham, Solway salmon, and a splendid mixed grill, with perhaps bread pudding or some other old-fashioned sweet for afters. Children can have burgers or fish fingers, and there are high teas from 4.30 to 6. *Typical prices:* Pork fillet in tomato & onion sauce £2.95   Solway salmon £3.85 (Last bar food 7pm) 🅟

ACCOMMODATION 5 bedrooms £C
Check-in: all day

The simple bedrooms with functional units and TVs share a bathroom. Residents have an agreeable first floor lounge, and there is also an attractive patio for summer drinking.

Onich *(B & B)*

Onich Hotel

Near Fort William · *Highland* · Map 1 B2
Onich (085 53) 214

Owners Linleven Hotel Company
Landlords Messrs I. & R. Young
Children welcome
Credit Access, Amex, Diners, Visa
🍺 Arrol's 70/-, 80/-, Special; Guinness; Skol; cider.
ACCOMMODATION 27 bedrooms £A
Check-in: all day

An enviable position on the banks of Loch Linnhe is enjoyed by this substantial hotel. Well-kept public rooms include a comfortable main bar, two panelled lounges with huge picture windows, plus games, TV and writing rooms. Other facilities include a solarium and whirlpool bath. Bedrooms have been up-graded and all now feature pretty wallpaper, lightwood furnishings, TVs and gleaming tiled bathrooms. Garden.

Portree *(B & B)*

Rosedale Hotel

Isle of Skye · *Highland* · Map 1 B2
Portree (0478) 2531

Free House
Landlord Mr H. M. Andrew

Children welcome (lunchtime)
🍺 McEwan's Lager; Tennent's Lager; cider. *No real ale.*
ACCOMMODATION 21 bedrooms £C
Check-in: all day

Neat and bright sums up this sparkling harbourside hotel – originally three 19th-century fishermen's cottages – which has been run in friendly, efficient style by the Andrews family for the last 30 years. There are two bars and two simple lounges, and a maze of corridors and stairways leads to the spotless bedrooms. All but two have their own bathrooms. The hotel is closed from October to mid May.

Spean Bridge   (B & B)   *Letterfinlay Lodge Hotel*

Highland · Map 1 B2
Invergloy (0397) 84222

Free House
Landlords Forsyth family

Children welcome
Credit Access, Amex, Diners, Visa
🍺 Alloa's Export Bitter; Löwenbräu; cider. ♀
ACCOMMODATION   15 bedrooms   £B
Check-in: all day

The friendly Forsyth family own and run this welcoming, traditional hotel, which stands some seven miles north of Spean Bridge by lovely Loch Lochy. Picture windows in the lounge enhance the scenic setting, and there's a cosy bar displaying world bank-notes. Spotless bedrooms provide modest, but very comfortable accommodation; five have private bath or shower, the rest share old-fashioned bathrooms with splendid Victorian fittings. Closed December to February.

Strathblane   (B & B)   *Kirkhouse Inn*

Near Glasgow · *Central* · Map 2 C3
Blanefield (0360) 70621
Free House
Landlord R. W. Cairns
Children welcome
Credit Access, Amex, Diners, Visa
🍺 McEwan's Export; Younger's Tartan; Guinness; Carlsberg Light, Hof; Tennent's Lager; cider. ♀
ACCOMMODATION   18 bedrooms   £A
Check-in: all day

On the A81 about ten miles north of Glasgow, this slate-roofed inn has been considerably modernised over the years. A log fire banishes winter from the foyer-lounge, and there's a choice of bars for young and old. Overnight accommodation comprises ten traditional bedrooms sharing three bath-rooms and eight more modern ones with private facilities en suite. All have colour TVs, radios and telephones. Some refurbishment throughout would be welcome.

Tarbert   (Food, B & B)   *West Loch Hotel*

Loch Fyne · *Strathclyde* · Map 2 B3
Tarbert (088 02) 283   *Free House*   *Landlords* Thom family
Children welcome   *Credit* Access
🍺 McEwan's Export; Younger's Pale Ale; Guinness; Carlsberg; cider. *No real ale.*

At the head of West Loch Tarbert, on the main A83 Campbeltown road, this old black and white coaching inn offers a warm welcome and superb home cooking available at lunchtime in its neat, comfortable bars. The menu changes daily and is full of interest – choices like tagliatelle in a creamy sauce with fresh herbs and tomato or lovely home-made soup and crusty bread make way for such appealing main courses as duck casseroled in red wine, venison burger and salad or grilled fresh herrings served with mustard butter. Tempting sweets, too – perhaps tangy lemon tart or rhubarb and orange ice cream. *Typical prices:* Tagliatelle Alfredo £3.50   Venison burger £3.65. (No bar food eves)

ACCOMMODATION   6 bedrooms   £C
Check-in: all day

Most of the six well-kept bedrooms enjoy splendid loch views. There are two public bathrooms and all rooms have wash basins. There's a pleasant first-floor lounge with TV for residents' use. Pub closed November.

Tayvallich   *(Food)*   *Tayvallich Inn*

Near Lochgilphead · *Strathclyde* · Map 2 B3
Tayvallich (054 67) 282

Free House
Landlords Pat & John Grafton

Children welcome
Credit Access, Visa
🍺 Ind Coope Alloa Export, Heavy; Arrols 70/-;
Guinness; cider. ♀

This cheery little pub stands on the shores of
Loch Sweet. The fare on offer in the cosy
public bar includes soup of the day, steaks,
burgers, salads and popular fish items such
as plump mussels and Dublin Bay prawns.
Home-made sweets like fruit crumble and a
rich chocolate nut slice. *Typical prices:* Mussels £2.25   Jumbo prawns £4.50 (Last bar
food 7pm) ⊖

Troon   *(Food)*   *Sun Court Hotel*

Crosbie Road · *Strathclyde* · Map 2 B4
Troon (0292) 312727

Free House
Landlord Mr Alistair Breckenridge

Children welcome
Credit Access, Amex, Diners
🍺 McEwan's Tartan; Carlsberg. *No real ale.* ♀

Overlooking the Royal Troon golf course,
this converted Edwardian house offers enjoyable snacks in its cosy bar and lounge. At
lunchtime your choice might be soup followed
by spaghetti bolognese, chicken curry or
quiche, while evening options include rare
roast topside chasseur and lamb cutlets.
Simple sweets like apple tart and pancakes
to finish. Terrace. *Typical prices:* Quiche
lorraine £2.75   Ploughman's £3.50 (Last bar
food 9.30pm) ⊖

Uig   *(B & B)*   *Ferry Inn*

Isle of Skye · *Highland* · Map 1 A2
Uig (047 042) 242

Free House
Landlords John & Betty Campbell
Children welcome
Credit Access, Visa
🍺 McEwan's Export; Younger's Tartan, Special;
Guinness; Tennent's Lager, Superior; cider. ♀
ACCOMMODATION 6 bedrooms £D
Check-in: all day

Perched above Uig Bay, with splendid views
of the harbour below, this friendly little pub is
a favourite haunt of local fishermen, who like
to gather in the simple public bars. There's
also a cosy lounge bar and a TV lounge.
Modest, well-kept bedrooms have tea-
makers and central heating; one offers private facilities, the rest share two public
bathrooms. Patio.

Ullapool   *(B & B)*   *Argyll Hotel*

Argyle Street · *Highland* · Map 1 B1
Ullapool (0854) 2422

Free House
Landlord Mr Ian Matheson
Children welcome
Credit Amex
🍺 McEwan's Export, 80/-, Lager; Guinness;
Harp; cider.
ACCOMMODATION 8 bedrooms £D
Check-in: all day

One street up from the harbour stands this
unpretentious little white-painted hotel. It's a
friendly, sociable place, and in the evening
the bars frequently ring with the sound of
chatter, laughter and music (the residents'
lounge with TV is a quieter retreat). Spotlessly
kept bedrooms share three old-fashioned
bathrooms that are also spick and span.
Whopping breakfasts are served in a pleasant, airy dining room.

Weem   *(Food, B & B)*   *Ailean Chraggan Hotel*

By Aberfeldy · *Tayside* · Map 2 C3
Aberfeldy (0887) 20346

Free House
Landlords Gillespie family

Children welcome
🍺 Younger's Tartan; Carlsberg Hof; cider.
No real ale. ♀

The Gillespie family has looked after this friendly pebbledash pub for over 20 years. The comfortable, cosy bar opens on to a picture-windowed eating area where you can admire the fine view as you tuck into a simple but tasty snack. The daily specials feature seafood choices like prawn tails in garlic butter, grilled herring fillet and local mussels, while the standard menu has soups, salads and omelettes, casseroles, grills and ice cream desserts. *Typical prices:* Fillet of brill and mushrooms £3.65   Lasagne £2.20 (Last bar food 10pm, 8.30pm in winter) ⊖

ACCOMMODATION   3 bedrooms   £C
Check-in: restricted

Accommodation is of an extremely high standard here. Two of the smartly decorated bedrooms boast separate dressing areas and all have good antique pieces, colour television and large bathrooms. Beds are turned down at night and fresh milk is provided with the tea-makers in each room. Family room.

Wester Howgate   *(Food)*   *Old Howgate Inn*

Near Penicuik · *Lothian* · Map 2 C3
Penicuik (0968) 74244

Free House
Landlord Mrs McIntosh Reid

Credit Access, Amex, Diners, Visa
🍺 McEwan's 80/-; Belhaven 80/-; Theakston's Best Bitter; Greenmantle Ale; Guinness; Carlsberg; cider. ♀

Alongside the A6094, this former coaching inn caters for dainty appetites, with elegant finger sandwiches and quail's eggs the only choice of food in the attractive white-panelled bar. The seven different varieties of Danish open sandwiches include gravad lax with dill mustard, chicken liver pâté with mixed pickles and a gourmet plate which enables you to try a taste of each. *Typical prices:* Danish herring on rye bread £1.20   Quail's egg 30p (Last bar food 10pm).

WALES

Aberaeron   *(Food)*   *Harbourmaster Hotel*

Quay Parade · *Dyfed* · Map 8 B1
Aberaeron (0545) 570351

Free House
Landlord Mr G. Flynn

Children welcome
Credit Access, Visa
🍺 Flowers IPA; Whitbread Welsh Bitter, Best
Bitter; Guinness; Heineken; cider.

Seafood is the speciality at this delightful
19th-century quayside pub, with plaice,
whitebait, prawn and crab all popular choices.
Meaty alternatives include chicken curry and
cottage pie, and there's soup, pâté, sandwiches and salads, too. Enjoy your snack on
the harbour wall or in the garden when it's
fine, or keep snug in the handsome little
panelled bar. Closed Sun. *Typical prices:*
Grilled skate £2.45   Lasagne & chips £2.10
(Last bar food 10.30pm) ☺

Abergavenny   *(Food, B & B)*   *Crowfield*

Ross Road · *Gwent* · Map 8 C2
Abergavenny (0873) 5048

Free House
Landlords George & Sasha Crabb

🍺 Bass; Worthington Best Bitter; Carlsberg Hof.

Situated on the southern slopes of the Skirrid
mountain in the Brecon Beacons National
Park, this 17th-century farmhouse today
makes a charming inn where Sasha Crabb's
appetising home cooking is a delightful
bonus. Sit by the fire in the cosy beamed bar
and tuck into creamy soup served with
wholemeal bread followed by, say, fresh local
salmon, kidneys in cream and sherry or spicy
pepperpot beef. Memorable sweets – from
fresh fruit ice creams to hot winter warmers
– make a fine finale. *Typical prices:* Roast
duck £8   Pork Churchill £5.25 (Last bar food
9.30pm. No bar food Sun) ☺

ACCOMMODATION 5 bedrooms £B (No dogs)
Check-in: all day

The five spacious, smartly furnished bedrooms are housed in an annexe which has its
own sitting room (with TV) and elegant
breakfast room. All offer thoughtful extras
like tissues and sewing kits, as well as large
carpeted bathrooms. No children under 12
overnight; the accommodation is closed 1
week at Christmas.

Abergavenny   *(Food, B & B)*   *Llanwenarth Arms*

Brecon Road · *Gwent* · Map 8 C2
Abergavenny (0873) 810550

Free House
Landlords D'Arcy & Angela McGregor

Children welcome
Credit Access, Amex, Diners, Visa
🍺 Robinson's Best Bitter; Wadworth's 6X;
Worthington Best Bitter; Tennent's; Carling
Black Label; cider. ♀

Above the Usk (where the hotel owns two
stretches of salmon and trout fishing), this
whitewashed 16th-century inn enjoys fine
valley and mountain views. Two traditional
bars and the new conservatory are the
agreeable settings for a wide range of
appetising snacks. As well as standard
favourites like soup, chilli con carne, meat
pies and salads, there's an interesting sup-
plement of weekly seasonal specialities such
as mixed seafood hors d'oeuvre, melon

and fresh crab in creamy mayonnaise or lamb steak marinated in rosemary and garlic. Inviting sweets to finish. *Typical prices:* Mushrooms & prawns au gratin £2.75 Steak & kidney pie £4.75 (Last bar food 10pm) ☺

ACCOMMODATION 18 bedrooms (No dogs)
Check-in: all day

Smartly decorated bedrooms in a separate extension with its own lounge are nicely furnished and equipped with a full range of modern accessories – radio-alarms, colour TVs, phones, tea-makers, even hairdryers. All have neat, fully-tiled bathrooms.

Babell *(Food)*   Black Lion Inn

Near Holywell · *Clwyd* · Map 3 B4
Caerwys (0352) 720239

Free House
Landlord Mr H. G. E. Foster

Credit Amex, Diners, Visa
🍺 Stones Best Bitter; Carling Black Label; cider.
No real ale. ♀

Mrs Foster's excellent cooking makes it well worth while seeking out this homely inn enjoying a peaceful country setting. Everything is beautifully fresh and full of flavour, from her soups and pâtés to delicious main courses such as home-baked ham with parsley sauce, guinea fowl bordelaise or a roast beef salad. The restaurant is open daily except Sat lunch & all Sun, and food is served in the bar at lunchtime in summer. *Typical prices:* Country pie £4.15 Roast duckling £5.50. ☺

Beaumaris *(Food, B & B)* `New Entry`   Liverpool Arms

Castle Street, Anglesey · *Gwynedd* · Map 3 A3
Beaumaris (0248) 810362

Free House
Landlords Allan & Margaret Jones

Credit Access, Diners, Visa
🍺 Younger's IPA; Scotch Bitter; Mild; Guinness; McEwan's Lager; cider.

A nautical theme runs through this delightful hotel, which Allan and Margaret Jones have renovated with loving care. Among the mass of marine memorabilia in the bar you can enjoy some tasty, satisfying snacks, from soup and sandwiches to prawn curry, roast chicken and a very good steak and kidney pie served with jacket potatoes and a generous salad garnish. Daily specials like chicken and mushroom pancakes provide further choice, and there are some simple sweets. *Typical prices:* Stuffed peppers with brown rice £2.45 Chicken, ham & leek pie £2.95 (Last bar food 9.30pm)

ACCOMMODATION 10 bedrooms £B (No dogs)
Check-in: all day

An original staircase, preserved by Ancient Monuments of Anglesey, leads up to ten spotless bedrooms, each named after an admiral and each with a skilfully designed private bathroom. Colour TVs, direct-dial phones and hairdryers are standard accessories, and one particularly nice room boasts a four-poster. Lots of choice for breakfast. Children not accommodated.

Betwys-yn-Rhos *(Food)* | *Ffarm Hotel*

Near Abergele · *Clwyd* · Map 3 A3
Dolwen (049 260) 287

Free House
Landlords Lomax family

Children welcome
🍺 Ind Coope Bitter; Tetley Bitter, Dark Mild;
Wrexham Lager; cider.

Simple starters pave the way for satisfying main courses at this Victorian Gothic pub which is only open in the evening. Fare ranges from steaks and spicy chicken dishes to local trout and baked ham, with homely fruit pies and sherry trifle for afters. *Typical prices:* Kidneys Madeira £3.95 Gratin aux fruits de mer £4.50 (Last bar food 10pm) Closed Sun & Mon October–mid March. ⊖

Bodfari *(Food)* | *Dinorben Arms Inn*

Near Denbigh · *Clwyd* · Map 3 B4
Bodfari (074 575) 309

Free House
Landlord Mr G. T. Hopwood

Credit Access, Visa
🍺 Webster's Yorkshire Bitter; Whitbread Mild;
Younger's Scotch Bitter; Wilson's Bitter;
Guinness; Foster's; Wrexham Lager; cider. ♀

The terraces of this delightful 17th-century inn command fine views of the countryside, while the cosy beamed interior is equally inviting. At lunchtime there's an impressive selection of cold cuts and salads, plus snacks like soup, ploughman's and jacket potatoes. The choice extends at night to include daily specials such as duck à l'orange and entre-côte chasseur. *Typical prices:* T-bone steak £6.95 Salmon meunière £4.75 (Last bar food 10.15pm) ⊖

Cardigan *(B & B)* | *Black Lion Hotel*

High Street · *Dyfed* · Map 8 B2
Cardigan (0239) 612532
Free House
Landlord Mr R. Bassett
Children welcome
Credit Access, Amex, Diners
🍺 Flowers IPA; Whitbread Best, Welsh Bitter;
Heineken; Stella Artois; cider.
ACCOMMODATION 11 bedrooms £C (No dogs)
Check-in: all day

Visitors were first welcomed on this site in 1105, and this much-enlarged inn later became an important coaching stop. Now, a red-brick Georgian facade hides a wealth of beams and rustic charm in the bars, one of which boasts some linenfold panelling. Up-stairs, there's a TV room and a little writing room. Bedrooms, all with private bath or shower, have attractive modern pine fittings. Closed Sunday.

Cenarth *(Food)* | *White Hart*

Near Newcastle Emlyn · *Dyfed* · Map 8 B2
Newcastle Emlyn (0239) 710305

Free House
Landlord Terry Parsons

Children welcome
🍺 Buckley's Best Bitter; Courage Best,
Directors, Dark, Mild; Hofmeister, Kronenbourg;
cider.

An agreeable old inn near the river Teifi where Terry Parsons offers an appetising range of food in his two appealing bars. Typical choices might include Welsh broth, locally-caught salmon and Anglesey eggs (served au gratin with leeks and potatoes). There are vegetarian choices, too, with sandwiches and salads for lighter bites and nice sweets like sherry trifle. *Typical prices:* Anglesey eggs £3.25 Steak & kidney pie £3.50 (Last bar food 9pm) ⊖

Egon Ronay's
guide to
THE LAKE DISTRICT
and YORKSHIRE DALES

This unique guide is a passport to over 200 carefully selected hotels, restaurants, wine bars, inns and tearooms providing exceptionally high standards of cooking and accommodation.

To help memories live on until the beautiful dales and fells can be visited again, Egon Ronay's Guide to the Lake District and Yorkshire Dales also offers some recipes from the top chefs of the area.

Available from AA Centres and booksellers everywhere at £5.95 or £6.95 including postage and packing from:

Mail Order Department
PO Box 51
Basingstoke
Hampshire
RG21 2BR

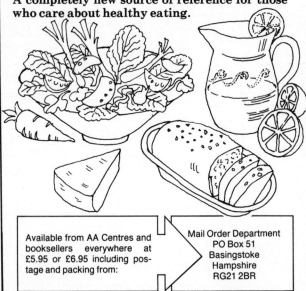

Chepstow *(Food, B & B)*   *Castle View Inn*

16 Bridge Street · *Gwent* · Map 8 D2
Chepstow (029 12) 70349

Free House
Landlords Mervyn & Lucia Gillett

Children welcome
Credit Access, Amex, Diners, Visa
🍺 John Smith's Bitter; Marston's Pedigree;
Kronenbourg. ♀

Mervyn and Lucia Gillett foster a very friendly
and welcoming atmosphere at their 300-
year-old inn, where alterations have added
to the comfort without lessening the period
appeal. One of the reasons for the inn's
popularity is the splendid range of bar food
available lunchtime and evening: sandwiches, pâté and devilled crab for quick
snacks; omelettes, burgers, salads and
grilled dabs for tasty light meals. There's also
a choice of vegetarian dishes, plus sweets
from the restaurant menu. Delightful walled
garden. *Typical prices:* Fresh salmon &
prawn flan £2.75   Vegetable lasagne with
cream sauce £3.50 (Last bar food 9.30pm) ⊖

ACCOMMODATION 11 bedrooms £B
Check-in: all day

Centrally heated bedrooms are well equipped
and all have private bath or shower rooms
fitted with hairdryers. In a recently incorporated cottage there's a double bedroom with
its own lounge, a residents' room, and a
reception area.

Cowbridge *(B & B)*   *The Bear*

High Street · *South Glamorgan* · Map 8 C2
Cowbridge (044 63) 4814

Free House
Landlord Mr J. Davis
Children welcome
Credit Access, Amex, Diners, Visa
🍺 Brain's SA, Bitter; Robinson's Best Bitter;
Worthington HB: Faust; cider.
ACCOMMODATION 37 bedrooms £C
Check-in: restricted

Dating back in parts to the 12th century, this
handsome coaching inn offers comfortable
overnight accommodation both in the recent
annexe and original building – where you will
also find the plush lounge bar, public and
resident's bars. Spacious annexe rooms with
good fitted units offer TVs, tea-makers and
hairdryers in the modern bathroom. Older
bedrooms, some beamed, are more homely
and traditional. Patio.

Crickhowell *(Food, B & B)*   *Bear Hotel*

Powys · Map 8 C2
Crickhowell (0873) 810408

Free House
Landlord Mrs J. Hindmarsh

Children welcome
Credit Access, Visa
🍺 Bass; Flower's Original; Stella Artois;
Heineken; Taunton cider.
ACCOMMODATION 12 bedrooms £C
Check-in: all day

A coaching inn with tremendous character
and a history that goes back 500 years. The
cosy bar serves tasty, satisfying snacks that
include savoury pies and pancakes, garlicky
prawns and the speciality lasagne verdi.
Lovely strawberry gâteau for a sweet. Most
of the comfortable bedrooms have private
bath or shower, and there's a TV lounge and
a delightful garden. *Typical prices:* Lasagne
£3.95   Guinea fowl £4.25 (Last bar food
10pm) ⊖

Crickhowell *(Food)*   *Nantyffin Cider Mill Inn*

Powys · Map 8 C2
Crickhowell (0873) 810775
Free House
Landlord Mrs Barbara Ambrose

Children welcome
Credit Access, Visa
🍺 Marston's Pedigree; Worthington Best Bitter; John Smith's Bitter; Carlsberg Hof; cider. ♈

Pork and cider pie and cider syllabub are two of the highly appropriate specialities offered at this former cider mill, a relaxed and civilised establishment to the west of Crickhowell. The imaginative menu also embraces flavoursome terrine and honey-barbecued chicken, cold meats and salads, quiche and lovely old-fashioned treacle tart. *Typical prices:* Smoked haddock kedgeree £2.85 Chicken & mushroom pie £2.95 (Last bar food 10pm) ☕

Dolgellau *(B & B)*   *Gwernan Lake Hotel*

Cader Road · *Gwynedd* · Map 8 C1
Dolgellau (0341) 422488

Free House
Landlords Mr & Mrs Coomber

Credit Access, Visa
🍺 Marston's Border Bitter, Pilsner. *No real ale.*
ACCOMMODATION 8 bedrooms £C (No dogs)
Check-in: all day

The Coombers are undertaking an improvement programme at their remote fishing hotel by Lake Gwernan (check directions when booking). Much has been done on the exterior, and some of the bedrooms have been provided with new carpets, curtains and duvets. Future plans include some private bathrooms (there are two shared ones at the moment). There's a TV lounge. No children under seven overnight. Closed mid January–mid March.

East Aberthaw   *Blue Anchor*

John Coleman and his son John have created a marvellous atmosphere at this ancient thatched and creeper-clad inn, the haunt of smugglers in the days when the estuary came almost to the front door. Today, the rustic low-beamed bars are crowded with regulars who come to enjoy the fine ales and warm Welsh welcome.

Near Barry · *South Glamorgan* · Map 8 C2
St Athan (0446) 750329   *Free House*   *Landlord* John Coleman
Children welcome
🍺 Wadworth's 6X; Robinson's Best Bitter; Archers Headbanger; Theakston's Old Peculier; Brain's SA; Guinness; cider.

Felindre Farchog *(Food, B & B)*   *Old Salutation Inn*

Crymych · *Dyfed* · Map 8 B2
Newport (0239) 820564

Free House
Landlords Richard & Valerie Harden

Children welcome
Credit Access, Visa
🍺 Bass; Worthington Best Bitter; Allbright Bitter; Guinness; Tennent's Lager; cider. ♈

It is just over a year since the Hardens took over this pleasant whitewashed inn, and improvements continue apace. The public bar remains rustic, practical and popular with local farmers, while the lounge bar is more comfortably furnished. Bar food is straightforward, with a tasty home-made soup, freshly prepared sandwiches, pâté, quiche or salads, as well as more substantial fare like home-made lasagne or chicken paprika. Creamy scrambled egg, hot toast and strong fresh tea make for enjoyable breakfasts. *Typical prices:* Sirloin steak with chips £5.80 Steak & kidney pie £2.80 (Last bar food 10pm) ☺

ACCOMMODATION 8 bedrooms £D
Check-in: all day

Eight of the twelve spacious bedrooms have been newly carpeted, redecorated and now have their own modern bathrooms, TVs and tea-makers. There is a peaceful residents' lounge. Those who fancy outdoor activity will be interested in 3½ miles of game fishing rights on the river Nevern which flows at the bottom of the garden.

Felingwm Uchaf   *(Food, B & B)*   **New Entry**   *Plough Inn*

Nantgaredig, Carmarthen · *Dyfed* · Map 8 B2
Nantgaredig (0267 88) 220

Free House
Landlord Leon Hickman

Credit Access, Amex, Diners, Visa
🍺 Felinfoel Double Dragon, Bitter; Buckleys Mild, Bitter; Guinness; Löwenbräu; cider.

The pub and restaurant are set in linked 16th-century buildings on a steep incline. It's a serious eating place, and the owner once worked for Robert Carrier at Hintlesham Hall. The bar meal menu provides sandwiches, ploughman's, salads and hot dishes like trout, chicken and gammon steak. You can also eat from the restaurant menu in the bar: this widens the choice considerably, with lots of starters, crab (fresh-dressed or au gratin), salmon and steaks, plus daily specials such as lobster Thermidor, duck en croûte or beef curry. There's a good cheeseboard, and sweets include home-made ice cream and a splendid liqueur gâteau. *Typical prices:* Crab au gratin £2.95 Duck en croûte £8.25 (Last bar food 9.30pm) ☺

ACCOMMODATION 5 bedrooms £C (No dogs)
Check-in: all day

Five spacious, very attractively decorated bedrooms, one a family room, are in a house across the street. Two have their own bathrooms, the others share a facility. There's a panelled reception area, plus kitchen and breakfast room.

Ffairfach   *(Food)*   **New Entry**   *Torbay Inn*

Llandeilo · *Dyfed* · Map 8 B2
Llandeilo (0558) 822029

Free House
Landlords Callum & Vera Mackay

Children welcome
🍺 Buckley's Bitter; Whitbread Mild, Welsh Bitter; Heineken; cider.

A really tiny pub, built of stone, painted pink and frequently bursting at the seams with contented quaffers and snackers. The bar food is very good and varied, with local fish, savoury pies and casseroles among the robust favourites. Our vegetable soup, served piping hot in a huge crockpot, was one of the best of the year. *Typical prices:* Chicken chasseur £2.25 Turbot in prawn sauce £3.95 (Last bar food 9.30pm. No bar food Sun lunch). Closed Sun eve. ☺

Glanwydden *(Food)* `New Entry`   *Queen's Head*

Llandudno Junction, near Penrhyn Bay
Gwynedd · Map 3 A3
Llandudno (0492) 46570

Brewery Ansells
Landlords Robert & Sally Cureton

🍺 Ind Coope Burton Bitter, Best Bitter; Tetley's Bitter; Guinness; Skol Special; cider.

The kitchen is in full view at this stone-walled, beamed pub reached by country lanes off the A546. Daily specials increase the scope of ever-changing menus of traditional favourites – soup, salads, pizzas and quiche – and more adventurous dishes at night might include lobster or sweetbread vol-au-vent. Luscious sweets. *Typical prices:* Steak & mushroom pie £3.25   Liver & bacon £3.75 (Last bar food 9pm. No bar food Sun eve) ⊖

Hay-on-Wye *(Food, B & B)*   *Old Black Lion*

Lion Street · *Powys* · Map 8 C2
Hay-on-Wye (0497) 820841

Free House
Landlords Mr & Mrs Colin Vaughan

Credit Access
🍺 Felinfoel Double Dragon; Flowers Best Bitter; Whitbread Welsh Bitter; Guinness; Carlsberg Export; cider. ♀

Dating back to the 13th century, this former coaching inn on the border between Wales and England abounds in period charm. The low-ceilinged, darkly beamed bar makes an atmospheric setting for simple but appetising snacks like home-made soup served with lovely wholemeal bread, moist, whisky-enriched pâté, fresh mackerel with mustard sauce, and exotic Hawaiian turkey with rice. Imaginative sweets might include rich pear and mocha gâteau, and there's a well-kept selection of English cheeses. There's also a restaurant, with a menu full of interest. *Typical prices:* Steak & kidney pudding £3.95 Moussaka £2.25 (Last bar food 10pm) ⊖

ACCOMMODATION   10 bedrooms   £C
Check-in: all day

Universally comfortable bedrooms – no two alike – range from traditional and characterful in the original building to brightly modern in the courtyard annexe. Eight rooms have private bath/shower rooms. Patio.

Henllan *(B & B)*   *Henllan Falls Hotel*

Near Llandysul · *Dyfed* · Map 8 B2
Velindre (0559) 370437

Free House
Landlords John & Lorraine Ellis
Children welcome
🍺 Felinfoel Double Dragon Bitter; Tetley's Bitter; Whitbread Welsh Bitter; Ind Coope Mild; Guinness; Löwenbräu; cider.
ACCOMMODATION   4 bedrooms   £D
Check-in: all day

Two stretches of trout fishing on the nearby river Teifi make this agreeable little pub a popular choice among fishermen. Cheerful, centrally heated bedrooms all offer tea-makers and washbasins and share an up-to-date bathroom. There's a comfortable residents' lounge and two simple bars, one with notices from the Great Western Railway. Pub closed Sunday.

Llanarmon Dyffryn Ceiriog   (B & B)   West Arms Hotel

Near Llangollen · *Clwyd* · Map 3 B4
Llanarmon Dyffryn Ceiriog (069 176) 665

Free House
Landlords Edge family
Children welcome
Credit Access, Amex, Diners, Visa
🍺 Younger's Scotch Bitter, Mild; McEwan's
Export; Harp; Carlsberg Hof. *No real ale.* ♀
ACCOMMODATION 13 bedrooms £C
Check-in: all day

This welcoming 400-year-old inn is situated
in a little village at the head of the lovely Glyn
valley (take the B4500). Its gardens run down
to the river Ceiriog and trout fishing is
available to guests, who can meet up in the
evening in the charming hop-garlanded bar
or retire to the peaceful lounge. Bedrooms,
some with fine views, are pleasantly cottagy;
six have private facilities. Garden.

Llandissilio   (Food)   Bush Inn

Dyfed · Map 8 B2
Clynderwen (099 12) 626

Free House
Landlords Mr & Mrs Honeker

Children welcome
Credit Amex, Diners, Visa
🍺 Brennin Bitter; Worthington 'M' Bitter; Crown
Bitter; Guinness; Harp; Pils Lager; cider. ♀

Home-made salads – potato, coleslaw,
pickled cauliflower, mushroom à la grecque
– steal the show at this simple little pub on
the A478. Try them with tasty turkey or
smoked trout, or go for something warming
like casserole or curry. Soup comes in a
generous portion that's a meal in itself, and
there are prime English cheeses or apple pie
for afters. *Typical prices:* Chilli con carne £3
Lasagne with salad £3 (Last bar food
10.30pm) ☕

Llandogo   (B & B)   Sloop Inn

Near Monmouth · *Gwent* · Map 8 D2
Dean (0594) 530291

Free House
Landlords Grace Evans & George Morgan
Credit Access, Amex, Diners, Visa
🍺 Smiles Best Bitter; Wadworth's 6X;
Worthington Best Bitter; Guinness; Carlsberg;
Stella Artois; cider.
ACCOMMODATION 4 bedrooms £C
Check-in: all day

Grace Evans and George Morgan are the
friendliest and most jovial of hosts at this
modernised inn, which takes its name from
the barges that once sailed here from Bristol.
Homely bedrooms are spotlessly clean and
offer TVs and tea-makers, plus tidy modern
bathrooms. There are two bars, public with
pool table, darts and jukebox, lounge with a
more restful ambience and some lovely
views. Garden.

Llandovery   (B & B)   King's Head Inn

Market Square · *Dyfed* · Map 8 C2
Llandovery (0550) 20393

Free House
Landlords Mr & Mrs D. P. Madeira-Cole
Children welcome
🍺 Worthington Dark Mild, Best Bitter;
Hancock's HB; Allbright; Guinness; Carling
Black Label; cider.
ACCOMMODATION 4 bedrooms £B
Check-in: all day

The Madeira-Coles are welcoming hosts at
this pleasant little inn on the market square.
Dating back in parts to the early 17th century,
its delightful rustic bar is a particularly cosy
and convivial spot and there's a comfortable
lounge bar as well as a spacious first-floor
residents' lounge. The four bedrooms have
a bright, modern appeal, with neat fitted
furniture and tiled bathrooms.

Llanfihangel Crucorney *(Food)*   *Skirrid Inn*

Near Abergavenny · Gwent · Map 8 C2
Crucorney (0873) 890 258   *Free House*   *Landlords* Foster family
Children welcome   *Credit* Amex, Diners
🍺 Robinson's Bitter; Wadworth's 6X; Felinfoel Bitter; Allbright;
Guinness; cider. ♀

★ Hospitality has been dispensed at this marvellous old pub for over 800
years, and for many justice, too, as it was once the local courthouse.
Flagstones and beams are very much the order of the day, and in the
characterful bars visitors can enjoy a very extensive range of snacks
served by the Foster family. Their meat pies are something of a speciality,
and other offerings include poached eggs served with various accom-
paniments; curries and casseroles; fish dishes and a marvellous array of
sweets, including home-made ices and old-fashioned English puds.
Typical prices: Cottage pie £3.60   Poached eggs on laver bread £3.40
(Last bar food 9.30pm) ★

---

*Our inspectors never book in the name of Egon Ronay's Guides;
they disclose their identity only after paying their bills.*

Llanfrynach *(Food)*   *White Swan*

Near Brecon · Powys · Map 8 C2
Brecon (0874) 86276

Free House
Landlords David & Susan Bell

Children welcome
🍺 Brains Bitter; Flowers IPA; Whitbread Welsh
Bitter; Guinness; Heineken; Stella Artois;
cider. ♀

Look for this ancient, appealing pub opposite
the largest graveyard in Wales. The spacious
bar is full of character and here you can
sample Susan Bell's tasty meat and fish pies,
her casseroles, curries and juicy steaks.
Lighter alternatives include ploughman's and
lasagne. Nice sweets, too. Pretty garden.
Typical prices: Ploughman's £1.90   Ratatouille au gratin £2.25 (Last bar food 10.15
pm. No bar food Mon). Closed Monday
lunchtime & last 3 weeks January. ☕

Llangollen *(B & B)*   *Britannia Inn*

Horseshoe Pass · Clwyd · Map 3 B4
Llangollen (0978) 860144

Free House
Landlords Mr & Mrs M. Callaghan
Children welcome
Credit Access, Amex, Diners, Visa
🍺 Webster's Yorkshire Bitter, Green Label;
Guinness; Carlsberg; Foster's; cider. *No real ale.*
ACCOMMODATION 7 bedrooms £C (No dogs)
Check-in: all day

A delightful 15th-century inn at the foot of the
Horseshoe Pass with mountain views and
terraced gardens among its charms. Nicely
appointed bedrooms, nestling under eaves,
have fitted units, colour TVs and coffee-
makers, and share three modern bath/
shower rooms. The low-beamed, rustic bars
with their massive fireplace are a popular
meeting place. Staff are friendly.

Llangorse   *(B & B)*   *Red Lion*

Near Brecon · *Powys* · Map 8 C2
Llangorse (087 484) 238

Free House
Landlords Mr & Mrs C. Cocker
Children welcome
🍺 Flowers IPA; Robinson's Best Bitter;
Whitbread Best Bitter, Welsh Bitter; Guinness;
Stella Artois; cider.
ACCOMMODATION 10 bedrooms £C (No dogs)
Check-in: all day

The Cockers are friendly, enthusiastic landlords, and their jolly little pub opposite the
church has its own babbling brook. Locals
crowd into the stone-walled bars to play
darts, pool and dominoes; so expect a certain
amount of good-humoured noise. Neat bedrooms, with private bathrooms or showers,
are being refurbished in cheerful floral style.
All have TVs. Patio and garden.

Llangurig   *(B & B)*   *Blue Bell*

Near Llanidloes · *Powys* · Map 8 C1
Llangurig (055 15) 254
Free House
Landlords Bill & Diana Mills

Children welcome
Credit Access, Visa
🍺 Sam Powell Best Bitter; Banks's Bitter;
Whitbread Best Bitter; Stella Artois; Heineken.
ACCOMMODATION   10 bedrooms   £D
Check-in: restricted

The Millses are friendly, welcoming hosts at
this charming old roadside inn, whose cosy
bar is very much the centre of village life.
There's a pool room, the games room has
darts and skittles, and next to it is a residents'
lounge with TV. Steep stairs and narrow
corridors give a cottagy feel, and the bedrooms (front ones with views of the church)
are neat, simple and homely. All have tea-
making facilities, one an en suite bath.
There's a garden.

Llangurig   *(B & B)*   *Glansevern Arms*

Pant Mawr · *Powys* · Map 7 C1
Llangurig (055 15) 240

Free House
Landlord Mr W. T. O. Edwards

🍺 Bass Bitter; Worthington Dark Mild;
Carlsberg Hof.

ACCOMMODATION 8 bedrooms £B (No dogs)
Check-in: all day

This spotless little inn on the A44 Aberystwyth
road four miles from Llangurig is surrounded
by the superb scenery of the Plynlimon
range. The Edwards are welcoming hosts, and
make guests feel really at home in their
characterful little bar and relaxing cottagy
lounge, which has lovely Wye Valley views.
Neat, traditionally furnished bedrooms have
colour TVs and smart wooden bathrooms.
Excellent breakfasts. Accommodation
closed 20–30 December.

Llangwm   *(Food)*   **New Entry**   *Bridge Inn*

Near Usk · *Gwent* · Map 8 D2
Wolvesnewton (029 15) 249

Free House
Landlords John & Fran Worbey

🍺 Bass; Worthington Best Bitter; Allbright
Bitter; Carling Black Label; cider.

Bar food here is eaten in a brightly lit area
with old prints, pew seats and views of the
Usk Valley and the pub's terraced garden.
The cold cabinet is very tempting, or you can
order something hot from the blackboard list
– perhaps grilled crawfish, lamb noisettes or
mallard with an excellent redcurrant sauce.
Sweets or cheese to finish. *Typical prices:*
Poached Wye salmon in tomato sauce £7
Chicken Kashmir & rice £5.50 (Last bar food
9.30pm). Closed Sunday evening. 🍽

Llannefydd   *(Food, B & B)*   ### Hawk & Buckle Inn

Near Denbigh · *Clwyd* · Map 3 A4
Llannefydd (074 579) 249

Free House
Landlords Johnson family

Credit Access, Amex, Diners, Visa
🍺 Wilson's Original Bitter, Special Mild;
Carlsberg; Foster's; cider. *No real ale.* ☿

Escape from the crowded tourist spots
nearby to this peaceful, stone-built inn with
panoramic views over the surrounding countryside. There are two bars in the original
building, and a newer extension houses a
residents' bar and restaurant area where
tasty snacks are served. The choice ranges
from pâté and ploughman's to steak, gammon, fish and chips and some vegetarian
dishes. *Typical prices:* Chicken provençale
£3.45   Steak & kidney pie £2.55 (Last bar
food 10.30pm). Closed weekday lunchtimes
November–Easter. ☕

ACCOMMODATION 10 bedrooms £C (No dogs)
Check-in: restricted

Seven of the ten bedrooms are situated in an
extension at the back of the inn. These are
all modern, whereas rooms in the original
building are traditional in style. All rooms
offer every convenience, from good writing
areas and dimmer controls for lighting to
excellent towelling – even a bath sheet.
Children not accommodated overnight.

*Any person using our
name to obtain free
hospitality is a fraud.
Proprietors, please inform
the police and us.*

RECEPTION

Llanrug   *(Food)*   ### Glyntwrog Inn

Gwynedd · Map 3 A4
Caernarfon (0286) 2191

Brewery Lloyd & Trouncer
Landlords Dave & Gill Rochell

Children welcome
🍺 Ind Coope Burton Bitter; Ansell's Bitter, Mild;
Double Diamond; Guinness; Oranjeboom; Skol;
cider.

There's plenty of seating in the pleasant
garden of this lively pub a few miles outside
town on the way to Snowdonia. The bar food
– similar choice lunchtime and evening – is
good and tasty and ranges from taramasalata
and excellent hamburgers to ploughman's,
salads, sandwiches and fresh fish such as
salmon or whitebait. *Typical prices:* Lamb
kebabs with pitta bread £1.90   Chicken in
barbecue sauce £2.70 (Last bar food 9pm) ☕

Llantilio Crossenny *(B & B)*

Near Monmouth · *Gwent* · Map 8 D2
Llantilio (060 085) 278

Free House
Landlords Mike & Pauline Parker
Children welcome
🍺 Ushers Best Bitter; Triple Crown Bitter;
Webster's Yorkshire Bitter; Carlsberg; Holsten
Export. ♊
ACCOMMODATION 2 bedrooms £D
Check-in: restricted

Hostry Inn

Mike and Pauline Parker are the new hosts
at this 15th-century black and white inn
between Monmouth and Abergavenny. The
bars are tiny and cosy, and you really have to
stoop as you climb the stairs to the bedrooms.
These are very much part of the household,
a double and a twin room that share a shower
and separate toilet. There's a nice little
garden.

Prices given are as at the time of our research
and thus may change.

Llantrissent *(B & B)*

Near Usk · *Gwent* · Map 8 D2
Usk (029 13) 2632
Free House
Landlord D. W. H. T. Gascoine
Children welcome
Credit Access, Visa
🍺 Wadworth's 6X; Flowers Original; Felinfoel
Double Dragon; Welsh Bitter; Heineken; Stella
Artois; cider. ♊
ACCOMMODATION 23 bedrooms £B (No dogs)
Check-in: all day

Royal Oak Inn

It's well worth the effort to find this 15th-
century village inn in the Usk valley (ask for
directions when booking). The delightful
beamed bar, with an open fire, is matched by
characterful bedrooms in the original building. Try the converted cottage, or the motel
block for something more modern. All have
practical units, colour TVs and telephones,
and most have their own bath/shower rooms.
Large garden.

Llowes *(Food)*

Radnor Arms

Near Hay-on-Wye · *Powys* · Map 8 C2
Glasbury (049 74) 460 *Free House* *Landlords* Brian & Tina Gorringe
🍺 Felinfoel Bitter; Everards Tiger Bitter; Burton Bitter; Guinness;
Löwenbräu; cider. ♊

Brian Gorringe received the MBE for his catering for Whitehall chiefs
during the Falklands War and the marvellous food served at his delightful
little stone pub is certainly award-worthy in his appreciative customers'
eyes. Over 100 different dishes appear on the imaginative menu every
week, all home prepared from the finest local produce. Superbly flavoured
★ carrot and orange soup or pickled salmon with brandy and pepper might ★
be followed by succulent beef and mussel pie, fresh fish or an omelette
filled with kidneys in red wine sauce. Tempting sweets like treacle and
walnut tart or profiteroles with cream to finish. Excellent cheeses, too.
Garden. *Typical prices:* Beef & mussel pie £5.95 Pigeon & walnut pâté
£2.60 (Last bar food 10pm)

325

Llyswen *(Food, B & B)* *Griffin Inn*

Powys · Map 8 C2
Llyswen (087 485) 241

Free House
Landlords Richard & Di Stockton

Credit Access, Amex, Diners, Visa
🍺 Flowers Original Bitter; Brains Best Bitter;
Whitbread Best Bitter, Welsh Bitter; Guinness;
cider. ♀

The Stocktons' attractive old inn on the A470 is kept in tip-top condition throughout. Black beams contrast with white walls in the convivial bar, where a log fire and gleaming horse brasses add to the appeal. Consult the blackboard for the tasty fare on offer – perhaps smooth chicken liver pâté or vegetarian minestrone to start, followed by, say, generously served garlic mushrooms on rice, haddock and prawn cheese or mutton pie. To finish, there are enjoyable home-made sweets like raspberry Pavlova and crème brûlée, and there's an excellent cheeseboard. *Typical prices:* Griffin curry £2.95 Treacle tart 95p (Last bar food 9pm. No bar food Sun eve) ℮

ACCOMMODATION 6 bedrooms £C
Check-in: all day

The six airy, attractively furnished bedrooms are named rather than numbered and all have private bath/shower rooms as well as tea-maker, radio and hairdryer. There's a little upstairs residents' lounge, too. Patio.

Menai Bridge *(B & B)* *Gazelle Hotel*

Glyn Garth · Gwynedd · Map 3 A4
Menai Bridge (0248) 713364

Brewery Robinson
Landlords Mr & Mrs Clark
Children welcome
Credit Access, Visa
🍺 Robinson's Best Bitter, Mild, Old Tom;
Guinness; Einhorn Lager; cider. ♀
ACCOMMODATION 14 bedrooms £B
Check-in: all day

Splendid views across the Menai Straits can be enjoyed from many of the bedrooms at this lively quayside pub. Neat and modern, all rooms have TVs and tea-makers, half their own private bathroom. Downstairs, you can rub shoulders with fishing and yachting enthusiasts in the large, cheerful bar or retire to the cosy little sitting room. Decent breakfasts. Patio for outdoor drinking.

Monmouth *(B & B)* *Queen's Head Hotel*

St James' Street · Gwent · Map 8 D2
Monmouth (0600) 2767

Free House
Landlords Margaret & Alan Statham
Credit Access, Visa
🍺 Piston Bitter; 1036 Bitter; Flowers Best Bitter;
Whitbread Welsh Bitter; Guinness; Tennent's
Extra Lager; cider. ♀
ACCOMMODATION 3 bedrooms £C
Check-in: all day

One of the few pubs that can boast its own brewery, this splendid black-and-white timbered building stands by the A40 near the town centre. The lounge bar is well furnished and traditional, and there's a little public bar. Comfortable overnight accommodation is provided in three centrally heated bedrooms with TVs, tea-makers and hairdryers. One has a bathroom en suite, the others showers. Cot available.

Nottage *(B & B)*   *Rose & Crown*

Near Porthcawl · Mid Glamorgan · Map 8 C2
(065 671) 4850
Owner Westward Hosts
Landlords Mr & Mrs Chris Rout
Children welcome
Credit Access, Amex, Diners, Visa
🍺 Usher's Best Bitter, Triple Crown; Webster's
Yorkshire Bitter; Guinness; Holsten Export
Lager; cider. ☿
ACCOMMODATION 7 bedrooms £B
Check-in: all day

An attractive old Welsh-stone pub with a whitewashed frontage, colourful window boxes and three cosy carpeted bars. Bedrooms, all in a more recent extension, are airy and comfortable, even if very modestly furnished, and all have TVs, tea-makers and en suite bathrooms. It's under new management, and there are plans to improve the bedrooms and to convert the TV room into an eighth bedroom.

Pembroke *(B & B)*   *Old King's Arms Hotel*

Main Street · Dyfed · Map 8 A2
Pembroke (0646) 683611
Free House
Landlords Mr & Mrs Wheeler
Children welcome
Credit Access, Amex, Visa
🍺 Courage Directors Bitter; Worthington Best
Bitter; Tetley's Yorkshire Bitter; Guinness;
Carlsberg Hof, Pilsner; cider.
ACCOMMODATION 21 bedrooms £C
Check-in: all day

The Wheelers have been welcoming visitors over 30 years to their extended coaching inn. They offer comfortable accommodation both in the original building (compact and pine furnished) and in the extension, where the rooms are more spacious, with fitted units. All have telephones, TVs and up-to-date private facilities. There's a relaxing residents' lounge and two bars, one cosily rustic. Patio.

Penllyne *(Food)*   *The Fox at Penllyne*

Near Cowbridge · South Glamorgan · Map 8 C2
(044 63) 2352

Free House
Landlords Michael & Barbara Taylor

Credit Access, Amex, Visa
🍺 Bass; Hancocks HB Bitter; Worthington Best
Bitter; Carling Black Label. ☿

A friendly, white-shuttered pub serving splendid cooked-to-order bar lunches, plus restaurant dinners. In the bar you eat at gingham-clothed tables under the eye of a stuffed fox. Fresh fish is a speciality (our grilled sardines were superb), and there's soup, home-baked wholemeal bread, pasta and pancakes, steaks and chicken, with a yummy chocolate mousse for sweet. *Typical prices:* Mushroom soup £1.25 Grilled trout £4.95 (No bar food eves) Closed Sun. ©

Penmaenpool *(B & B)*   *George III Hotel*

Near Dolgellau · Gwynedd · Map 8 C1
Dolgellau (0341) 422525
Free House
Landlord Gail Hall
Children welcome
Credit Access, Amex, Diners, Visa
🍺 Border Bitter; John Marston's Bitter;
Younger's Tartan; Guinness; Carlsberg Hof;
cider. ☿
ACCOMMODATION 12 bedrooms £C
Check-in: all day

This characterful old inn enjoys a superb situation at the head of the Mawddach estuary. It has its own moorings and there's fishing, too. Inside, prints, brassware and an old-fashioned Welsh dresser create a homely atmosphere in one bar, while the beamed cellar bar is quaintly rustic. There's a cosy lounge, too. Main-house bedrooms are compact and comfortable; those in the nearby lodge all have their own bathrooms. TVs and tea-makers throughout. Patio.

Pentwynmawr *(Food)* `New Entry`   *Three Horseshoes*

High Street · *Gwent* · Map 8 C2
Newbridge (0495) 243436

Brewery Whitbread
Landlords Ann & Peter Reynish

Children welcome
🍺 Flowers Original; Whitbread Best Bitter;
Welsh Bitter; Guinness; Heineken; cider. ⵌ

Lovingly restored by the Reynish family, this splendid village pub on the A472 offers a friendly welcome and some excellent bar snacks. A crusty sandwich filled with pâté, Cheddar and ham, crispy mushroom corn bake and shepherd's pie with lentils are typical of the tasty range. Lovely rhubarb pie to finish. Garden. *Typical prices:* French ploughman's £2.25 Sweet & sour almonds with rice £2.95 (Last bar food 10pm. No bar food Sun) ⵣ

Penybont *(B & B)*   *Severn Arms*

Near Llandrindod Wells · *Powys* · Map 8 C1
Penybont (059 787) 224

Free House
Landlords Geoff & Tessa Lloyd
Credit Access, Visa
🍺 Bass; Whitbread Welsh Bitter; Worthington
Best Bitter; Welsh Brewers Allbright Bitter;
Guinness; Tennent's; Carling Black Label; cider.
ACCOMMODATION 10 bedrooms £C
Check-in: all day

Geoff and Tessa Lloyd are the friendly hosts at this old whitewashed inn on the A44. Two characterful bars provide a choice for the thirsty, and there is also a residents' lounge with TV and a games room. Spacious, comfortable bedrooms have tea-makers and good bathrooms; ten have colour TVs. Across the garden is a sports field where ponytrotting races are a regular feature. Accommodation closed 1 week Christmas.

Raglan *(Food, B & B)*   *Beaufort Arms Hotel*

High Street · *Gwent* · Map 8 D2
Raglan (0291) 690412

Free House
Landlords Jeanes family

Children welcome
Credit Access, Amex, Diners, Visa
🍺 Ansells Traditional Bitter; John Bull Bitter;
Smiles Traditional Bitter; Double Diamond;
Guinness; cider. ⵌ

Situated in the centre of the village, this inn dating from the early 15th century is lovingly tended by the Jeanes family. A magnificent inglenook fireplace and some original Tudor timbers are noteworthy fixtures in the bars. These, together with the exposed stone walls, give a pleasant, traditional atmosphere in which home-made dishes are served to appreciative customers. The snacks range from an excellent vegetable soup, pâté and burgers to more substantial meals of steak, fish or chicken followed by a delicious dessert like apple strudel. Vegetarian dishes are available on request. *Typical prices:* Mussels provençale £2.70 Beef curry £3.29 (Last bar food 10pm). ⵣ

ACCOMMODATION 12 bedrooms £B
Check-in: all day

The bedrooms are pleasingly decorated in traditional style. Ten of them have private bathrooms; all are centrally heated and have colour TVs and tea-making facilities. There are two public bathrooms. Patio.

Swansea *(Food)* · St George Hotel

30 Walter Road · *West Glamorgan* · Map 8 C2
Swansea (0792) 469317

Brewery Welsh Brewers
Landlords Michel & Valerie Amirat

🍺 Bass; Worthington Dark, Best Bitter;
Allbright; Carling Black Label; Tennent's
Extra. ⚲

Tempting dishes from landlord Michel Amirat's native France have won the hearts – and stomachs – of the local business community, who flock to his pub at lunchtime. Succulent ham, salami, smoked fish and savoury flans go beautifully with tangy salads, while from the hot counter you could have, say, garlicky frog's legs or deliciously sauced pasta. *Typical prices:* Chicken à la crème £2.20 Mussels provençale £2.80 (No bar food eves or all Sat & Sun) ⊖

We welcome complaints and bona fide recommendations on the tear-out pages for readers' comments. They are followed up by our professional team. Please also complain to the management instantly.

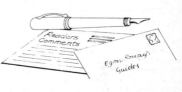

Three Cocks *(Food, B & B)* · Three Cocks Hotel

Near Brecon · *Powys* · Map 8 C2
Glasbury (049 74) 215

Free House
Landlords Michael & Marie-Jeanne Winstone

Children welcome
Credit Access, Visa
🍺 Flowers Best Bitter; Stella Artois.

Michael Winstone and his Belgian wife Marie-Jeanne run this delightful ivy-clad hotel and restaurant, which is situated near the famous Brecon Beacons. The oldest parts date from the 15th century, and under the sturdy oak beams you can enjoy some excellent snacks, from garlic mushrooms and lasagne to toasted sandwiches, chicken waterzooi and a warm dish of goat's cheese and honey. Good sweets, too. *Typical prices:* Lasagne £2.75 Ploughman's £2.25 (Last bar food 9.30pm) ⊖

ACCOMMODATION 7 bedrooms £C (No dogs)
Check-in: all day

The seven bedrooms are appealingly traditional, with the reassuring solidity of beams and oak furniture. Marie-Jeanne's eye for style shows in the pretty fabrics, and housekeeping is a matter of real pride. The bedrooms share three neat public bathrooms, and there's a relaxing panelled lounge. A final delight comes in the form of super breakfasts with fresh orange juice, spot-on scrambled eggs and good fresh coffee. Pub closed January.

Trecastle   (Food, B & B)   Castle Hotel

Near Sennybridge · Powys · Map 8 C2
Sennybridge (087 482) 354

Free House
Landlords Dick & Joan Ward

Children welcome
Credit Access, Visa
🍺 Usher's Founder's Ale, Best Bitter; Ben Truman; Guinness; Holsten; Carlsberg; cider. ♀

ACCOMMODATION 6 bedrooms £D (No dogs)
Check-in: all day

A welcoming fire burns in the appealing bar of this sturdy grey-painted inn at the heart of a village on the A40. Snacks can also be enjoyed in a summery conservatory, a comfortable lounge where children are welcome, or in the garden. Dick and Joan Ward are friendly hosts, and their wholesome, tasty bar food is much appreciated. Sandwiches and salads provide light bites, while lamb curry is a particular favourite among the hot dishes. *Typical prices:* Lasagne with salad £3.15   Lamb curry & poppadoms £3.80 (Last bar food 9.45pm) ☺

Attractive, spacious bedrooms, with pretty floral wallpaper and practical modern furniture, share three well-equipped bathrooms (only one has its own bathroom en suite). All have TVs and tea-makers. Pub closed 3 weeks in January.

*Prices given are as at the time of our research
and thus may change.*

Whitebrook   (Food, B & B)   Crown at Whitebrook

Near Monmouth · Gwent · Map 8 D2
Monmouth (0600) 860254

Free House
Landlords John & David Jackson

Children welcome
Credit Access, Amex, Diners, Visa
🍺 Flowers IPA; Heineken. ♀

ACCOMMODATION   12 bedrooms   £B
Check-in: all day

The river Wye is but a mile from this remote restaurant-cum-hotel and village inn, which stands in sloping gardens in a steeply wooded valley. Bar snacks – starters from the restaurant menu – are served in the lounge, and the interesting choice ranges from a tasty duck terrine and cucumber and cheese mousse, to savoury buckwheat pancakes and tartelette alsacienne, with homemade ice creams or sorbets for afters. *Typical dishes:* Savoury pancake £2.35   Duck terrine £2.95 (Last bar food 10pm) ☺

Charming bedrooms have smart modern units, pretty furnishings, and spotless well-equipped bathrooms. There are direct-dial telephones, lots to read, and continental breakfast in bed if you want a leisurely start to the day. Terrace.

Wolf's Castle *(Food, B & B)* | *Wolfe Inn*

Near Haverfordwest · *Dyfed* · Map 8 B2
Treffgarne (043 787) 662

Free House
Landlords Mr & Mrs Fritz Neumann

Children welcome
Credit Visa
🍺 Felinfoel Double Dragon; Worthington Best
Bitter; George Best Bitter; Guinness; Holsten;
Carling Black Label; cider. ♀

It would be worth making a detour to visit this
well-kept stone inn just off the A40. Landlord
Fritz Neumann has worked in the restaurant
business for over 25 years. His small public
bar buzzes with locals and the stone-walled
lounge bar with its attractive dining area is
ideal for sitting and sampling the wholesome
snacks. There are home-made soups and
pâté, sandwiches and salads plus more
substantial fare like the popular steak with
garlic butter sauce. Home-made desserts
include profiteroles and gâteaux. *Typical
prices:* Steak chasseur £6.50   Chicken Kiev
£4.25 (Last bar food 10pm No bar food Sun
& Mon eves & all Mon in winter) ⊖

ACCOMMODATION 1 bedroom £D (No dogs)
Check-in: restricted

In a converted outbuilding attached to the inn
there is a spacious twin-bedded room (with
space for a child's bed). It has its own private
bathroom and kitchen and a TV. Breakfast of
fresh orange juice and scrambled egg is
served in the bedroom.

JUST A BITE
Egon Ronay's **PG**tips
1987 GUIDE

Light meals and snacks to suit all pockets and palates in some 950 wine bars, tearooms, pizzerias, coffee shops, cafés

New features:

- **Place of the Year, an annual award for all-round excellence**

- **a colourfully illustrated children's section of parties, special menus, Junior Inspectors for a day**

Available from AA Centres and booksellers everywhere at £4.95 or £5.95 including postage and packing from:

Mail Order Department
PO Box 51
Basingstoke
Hampshire
RG21 2BR

CHANNEL ISLANDS

Pleinmont   *(B & B)*   *Imperial Hotel*

Torteral · *Guernsey* · Map 9 C4
Guernsey (0481) 64044

Brewery Randall
Landlords Mr & Mrs J. W. Hobbs
Children welcome
Credit Access, Visa
🍺 Randall's Bitter; Worthington 'E'; Guinness;
Breda; cider. *No real ale*
ACCOMMODATION   16 bedrooms   £C
Check-in: all day

Within easy reach of fine sandy beaches and
clifftop walks, this cheerful white-painted inn
is a popular choice with families. Two residents' bars enjoy excellent views from picture
windows and the convivial public bar is a
popular local meeting place. The bright, airy
bedrooms have functional modern furniture;
all offer TVs and tea-makers and most have
private facilities. Patio and garden.

St Aubin's Harbour   *(Food, B & B)*   *Old Court House Inn*

Jersey · Map 9 D4
Jersey (0534) 46433

Free House
Landlords Jonty & Vicky Sharp

Children welcome
Credit Access, Visa
🍺 Mary Ann Special; John Smith's Bitter;
Guinness; Harp; cider. *No real ale.* ♀

This exceedingly popular inn, built in the 14th
century, overlooks the yacht-filled harbour of
St Aubin. Low oak-beamed ceilings, exposed
stone walls, roaring fires and even a floodlit
well provide oodles of character in the
ground-floor bars. A second bar on the first
floor – panelled to resemble the stern of a
ship and decorated with sailing artifacts –
makes a pleasant spot from which would-be
sailors can gaze out over the harbour. The
good, simple snacks announced on a blackboard range from home-made soup, lasagne,
cannelloni and frankfurters to other dishes
like spare ribs, outstanding moules marinière
and seafood salad. There are also choices
suitable for vegetarians. *Typical prices:*
Moules marinière £2.75   Spare ribs £3.25
(No bar food eves or all Sun) ⓒ

ACCOMMODATION   9 bedrooms   £A
Check-in: all day

Homely bedrooms with antique pine furniture
have en suite bathrooms, colour TVs and
radios. Most have good sea views – the best
being from the penthouse suite. Accommodation closed February.

ISLE OF MAN

Kirk Andreas *(Food)*   *Grosvenor*

Isle of Man · Map 3 A2
Kirk Andreas (0624 88) 576

Brewery Heron & Brearly
Landlord Mr J. P. Legat

Credit Access, Visa
🍺 Okells Bitter, Mild; Guinness; Harp; cider.

Bar snacks bring the crowds to this well-kept modern pub not far from the sea. Toasted baps with grilled steak or gammon are very popular, as are black pudding, fishy things such as cockles and crab salad, and a good meaty steak and kidney pie served with super chips. To finish, a selection of familiar sweets from the trolley. *Typical prices:* Avocado with prawns £1.75   Steak & kidney pie £2 (Last bar food 8pm. No bar food Sun) ℮

Peel *(Food)*   *Creek Inn*

The Quayside · *Isle of Man* · Map 3 A2
Peel (062 484) 2216

Brewery Okells
Landlords Robert & Jean McAleer

Children welcome
🍺 Okells Bitter, Mild; Guinness; Harp; Carlsberg; cider. ♀

Down on the harbour amidst the bustle of the boats, this welcoming pub is a convivial place to meet for a drink and a snack at any time of day. Sandwiches, salads and pizzas are favourite choices, and an ever-changing blackboard menu announces specials like lasagne, scallops mornay and the popular Creek pie – a delicious concoction of sausage meat, onions, apples and potatoes. *Typical prices:* Kipper pâté £1.75   Seafood platter £3.95 (Last bar food 10.45pm) ℮

AN OFFER FOR ANSWERS

A DISCOUNT ON THE NEXT GUIDE

Readers' answers to questionnaires included in the Guide prove invaluable to us in planning future editions, either through their reactions to the contents of the current Guide, or through the tastes and inclinations indicated. Please send this tear-out page to us *after you have used the Guide for some time*, addressing the envelope to:

Egon Ronay's Pub Guide
Second Floor, Greencoat House, Francis Street
London SW1P 1DH, United Kingdom

As a token of thanks for your help, we will enable respondents to obtain the 1988 Guide post free from us at a 33⅓% discount off the retail price. We will send you an order form before publication, and answering the questionnaire imposes no obligation to purchase.
All answers will be treated in confidence.

This offer closes 30 June 1987 and is limited to addresses within the United Kingdom.

---

1. Are you   *Please tick*

    male? [   ]   Under 21? [   ]   31–45? [   ]
    female? [   ]   21–30? [   ]   46–65? [   ]
                                                   over 65? [   ]

---

2. Your occupation ....

---

3. Do you have any previous editions of this Guide?
    1984 [   ]   1985 [   ]   1986 [   ]

---

4. Do you refer to this Guide
    four times a week? [   ]   once a week? [   ]
    three times a week? [   ]   once a fortnight? [   ]
    twice a week? [   ]   once a month? [   ]

---

5. How many people, apart from yourself, are likely to consult this Guide (including those in your home and place of work)?

    male ....   female ....

6. Do you have our Hotel & Restaurant Guide?

    1985 [   ]   1986 [   ]   1987 [   ]

7. Do you have our Just a Bite Guide?

    1985 [   ]   1986 [   ]   1987 [   ]

8. How many times have you travelled overseas in the past year?

    ....

9. How many nights have you spent in hotels during the past year?

    ....

10. Do you occupy more than one home?   [Yes | No]

     Do you own the house you live in?   [Yes | No]

11. Your car

     type .... year ....

12. What is your daily newspaper? ....

13. Which of the following credit cards do you use?

              Access [   ]   Diners [   ]

     American Express [   ]   Visa [   ]

14. What fields would you like us to survey or what improvements do
     you suggest? ....
     ....
     ....

Please *print* your name and address here if you would like us to
send you a pre-publication order form for the next Guide.

Name ....

Address ....

....

Readers' comments

Please use this sheet to recommend bar snacks or inn accommodation of very high quality – *not* full restaurant or hotel facilities. Your complaints about any of the Guide's entries are also welcome.

Please post to:
PUB GUIDE 1987
Egon Ronay's Guides
Greencoat House,
Francis Street,
London SW1P 1DH

NB We regret that owing to the enormous volume of readers' communications received each year, we will be unable to acknowledge these forms but they will certainly be seriously considered.

Name and address of establishment (*Please state whether food or accommodation*)

Your recommendation or complaint

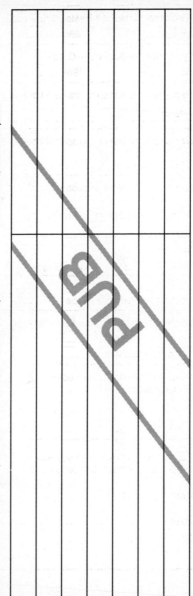

Name of sender (in block letters) _____

Address of sender (in block letters) _____

Readers' comments

Please use this sheet to recommend bar snacks or inn accommodation of very high quality – *not* full restaurant or hotel facilities. Your complaints about any of the Guide's entries are also welcome.

Please post to:
PUB GUIDE 1987
Egon Ronay's Guides
Greencoat House,
Francis Street,
London SW1P 1DH

NB We regret that owing to the enormous volume of readers' communications received each year, we will be unable to acknowledge these forms but they will certainly be seriously considered.

Name and address of establishment (*Please state whether food or accommodation*)	Your recommendation or complaint

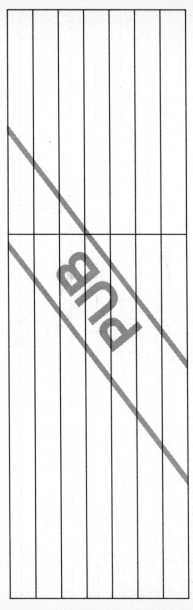

Name of sender (in block letters) _____

Address of sender (in block letters) _____

Readers' comments

Please use this sheet to recommend bar snacks or inn accommodation of very high quality – *not full restaurant or hotel facilities*. Your complaints about any of the Guide's entries are also welcome.

Please post to:
PUB GUIDE 1987
Egon Ronay's Guides
Greencoat House,
Francis Street,
London SW1P 1DH

NB We regret that owing to the enormous volume of readers' communications received each year, we will be unable to acknowledge these forms but they will certainly be seriously considered.

Name and address of establishment (*Please state whether food or accommodation*)	Your recommendation or complaint

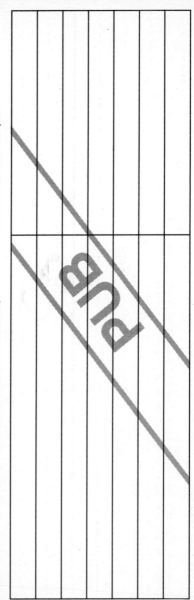

Name of sender (in block letters) _____

Address of sender (in block letters) _____

Readers' comments

Please use this sheet to recommend bar snacks or inn accommodation of very high quality – *not* full restaurant or hotel facilities. Your complaints about any of the Guide's entries are also welcome.

Please post to:
PUB GUIDE 1987
Egon Ronay's Guides
Greencoat House,
Francis Street,
London SW1P 1DH

NB We regret that owing to the enormous volume of readers' communications received each year, we will be unable to acknowledge these forms but they will certainly be seriously considered.

Name and address of establishment (*Please state whether food or accommodation*)

Your recommendation or complaint

Name of sender (in block letters)

Address of sender (in block letters)

Readers' comments

Please use this sheet to recommend bar snacks or inn accommodation of very high quality – *not* full restaurant or hotel facilities. Your complaints about any of the Guide's entries are also welcome.

Please post to:
PUB GUIDE 1987
Egon Ronay's Guides
Greencoat House,
Francis Street,
London SW1P 1DH

NB We regret that owing to the enormous volume of readers' communications received each year, we will be unable to acknowledge these forms but they will certainly be seriously considered.

Name and address of establishment (*Please state whether food or accommodation*)

Your recommendation or complaint

Name of sender (in block letters) _____

Address of sender (in block letters) _____

Readers' comments

Please use this sheet to recommend bar snacks or inn accommodation of very high quality – *not* full restaurant or hotel facilities. Your complaints about any of the Guide's entries are also welcome.

Please post to:
PUB GUIDE 1987
Egon Ronay's Guides
Greencoat House,
Francis Street,
London SW1P 1DH

NB We regret that owing to the enormous volume of readers' communications received each year, we will be unable to acknowledge these forms but they will certainly be seriously considered.

Name and address of establishment (*Please state whether food or accommodation*)	Your recommendation or complaint

Name of sender (in block letters) _____

Address of sender (in block letters) _____

Egon Ronay's *CELLNET GUIDE 1987*

HOTELS, RESTAURANTS & INNS IN GREAT BRITAIN & IRELAND

Egon Ronay's Cellnet Guide 1987 includes detailed descriptions of over 2500 of the best hotels, inns and restaurants in Great Britain and Ireland.

Restaurants serving outstanding food are awarded stars, and wine comments are included in many entries. There's an extensive section on bargain breaks and lower-priced London restaurants and hotels.

Many new features make the Guide more useful than ever for anyone who travels on business or for pleasure. Among them are

- Town house hotels
- Starred restaurants and high-grade hotels near the motorway network
- Countrywide listing of theatres

Available from AA Centres and booksellers everywhere at £9.95 or £10.95 including postage and packing from:

Mail Order Department
PO Box 51
Basingstoke
Hampshire
RG21 2BR

English beers, Flemish settlers.
And probably the best lager in the world.

A Short Guide To What Goes Into Your Drink

Ale – Originally a liquor made from an infusion of malt by fermentation, as opposed to beer, which was made by the same process but flavoured with hops.

Beer – "Beer" and "Ale" were the words to describe all malt liquors until the 16th Century, when Flemish settlers re-introduced hops for flavouring. The hopped variety was then called "Beer" and the unhopped liquors were called "Ale."

Bitter – The driest and one of the most heavily hopped beers served on draught.

Burton – A strong ale, dark in colour, made with a proportion of highly dried or roasted malts. It is not necessarily brewed in Burton and a variety of strong or old ales were given the term.

Carlsberg – A Danish lager brewery, founded in 1847, based in Copenhagen and specialising solely in the production of lagers. The company has a major brewery at Northampton, England, where these lagers are produced by Danish brewers. Carlsberg is unique because it is owned by a philanthropic foundation which gives all its profits to art, scientific and medical research.

India Pale Ale – The name given to a fine pale ale first made for export to the troops in India. The term became popular with a number of brewers for their bottled pale ales.

Lager – Light coloured beer brewed principally on the Continent. Fewer hops are used than in English beer, and fermentation is carried out at a much lower temperature. Bottom fermentation is caused by special yeasts which descend to the bottom of the fermenting vessels, and character is achieved by the length of the fermentation and storage.

Mulled Ale – A hot drink for cold weather. Beer flavoured with sugar and spices and sometimes the yolk of an egg.

Pale Ale – Also known as light ale. Made of the highest quality malts, it is dry and highly hopped.

Pilsner – The German name for the Czechoslovakian town of Plzen which gave its name to Pilsner. Carlsberg first exported a pilsner type lager from Copenhagen to Scotland in 1868.

Special Brew – A strong, high quality lager produced by Carlsberg. First introduced to commemorate a visit by Winston Churchill to Copenhagen in 1950.

Stout – Heavy dark beer prepared with well roasted barley or malt, and sometimes caramel.

Carlsberg Brewery Ltd. Tel 0604 21621.